# O.C. Seltzer

The Gilcrease–Oklahoma Series
on Western Art and Artists

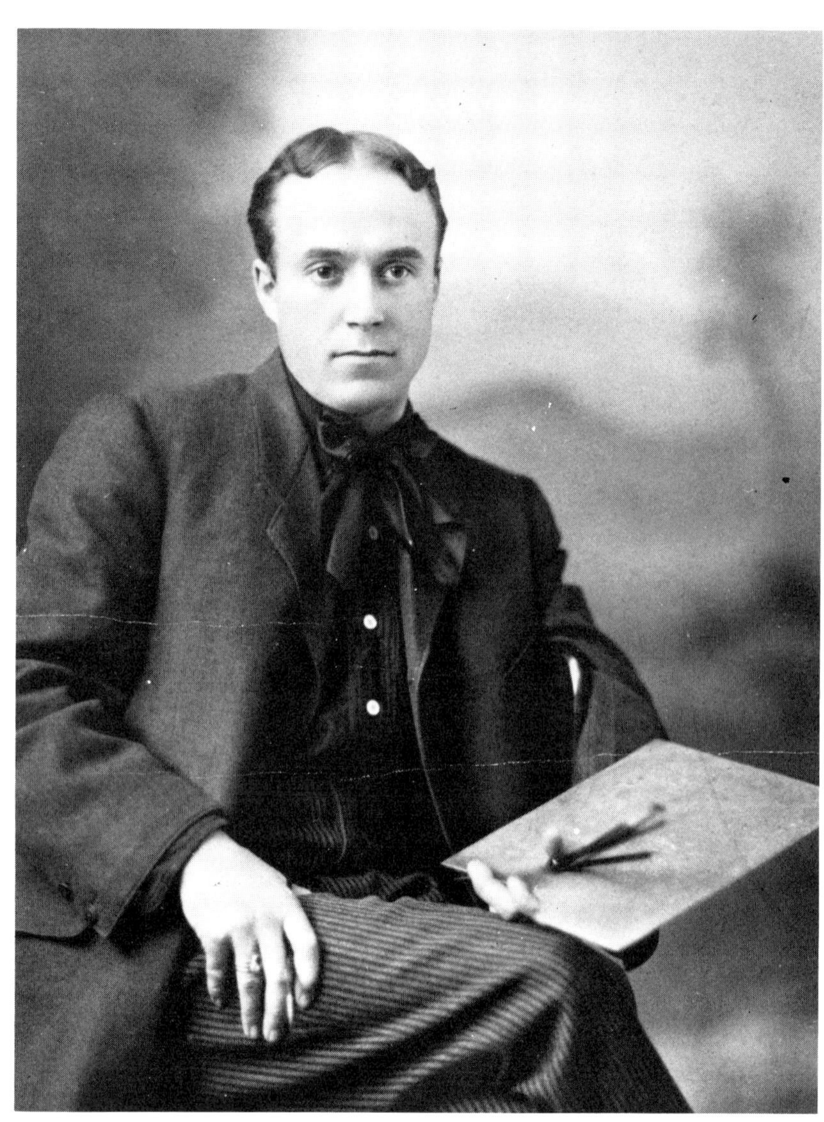

Seltzer at thirty-two.
Courtesy of Carl C. Seltzer.

# O. C. SELTZER
## Painter of the Old West

By Mildred D. Ladner

*Foreword by Fred A. Myers*

University of Oklahoma Press   :   Norman
and
Thomas Gilcrease Institute of American History and Art   :   Tulsa

Library of Congress Cataloging in Publication Data

Ladner, Mildred D.       1918–
    O. C. Seltzer, painter of the Old West.

    Bibliography: p. 211
    Includes index.
    1. Seltzer, Olaf  C.,  1877–1957.  2.  Paint-
ers—United  States—Biography.   3. The  West
in art.   I.  Seltzer, Olaf C., 1877–1957.   II. Title.
ND237.S4375L3   759.13 [B]          78–21379

*For*
*my husband, John Ladner,*
*and*
*my father, the late Orlando Diefenderfer,*
*men with whom O. C. Seltzer would have felt at home*

# Contents

# Illustrations

## COLOR PLATES



## BLACK-AND-WHITE ILLUSTRATIONS

# Foreword

BY FRED A. MYERS, DIRECTOR
*Thomas Gilcrease Institute of American History and Art*

THE PUBLICATION of this book on the life and work of Olaf Seltzer is the occasion for rejoicing on a number of accounts. The book puts before a large audience material that was previously difficult to get at. As Mildred Ladner's scholarship revealed, there is a good deal of original Seltzer source material. Seltzer died only recently, after all, and did not live a life of impenetrable obscurity. Yet, for reasons that Mrs. Ladner suggests, until now much of the original material had not been published, nor have the paintings of this estimable artist been as widely known as they deserve to be. This book brings the material to the light of day in orderly fashion; it will go a long way toward focusing proper attention on Seltzer and his art.

Another reason for rejoicing is that this book will in some measure focus attention on the Thomas Gilcrease Institute of American History and Art. There are 340 works by Seltzer in the Gilcrease Collection. A book about Seltzer is thus a book about the Gilcrease Institute.

There has never been a better time for research and publication of the efforts of American artists. Slow to develop because of what might be called "Europe envy," appreciation of American art is burgeoning. The celebration of the Bicentennial Year merely gave impetus to a process that began after the close of World War II. Artists are now paying attention to American art as a suitable heritage, writers and critics are paying attention to American art old and new, art collectors are paying attention, art sellers likewise, of course; most importantly, the public is paying attention. In our era of lifelong learning the kind of learning that happens in museums—self-started and self-paced—appeals to more and more people. Books to extend this kind of learning are newly needed today.

So all is ripe, the art, the scholarship, the publication, the audience. I applaud Mrs. Ladner and her book as a harbinger of Gilcrease participation in the maturation of American art and art awareness.

# Acknowledgments

I AM INDEBTED to admirers of O. C. Seltzer who have helped to reconstruct his life and times.

Special thanks are due Carl C. Seltzer, older son, unwearying researcher never wanting in time or patience; and the other Seltzers—daughter-in-law, Lillian; granddaughters, Ruth Teddy and Sue Erwin; younger son, Walter, and his wife, Della, and their children, particularly W. Steve Seltzer.

Grateful acknowledgment is accorded to Patricia McAndrew, of Bethlehem, Pennsylvania, a former Fulbright scholar in Denmark, for her invaluable assistance in reconstructing the Copenhagen that Olaf Seltzer knew, her sensitive translations, and her guidance toward valued sources, such as Inger Marie Hansen and Inge Winkelmann, of the Danish Information Office in New York City; Harald Jørgensen, director of Landsarkivet for Sjaelland (Regional Archives for Zeeland); and Sigurd Jensen and Jeppe Rasmussen, of the Kobenshavens Stadsarkiv (Copenhagen Municipal Archives).

Former Gilcrease Director W. R. Best; the present Director, Fred A. Myers; Senior Curators Dan McPike and Pat Edwards; Registrar Jeanne Snodgrass King; former Librarian Marie Keene; former Art Curators Carolyn Bradshaw and Betsy Olson; Art Curator Anne Roden; former gift-shop manager Rubye Kramp; Susan Regur; and especially photographers Oliver Willcox and Mark Haynes, for their painstaking efforts to reproduce the Seltzer art with fidelity.

The Gillies of Gilcrease Museum, particularly Janice Daniel, who spurred this project, and Sally Campbell, Jean Devlin, Nancy Robertson, and Marjorie Blocksom.

Eudotia Teenor, Secretary of the Gilcrease Foundation; Lindsay L. Alexander and Paul H. Johnson, former Presidents of the Gilcrease Museum Association, and Bob Biolchini, President; David Carlson and Cecille Bales, of the Tulsa Parks and Recreation Board and trustees of Gilcrease. Martin Wiesendanger and David R. Milsten deserve special thanks, along with David C. Hunt, of Missoula, Montana; James Taylor Forrest, of Laramie, Wyoming; and Paul A. Rossi, of Woodland Park, Colorado, all former Gilcrease associates who earlier carried on research on Seltzer.

Montanans Jean Morrison Thomas and Julia Morrison, of Billings; Richard Williams, of Big Timber; Cato Butler, of Helena; Mrs. T. D. Barry, of Lakeside; the Con Lundgrens, of Kalispell; Helen Clark, of Butte; and Thor Halseth, of Great Falls, along with Montana Historical Society staff and supporters, such as Harriett C. Meloy, Librarian; Sam Gilluly, former Director; and E. E. MacGilvra, of Butte, and his wife, Edna, for their continuing flow of information.

Old friends who remember, such as North Dakota Stark, of Vancouver, Washington; Alice Marks, of Seattle; J. Kenneth Ralston, of Billings, Montana; Sandy Ingersoll, of Stevensville; Kermit Rasmussen, of Harlem; E. B. Craney, of Butte; Frank Curry, of Great Falls; and Walter Foresman, of Apgar.

Members of the family of Dr. Philip G. Cole, especially Philip G. Cole, Jr., of Colorado Springs and Kihei, Hawaii; and Kay Cole Worden, of Weston, Massachusetts.

Librarians and staff members of the Amon Carter Museum of Western Art, Fort Worth; the

Charles M. Russell Museum, Great Falls; the Harry S Truman Library, Independence, Missouri; and the public libraries of Tulsa, Dallas, Billings, Great Falls, and Manhattan, with special thanks to Bonnie Marquard, of the New York Public Library reference room.

Art-gallery personnel, such as Eugene Coulon, of Kennedy Galleries; Sidney Hill, of Berry-Hill Galleries; Leonard A. Lombardo, of Fairfield Gallery; and Michael Frost, of J. N. Bartfield Art Galleries, New York City; Robert Rockwell, of Corning, New York; Harry A. Lockwood, of Cincinnati; and Harold Ruth, of Billings, with special gratitude to J. N. Bartfield for permitting publication of the doggerel on the C. M. Russell Christmas card.

Personal friends, such as Cathy Kellough and Elizabeth Allen Thompson, in Tulsa; Dr. Margaret Heimberger, in Victoria, British Columbia; Margo Reich, in Seattle; Florence Drumright, in Poway, California; Betty Sue Morgan, in Scottsdale, Arizona; and Florence Rossi, in Phoenix, Arizona; Mary Thompson, in Southbury, Connecticut; David C. Frailey and Harold Kuebler, in New York City; and Malvina Stephenson, in Washington, D.C. New acquaintances, such as Glenn Godsey, of the University of Tulsa Department of Fine Arts; W. B. Putman and the Obert Undems, of Fayetteville, Arkansas; Nina von Dolar, of Copenhagen; and E. W. O'Neill, of Tulsa. A visit to Zeeview was made possible by Phyllis K., Yamato, of the Unification church staff.

Loving thanks are due Mary Pat Ladner Robertson and Helen L. Ladner for assistance in research in New York City; Ovanda Dell Ladner, for typing; and Edward D. Ladner, for photographic work in Montana.

MILDRED D. LADNER

*Tulsa, Oklahoma*

# O.C. Seltzer

# Chapter 1
# Early Years

ALL I REMEMBER is being so damned poor, and that my mother was sick all the time, and had to work so hard."

These few words, spoken impatiently, were O. C. Seltzer's stock answer to inquiries about his boyhood in Denmark. They summarized a time remembered with bitterness.

In 1877, the year Seltzer was born in Copenhagen, Sigmund Freud was a medical student in Vienna. Psychology was in its infancy. The concept of psychic scarring was unknown. A pragmatic man whose scientific interests were confined to the chemical properties of paint and the wondrous phenomena of the insect world, Seltzer may never have brooded over the effects upon his psyche of a deprived childhood. Yet the youth who would become a foremost artist of the American West crossed the Atlantic bearing the stigmata of an insecure childhood. In later life they showed in his attitude of crusty independence. He bore them throughout his eighty years. Of the several thousand oils and watercolors Seltzer painted during sixty-five years in Montana, only one—a 13″ × 16″ oil entitled *Danish Fishing Boat*—has his native land for its setting.

Because of Seltzer's reluctance to recall the past, details of his early years are sketchy. A half-dozen documents, a school primer and a *karacter bog* (mark book), a sailing schedule, and a thin folder of clippings and etchings from Danish newspapers are his only mementos of those years. Official records in the Danish archives add enigmatic scraps of data.

The long trail that brought Olaf Seltzer to the Montana frontier in 1892 began in Denmark forty years earlier, when his maternal grandparents moved to Copenhagen from their rural home in Slagelse, about eighty kilometers southwest of the city. His grandfather, Niels Børge Sørenson, eked out a livelihood for his wife (born Sidse Marie Jensdatter) and their three children, Olaf Peter, Julie Auguste, and Laura Constance.

In the Danish capital the Sørenson family settled in a tenement area marked by rows of nondescript flats over ground-floor shops. Copenhagen was expanding rapidly to meet the demands of workers lured to the city by dreams of a more secure future in an industrialized society and of better education for their children.

Among the many German immigrants crossing the Bay of Mecklenburg with the same objectives were Ludwig Friedrich Christian Seltzer and his wife (born Caroline Albrecht) with their infant son. The Seltzers arrived in Copenhagen in 1857 and found a niche in the German community, which centered about the Lutheran congregation of Sankt Petri (Saint Peter's) Church. The elder Seltzer was a journeyman tailor from Malchin, in Mecklenburg-Schwerin.

Young Carl Christian August Seltzer was reared and educated within the strict confines of the German Lutheran parish. Before he was twenty, he was working as a cut-glass maker. When work was slack, he sorted cigars in a factory, where he met Julie Nielsen, a cigar maker five years his senior.

A photograph of Julie as a young girl reveals a face of striking Nordic beauty. Her flaxen hair is brushed in shining wings drawn up from high temples. Intense, fiery eyes flecked with gold lights and a square, firmly set jaw are softened by the delicate curve of her retroussé nose. On

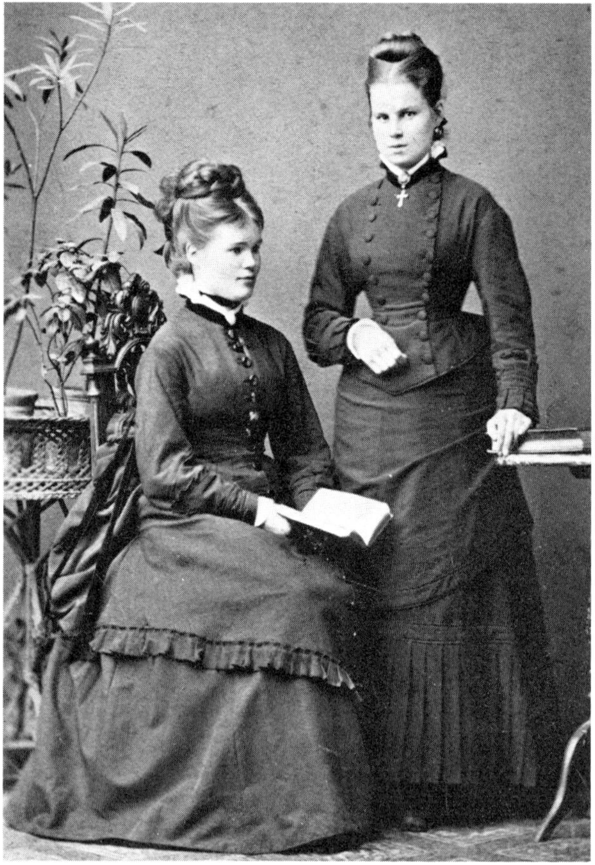

Julie and Laura Nielsen
ca. 1874
Courtesy of Carl C. Seltzer.

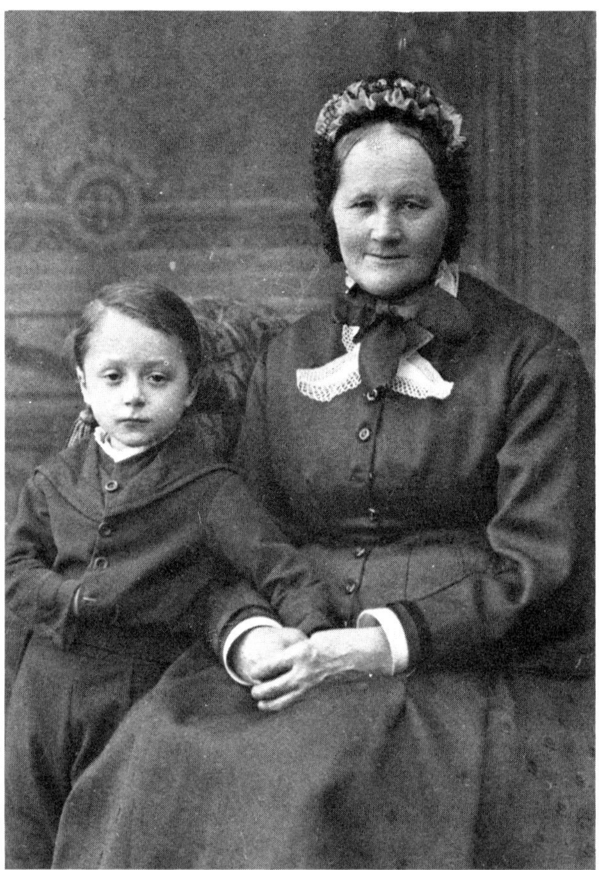

Olaf and his grandmother, Sidse Marie
ca. 1885
Courtesy of Carl C. Seltzer.

pasteboard she overshadows her younger sister, Laura, also shown, whose pale countenance reveals no matching spark of personality. In spite of her wholesome and energetic appearance, however, Julie suffered a hacking cough for most of her lifetime.

Carl and Julie's son was born on August 25, 1877, and three months later was christened Olaf Carl Børre Seltzer in Saint Matthew's Church. He would never use his third name.

Details of the young couple's life together are shrouded in mystery. Carl disappeared sometime after his infant son was christened. Whether he deserted, was shanghaied, or returned to Germany remains a matter of conjecture.[1]

Olaf was reared in a matriarchal household, with his widowed grandmother assuming respon-

sibility for his upbringing while his mother worked. During Olaf's early years there were frequent changes of living quarters, brought about by periods of unemployment. In 1881, when the lad was four, his mother was working as a seamstress and sharing a flat with her mother and her brother, Olaf, a waiter. Three years later Olaf was living alone with his grandmother.

Olaf's grandmother assumed the role of guardian for the boy, signing his monthly reports throughout his school years.[2] The Copenhagen public schools of the period were operated on a dual system, with better instruction available in the *betalingskole* (fee-paying school) than in the *friskole* (free school). Young Olaf's family managed to raise the monthly krøne to keep him in the Gasvaerksvejen (Gasworks Way) Betalingskole from 1885, when he was eight years old, until he was graduated in May, 1891.

The *betalingskole* had a standardized curriculum with daily classes in religious studies, book and manuscript reading, writing, spelling and grammar, style, drawing, Danish and world history, and mental and slate arithmetic at various levels. Geography and natural history were taught in the elementary levels; Latin and German were available in advanced levels.

From the beginning the alert boy with over-sized round eyes made excellent grades in religious studies, reading, history, geography, and slate arithmetic and only a slightly lower mark in conduct. By the end of his first school year, he had risen from tenth to third in the class of thirty-six students.

Early in his schooling Olaf developed a keen interest in natural history, particularly in entomology. He made friends with foreign deck hands on ships tied up on the Copenhagen waterfront and shared with them his enthusiasm for insect life. Intrigued by the boy's insatiable curiosity, his sailor friends brought him butterflies from the Amazon and beetles from Central Africa to add to his collection.

In 1887, when he was ten years old, Olaf was first given a grade for his drawing classes. On a scale of six he was marked consistently at five during his first two sessions of formal drawing instruction in the *betalingskole*. The daily drawing session was a period of pure joy to the boy, who had amazed his family with his sketching ability from the time he first held a piece of chalk. His drawing teachers soon discovered his talent. Through their efforts he was permitted to enter the Tekniske Selskabe (Technical Society Institute) for special instruction in 1890, shortly before he turned thirteen.[3] Although designed for the development of artisans, the institute provided elementary instruction for promising young artists who were considered to be potential material for the Royal Academy.

Olaf attended the institute part time during the first season, pending completion of his final year at the *betalingskole*. His dual attendance was reflected in his grades; he dropped from first in his class to fifteenth, although his examination scores continued to be noted as "excellent."

At the institute the precocious Olaf worked and fraternized with artists twice his age, enjoying their expertise and reveling in his exposure to the

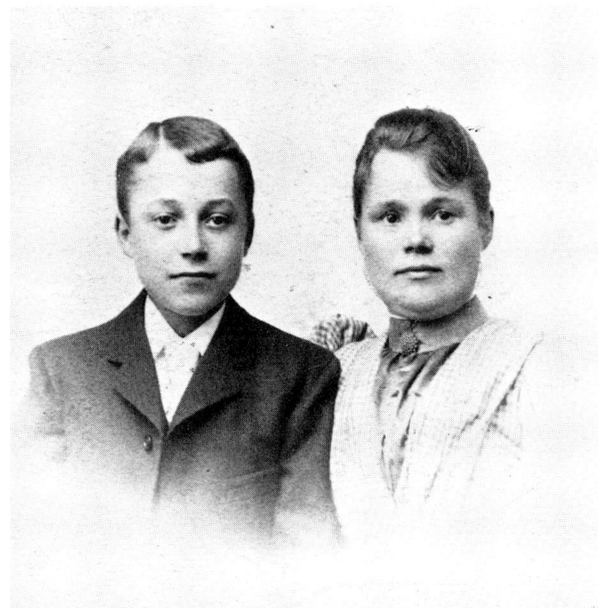

Olaf and his mother, Julie
ca. 1889
Courtesy of Carl C. Seltzer.

world of art and creative talent. Eager to be accepted in this rarefied atmosphere, he disciplined himself in patience, spending hours drawing objects from every possible angle to acquire skill in draftsmanship. Danish art instruction placed a high priority on draftsmanship; virtually every outstanding painter and sculptor of the nineteenth century was also a superb draftsman.

There is little question that Olaf would have moved from drawing classes at the institute to painting classes at the Royal Academy had it not been for an upheaval in his home life. His mother's sister, Laura, had married a man named Louis Jensen, and during Olaf's early adolescence the Jensens lived with Olaf, his mother, grandmother, and Uncle Olaf. Jensen, ill at ease in such crowded circumstances, spent most of his free time in waterfront saloons.

In the late 1880's, when Jensen's drunkenness made their living conditions unbearable, the sisters arranged for him to be removed from the scene. As a child Olaf probably failed to understand fully the disappearance of his Uncle Louis.

He was smuggled aboard a ship bound for America by sailors hired by Laura and Julie.

Months later a letter arrived from Great Falls, Montana. Jensen reported that he was in good health, working full time, and saving money on his new job. He now considered that the misfortune that had befallen him when he was shanghaied on the Copenhagen waterfront had been an unparalleled blessing.

When the ship docked in New York, Louis reported, agents for the Great Northern Railway were on hand to make tempting offers to the immigrants. A Canadian railroad builder named James J. Hill was spanning the new state of Montana with tracks to link the Great Lakes with the Pacific Northwest. He had plenty of jobs for laborers who would go west. Louis signed on, crossed the broad American continent, and was excited about the new land. The work was backbreaking, but the pay—two dollars a day!—made his efforts worthwhile. He was eating eggs for breakfast every morning.

Louis outlined plans for his wife to join him in Montana. Together they could save money to bring Julie and the boy; the dry Montana air might help Julie's chronic cough. A few months later Laura Jensen set out to join her husband, promising to send for Julie and Olaf as soon as arrangements could be made.[4]

With the beckoning promise of a new life in the romantic American West, Olaf was eager to finish his schooling and take leave of Denmark. In August, 1891, he was presented with a simple handwritten certificate bearing the elongated seal of the Gasvaerksvegen Betalingskole. Principal V. Borgen, in florid handwriting, attested that "Olaf Seltzer, being confirmed, is graduated from this school."

Now that his formal schooling was behind him, young Olaf had more time to spend at the institute, making dozens of drawings from the plaster casts provided. Here was planted the concept that would remain with him: The fundamental outline is the most important element in a work of art. He would later explain in pragmatic terms: "You cannot paint a house before it is built."

An avid reader, Olaf dreamed of the day when he could use live buffalo and antelope in their native habitat as subjects to replace the classroom models. In the meantime he sketched the dray horses plodding over Copenhagen's cobblestoned avenues and the tame deer in Deerhavn (Deer) Park.

In the spring of 1892, Julie sent her son to the wedge-shaped building, across the street from the Academy of Art, that housed the ticket office for Thingvalla Lines, which offered service "direkte to America" on four passenger ships. Olaf proudly signed the sailing schedule, adding his current address—"Freundsgade (Friend's Street) 9, 2d floor." He kept the schedule throughout his lifetime as a talisman of hope.

Mother and son pored excitedly over the self-proclaimed advantages of the Thingvalla Lines:

*   Passengers traveling with this line are transported *directly* to America, whereby all changes, stays in foreign lodging-houses, customs, inspection of baggage in intermediate ports, etc., are avoided.

*   The ships' provisions are wholesome and abundant.

*   Every ship is accompanied by a *Danish* physician appointed by the Commissioner of the Copenhagen Police, who in case of illness will give medical help to the passengers gratis.

*   Before departure, every ship will be inspected by the Authorities, who will attest to the fact that the ship is *completely seaworthy and abundantly provisioned.*

*   Passengers will be received in New York by *Danes* who will instruct the passengers upon arrival and see to the further transport of those passengers who are provided with inland railway tickets.

Julie and Olaf booked passage on the *Island (Iceland)* and on the afternoon of June 21, 1892, joined other emigrants at the ship's rail for a last farewell to their native land. The ship docked at Frederikshavn the next morning to take on passengers and cargo and at Christiansand, on the southern tip of Norway, the following day.

At first Olaf enjoyed the novelty of shipboard life, particularly the sighting of a herd of whales. But a few days later a horrendous storm moved across the North Atlantic, terrifying the Danish and Norwegian passengers. The swells were so high that the passengers were convinced the floundering ship would be engulfed in the frigid, steel-colored waters. Both Olaf and his mother were miserably ill. Julie, worn out by the chores connected with their departure, suffered intensely from the effects of the storm and seasickness. With her chronic cough she could ill afford to be undernourished. By the time the *Island* reached New York City three weeks later, mother and son were bruised and exhausted. Before them lay a five-day rail journey with tiring layovers in Chicago and Saint Paul before they would reach Great Falls, to be met by the Jensens.

As the transcontinental train crossed the northern plains, Olaf was captivated by the beauty of the undulating prairies neatly hemmed by serrated mountains and textured with buttes. He whiled away the long hours watching for wildlife and doing rough sketches.

Olaf's aunt and uncle were living in a rented cabin in Giant Springs, a hamlet eight miles east of Great Falls on the south bank of the meandering Missouri River. By the time Julie and Olaf arrived, Louis Jensen had left the Great Northern for less strenuous work as a laborer in the old silver smelter in Giant Springs.

Here Olaf had his first contact with American children and their carefree ways. A two-room shack barely twenty feet from the Jensens' cabin housed the Hansen family, which included eleven- and nine-year-old sons. Olaf learned that Halder Hansen, the older boy, had been waiting impatiently for weeks for Olaf's arrival, and he was eager to include the newcomer in the village youngsters' swimming parties in the river slough and on hikes out on the prairie. But Olaf's natural shyness was intensified by the strange surroundings and his inability to talk with the youngsters of Giant Springs. Although small enough in stature to fit in with the eleven- and twelve-year-olds, the self-conscious Danish lad had the quiet reserve of an older boy. He gave the impression of being disinterested in the other boys' activities, preferring to sit for hours in the strong sun of August, sketching the mountains and coulees and drawing the horses and cattle pastured near the tiny community.

When Halder realized that Olaf's silence was a deliberate effort to hide his clumsiness in using the English language, the younger boy began to help the newcomer build his vocabulary. As Olaf became familiar with the language, he lost much of his shyness. He soon felt enough at home with the local boys to show them his butterfly and beetle collection. Housed in a glass-covered box of his making, it was the most precious possession Olaf had brought with him from Copenhagen. Basking in the admiration of his new friends, Olaf soon was helping them make butterfly nets of their own from scraps of string and guiding their collecting efforts.[5]

The weeks following Olaf's arrival in Montana

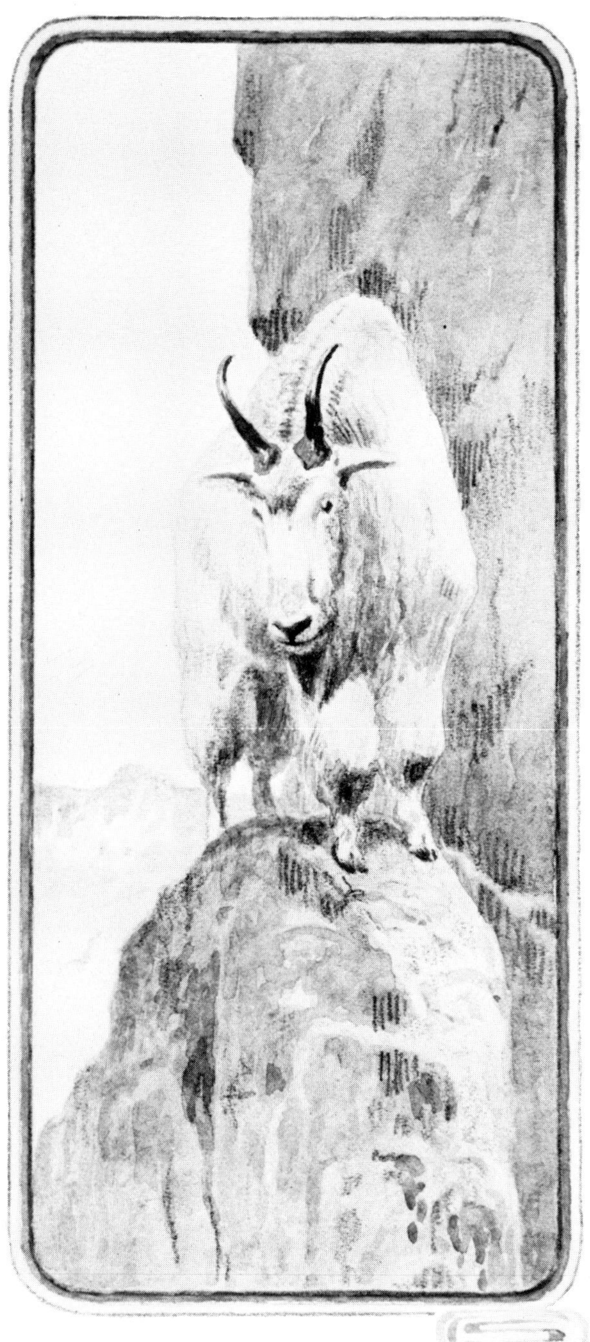

*Mountain Goat*
1926
Watercolor, 9½″ × 6¾″
Gilcrease Collection

(Unless otherwise noted, all paintings reproduced in this book are in the Gilcrease Collection, Thomas Gilcrease Institute of American History and Art, Tulsa.)

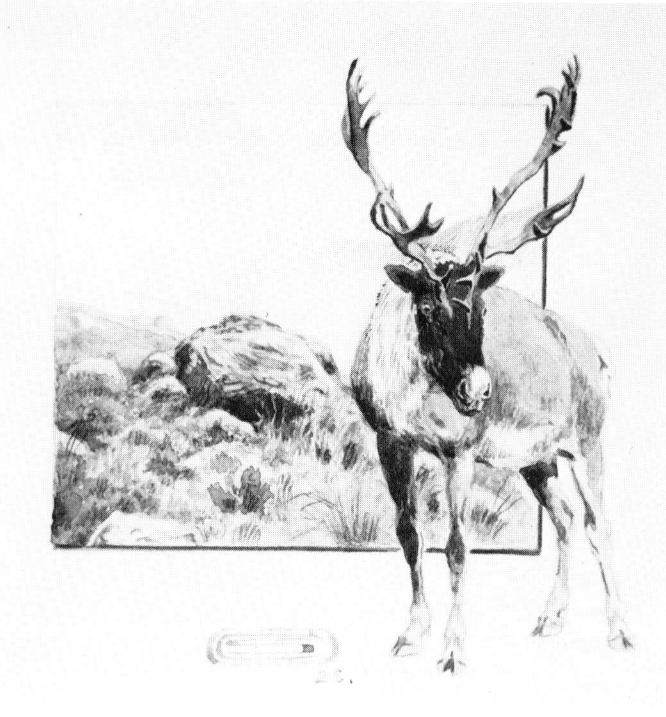

*Elk*
1926
Watercolor, 7½″ × 8¾″

and sensitive disposition, were his most commanding feature. Guileless and naïve, he bore the brunt of many a joke during his greenhorn days. But his delight in western ways and in the spectacularly beautiful new land endeared him to even the toughest saddle pounders. Chameleonlike, Olaf quickly picked up the ways of his fellow workers. He set out determinedly to be one of the boys.

In his eagerness to be accepted by his peers, Olaf quickly adopted their speech patterns, learning expletives as fast as he did English verb forms. When riled, he could swear like a mule skinner. He used his new language expressively, with a vocabulary far greater than that of the herders with whom he spent most of his time in that first season and with a minimum of grammatical errors. Within a few years he would be speaking English without a trace of foreign accent and would be able to write convincing dialogue filled with colorful western colloquialisms.

During Olaf's first year in Montana he worked for Pete Hansen, a supplier of horses for the Yellowstone Park Stage Line, and for the H. H. Hartman and the Valentine Lobenheimer horse outfits. Few details of western horsemanship and range customs were lost on the perceptive lad, whose sketching pad went everywhere with him. He began almost immediately to study and collect Montana brands, details he would use later in some of his paintings of activities on the huge spreads given over to cow outfits.

Olaf soon discovered that the job of breaking horses was not for him. Montana horse breeders of the period often halterbroke their two-year-old broncs just enough to turn them over to a cow outfit in a condition described as "green broke." These young horses were far from completely trained for all-around ranch work. Olaf steered clear of breaking, partly because, as a city-bred youth, he stood in awe of the powerful range-bred beasts, and partly because of his love for animals. He could not stand even to watch some of the cruel practices employed in breaking horses. Whenever possible he chose to ride as a corral helper, riding alongside the handler to help him out if the going got rough.[6]

Years later Olaf Seltzer prepared the following description to accompany the historical miniature he painted to commemorate the bronco buster:

*The broncho buster's idea was to "break the pony's heart" on the first ride. For if then the idea*

were idyllic. He spent most of his free time on the fringes of Giant Springs. As he wandered along the south bank of the twisting river, his sharp eyes searched for the remnants of buffalo herds. Frequently he sighted deer and antelope, noting for future reference their graceful movements and studying the effects created by the clear prairie light.

After a few months with the Jensens, during which Olaf turned fifteen and was exposed briefly to American schooling, his mother went to work as a servant in Great Falls, and Olaf joined the first of several horse outfits with which he would spend most of the coming year.

Young Seltzer had by now achieved his full height, five feet seven inches. He was lean and wiry, with trigger-quick reactions that served him well when he was bucked from a half-broken horse or, on one memorable occasion, catapulted from the roof of a stagecoach as it plunged across an icy stream.

Olaf's deep-set dark eyes, reflecting a gentle

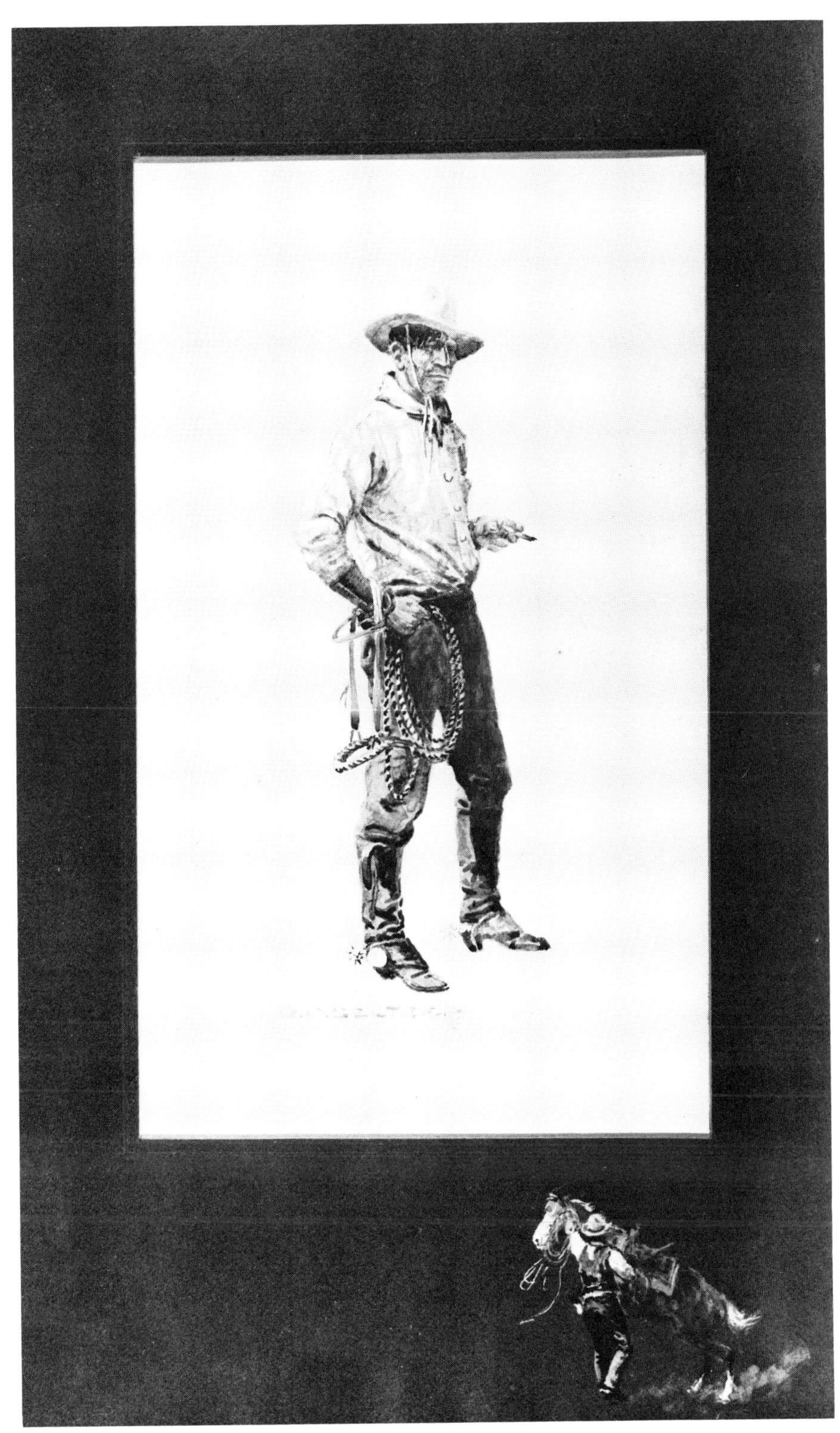

*Bronco Buster*
1928
Western Character watercolor, 18″ × 11½″
exterior, 12″ × 7″ interior

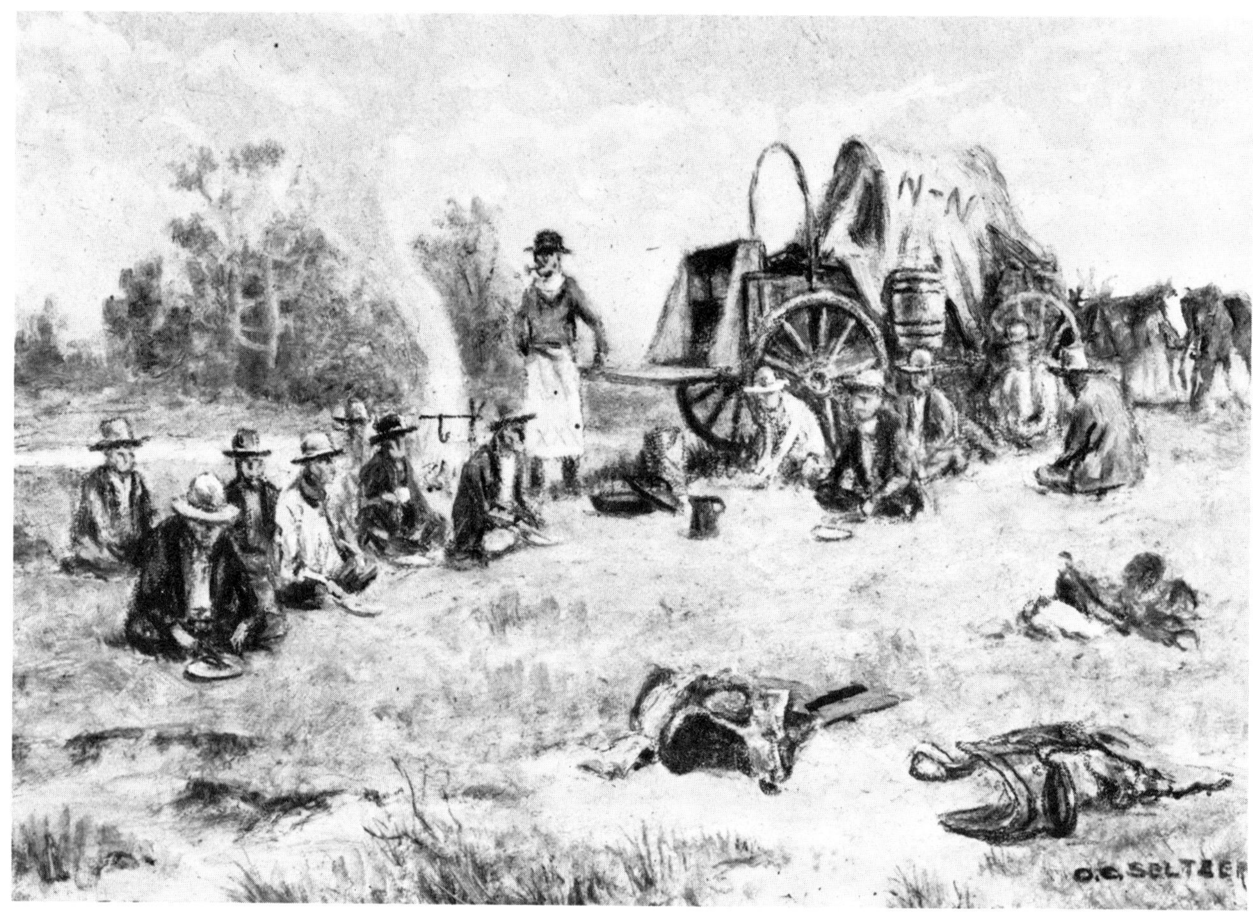

*Grub Pile—The N-N Outfit at Judith Basin About 1891*
1933
Miniature oil, 4″ × 6″
Miniature oils range from 3½″ × 5″ to 4½″ × 6″,
with most either 4″ × 6″ or 6″ × 4″.

*of human supremacy could be impressed upon an animal physically exhausted from its own efforts to the point of staggering and mentally dejected from the failure of its confident expectation, it was a surety it would never again make such a violent effort. True, it might buck again, but never so fiercely. The dread of man would cloud every subsequent plan to pitch.*

*To create this dread, the broncho buster brought down the quirt and scratched at every jump the pony made. The broncho buster "Busted, Broke, Peeled, Twisted, or Gentled" ac-*

*cording; as "busting wide open, quirting aplenty, shoving in the steel and scratching."*

Some critics have contended that the horses Seltzer painted bear a resemblance to European horses in their girth, rather than to the scrawny cayuses ridden by Montana's Indians. Actually, in order to buck the winter snowdrifts, Montana's cowpunchers needed a stouter, larger-boned, and longer-legged horse than the cow ponies commonly used by Texas-based trail outfits. Montana horse breeders preferred the Morgan breed, or a

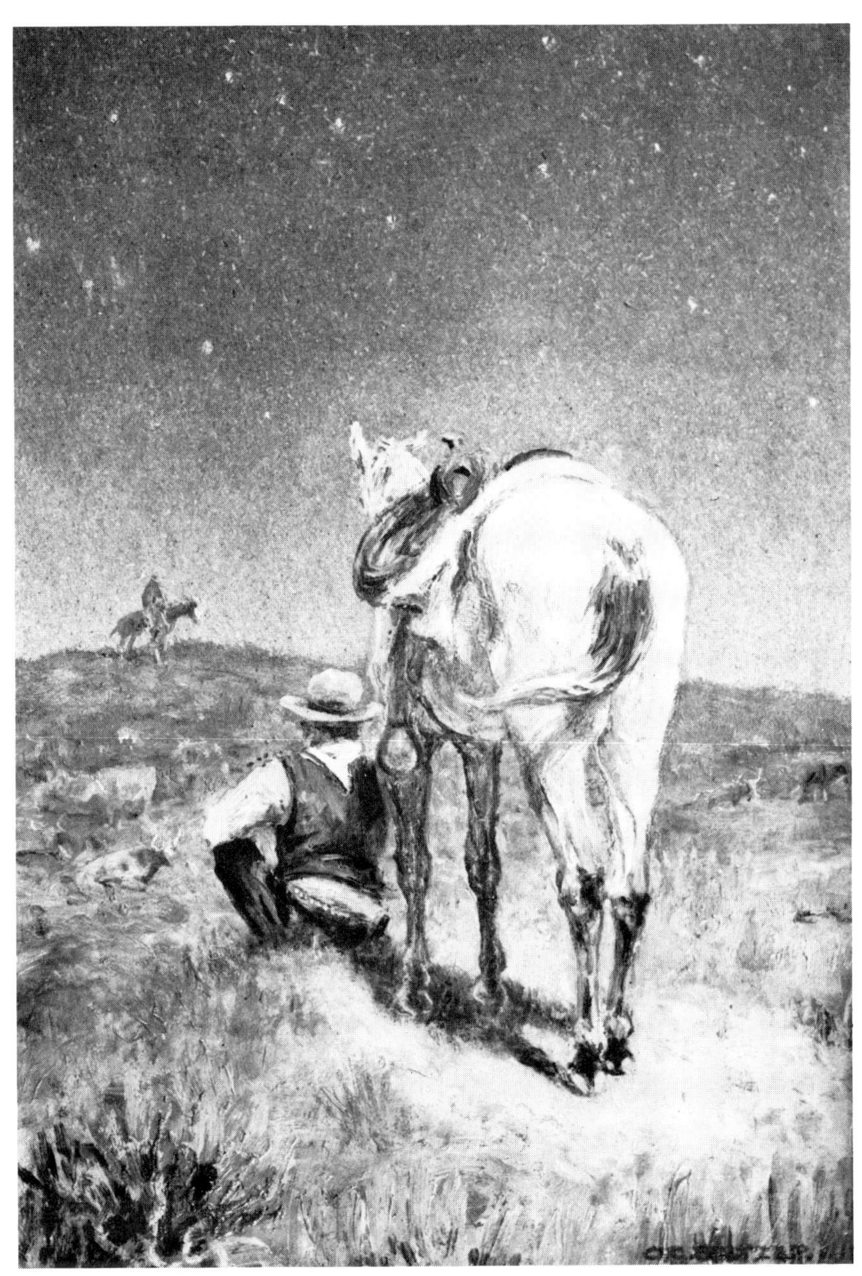

*Night Herder's Clock*
ca. 1934
Miniature oil

cross between a Percheron stallion and a Hambletonian mare of the trotting type. Mares of the Appaloosa breed, sturdy horses developed by the Nez Perces, often were bred to Morgan studs to produce "circle" horses strong enough to carry riders up to thirty miles a day on a cattle drive.[7]

After some practical experience in breaking broncs, the teen-aged Olaf gladly took over the duties of nighthawk, the herder who tended the horses from early in the evening until four in the morning, rounding up strays and investigating disturbances that caused restlessness among the animals during the long prairie nights.

Years later Olaf painted a 6″ × 4″ miniature in oil, which he titled *The Night Herder's Clock*. It features a young hand hunkered down by his saddle horse under a star-studded sky of midnight blue. He added this explanatory note based on his own youthful experience: "Looking upon this painting and knowing the title, a graphic story is told. You are looking due north with the moon behind your back. You see the 'Night Herder's Clock'—the big dipper in the northern sky. The position being ten o'clock on about the 25th of September somewhere in Montana."

In the small painting it is possible to make out a mounted rider on a bluff in the distance and a herd of cattle bedded down for the night in a valley between the two herders. The construction of the scene is similar to that of Frederic Remington's *The Herd at Night*. Remington also portrayed the nighthawk from a rear view, but his herder is mounted on a horse as he surveys the herd.[8]

His season on the range was young Olaf's first and last experience of outdoor work. The sixteen-year-old was still attracted by the beauty of the prairie country and the romance of working with horses, but he was fully aware of his responsibility to support his ailing mother. Julia, as she became known after her name was anglicized, worked when she was able in some of the affluent homes of Great Falls, but she returned often to the little cabin in Giant Springs, where her sister looked after her during recurrent seizures of lung inflammation. Young Olaf knew that he could not afford the winter layoffs customary among those who made their living on the open range. He needed a dependable income to support his mother.

But Olaf had fallen in love with the subtle coloring of the prairie, its tawny grasses and mauve buttes, the dull, silvery cast of the sagebrush, the smoky blue shadows enveloping the distant mountains, and the diamond-hard glare on fresh snow cast over miles of undulating plains. In a single round of seasons in Montana, Olaf Seltzer had put aside his boyhood to prepare for a long stay in the new land. He had found his home.

# Chapter 2
# Apprentice to Machinist

ON OCTOBER 3, 1893, Olaf Seltzer signed on as an apprentice machinist in the red-brick locomotive shops of the Great Northern Railway, across the river from downtown Great Falls. Now that he had decided on his future, he applied himself to his apprenticeship with the unflinching conscientiousness that was his distinctive trait.

In exchanging the grime and clatter of the machine shop for the boundless skies of the open prairie, Olaf gained the advantage of regular ten-hour shifts and instruction in the use of complicated tools. The apprenticeship also assured him of being in town for most of the next three to four years, for his mother's health weighed heavily on the youth's mind.

Olaf's choice of a trade was based on job availability rather than inclination alone, but it was a fortunate one, because the same perfectionism and insistence upon accuracy of detail that would later mark his paintings were basic requirements in a topnotch skilled machinist.

After his introduction to the plant through a series of unpleasant cleanup jobs, Olaf began practice work on the pin-drill press, grinder, slotter (vertical shaper), planer, and milling machine. At least half of his apprentice training was with machines. During this time he learned how to taper a hundred or more kinds of locomotive bolts, each individually reamed to measurements as fine as 1.5 thousandths of an inch by use of calipers. Bearings and brake shoes also had to be painstakingly ground until they were a precise fit.

Such assignments took unlimited patience and a native mechanical skill, along with a high degree of dexterity, a sense of spatial relationships, and a willingness to stay with a trying task until it was completed. Olaf measured up on all scores. His wiry build and quick reflexive responses came in handy when he was called upon to help a journeyman machinist with a fast-moving and often dangerous job, such as pulling the superheaters out of still-hot flues in a locomotive just in from the tracks, always one of the most unpleasant chores facing a roundhouse crew of the late nineteenth century.

An eager learner, Olaf absorbed the one-to-one tutelage he received from the shift foreman and assistant foreman, including instructions on analyzing the complex blueprints distributed by the Baldwin and the American locomotive works for the guidance of repair and maintenance crews. He quickly developed an expertise in mechanical drawing—before Olaf left the railroad, a course in mechanical drawing would be required for all prospective rail-machinist apprentices—and this gave him an advantage over his peers, as did his practiced eye for working with scaled-down detail.[1]

Young Seltzer felt at home in the rugged atmosphere of the roundhouse. A number of other Danes were employed there, and he enjoyed the chance to talk with them in his native tongue. The regularly scheduled shifts provided him with more time for drawing, even though he was working a six-day week. Whenever possible during the next thirty years, he chose to work the night shift so that he could spend time on his artwork in the morning after leaving the job; he preferred working at his easel in early-morning light.

In mild weather Olaf spent his leisure time out on the prairies, which stretched endlessly in

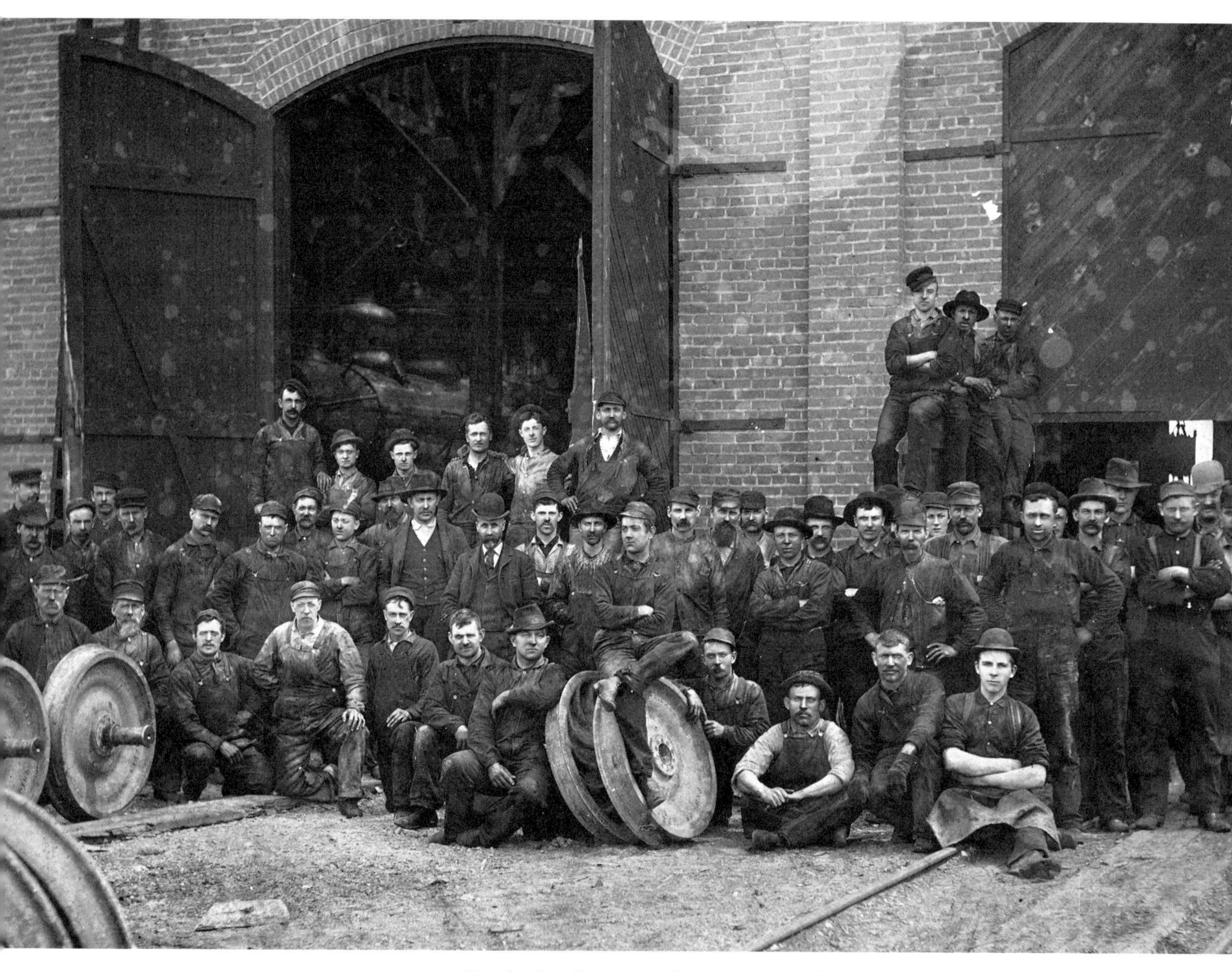

"Back-shop" crew at the Great Northern
ca. 1896
Olaf Seltzer, at nineteen, arms folded, the first of the three men seated in upper-right corner.
Courtesy of Carl C. Seltzer.

every direction from the fledgling rail center. His expeditions to sketch animals against backgrounds of undulating grasslands and jagged mountain ridges were made easier when, in September, 1894, he bought a saddle horse from J. W. Guyella for twenty dollars.

Riding the Kid across the plains in the slanted light of a wintry daybreak or in the mellow gold of an Indian summer dusk, Olaf framed the sentiments that he put into a few lines of verse and used with slight variations again and again in letters and greeting cards he illustrated for friends:

I oft times feel a pity and regret
For those who never knew
That wide and open space
Which lies between the sunset and the dawn;
The Prairie.

During the long, bitterly cold winters Olaf had time to refine the rough sketches he had made on the plains into pen-and-ink drawings distinguished by their fine linear composition. He experimented with colored inks, striving for brighter touches in his work.

By 1896, Seltzer felt secure enough in his progress as an apprentice machinist, and with the modest but regular increases in his pay envelope, to provide his mother with a home of her own at Black Eagle, just across the river north and east of Great Falls. Known then as Little Chicago, Black Eagle was settled largely by Scandinavian immigrant laborers and their families who chose to be close to the Boston and Maine Smelter, which was later taken over by the Anaconda interests.

At the time Little Chicago was largely a collection of tar-paper-roofed shacks along the riverbank. Housewives carried water from the river for their cooking and washing. In rainy seasons the main street of the settlement—Smelter Avenue—would be ankle-deep in mud. Nonetheless, living in her own home on the edge of Great Falls was a boon for Olaf's mother after her rootless years working in the homes of others. In the Little Chicago community she was among those who spoke her language and knew her ways. The air would not have been good for her health, however, or for her bouts of lung congestion. The sulfurous wastes spewed from the smelter most likely added to her problem.

With the knowledge that his mother was settled, Olaf finished his apprenticeship and late in 1896 began a long period of itinerant work as a journeyman machinist for various railways and for the ironworks and smelters in the area. Plying the machinist's trade on the expanding Canadian rail system took Olaf as far as Medicine Hat, Alberta, along the South Saskatchewan River nearly 250 miles northeast of Great Falls. Because of Medicine Hat's location in the Chinook belt of warm winds, there was a wide variety of wild animals in the area. Olaf observed and sketched to his heart's content, and the more familiar he became with varieties of deer, elk, moose, cougar, and coyote the more upset he became at the prospect of their eventual disappearance from the prairies as a result of unlimited hunting.

While working in Lethbridge, Alberta, not far from the international boundary line, Olaf frequently visited the nearby Belly River Reservation of the Bloods, an offshoot of the Blackfoot tribes. There he made detailed sketches to remind him of tribal ways. In Lethbridge he developed a great respect for the Canadian Mounted Police. Visiting the police barracks on the edge of town on Sunday afternoons, he would hobnob with the Mounties as they groomed their sleek, powerful horses. Olaf's admiration was based as much on the Mounties' respect for their horseflesh as for their reputation in enforcing the law.

Traveling back and forth on a narrow-gauge railroad known as the Turkey Trail, which connected Great Falls with the frontier towns of Alberta, Olaf had time to bring out his sketch pad. His quickly executed sketches and inexhaustible curiosity about the area caught the attention of George Waghorn, a well-known Turkey Trail conductor, who took a liking to the talented youth.

"Wag," as he was called by the regular passengers, particularly admired a drawing of Olaf's that showed the Turkey Trail's engine against recognizable scenery at Shelby, Montana, midway between Great Falls and Lethbridge. Late in 1896 the conductor took the Turkey Trail drawing, which Seltzer had given him, to A. J. Trigg for display behind the bar in Trigg's Brunswick Saloon in Great Falls. Among the regulars at the Brunswick was the established cowboy artist Charles M. Russell.

The young itinerant machinist and the already

legendary Russell had not met, for Russell had settled in Great Falls only recently. Since both enjoyed the conviviality of the Great Falls "watering holes," it was fitting that they should meet in one of them. The saloons, with their polished mahogany bars, prints of sporting figures, and samples of local artwork, were the social centers for range riders and railroaders, as well as local tradesmen. Seltzer's favorites were the Silver Dollar and the Brunswick.

William H. (Billy) Rance, proprietor of the Silver Dollar, hung Russell's work in his barroom and proudly displayed the illustrated letters Charlie had sent him. Trigg, whose saloon boasted a back room that Russell used as a studio until he had one of his own, also hung the cowboy artist's paintings behind the bar. (Several years later, the Russells purchased a clapboard house next door to the Trigg residence on tree-lined Fourth Avenue North, and the two families formed an enduring friendship. Charlie's log-cabin studio was erected between the two homes, and the Charles M. Russell museum now occupies the site of the Trigg residence.)[2]

Olaf Seltzer often told his family and friends that, when he crossed the coin-studded entry to the Silver Dollar on a blustery late-winter day in 1897, he took the step that would most profoundly change the course of his life. He entered the Silver Dollar a machinist with a hobby of sketching; he left with a glimmer of hope that he might someday become an artist like his newfound friend. March 19, 1897, marked the thirty-third birthday of Charles Marion Russell, and nineteen-year-old Olaf Seltzer happened in on a boisterous birthday celebration for the artist, who was even then a Montana celebrity whom Olaf had long looked forward to meeting.

Magnanimous by nature, Russell could afford to be generous in his praise of the promising young draftsman whose pen-and-ink sketch of the Turkey Trail he had seen in Trigg's bar. Words of praise from an accomplished artist like Russell, who was even then selling some paintings for reproduction on calendars, opened new vistas for young Olaf.

The freewheeling Charlie, only recently domesticated by his venture in "double harness" with beautiful eighteen-year-old Nancy Mann Cooper, welcomed his encounter with the young man who had drawn the Turkey Trail. There was an immediate rapport between the artist who had put aside his roaming ways to live in town and

spend regular hours at his easel and the young machinist who dreamed of the distant day when he could afford to do likewise.

Olaf was transported with joy to be accepted as a drinking companion of such a renowned artist and raconteur as Russell. Charlie, for his part, recognized in the fresh-faced youth with the contemplative dark eyes and quick smile a kindred soul with whom he could talk about his craft and share his dream of preserving on canvas the ways of the Old West, so changed since his arrival in the Judith Basin east of Great Falls seventeen years earlier.

Their shared interest in depicting western scenes and conserving the wildlife of the plains and the high country was a bond between them. Both despised wanton killing and earnestly applied their talents to protecting the wilderness and its primitives. Both considered themselves "square shooters" and deplored sham and pretension, yet each had a touch of vanity in his makeup. It was more obvious in Russell, with his many rings and his woven voyageur's sash of bright colors (cerise silk for dress occasions), but Olaf was not averse to posing for his photograph a few years later wearing a flowing silk tie and balancing a palette on his knee.

Both were perfectionists, striving for depictions that would be correct down to the most minute detail. Yet their attitudes toward the discipline of formal training were poles apart. Russell, the school dropout from a wealthy family, had endured three days of art lessons as a boy of fifteen in Saint Louis, during which he was required to make many sketches of a cast of a human foot. "Three days of lookin' at that hunk of plaster was all I could stand and I walked out," he told friends.[3] Later he turned down a Philadelphia patron's offer to stake him to a European study trip, and when his wife persuaded him to visit the Continent, following a London exhibition years later, he quickly lost interest in gallery trotting and insisted that they shorten their trip and return to Montana.

As an impoverished adolescent, Olaf had applied himself to drawing inanimate objects at the Technical Society Institute for days on end, patiently striving for a realistic reproduction. He felt keenly the need for additional art training and for more general education, never passing up a chance to visit museums and art galleries in the hope of overcoming these deficiencies.

Charlie, the extrovert, sought the knowledge of

authentic ways in the skin lodges of the Bloods, with whom he lived for six months in 1888, and in barrooms and bunkhouses across the state of Montana. Olaf, the introvert, turned to books for his continuing self-education, haunting the public library and scanning years of issues of periodicals in his methodical research.

Russell lived happily in a world of his own creation, enjoying the use of rustic colloquialisms. When he turned to writing for publication as a means of selling illustrations, his haphazard punctuation and phonetic spelling never bothered him. It has been claimed that he could write as correctly as the average person of his time and that his careless use of language was for folksy effect. But the atrocious misspellings in his last, exquisitely illustrated letter raise some doubt about this claim.[4]

Seltzer worked at his new language until he lost all telltale pronunciations that would mark him as an immigrant. In his writing, his grammar, though marked by a personal idiosyncrasy, the frequent use of colons followed by dashes, was generally correct and consistent, particularly when he was writing to patrons.

The greatest single stroke of luck to befall the happy-go-lucky Charlie was his marriage to the young girl who was to devote her life to assuring him fame and fortune. Because of her unusually keen business sense, coupled with charm and rare beauty, Nancy Russell was able to assume total responsibility for Charlie's career beyond the actual creation of the paintings. It was she who urged him to take his beeswax molding more seriously after reading an article on Remington's bronzes, thus expanding the role her talented husband would play in the world of American western art. She throve in her role as his manager, and Charlie was delighted and everlastingly grateful to be able to turn all such duties over to her so that he could be free of any concern for business matters, particularly when it came to pricing his work.

Olaf Seltzer, by contrast, was insecure and easily discouraged. He too married a woman with exceptional qualities and an abundance of tact, but he nurtured a typically European nineteenth century view of woman's role. Only when his health began to fail did he welcome his wife's cooperation. In his later years he bought her a typewriter so that she could help with his growing correspondence, which up to that point he had been answering by hand.

Charlie, easygoing and unhurried, radiated what is today called charisma. Olaf, who operated on a schedule and could not abide being kept waiting, had no patience with slothful habits. His friends knew him to be pleasant, witty, and delightful company, but as he grew older, he acquired the reputation among those who incurred his displeasure of being something of a curmudgeon. His family knew him to be warm and affectionate.

But the traits for which both men are remembered had barely surfaced on March 19, 1897, when friends of the celebrating painter, now including the young machinist, raised their glasses to *skoal* Charlie Russell into a new year.

A few months earlier Russell had written a friend to let him know that "the Gospel Wrangler had caught him and necked him," the phrase referring to the practice of tying a wild horse to a gentle one, forcing the bronco to go wherever the tamed horse led.[5] The gentling process got under way during the first year of the Russells' marriage when Nancy began to break her husband of his longtime habit of selling or trading his paintings over the bar in the saloons for five or ten dollars, or even for a round of drinks. One can imagine the warmth and feeling of relief with which she welcomed a younger would-be artist come to work with Charlie in the room he used as an improvised studio and to accompany him on sketching trips into the wilderness.

Seltzer became a frequent guest in the Russells' first rented quarters, and was presented with one of the oval-shaped wedding photographs showing the head and shoulders of a grimly serious Russell at the right of his comely bride in her handmade dark polka-dot wedding dress.

The two men enjoyed drawing each other. A line sketch of Olaf done by Charlie shortly after they met shows the Dane wearing a wide-brimmed slouch hat with a kerchief tied at the nape of his neck—a rare pose for Seltzer, who generally was critical of the wearing of western garb by those not actually working on the range. The sketch was done when Olaf accompanied Charlie and several of his cronies on a trip down the Missouri River. Perhaps Olaf was posing for one of Russell's storytelling paintings, such as *Through the Alkali*, which illustrated the cowpuncher's practical use of his neckerchief, or bandanna.

In one of the pocket notebooks that Olaf Seltzer kept during the latter years of his life, he noted in

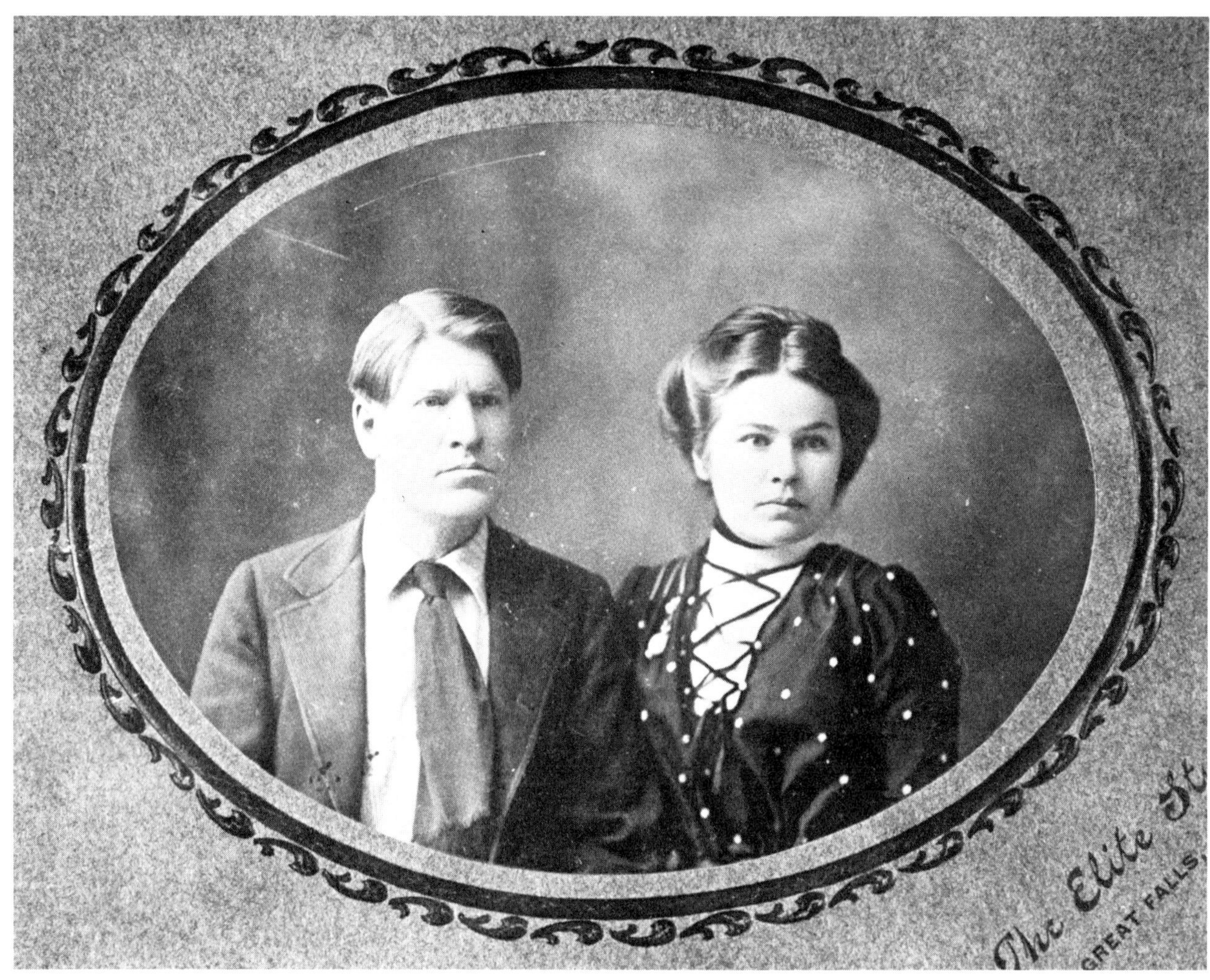

Nancy and Charlie Russell's wedding picture.
Courtesy of Carl C. Seltzer.

his tiny, precise script that on November 14, 1947, he turned up, forty-nine years after it was done, "an old CMR watercolor sketch painted on trip of 1898. . . . Also a small watercolor sketch by Charley of himself on old Monty painted on the flyleaf of one of Wallace Coburn's books entitled 'Rimes of the Round-up.' "

On the Circle C Ranch, the Coburn spread near the Fort Belknap Indian Reservation on Beaver Creek outside Zortman, Montana, E. E. (Boo) MacGilvra came across a watercolor signed by Russell with his name and that of "O. Seltzer" (this is a rare example of Seltzer's work signed with only the initial of his first name and the only

known collaboration). MacGilvra, the winner of a bunkhouse poker game, was asked by an old-time cowboy if he would take a picture to satisfy a poker debt. When MacGilvra agreed, the cowhand produced a rolled-up and fly-specked 14″ × 20″ watercolor depicting a party of mounted braves riding at the head of a war party against a background of buttes and distant mountains touched with soft pink. The general effect is impressionistic, but four of the horses in the advance party are clearly defined, their trappings well marked.[6]

MacGilvra, an authority on the Lewis and Clark Expedition, sought authentication from Olaf Selt-

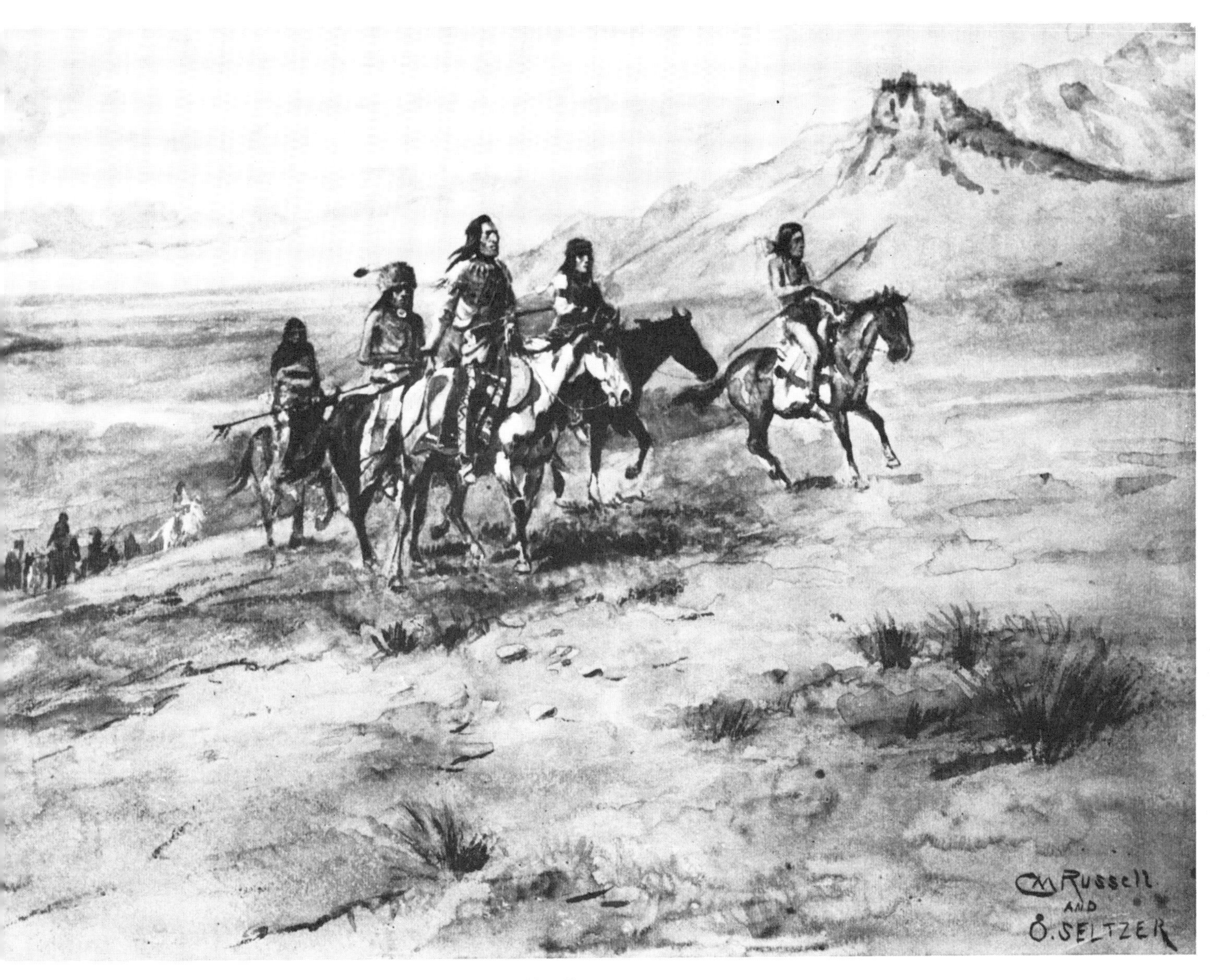

*War Party*
1900–1901
Watercolor, 14″ × 20″
The only known collaboration of Charlie Russell and Olaf Seltzer.
On loan to the Montana Historical Society Museum, Helena, Montana.
Copyrighted by E. E. and Edna MacGilvra, Butte, Montana.

zer's older son, Carl, who wrote him on September 11, 1971:

*Your watercolor "War Party" painted by my father and Russell is very rare. It was done "Just for the hell of it," to give the natives something to talk about and to see if they could figure out who painted which part, of course, no one could tell. They got a big kick out of it, my father told me.*

*Charlie and my father were very close friends and they worked on their painting in Russell's cabin on many occasions. . . .*

*The two artists made many pack trips to sketch, watch the wild game, see the country and observe the Indians who were continually on the move headed for the Judith Basin. It was on one of these trips (1900–1901) to the Basin that Charlie suggested they paint one together. The sketches were made on this trip. C.M.R. made the sketch and O.C.S. did the painting.*

*The two friends would do some hunting for meat in the pan and carry fire water for snake bite. They enjoyed each other's company, seeing the great game animals and the country. The wild game were among their artistic and humanitarian enthusiasms.*

In rough notes made for a talk given shortly after Russell's death in 1926, Olaf reminisced about his meeting with Charlie in the Silver Dollar:

*. . . From that time on for twenty-four years . . . we enjoyed a continuous friendship and close association.*

*. . . That raw March day in 1897 when we first met was no doubt a turning point in my life. . . . by reason of that meeting and the subsequent association, my future was to a great extent molded.*

At the time of their meeting Olaf Seltzer had not begun to work with oil paints, although he was experimenting with watercolors. *Mad Steer or Green Cowhand*, 12¾″ × 17½″, is dated 1897 and signed with the tiny oblong palette pierced with three brushes that Olaf fancied beneath his name in his early years of painting; several early watercolors of hunters and their prey are similarly signed. His early watercolor work was far less clearcut and definitive in detail than his later work.

Russell imparted to the younger artist some tips for working with oil paints during their visits in the Russell home, but Olaf's acknowledged first full-scale attempt at working with oils on canvas took place a year later, in the spring of 1898, while he was employed as a machinist on the narrow-gauge railroad at Lethbridge.

Young Olaf struck up a friendship with Frederick D. Downer, a partner in the Lethbridge House, with whom he became acquainted while looking for a place to stay. Downer, formerly the proprietor of the Grand Hotel in Great Falls, had brought his family to the Alberta boom town only a few months earlier.

Itinerant workers were well aware of the overcrowded conditions in Lethbridge. It was an almost nightly experience for late arrivals to sleep on the billiard and pool tables in the main hotel, the English-style Lethbridge House. Workers poured into the coal-mining town of thirty-five hundred, headquarters for crews working on the construction of the Crow Nest branch of the Canadian Pacific Railway. When Olaf arrived on the 10:30 train from Great Falls on a Saturday night in March, 1898, he took his place in the queue of men awaiting the assignment of space in the inn or referral to private homes. To his surprise Olaf was given an attic room in the Lethbridge House.

The following afternoon Olaf went to the hotel office to thank Downer for his courtesy, and the two began talking. In his reminiscences written years later, Downer noted that there was something about this "fine-looking boy" that set him apart from the rough laborers and prompted the innkeeper to relinquish one of two attic rooms he had been holding back for an emergency. After explaining that he had come to work as a machinist in the roundhouse, Olaf produced a handful of pen-and-ink drawings on foolscap for Downer's inspection.

Downer asked Seltzer if he had ever taken any painting lessons.

"A few," Olaf answered. "A painter named Charlie Russell down in Montana showed me a few tricks."

The drawings, "wild and wooly westerns" in Downer's words, reminded him of Russell's work. He offered to sell the drawings at fifty cents apiece over the bar, and Olaf's work sold easily.

A few weeks later Downer asked Olaf whether he had ever painted in oils. When he learned that the young machinist had never been able to afford such luxuries, the hotelman asked conductor Waghorn to visit the Como Store on his next run to Great Falls to pick up some supplies for Olaf's use. Downer was specific in his order: he wanted a canvas "stretched on a frame about three feet by four feet, paint, brushes, palette, etc., and to have the canvas put into a wide gilt frame."

Since some of the hotel's regular guests had taken an interest in the fledgling artist, there was considerable excitement at the bar when Wag returned with Downer's purchases. Seltzer immediately rearranged his attic room to get the maximum light from the north and asked Downer what he wanted painted on the framed canvas. Recalling the episode, Downer wrote:

*I told him I thought a war party of Indians on a fairly high bluff looking down on a valley with an immigrant train of wagons... crossing the Sun River [in Montana] would make a very appropriate picture. He started on a Sunday morning ... Propping the canvas on the bureau he made a rough sketch with a pencil and then asked me to check it over, and it was perfectly done. Then the work with the oil paints started.*

After the painting was completed, Downer pointed out that the artist had forgotten to put a medicine man in the war party. Seltzer added one. "Anyone viewing it would think it was done by Charles Russell," Downer concluded in his reminiscence.

Seltzer's first oil painting was, indeed, in the heavy tones of bronze, olive, mustard, and gray-green of Russell's earlier work, with small splashes of bright red to enliven its somber effect.

It was July before the painting was completed to the artist's satisfaction. Olaf presented it to his delighted benefactor. "The perspective was excellent and the painting itself was carefully done, even to the red patch on the hip of one of the Indian ponies," Downer wrote. "I was a little doubtful on this point and questioned Olaf closely, but he assured me it was true to the Indian practice of marking a stolen pony."

Soon after finishing the painting, Seltzer moved on to Butte, Montana, without leaving a forwarding address. Downer never heard from the artist until Olaf paid him a surprise visit thirty years later, and the painting remained unnamed until the last decade of the artist's life.

But *The Scout* in its gilded frame had worked its magic in giving young Olaf Seltzer the confidence to continue working with oils.[7] By 1901 he had painted at least two notable oils: *Elk Hunt in Winter*, an 11" × 22" snow scene laid in Canada that depicts an Indian on bended knee taking aim on an elk, with huskies and sled in the background, and *Indian Maiden at Rock*. The latter, 22" × 11" and signed with the tiny palette, features a romanticized maiden in a pose similar to several painted by Russell after his time in residence with the Bloods north of the Canadian border. The subtle use of color that would become a characteristic of Seltzer's work is detectable in these paintings.

Olaf Seltzer had yet to develop a style unmistakably his own, but by the turn of the century the strands of his uprooted existence were coming together. He now had a dependable way of making a living and, thanks to the encouragement of new friends, the confidence to know that he could be an artist. He had found his *métier*.

Chapter 3
# Itinerant Years

FOR EIGHT YEARS Olaf Seltzer continued his itinerant way of life, moving back and forth across Montana and as far west as the shipyards of Seattle during railroad layoffs. He seldom was unemployed for more than a few days at a time. Skilled machinists were in demand in the burgeoning industries of the area. As soon as he was notified of a work shutdown in the locomotive shops of the Great Northern, he would pack his bag and take the day coach to Tuttle or Butte or Anaconda, working for brief intervals on narrow-gauge industrial rail lines or in the copper-refining or iron industry until he got word that the Great Northern was rehiring.

Seltzer was back in Great Falls shortly after he left Lethbridge for Butte in 1898, remaining in the railroad shops until October, 1899, when he signed on with the Great Falls Iron Works. For a lengthy interval he was able to be with his mother in Black Eagle or with the Jensens in Giant Springs. He stayed with the ironworks until March, 1900, when he returned to the locomotive shops, where he worked until mid-July. He finished out the year in the employ of the American Refining and Smelting Company in Giant Springs. Between January, 1901, and May, 1902, he was employed steadily by the Great Northern, except for a five-month layoff because of a strike in the summer of 1901.

In the spring of 1902 he moved on to Tuttle, then to the copper community of Anaconda, about twenty miles west of Butte, from which he returned in the autumn on call from the Great Northern. Olaf added watercolors (and perhaps gouache) to the gear he carried with him on his out-of-town jobs. Watercolors required less equipment than oil paints; the drying process was simpler and faster. It was a natural progression for a young artist to make in his creative development.

Olaf took advantage of his relative freedom during this seminomadic period to spend as much time as possible in the wilderness, filling sketchbooks and wrapping-paper rolls with sketches of all manner of wild game, from the furtive wolf to the majestic buffalo. He studied their individual features closely, discovering at first hand that a bison's tongue is black, not red and learning to identify hoof and paw prints. These he would use effectively as decorative touches on the dozens of wild-animal pictures he had begun painting in oil and watercolor.

The sketching expeditions with Charlie Russell into the Montana mountains continued. Sometimes their parties were augmented by their mutual friend, young Bill Marks, or some of Charlie's cronies among the business and professional men of Great Falls. Whatever the purpose of the pack trip, Seltzer and Russell always carried their sketching paper and drawing materials in the same spirit that contemporary safari hunters arm themselves with telephoto lenses and high-speed cameras. Neither countenanced trophy hunting, although they carried guns for protection and occasionally to provide their party with fresh meat.

*Flagging Antelope*, an 18″ × 25″ Seltzer watercolor, depicts two hunters crouched behind a hillock, waving a red bandanna to arouse the curiosity of a herd of antelope and lure them closer, a trick borrowed from Indian hunters. But when Charlie and Olaf indulged in this ruse, it was to watch the fleet-footed antelope leap to their escape after a confrontation with man, and not to bring them within rifle range.[1]

"Civilized man is the most cruel and purposeless killer under the cover of Sport," Olaf noted in a pocket diary some fifty years later. A man who found it hard to articulate his emotions, he depicted on paper and canvas his deep feelings about the vanishing herds of buffalo, antelope, and mountain goats. Animals, whether household pets or shy woodland creatures, always excited Seltzer and aroused his protective instinct. When he glimpsed a velvet-eyed creature peering from a break in the forested hills, he would be as excited as a city youngster on his first visit to a zoo.

Olaf called his small paintings of Montana's animals his "Wild Critters," and he posed the animals against appropriate scenic panels and shapes of bright colors, each with a smaller animal or complementary detail on the panel or the matte. He adapted some of the graphic modes of the day in hopes of selling his critters as magazine illustrations.

It was probably with the same objective in mind that Olaf was emboldened to write a short story in 1900, his only known literary effort other than the bits of verse he used in illustrated letters or on personal greeting cards. Perhaps he was inspired by an illustration Charlie Russell had already made, or perhaps he sought Charlie's help to make his story more salable—"A Bear Story," which appeared in the January, 1901, issue of *Rocky Mountain* magazine under the byline O. Seltzer, is jointly illustrated.

An entertaining account of a skirmish between a prospector and a grizzly bear, "A Bear Story" is illustrated at the beginning with a pen-and-ink drawing of a bear walking a log. The bear is placed between the letter "A" and the word "Story." This illustration carries the acknowledgment: "From Drawing by the Author." On the reverse side is a full-page (5″ × 8″) sketch of a grizzly bear embracing its frantic victim, captioned "From Wash Drawing by Russell." A bear-claw print serves as a final signature at the close of the account. Seltzer related the adventure as he may have heard it from the victim, Hank Winters, with some probable changes for humorous effect. The true incident occurred "just after the Yogo Stampede in '80," when Hank and his partner, Bed-Rock Jim, were prospecting on the south side of a Montana mountain range known as the Snows:

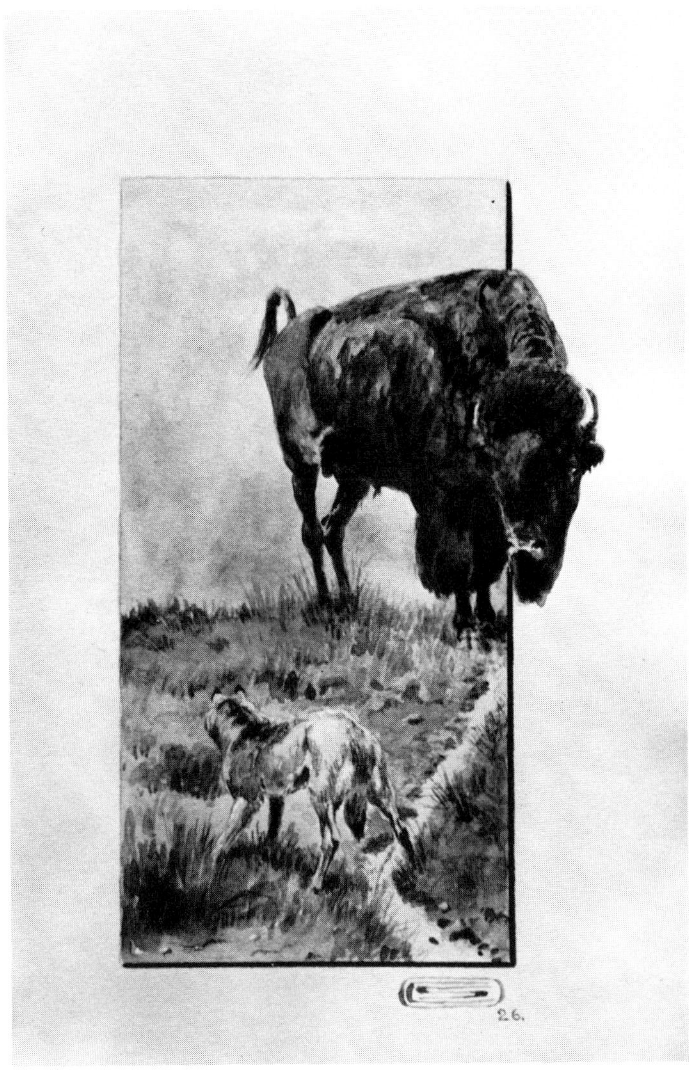

*Buffalo and Coyote*
1926
Watercolor, 9½″ × 6½″

*We're takin' it easy, not carin' much whether we find anything or not, bein' it's so easy to live. The country is lousy with game, them days—blacktail, mountain sheep an' elk in the mountains; antelope, white-tail an' buffalo in the vallies.*

*But we're stayin' pretty close in the mountains on account of Injuns. A couple of days before, we seed twenty of 'em, all on foot, and barrin' a breech cloth, their clothes consist of paint an' feathers.*

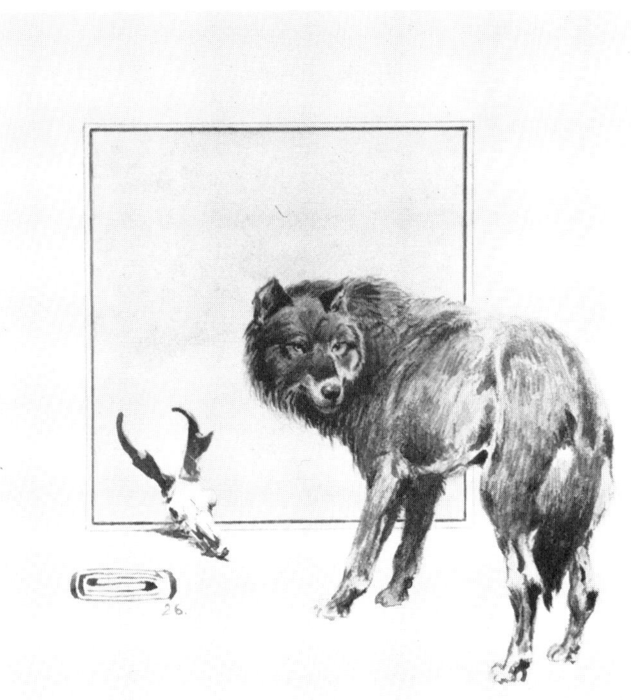

*Wolf and Skull*
1926
Watercolor, 7¾″ × 8¾″

*Bed-Rock says, "When you see geese goin'
south, it's a sign of cold weather; but it ain't
reliable. But when you see Injuns afoot, it's a sure
sign somebody else'll be afoot shortly . . ."*

*But me and' Bed-Rock don't figure on scatterin'
our locks among no bunch of savages to trim
leggins with, so we pulls for the head of Swimmin'
Woman creek. It's there I mix up with this bear.*

Hank Winters told his tale many times in
Montana's convivial bars; it became legendary.
Twelve years later Charles M. Russell painted
*The Price of His Hide*, described as "Russell's
interpretation of a story told by Hank Winters in
which a bear invaded his camp and almost killed
him before Bed-Rock Jim, his partner, killed the
animal."[2]

Olaf Seltzer's ear for the vernacular and his eye
for fine details of western life were equally well
trained. He had been in Montana only eight years
when he wrote "A Bear Story" in his newly acquired language.

The *Rocky Mountain* was short-lived, and so
was Olaf's literary career. But he continued to
paint Wild Critters, sometimes employing landscape backgrounds in soft pastel colors of the type
subsequently used as vignettes in his later Western Character Series, but more often placing the
animals on brilliantly colored panels decorated
with hoofprints, skulls, or small prairie animals.
Sometimes the featured animal appears to be
emerging from the panel, head and forelegs protruding into the unpainted margin area, while
the bulk of the animal's body is set off by the con-
trasting panel. Smaller animals, either natural
foes or companions to the central creature, are
used in effective graphic composition. The scenic
backgrounds vary from the tangled underbrush
of a windfall to a snow-covered forest or ice-
rimed trail above the timberline.

In *Coyote and Moon* the animal's paws clutch a
bone; prints are used on the matte. *Prairie Wolf
and Cow Skull* has a small circle as a background
for the skull and the wolf's head; paw prints are
arranged below. Seltzer placed another cow skull
against a square panel, adding a meadowlark
perched on the tip of one horn that protrudes
above the background. *Deer Grazing* has two
animals posed against an oblong panel with an
arrangement of hoofprints along the right side.
The artist depicts *Mountain Sheep* against a circular scene. *Timber Wolf*, another circular rendition, has paw prints against a targetlike background.

With the Wild Critters in their unique settings
Olaf Seltzer began to develop a style that would
give his work a certain dash, a force unlike that of
other western landscape painters. He gradually
began to sell the critters for a few dollars, although
he did most of his early animal paintings for
friends he wanted to please with the work of his
pen and brush. Commissioned some years later to
do twenty-five Wild Critters for a single patron,
Olaf sent along almost as many more as details on
illustrated envelopes, letters, and greeting cards.

During his itinerant years Olaf was putting
down roots for a future in Montana. Not the least
of his concerns, now that he was established as a
journeyman machinist and a union member, was
his eagerness to become an American citizen. On
April 3, 1903, when he was twenty-five years old,
he appeared in the Cascade County District
Court before the Honorable J. B. Leslie to take
his oath of citizenship. With saloonkeeper A. J.
Trigg and W. J. Forster as witnesses to affirm that

he had lived in the United States for five years and behaved as a man of good moral character, Olaf swore to uphold the Constitution of the United States and promised that he would "absolutely and entirely renounce and adjure all allegiance and fidelity to every foreign Prince Potentate, State or Sovereignty whatever and particularly to (the) King of Denmark." This oath would never be taken lightly. Olaf loved his adopted country and its system of government with unbounded enthusiasm and the intense loyalty characteristic of the foreign-born. He took a keen interest in politics, maintaining a conservative position.

A few months after taking his oath of citizenship, Olaf Seltzer stood before Justice of the Peace Ed. S. Walker in Helena, Montana, and repeated another set of vows that he would hold to until death, as the husband of Mabel Leora Cleeland. Their courtship was brief; they met at a dance in Luther's Hall, a Great Falls gathering place for properly reared young people, shortly after Olaf became a citizen. A fine-boned girl of twenty-one, with masses of light-brown hair and cornflower-blue eyes, Mabel was a telephone operator for the Great Falls central exchange. Known for her wit and warm, outgoing personality, she sang in the choir of the Episcopal Church and took an active part in community life.

Olaf was captivated. Not the least of Mabel's charms was her large, close-knit family. William M. and Eliza Ann (Evans) Cleeland began their westward trek from hamlets near Butler, Pennsylvania, after Sergeant Cleeland was discharged from Company G of the 155th Regiment, Pennsylvania Infantry, in 1865. The Cleelands lived in Breckenridge, Fort Abercrombie, and McCauleyville, Minnesota, before moving to Great Falls in 1889. Cleeland, a blacksmith and skilled cabinetmaker, took his family on to Basin, Montana, about the time that Mabel met her future husband.

Mabel was graduated with the class of 1899, one of three students in the first class to receive diplomas from Great Falls High School. Olaf was proud of her education and pleased that she enjoyed books as much as he did. She had a natural spunkiness of disposition, and she held her own in any showdown of a conflict of wills, another characteristic she shared with her husband.

No one recalls that Olaf and Mabel ever explained why they rode the train to Helena to be married, rather than exchanging vows in Great Falls. Since Basin was only twenty-four miles

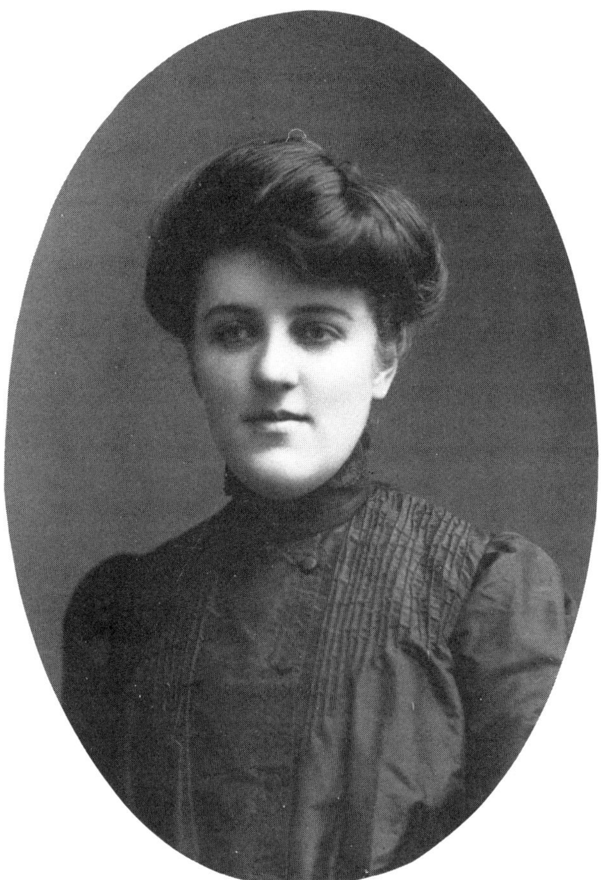

Mabel Cleeland Seltzer
ca. 1903
Courtesy of Carl C. Seltzer

farther than Helena, the newlyweds may have continued on to visit the Cleelands and Mabel's sister Elizabeth, whose husband, George Osborne, was stationmaster at Basin. It appears that no relatives attended the ceremony; the witnesses were Thomas B. Kirkendall and Maurice Weiss, manager of the Placer Hotel and an old friend of Olaf's.

Olaf grew very fond of his parents-in-law and of Mabel's three sisters and brother. The Seltzers exchanged frequent visits with the Osbornes and with a second sister and her husband, Annie Laurie and Jack Woodland, in Seattle (a third sister, Emily, died shortly after Mabel and Olaf were married). The artist used his father-in-law as his model for the Western Character sketch *Cowtown Smith*.

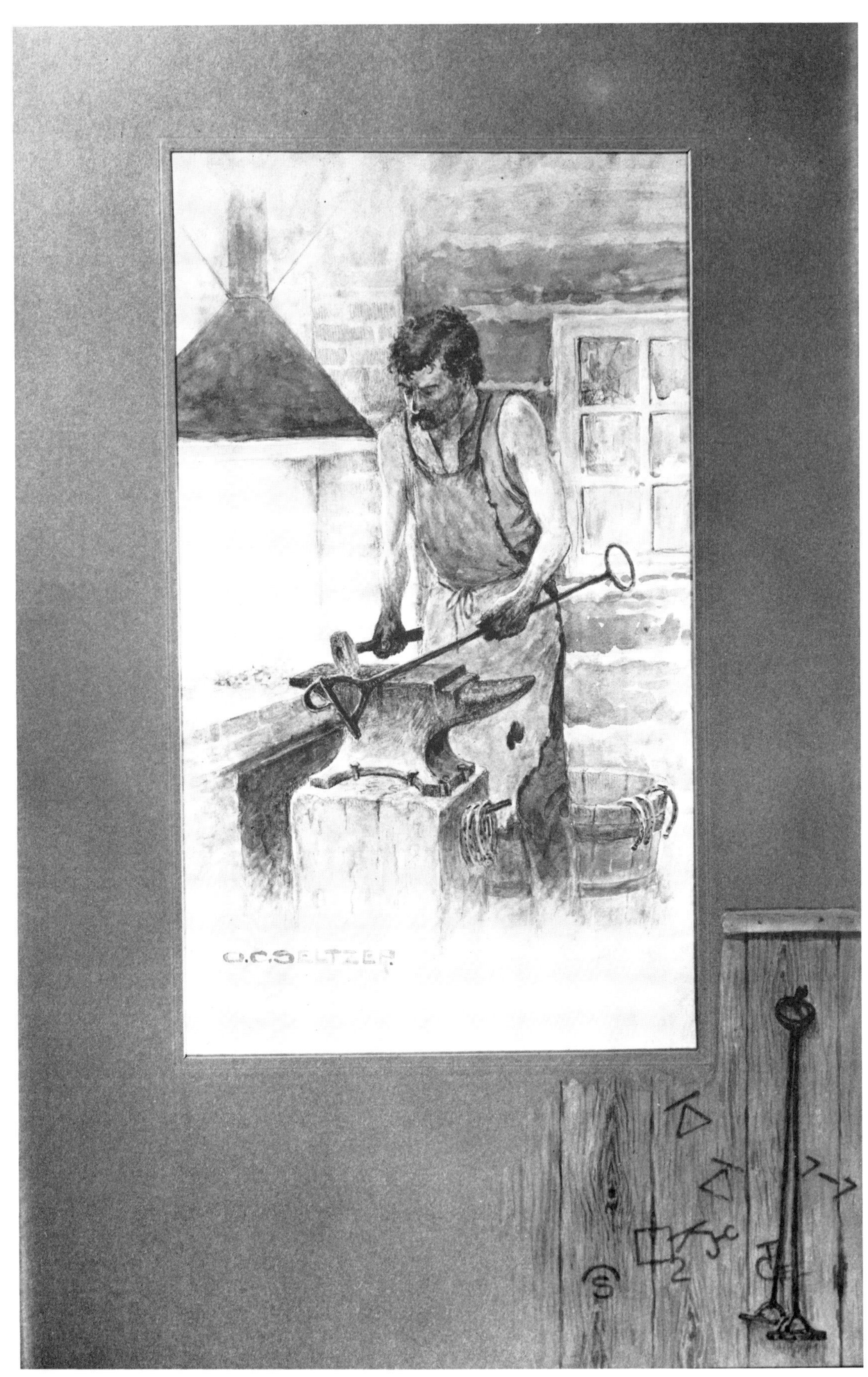

*Cowtown Smith*
1928
Western Character watercolor

Mabel was intensely proud of her "Oluff." With his firm, expressive mouth, deep-set dark eyes and classic nose, Olaf had a commanding appearance, though he never weighed more than 160 pounds. He was always immaculate about his person, and he dressed neatly.

Recognizing his genius, Mabel made many personal sacrifices so that her husband could have extra time to devote to his painting. She patiently tolerated his using the front room of their little home as a studio in the early years, although it meant that she could not entertain friends and family as much as she would have liked.

Olaf, who was not given to verbal compliments, showed his appreciation of his wife through gifts of lovely clothes whenever he could afford such luxuries. During the early years of their marriage he liked to see her wear picture hats with sweeping brims and luxuriant plumes.

At the time of their marriage Olaf was employed at the Boston and Maine Smelter. They settled in rented quarters in the downtown area of Great Falls. In November they boarded the Great Northern to visit the Woodlands in Seattle. Olaf easily found employment as a machinist in a shipbuilding yard, and the newlyweds were looking forward to a lengthy stay in the Puget Sound area when word reached them that Julia was dying. On December 21, 1903, at the age of fifty-two, Olaf's mother died of pneumonia. She was buried on a windswept slope in Highland Cemetery, south of Great Falls.

Saddened by his loss, Olaf found consolation in looking forward to becoming a father. The baby arrived sooner than expected, bringing both joy and trauma to the young couple. Carl Cleeland Seltzer arrived on March 14, 1904, premature and weighing a scant three pounds. At the hospital the baby was wrapped in hot packs, a common practice in the days before incubators. A nurse misjudged the temperature of a hot pack, and the infant suffered deep burns on his hip, causing a wound that took months to heal and left extensive scars.

While the baby was still hospitalized, Olaf was once more laid off by the railroad for a four-month period from April to mid-August. His friend Billy Rance offered him a job to tide the Seltzers over until work picked up in the railroad shops, and Seltzer became a bartender at the Silver Dollar (when asked in later years about his qualifications for tending bar, Olaf would chuckle and answer that he had no problems: "I had tended bar for so long from the other side that I knew just what to do").

Olaf would eventually do two Western Character watercolor sketches of bartenders. The first, *Saloon Keeper*, depicts a respectable-looking, polished barkeep with a handlebar mustache leaning on the bar in an attentive, hospitable fashion. A brass spittoon sits in front of the bar, and the complementary vignette on the matte features two glasses and a bottle labeled "Old Crow." This was drawn from the artist's own experience in the Silver Dollar in 1904, but it was too genteel a rendition to suit the taste of the purchaser, who wanted something more reminiscent of the rugged Montana frontier. Seltzer obligingly did a second version, *Barkeep*, showing a surly, heavy-jowled, unkempt bartender with unbuttoned shirt and a neckerchief in place of a tie. His western hat sits squarely on his head, and the mirror behind the bar has been shattered by a random shot. There is a crude box before the bar with cigar butts spilling out of it. The vignette depicts the exterior of the frame "Maverick Saloon," from which two cowhands are ambling away on their ponies under a star-studded sky. In both versions the bartender is smoking a cigar, the form of tobacco favored by Seltzer.[3]

It was probably during this stint behind the bar that Olaf met a fellow countryman, Holger Rosenberg, a travel writer for the Danish press, who drew him out about his experiences since leaving Denmark. Rosenberg was deeply interested in learning the stories of *emigré* Danes he came across in his wanderings on the North American continent. From such visits he drew models for characters in his popular books.

Herr Rosenberg published a book for boys entitled *Smuthans* (Dirty Hans), which appeared in 1905 after one of his trips to the United States. Its fictional hero is a small-statured lad from a Copenhagen working district who, in the opening pages, stands up to some bullies tormenting a little dog. Hans, a fifteen-year-old, emigrates to the United States and secures a job in a "locomotive factory," eventually becoming a stoker and a "locomotive-driver apprentice." Continuing westward, Rosenberg's fictional Hans works as a cowboy and eventually moves on to Mexico.

Although the experiences of others may have been woven into Hans's career, it appears that Rosenberg's imagination was sufficiently titillated by what he learned of Olaf's youthful experiences to make them the core of the plot of *Smuthans'*.

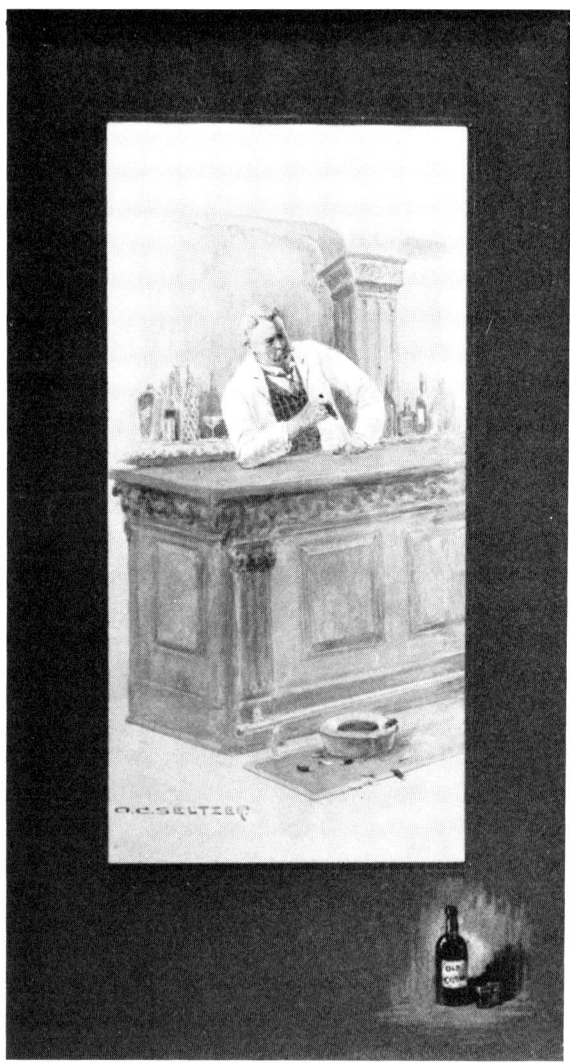

*Saloon Keeper*
1928
Western Character watercolor
Courtesy of Northwestern Bank, Great Falls, Montana.

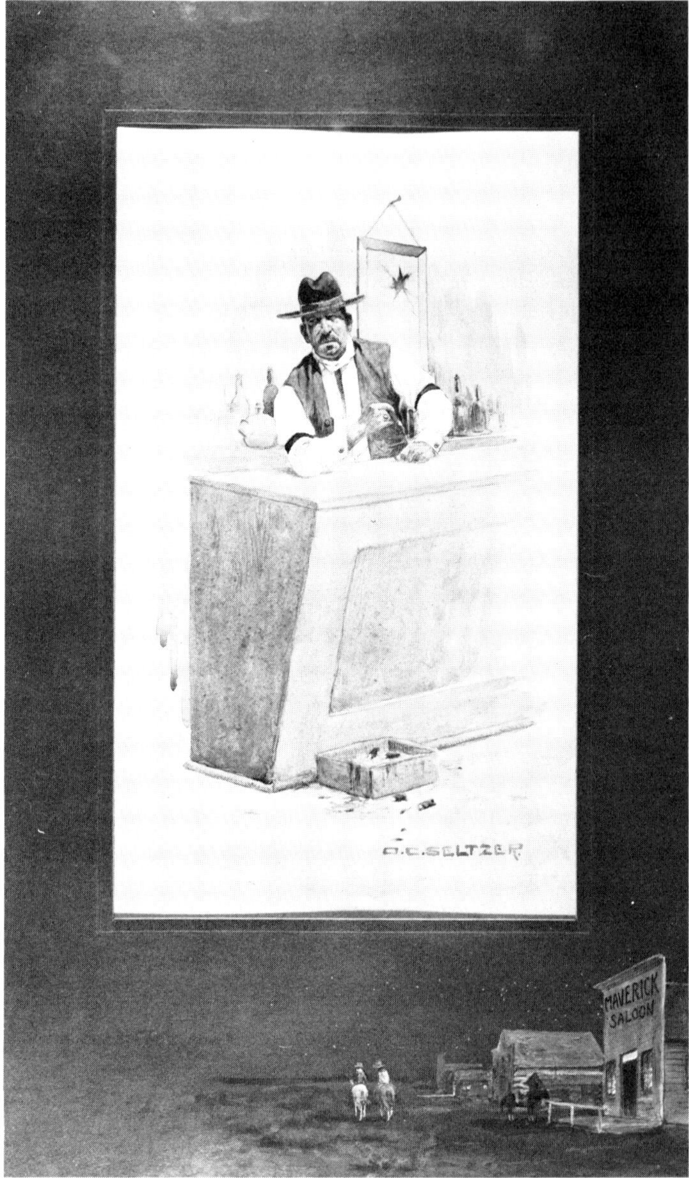


*Barkeep*
1928
Western Character watercolor

Olaf never knew that a fictionalized version of his early experiences had become a classic Danish Horatio Alger tale, which is still on the shelves of libraries in Denmark.

Before the year 1904 ended, Mabel was pregnant again. Work in the locomotive shops was unpredictable. The infant Carl was still in need of medical care for his burns. Olaf was hard put to figure out another means of income. He was not selling enough paintings to take up the gap between income and expenses.

A second son, christened Walter William, arrived in August, 1905. Olaf applied to homestead a 160-acre tract of land near Geyser, Montana, forty-six miles southeast of Great Falls in the vast Judith Basin. The prospect of owning his own land was appealing to Olaf, although he had no experience in cultivating prairie land.

The family stayed only briefly on the claim. When Olaf realized that the endless round of chores left him no time for painting, he began paying visits to the tract only on free days. Years later Olaf told his friend Frank Curry about one of his lonely visits to the Geyser tract, which he later gave up. A prominent cattleman was attempting to add to his grazing acreage by buying up homestead claims from settlers who grew discouraged in their attempts to cultivate the arid land. He would urge the disgruntled homesteaders to continue until the claim was legally theirs, when he could buy it from them. To help them stay, the rancher would grubstake the homesteaders' crude shelters with provisions—complete with a jug of liquor.

One wintry evening, as Curry told the story, Olaf left his quarters on the land, jug in hand, and walked to Geyser to catch the Lewiston–Great Falls stagecoach.[4] When the stage pulled in, every seat was occupied. Frenchy, the driver, offered to share the driver's seat with Olaf. Frenchy produced a stiff, bulky buffalo-hide coat to protect Seltzer from the biting wind, and the loaded stagecoach pulled out of Geyser at a brisk clip.

Naturally Olaf uncorked his jug and passed it to the driver for a companionable drink. Frenchy's stage picked up speed with every swig. The jerk-line outfit would plunge down a bank, jolt across a swollen stream, and gallop up the other bank without a break in pace. In celebration of another crossing Olaf would bring out his jug once more.

Inevitably Olaf concluded that Frenchy had better make an unscheduled stop.

"I'm not stopping until we get to Great Falls," the stage driver growled.

"Frenchy, you gotta stop."

"I don't gotta do nothin'," came the reply from the driver, who was becoming surly.

The buffalo-coated figures on the driver's bench now had another drink to contemplate Olaf's distress. It was then that Frenchy proposed that Olaf climb over the top of the stagecoach toward the baggage rack at the rear. Seltzer, as he later related the incident to Curry, was "just fool enough to do it."

While Olaf was making his shaky crawl across the roof of the jolting stagecoach, Frenchy took his team down an embankment to cross another creek, and Seltzer was catapulted into the icy water.

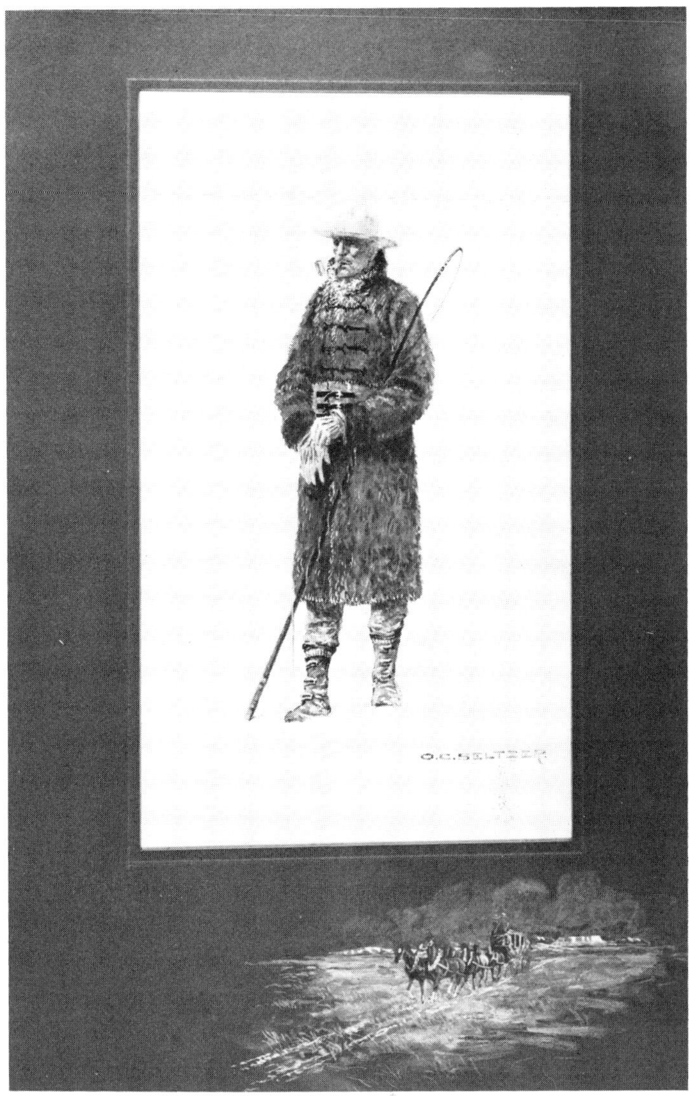

*Stage Driver*
1928
Western Character watercolor

Wet, bruised, and enraged, Olaf in his dripping hide coat slogged along in the rutted tracks of the departing stage, confident that Frenchy would wheel around the cumbersome rig and come back for him. But Frenchy's state was such that he had forgotten about his seat mate.

Olaf had hiked to the edge of the city before a rancher picked him up in the first rays of dawn and dropped him at his doorstep.

Never one to avoid a scrap when he had provocation, Olaf made two trips to the stage terminal to settle his score with Frenchy. Each time the driver was out on the road. Months passed before the two men met again. By then, time had lent perspective to the incident, and Olaf could view it with a degree of humor. Frenchy and his buffalo-skin coat were immortalized in *Stage Driver*, one of the Western Character watercolors.

Thirteen years had elapsed between the arrival of the youthful art student from Copenhagen and his eventual settling in Great Falls as husband and father of two young sons. Horse tending, barkeeping, homesteading, and itinerant machinist's jobs behind him, Olaf Seltzer would spend the next twenty years progressing in his trade and developing his art toward the anticipated day when he could put aside his daily shifts and spend full time at his easel.

Chapter 4
# "The Good Old Days"

IN THE PERSONAL LEXICON of Olaf Seltzer the "good old days" were the years between the time he finally settled down in Great Falls with Mabel and the boys and his break with Charlie Russell in 1925. The Seltzers occupied a succession of rented clapboard cottages close to the Missouri River, a neighborhood chosen so that Olaf could walk across the railroad bridge to and from the Great Northern shops. He began to adjust to his dual life as machinist and spare-time painter, dreaming of the day when he could sever his connection with the railroad, but pragmatically accepting the hard fact that, barring a miracle, that day was far in the future.

Olaf clung to one idiosyncrasy that indicates that he never committed himself totally to the life of an industrial worker: he refused to carry a lunch pail. Mabel would fix him a brace of sandwiches—one was invariably peanut butter—which he carried in a paper bag along with an apple or orange and table scraps to feed the stray cats around the shops. After his meal he would fold and pocket the sack so that he could walk home unencumbered by a lunch box and the servitude it symbolized.

Olaf got along well with his coworkers. A rough lot, doing an exacting job that demanded strength and vigor and that always held an element of danger, the railroad machinists cursed with imagination and frequently drank to excess. Seltzer could measure up on both scores. He never discussed his painting ambitions with the men in the shop, preferring to keep separate the two aspects of his life. Since he could hold his own with men bigger and sturdier than he was, this reluctance was hardly predicated on any fear of being misunderstood.

The Seltzers' social life was home-centered, because Olaf filled all his spare moments with his painting. As he grew more confident in the use of oils, he took to making small, genre paintings— quiet domestic scenes and romantic concepts of the French countryside during the Napoleonic period and of life in colonial America as he imagined it had been. The inspiration for many of the genre paintings came from the historical romances he checked out of the Great Falls Public Library for Mabel's and his reading pleasure. He would work at four or five such paintings concurrently, adding finishing touches and setting them about in the living room to dry at room temperature. This crowded the family's living quarters and put the improvised studio off limits to the little boys, who were trained by their mother to stay out of the front room.

The small oils, on illustration board (6″ × 7″ up to 9″ × 12″), were paintings Olaf did for his own satisfaction. He continued making such paintings of romantic subjects or family pets throughout his career, often using them as gifts for his loved ones. He early discovered that there was far less market for his brushworks of such subjects than there was for paintings of Indians on horseback and other variations on western themes. Whenever his genre paintings had outdoor settings, whether they featured hussars, Continental Army volunteers, Napoleon's troops, or Arab tribesmen, Seltzer always included horses. One of these paintings, *German Lancers*, he gave to Russell in 1905.

As his work progressed, Olaf experimented with different ways of signing his paintings. About 1905 he dropped the palette pierced with three brushes in favor of a stylized monogram with the

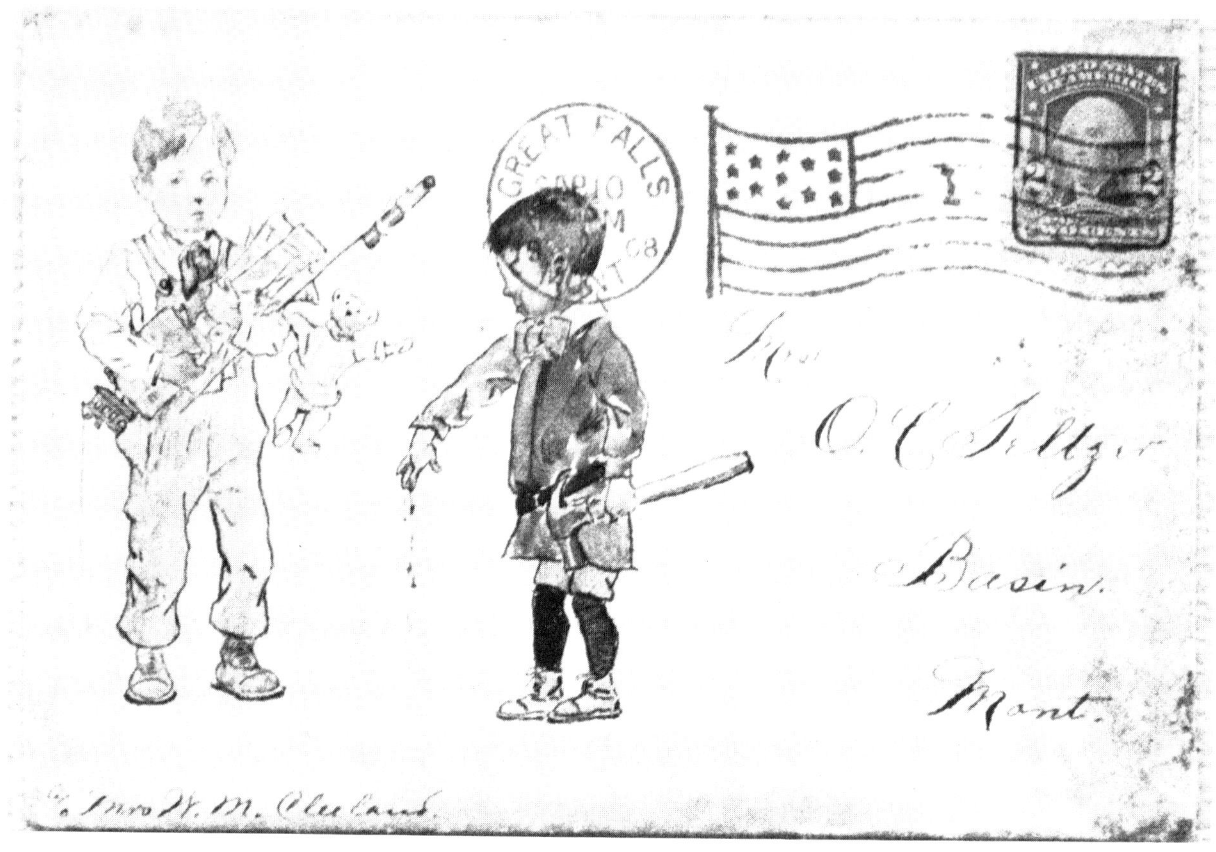



*Carl and Walt, Illustrated Envelope*
1908
Watercolor and ink, 4″ × 4″
Courtesy of Carl C. Seltzer.

*C* placed within an encircling *O* and the *S* within the arc of the *C*, following this monogram with the last two digits of the year in which the work was painted. When he spelled out his surname, he sometimes dropped the tail of the lower case *z* or extended the horizontal bars on a capital *Z* to give his signature a distinctive flourish. Eventually he settled on *O. C. Seltzer* with the letters growing slightly larger as his signature progressed through his surname. The signature was usually placed in the lower-right-hand corner. If there were dark tones in that corner, he signed the painting in the left corner.

After Olaf began signing his full name in 1907, he added the year of execution less frequently. For illustrative sketches Seltzer normally initialed the details. He never used his first name on paintings, although he signed his personal letters to friends "Olaf." A deviation from "O. C. Seltzer" appears on the *War Party* watercolor signed by Charlie on behalf of "C. M. Russell and O. Seltzer." Russell added a distinctive dot on top of the *O*, creating the effect of a prong-set ring.[1]

Examples of a lighter, humorous illustrative style, not unlike that of Olaf's later idol Norman Rockwell, are found in letters and cards he made for his family. An envelope addressed to Mabel, who with their sons was visiting her parents in Basin in September, 1908, is ornamented with a 4″ × 4″ watercolor of two little boys. The taller, a towhead of about four, has his hands full of firecrackers, toys, and picture books; a toy locomotive sticks out of the pocket of his overalls. The toddler, brown-haired, holds a hammer in one hand

and nurses a bloody finger on the other. In-cluded with Olaf's letter to Mabel, under a calico cat in watercolor, was a fond note for his sons.

When he was not at work or at the easel or on an outing with his family, Olaf was usually in the company of Charlie Russell and his buddies. In 1903, Nancy Russell had a log cabin built next to the Russell home as Charlie's special preserve. Soon after the cowboy artist moved his painting and camping gear into the studio, a group of his friends began drinking coffee there on Sunday mornings, a habit they continued for many years. Olaf was among them, as was the artist Jack Wryn and the builder George Calvert.

Charlie often rode over to see Olaf's progress on his painting, tying up his horse at a cottonwood in front of the Seltzer cottage, or Olaf joined Charlie on one of his afternoon visits to the color-ful downtown saloons, incurring Mabel's disap-proval.

Olaf's saloon visits were limited by his tight working schedule and tighter budget; most of his imbibing was done around the campfire on the pack trips Russell enjoyed organizing for his friends. These expeditions were the occasion for many a practical joke, and Olaf learned to bear the brunt of Charlie's humor good-naturedly and to perpetrate some mischief at Charlie's expense as well.

For one such trip Russell borrowed an extra saddle horse from the owner of the Como Store, who warned him that Chub would buck if spurred in the flanks. The episode was recounted later in an article on Charlie Russell:

*So C. M. R. was mindful of the chance to have fun with someone. During the trip each member of the party took a turn at wrangling horses. When it came to Olaf Seltzer's turn, he wanted to look the part, so he put on chaps and spurs before he climbed on old Chub to round up the other horses.*

*Chub, as usual took his time in getting started. Charlie Russell had told Mr. Seltzer to give him the spurs. Olaf followed instructions all right, and Chub piled him high, wide and handsome.*[2]

Carl Seltzer remembers his father's amuse-ment in recalling a trick he was inspired to pull—with Russell's willing assistance—one day when the two men were riding in the Sand Coulee area south of Great Falls. The pair came upon an elaborate livery-stable surrey, its horse tied to a fence post. A young couple, strolling hand in hand across the prairie, disappeared behind a low hill. The jokesters hid their horses in a near-by thicket. Unhitching the bay, they led him through a gate in the barbed-wire fence and re-hitched him so that the horse was on one side of the fence and the surrey on the other.

The culprits had ample time to enjoy their joke. It took the young Lothario, who must have been a new arrival in the West, quite a while to figure out what had happened. He was sadly inept in his attempts to bring the horse and surrey together again. The two artists were forced to remain in hiding for nearly three hours.

Not all of their joint experiences were amusing. Olaf liked to tell about the time he and Charlie, riding saddle horses in the company of a local physician, led a pack train into the Missouri brakes, an area of dense thickets along the mean-dering river. A rainstorm of cloudburst vehe-mence drenched them on their first night out. They wrapped themselves in their saddle blan-kets to keep dry and warm.

In the light of morning the three men discov-ered that the dye in the blankets had run. They agreed that they looked like a war party of Indi-ans. They also discovered, when the wind changed, that they were camped near a tree that held an Indian corpse. Olaf later used this experi-ence in painting a major oil in addition to the 4½" × 6" *Scaffold Grave* included in his Montana in Miniature series. His large (24" × 36") oil includes a decomposed horse, shot and left below the scaffold, as was the custom. Because Seltzer de-plored violence and cruelty to animals, his im-pulse to record a savage custom long since out-lawed must have overcome his repugnance in dealing with this scene.[3]

Camping near the scaffold was less unpleasant than being left on foot in the Highwood Mountains. According to Carl Seltzer, during a camping trip with a younger friend, Bill Marks, Charlie and Olaf awakened one morning to find their horses gone. They set out on foot to find the nearest settler. When the rancher's wife saw them coming, she bolted her door and would have nothing to do with them, because a rustlers' gang had been operating in the neighborhood, and she mistook the campers for outlaws.

The three men sat down to consider their plight. "We're a hundred miles from nowhere with nothing to eat, no horses to ride, and even a gentlewoman won't trust us," was Olaf's disgusted summary of the situation. Luckily, two horsemen

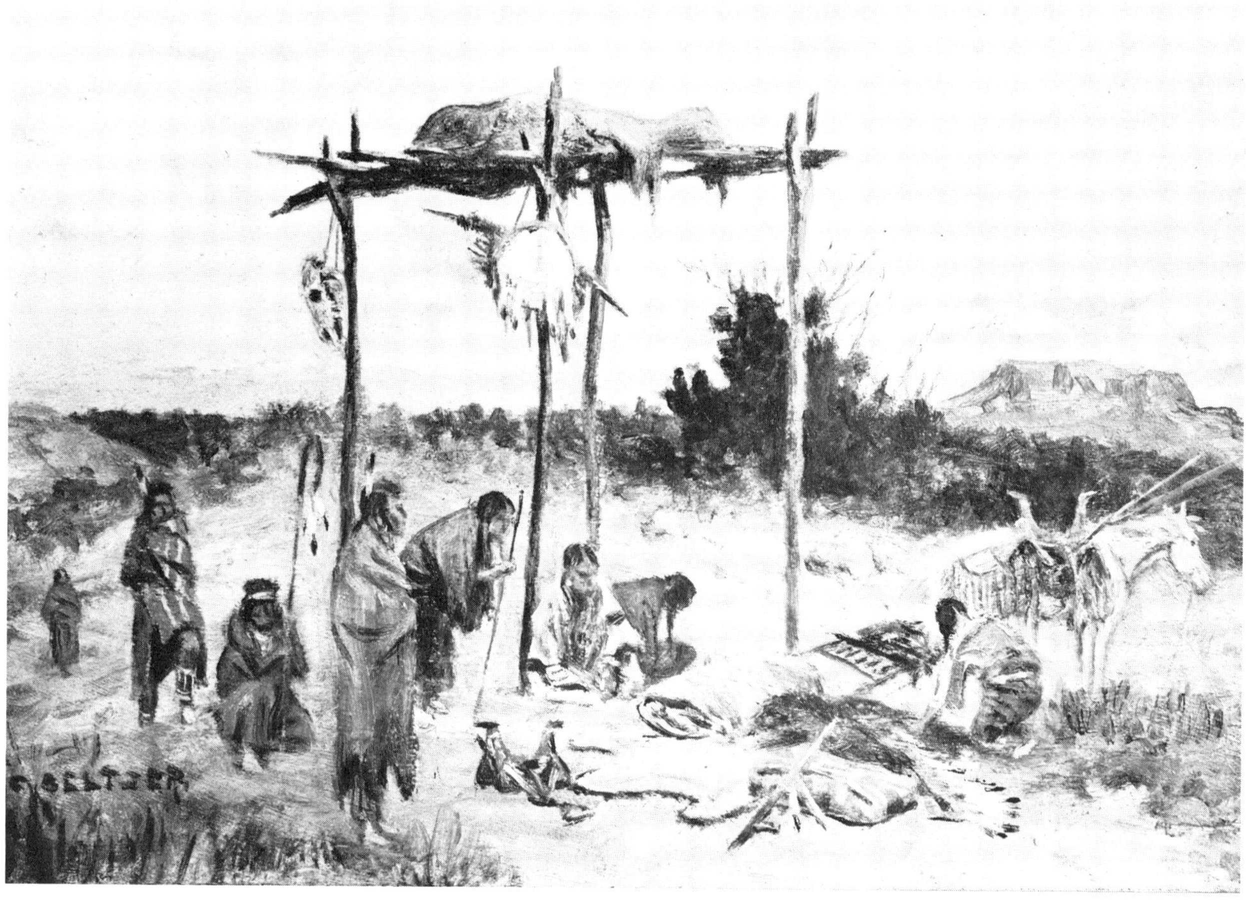

*Scaffold Grave*
1935
Miniature oil

who knew both Charlie and the ranchwoman happened to ride by. They assured the woman that Charlie and his friends were not outlaws but respected citizens of Great Falls. So the woman fed them a good breakfast and loaned them horses for the trip home. As the trio rode away, one of the horsemen shouted after them, "You three sure do fit the description of them rustlers."

Such shared experiences led to a number of portraits Seltzer made of Charlie and to several scenes that included him. In the collection at Gilcrease Museum alone there are at least five, ranging from a striking small oil named *Portrait of C. M. Russell* (on horseback with a cattle herd in the background) to a cartoon of a grinning Charlie sporting an academic robe and clutching a dip-

loma, captioned "Oh-h-h you Doctor!" This was Olaf's fondly teasing tribute when Russell was given an honorary doctorate of laws by the University of Montana in 1925.

A 12″ × 10″ oil entitled "*Charley Russell About 1891 with the N-N Outfit in the Judith Basin*" shows Russell seated, sketching, while five comrades watch intently. Horace Brewster, trail boss of the N-N and an acquaintance of Seltzer's, and the cook, Gros Ventre Johnny, who sports a flour-sack apron, are also identifiable. *Grub Pile—the N-N Outfit at Judith Basin about 1891* is a 4½″ × 6″ miniature featuring the same cast. It shows twelve of the hands seated cross-legged by the chuck wagon, which is presided over by Gros Ventre Johnny, the only standing figure. Both of these scenes resulted from stories Charlie told about his days with the N-N, described by Olaf as "the last of the great old-time cattle outfits."

Among the Western Character watercolors, at Gilcrease Museum is *A Picture Builder (C M R)*. Its complementary vignette contains the buffalo-skull symbol Russell used as his signature.

A Seltzer ink-and-watercolor sketch of 1909 depicts Russell standing against a brilliantly colored oblong panel that extends across the 19″ × 12″ picture. A tiny antelope is drawn on the panel, and hieroglyphics beneath it represent the Indian way of writing Aw-A-Kos (or Ah-Wah-Cous, antelope), the name by which Charlie was known among the Bloods in Canada. Olaf made several watercolors of Russell on his favorite horses. The earliest is *C. M. Russell with Red Bird*, dated 1902. *The Cowboy Artist with Nee-Nah* bears a 1917 date.

Perhaps the tenderest memorial to the friendship of the two men is the four-panel Christmas greeting in which Olaf set forth in teasing doggerel and clever cartoons his affection for the older painter. The watercolor cartoons are fitted within 13″ × 11″ cutouts in the shape of buffalo skulls, the symbol Charlie used with his signature, and mounted on gray mats.

The first panel features a caricature of Russell against an oblong panel of cardinal red bordered in black, on which is mounted a small toy horse on wheels. The smoke from Russell's omnipresent cigarette wafts upward to form in feathery letters the legend "Xmas 1906." Beneath, Seltzer printed in capital letters:

> You'r not what's termed a beauty
> But genius and clever
> And the worst that we can wish for you
> Is health and luck forever
> So here is to you and the ghost of your
> old pinto
> Who has crossed beyond the Big Divide
> We have never yet looked into.

One has the impression that this was probably the only greeting originally planned by Seltzer but that, once the muse was stirring him, he could not resist the urge to continue his conceit. The second panel features a figure on foot, leaning on a staff and trudging toward a sign pointing "To Divide." Beyond waits a pinto, sprouting wings. Under the aspiring figure's arm is a clutch of

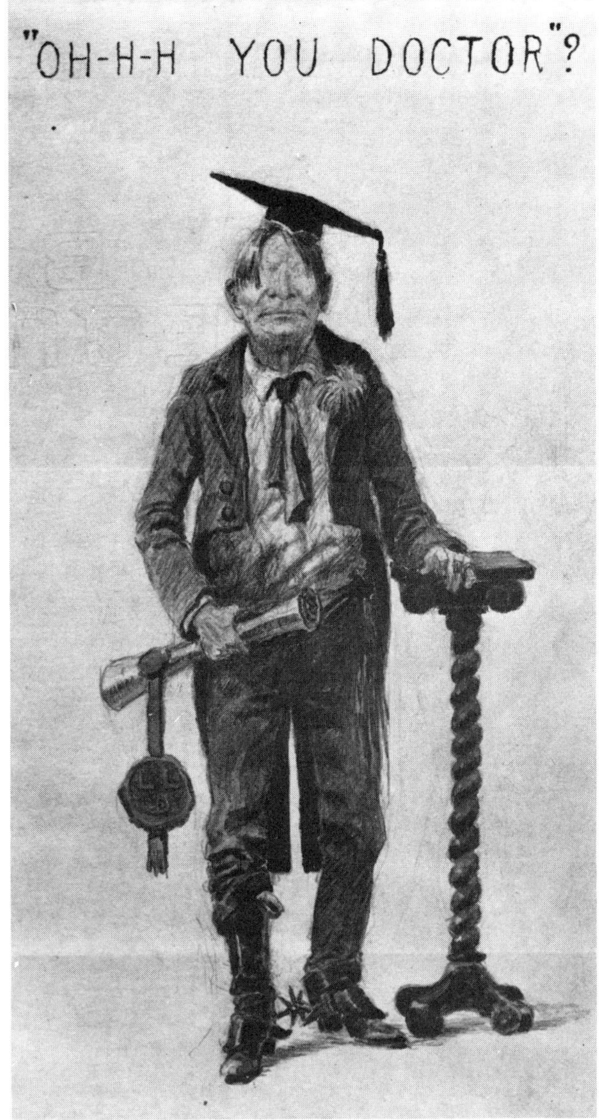



*Oh-h-h You Doctor*
1925
Watercolor and ink

manuscript sheet music showing the names of Bill Blair and Joe McComb, most likely a reference to an inside joke lost to the years. The lettering proclaims:

> But some day when we hit the trail
> To which we all must cater
> Old Monte will be waiting there
> To take you to Saint Peter.

The third panel features in the foreground the figure of Saint Peter, laden with the keys to the kingdom. The winged pinto approaches from a distance with his former owner astride:

> "Back up my friend," the saint will say
>      You'r in the wrong direction.
> For down on earth, although quite good
>      You never reached perfection.
> And yet,—we'd have to travel far
>      O'er plain—through city bustle
> To find a man just half as good
>      As—"Charlie Marion Russell."

Seltzer's elaborate attempt to amuse his friend continues in a postscript surrounded by illustrations on the fourth panel. In the upper-right-hand corner is a sketch of Charlie as a bareheaded angel, still booted and spurred and wearing a crimson sash. He looks down over the last of the text on a busy scene below:

> These verse and pictures
>      So unlimited rotten
>      Is the work of a friend
> With the head of a button.
>      "A friend": You'l say,
> "Has my memory grown fainter?"
>      Why of course, from your friend
>      The Lion-painter.

Seltzer caricatures himself in a gaudy checked suit and brightly colored tie, with a full head of hair (his was thinning), smoking a cigar. With one hand he is daubing green paint on the back of a seated lion. Between his rakish self-portrait and the docile animal is a jug labeled "Oil," and in the left margin is a large button with tag ends of thread protruding from it. The second panel is signed "O. C. Seltzer, 1906"; the first and third panels are initialed, but the postscript bears no signature.

Russell appears to have been the model for many of Seltzer's paintings, as Olaf was for some of Russell's works. In Olaf's renditions the Russell characteristics—square jaw, strawlike hairlock, omnipresent cigarette—are unmistakable. Seltzer struck poses for as many as three figures on a single Russell oil, but his features are not clearly defined. He became proficient at making himself up in some of the western gear Charlie kept in the studio so that he would be ready to pose on a few minutes' notice. It was not only Olaf who masqueraded for the other's benefit. In 1908, Russell, knowing Olaf's deep interest in the Napoleonic period, donned parts of a French officer's uniform for Seltzer's benefit. Olaf captured the antic in an amusing pencil drawing.

As the Seltzers' sons grew, they were sometimes pressed into service as models for the painting companions. Walt recalls squatting for an uncomfortably long time so that his thigh muscles could be noted—"the only problem being I didn't have any noticeable muscles at that age." Carl remembers being hustled off to the studio on a summer day. He says, "They sat me on a high bench and put a broom in my hand so they could get a hand around a coup stick just right."[4]

In spite of his constant activity Olaf Seltzer left his sons memories of a happy childhood. He would take them for Sunday walks, sharing with them his considerable knowledge of plant, animal, and insect life. He also imparted his enthusiasm for his collections, so that the boys joined in the fun of spotting butterflies and beetles and in adding to his stamp collection.

One unforgettable Christmas the Seltzers gave their sons a windup phonograph. The boys were delighted with the gift and with the chance to stay up far past their bedtime to play "Way Down Yonder in the Cornfield" over and over again. Shortly thereafter the records took a turn toward the classical, for Olaf was fond of Chopin and Mozart and cherished virtuosos of the violin.

The Seltzers lived simply and frugally, but there was always money for concerts and stage shows, particularly when the artists were of the caliber of Madame Schumann-Heink. The family also went to movies and vaudeville shows together.

Until he was well into his forties, Olaf Seltzer continued to live in two worlds: the clattering, grimy, physically demanding atmosphere of the roundhouse and the quiet milieu of artistic creation, where he found an outlet in his search for more delicately expressive color and relaxed to the soothing tones of classical music.

In 1909, when he was thirty-two, Olaf posed for a photographic portrait. He is seated, holding his palette and brushes (the palette, a simple rectangle, may be the same one Downer ordered for him in 1898, or its replacement since he preferred that kind to the traditional curved shape). He is wearing a soft silk tie with flowing ends and a dark coat over pinstripe vest and trousers. His hair is parted in the middle with slight waves on each side of his high brow. The camera captured his steady, somewhat brooding gaze and his full, sensitive mouth.[5] Within a few years he would resemble the screen actor Charles Boyer, a resemblance that pleased Mabel whenever it was mentioned. One would never know from this portrait that the artist had ever dirtied his hands with more than paint specks.

Austin Russell, who came from Saint Louis in 1908 to live with his Uncle Charlie and Aunt Nancy, recalled the conflict that Olaf Seltzer felt after being promoted to foreman in 1910. Seltzer was pleased to be making more money but "discontented because he wanted to be an artist. He would work at his easel a while and then get discouraged and quit."[6] Olaf may have exhibited these ambivalent feelings in the hope of eliciting encouragement from Charlie. It is doubtful that he had any serious thought of giving up painting. The prospect of added responsibility may have overwhelmed Olaf at the outset, but Charlie always bolstered him with compliments. Russell often told mutual friends that Seltzer was a better draftsman than he was and that as a watercolorist Olaf had no equal.

Shortly after he became foreman, Olaf began to have photographs made of his larger oil paintings. He knew that Russell, since the early years of the century, had made a modest but steady income from contracts with the Osborne Company and with Brown and Bigelow, both major calendar companies. Although Olaf maintained that he "could not afford the loss . . . of a single detail or color by letting his work be reproduced" because he worked too hard to perfect it, it is known that he made quiet overtures to some calendar companies, perhaps by sending them photo reproductions.[7]

Photographer Mike Ford did Olaf's reproduction work in his second-story studio on Central Avenue. There, on a gloomy Sunday afternoon in 1911, Olaf first encountered fifteen-year-old North Dakota Stark, Mike's apprentice, who would become Olaf's disciple and lifelong friend. North's family had moved to Great Falls from an isolated Bad Lands ranch in order to provide the children with a proper education. North dreamed of becoming a painter. Russell and Seltzer were his idols. He had ingratiated himself with Charlie,

who let the boy sit quietly in a corner of the log cabin watching him paint. But North's path had not yet crossed Olaf Seltzer's.

After Ford finished photographing Seltzer's painting of a stagecoach holdup, the three enjoyed a spirited visit, and Olaf invited the boy to come home with him. Now in his eighties and a resident of Vancouver, Washington, Stark remembers vividly their conversation on that first visit in Olaf's home and the seemingly completed watercolor—a white-tailed buck deer jumping over a windfall—to which Olaf kept adding touches.

"Olaf's house faced north," he recalled, "and the front windows furnished a north light for his painting. Not enough light . . . not a thing like Charlie's big skylight, but it suited Olaf just fine. I was to learn that he always painted by a small north window. Less light on your picture encouraged you to use stronger colors, Olaf claimed."[8]

Part of the conversation had to do with Seltzer's many trips to the public library to study, "not always about drawing, but the composition of each color, and which oil color or pigment would poison another and cause the sky to turn muddy after ten or twenty years," Stark said. "This will happen to the best of us, but I have never seen it happen to one of Olaf's oil paintings."

Mauve was the particular hue that Olaf was leery of and the subject of many a good-natured argument between him and Russell, according to Stark. Russell liked using purple tones. Several years after Russell's death Seltzer was asked to restore "four or five Russell canvasses gone muddy because of too much mauve."[9]

Differing views on the choice of materials was always a subject for badinage between Olaf and Chrlie. Charlie used linseed oil as a medium in his pigments; Olaf preferred poppy-seed oil, contending that it preserved color intensity and protected against yellowing. Although most experts agree with Russell on this point, claiming that poppy seed has a greater propensity for eventual yellowing, Seltzer's oils are prized for their clarity and true-color intensity. His direct, simple structural technique in applying an even thickness of paint may have enabled him to achieve a better effect with the poppy-seed oil.

Seltzer's handwritten notes indicate that, in addition to reading through volumes of *Scribner's*, *Harper's*, *Century*, and *National Geographic* in his search for additional knowledge in the fields of natural history, geography, art, and literature, he also diligently worked his way through *World Book, Masters of Art*, and the art magazine *International Studio*. He recommended a similar course of self-education to young North.

Olaf also annotated his own color discoveries and experimented with effects of light intensity. Cobalt blue he noted as "a fine reliable color of absolute permanency and probably the most widely used of all blue pigments." Under lemon yellow he jotted: "Chrome of barium. A fine opaque yellow of good body and permanence," while referring to rose dorée as a "delicate rose color inclining to scarlet, prepared from the genuine Madder root. Very permanent." Field's orange vermilion had "great brilliancy, much tinting strength and good permanency, although it will blacken if much exposed to direct sunlight." Terra rosa he marked as "an earth ochre . . . a fine red pigment ranking high for its permanence. He described terre verte as "a native green earth highly valued for its permanence and individual characteristic hue . . . fine glazing quality (olive tint.)"

Seltzer studied the effects of one color of paint in relation to another before he put them on canvas. He would daub small scraps of canvas and composition board with various colors and place them in a window where they would be exposed to direct sunlight for as long as six or seven months. Only after such testing would he feel safe in using new pigments.

Always neat and orderly in his working habits, Olaf kept a little book in which he jotted down reactions of paint, so that he would know the intensity needed for a red coat in the foreground as contrasted with one in the background, a matter of aerial perspective. This painstaking experimentation and study would be of value when it came to adding touches of color with minute strokes to lend detail to the historical miniatures.

At the end of each painting session he would scrape together the leftover blobs and use the conglomerate to build up a textured effect in the foreground, a trick used by Russell and sometimes by Remington. This lends a three-dimensional effect to sagebrush, cactus, and greasewood in western paintings but adds to the difficulty of cleaning such oil paintings.

Olaf studied the chemical makeup of pigments, whether vegetable or mineral, and how they worked with one another. In his search for perfection he believed that the best paints available were none too good. He used Devoe and Raynolds paints, which he bought at the Como Store, but his preference was for Winsor-Newton, an English import. When he could afford it, he preferred to paint on fine Belgian linen, but he also used various weights of canvas and composition board. Based on the succession of new products that came on the market during his painting career, his opinion was that paintings in the future would exceed those of the past in durability of color tone, provided that as much care went into their creation.

In his watercolor work Seltzer built from the top down. To avoid a streaked sky, he would put in the sky first, adding a little glycerine to the water to enable the color to slip along the surface. He would then turn the painting upside down until the color "washed in" to please him. The darker colors covered any of the blue that washed down, he reasoned, and the delicacy of the sky took precedence, in his opinion, over any other color consideration.

Light and shadow, space, the cross play of reflections on forms in movement—these were the facets of painting that Olaf Seltzer most enjoyed. He avoided trends and vogues in order to be consistent with what was essential to his nature. Integrity in his work was vitally important to him.

Olaf never ceased expressing his gratitude for all he had learned from Charlie Russell during their long association, but he knew the process had not been to his benefit alone. Russell's use of color brightened perceptively in the early years of the new century as Seltzer shared his findings with his friend. Their comradeship was a broadening experience for both.

In the autumn of 1914, eighteen-year-old North Dakota Stark painted a 20" × 30" copy of Russell's *The Cinch Ring*. He had previously copied *Bronc to Breakfast*. He sold both of them to Mike Ford, the photographer. North had been warned that the copying might enrage Russell. Instead, Charlie and Olaf made a special trip to Ford's studio to see the copies, and Stark seized this opportunity, with Ford's help and expertise, to take their picture together.

According to Russell scholars, Charlie gave up drinking in 1908, when he began to realize that his imbibing might affect his painting, and never took

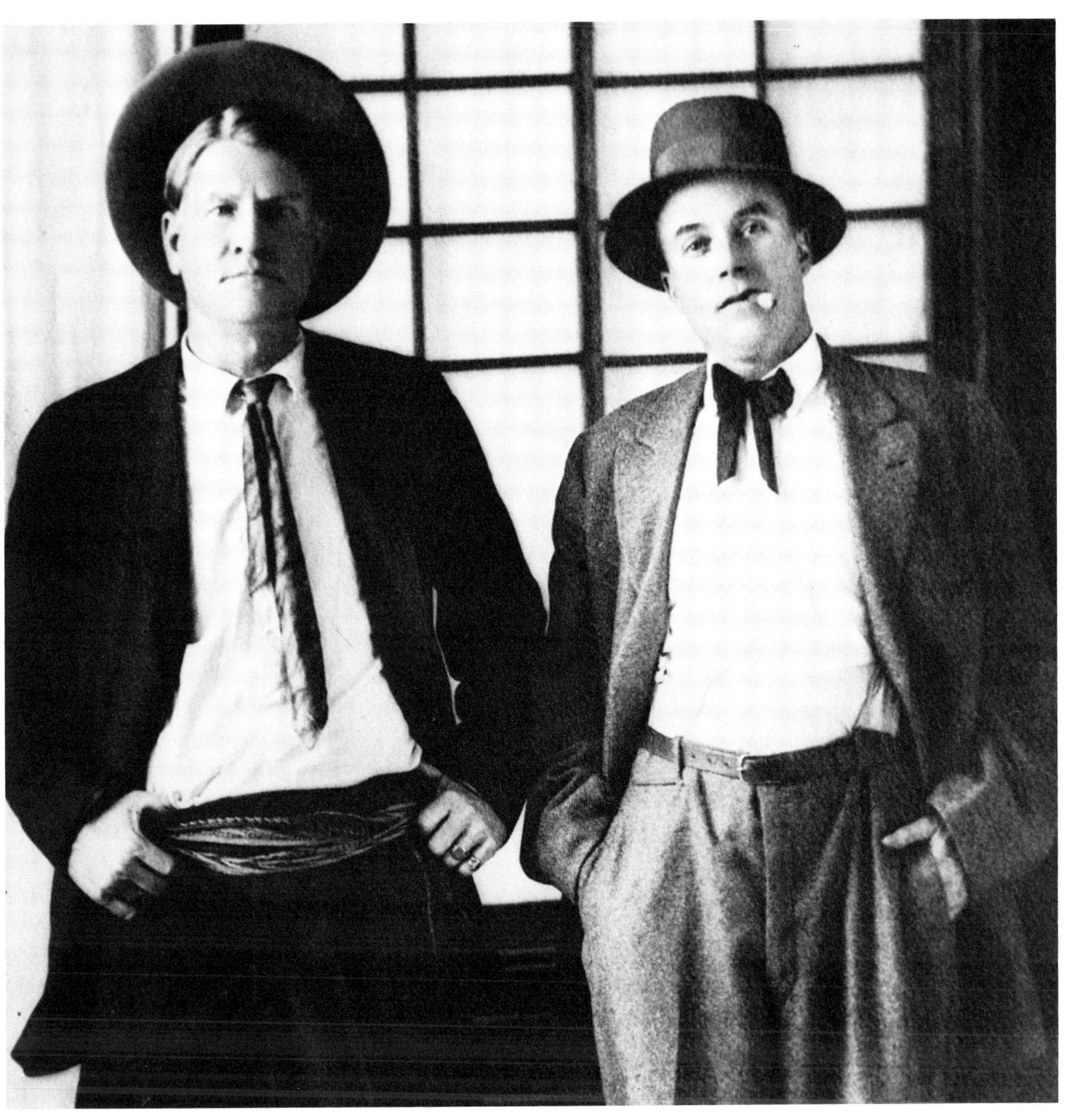

Convivial friends—Charlie Russell and Seltzer
1914
Courtesy of North Dakota Stark.

another nip. Those who knew him contend that he would slip from grace on rare occasions. The autumn visit to Ford's studio may have been one of these times, to judge from the jaunty pose Stark captured.

The artists are standing with feet apart, shoulders relaxed, hands in their pockets. Charlie's right thumb is hooked in his woven sash, his Stetson is pushed back, and his four-in-hand is loosely tied, but the expression on his face is as grimly serious as the one he wore in his wedding photograph. Olaf is wearing a tweed suit and a porkpie hat (the same apparel he wears in a more serious portrait that appears on Gilcrease Portfolio I of his Western Character sketches). His hat also is worn at a rakish angle, and he clutches the stump of a cigar between his teeth, managing a half-smile around it. Stark's camera caught a moment of high spirits—one of the best pictures ever taken of either painter—at the apex of their camaraderie. Russell was fifty at the time, and Seltzer was thirty-seven.

Forty years later, on the eve of his seventy-seventh birthday in 1954, when Russell had been dead for twenty-eight years, Olaf Seltzer recalled for an interviewer some of the experiences he and Russell had shared. He summarized his recollections on a wistful note: "Charlie was an interesting fellow. He was the most peculiar fellow; there was always something fascinating about him. Those were the good old days. I wish some of those days would come back."[10]

# Chapter 5
# "Start of the Finish"

LUMINOUS, LIMPID AND COOL, almost enamel-like."[1] Words such as these are often used to describe the oil paintings of Olaf Seltzer's mature years. They are also the words chosen by a foremost authority on Danish art to describe the naturalism of the father of Danish painting, Christoffer Wilhelm Eckersberg, who died in 1855. Eckersberg's influence can be traced in the exquisite colors and jewellike small paintings of his contemporary Christian Købke and in the work of three later painters: P. C. Skovgaard and Johan Thomas Lundbye, who did idyllic landscapes in the romantic style, and Theodor Philipsen, the animal painter who sought harmony with reality in nature and founded the Danish *plein air* school (the *pleinairistes* took their easels outdoors to capture transient atmospheric effects and to study the diffused effect of light).[2]

Philipsen was in his prime as an instructor at the Royal Academy in Copenhagen when young Olaf Seltzer attended the elementary classes at the Technical Society Institute, the incubator for Royal Academy students. Can such a slender thread be stretched to claim Danish influences on the work of a painter of the American West a quarter of a century after he left the cobblestoned streets and picturesque canals of Copenhagen for the rough frontier atmosphere of Montana? If so, such influence would have been subliminal. If the iridescent quality of Olaf Seltzer's painting and the wash of golden light that so often floods his paintings are the aftermath of early observations and impressions, he never shared that influence with friends or family.

More likely the similarity between Olaf's work and fine Danish painting originates in the skillful use of the strong light of the northern latitude, which illuminates with pure blondness, and from his unending fascination with the effect of light-intensity variations on western topography. At times his landscapes present distant detail with such clarity that he might be charged with artificiality by those who have never known the shining, crystal atmosphere of the western highlands. In other scenes distant landmarks acquire the softness of strong color filtered through a haze of prairie dust.

Whether through conscious knowledge of the *plein air* tradition or the patient discipline of his own observations, Olaf Seltzer mastered a subtle spectrum of color and marked it as his own. His cloud effects are so natural and indigenous to Montana that on certain sparkling days when random white clouds scud across mountain backdrops those who know his work refer to the "Seltzer sky."

One can only speculate on the inspiration for Olaf's lyrical expression. His respect for draftsmanship and linear composition are easier to account for, both from his early training and from statements he made from time to time lamenting the overemphasis that he felt was placed on color usage in the art classes of his day: "The most important factor in any painting is the outline, the basic foundation, whether it be the landscape, persons, animals, or objects. After one becomes proficient at that, then the coloring can be added and acquired." This he would follow with his oft-repeated homily, "One cannot paint a house before it has been built."[3]

It was during this time that Olaf Seltzer painted his first, and perhaps last, portrait. He had done a

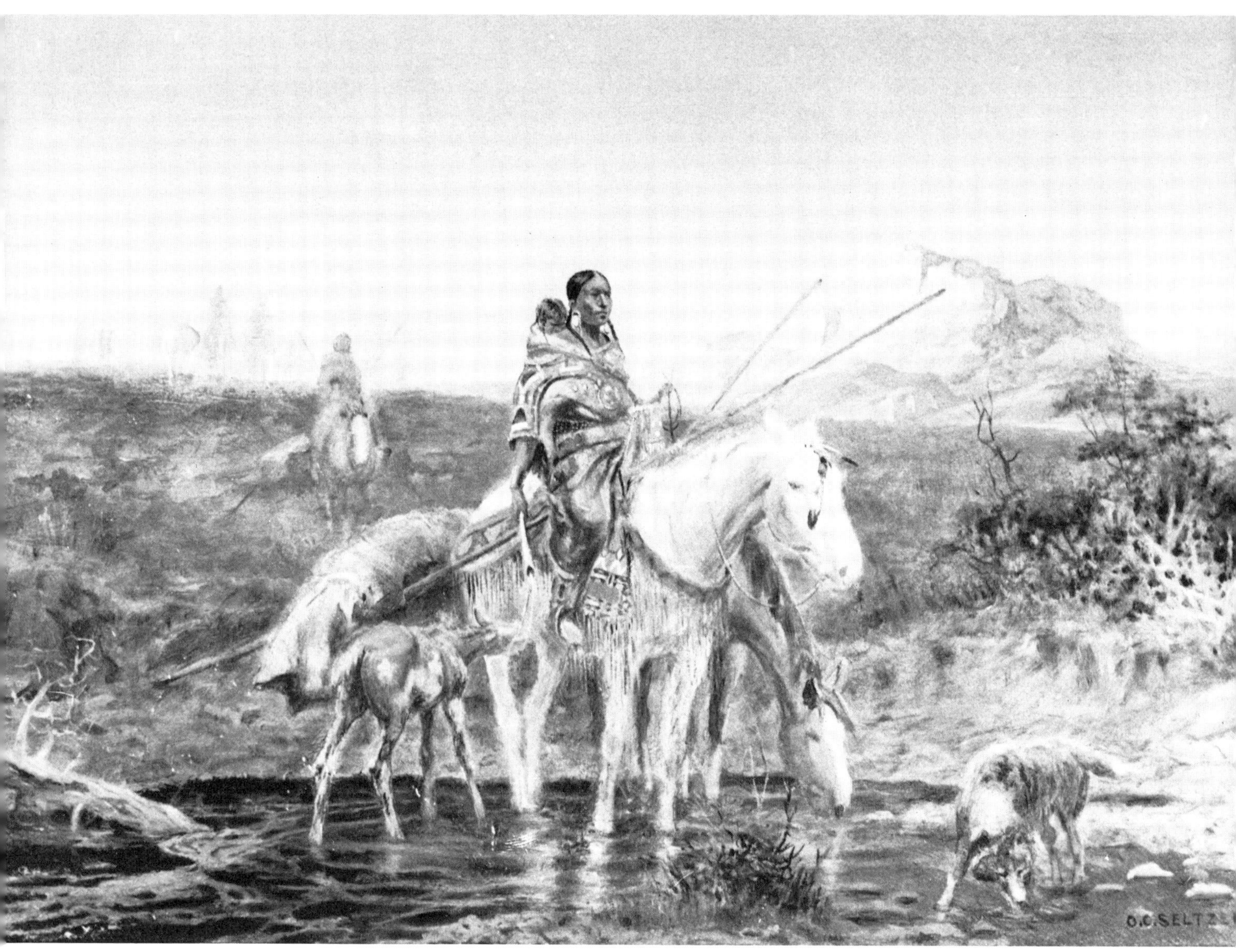



*Prairie Mothers*
ca. 1914
Author's Collection

few Indian heads—the Gilcrease collection includes a 7″ × 6″ study of *So-Ku-Yum* and an 8½″ ×
7″ entitled *Man Child—Cree Indian Brave*—but
his first remembered portrait is an upright 15″ ×
10½″ oil of Mabel.

This painting can no longer be viewed, except
on a poor photographic print from an X-ray taken
from the underside of a 10½″ × 15″ scene of
moving camp.

From what one can see of the portrait, Mabel is
wearing a toque ornamented with plumes, probably of ostrich feathers. Her shoulders are encased
in a lustrous stole of satin or taffeta. One dainty
hand holds her shawl in place over a high-necked
dark dress. Her deep-set eyes are shadowed by
the plumes. Although the portrait is well propor-
tioned, it does not appear to be a flattering likeness, for her mouth is pursed and tense, her eyes
guarded.

Very likely the portrait would not have been
remembered had I not purchased a Seltzer oil
painting in Chester, Pennsylvania in February,
1976, which I named *Prairie Mothers*. The central
figure is an Indian woman who is moving camp in

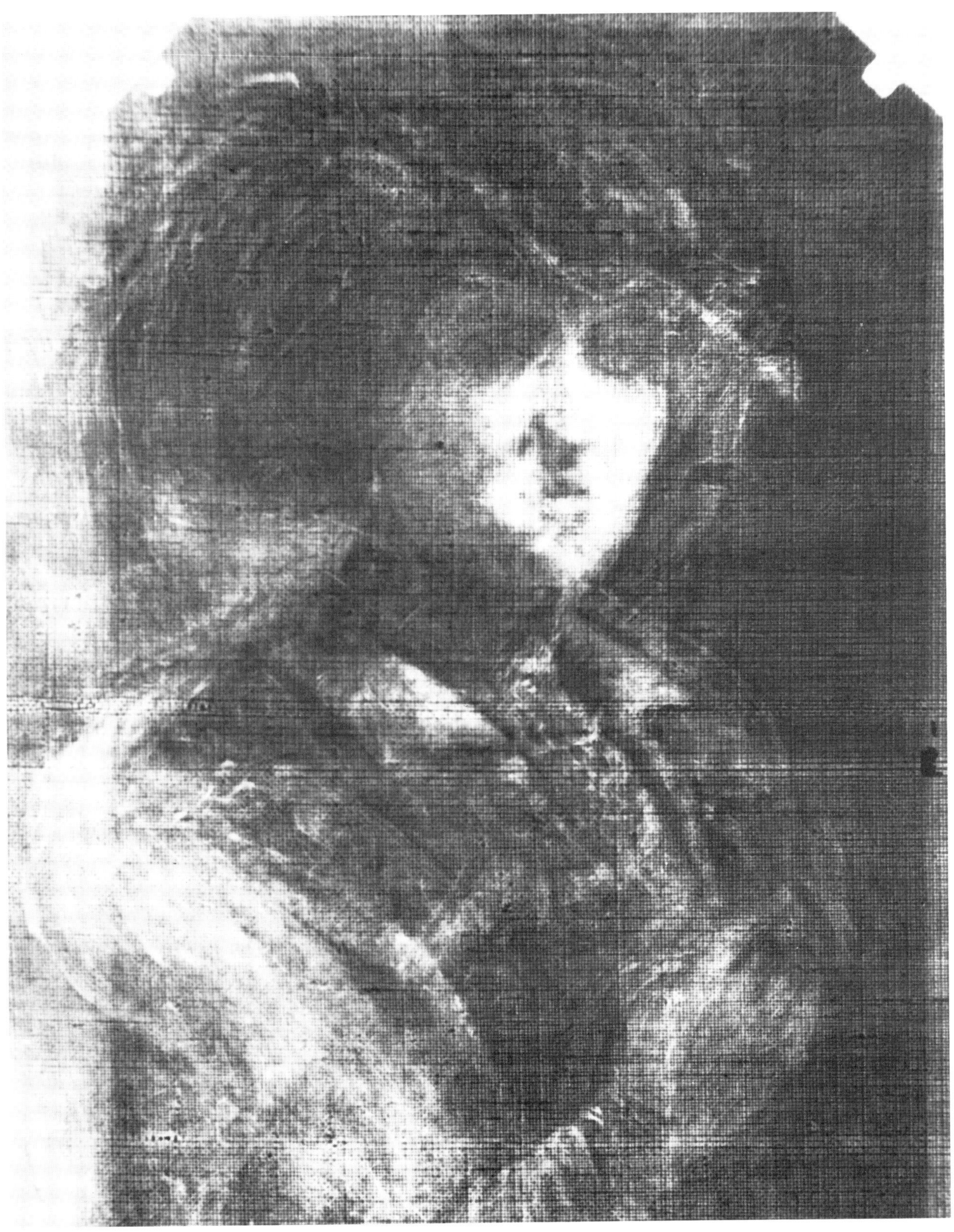

Mabel Seltzer's portrait under *Prairie Mothers*, as revealed by X ray.

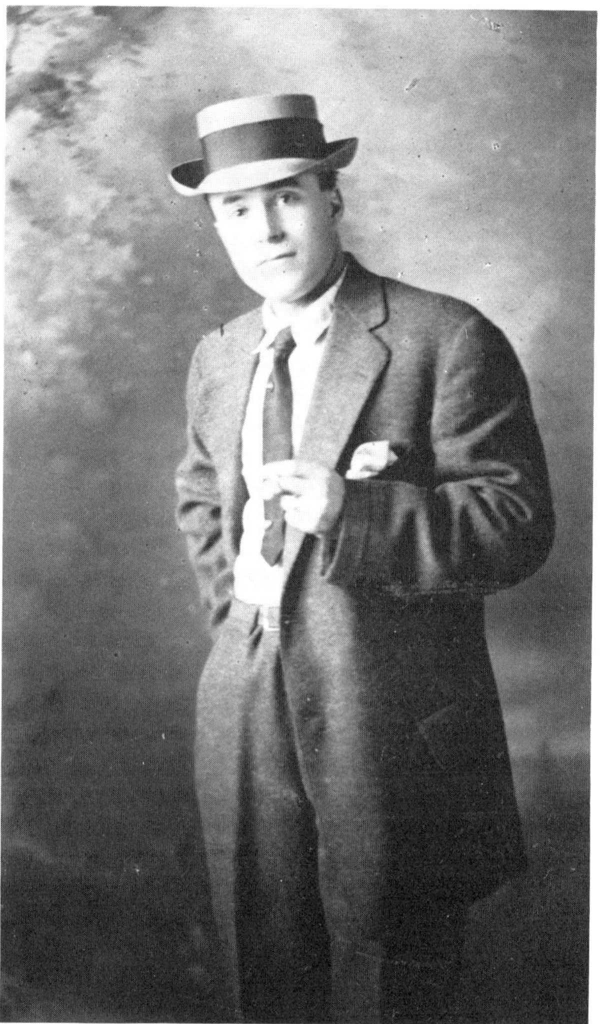

Seltzer about the time he painted *Prairie Mothers.*

all her tribal regalia. Mounted and carrying her papoose on her back, she waits patiently for her mare to drink at a water hole. The rest break provides a chance for the mare's colt to nurse. The peaceful scene is a gentle witness to motherhood.

Shortly after acquiring this western scene—one of gemlike coloring—I arranged to have it restored; a blow had caused a bit of the sky to flake away, disclosing white canvas beneath. The restorer, Ahmad Moghbel, of Norman, Oklahoma, discovered from the texture of brush marks on the right side of the canvas that there was a second painting under the scene. Sensing feather strokes, he judged it to be of an Indian.

After the X-ray disclosed that the portrait was of a woman, the question arose: was it Julie or Mabel? The question brought back Carl Seltzer's memory of the portrait episode.

"Pa did not like the painting . . . and decided he was not a portrait painter, so this was his first and last try in this field," wrote Carl, who remembers clearly that the artist covered the canvas with several coats of white paint and used it as the base for a 10½″ × 15″ landscape. Mabel's estimate of the portrait is not recorded, but her opinion may have entered into the artist's decision.

Apparently this attempt discouraged Olaf so completely that years later he would write to his patron, "I am surely no painter of she-types."

No one was as yet seeking Olaf Seltzer's philosophy of art in 1914, when he sold two of the largest paintings he had attempted: a 36″ × 48″ oil, *Squaws Watering Horses,* to Arthur Stephens and a 36″ × 30″ painting of an *Arab Sentinel,* which Olaf classified as genre. The Arab painting was his first recorded sale to Sylvia Bryant of Great Falls, who had a penchant for collecting art; she would become Seltzer's earliest steady customer for paintings.

Just as Olaf had arrived in Montana in time to observe the last of the wandering herds of wild-game animals, he also was on hand toward the end of another western phenomenon: the gaudy, rococo bordellos with their clublike atmosphere. Great Falls, its economy bolstered by a steady influx of smelter workers and railroaders, had no dearth of bawdyhouses, each with its bar and special attractions. Although none was as spectacular as the Butte houses, which boasted an international flavor with girls representing every continent, the Great Falls bordellos vied with each other in providing attractive atmospheres. One of them was noted for its ballroom with an immense crystal chandelier. Others collected antiques and western art.

Seltzer's painting effort was sidetracked for a time toward the end of 1914 by the death of his Uncle Louis Jensen and the subsequent arrangements that had to be made. After Jensen was laid to rest, next to the grave of his sister-in-law in Highlands Cemetery, his widow, Laura, decided to return to Denmark to live out her remaining years. She died in 1915 and was buried in the land of her birth.

Work in the Great Northern shops was being stepped up because of World War I. Olaf was busy with locomotive maintenance and repair, and he was short of skilled machinists as war production got under way. The responsibility for training apprentices and new journeyman machinists fell to him. There was little leisure time for sketching trips or painting sessions. The Seltzers were almost entirely home-based throughout the war years, and when Mabel and the boys wanted to visit Lizzie and George Osborne in Basin, along with their five sons who were favorite cousins of Carl and Walt, Olaf would have to send them alone. They also made some summer visits to Black Lake, Idaho, where the boys' grandparents, the Cleelands, then lived.

The entry of the United States into the conflict on April 7, 1917, inspired renewed dedication in the loyal, patriotic naturalized citizen. By now Olaf had been machine foreman and erecting foreman long enough to have developed self-confidence about his work. Although humble in his estimate of his painting, he had the cocky self-assurance of a conscientious and experienced worker when he tackled any task on a locomotive. The positions of others never intimidated him, and he was not one to sit back quietly and accept contrary orders if he believed he was right in his appraisal of a situation.

On one occasion Olaf's crew was working on Locomotive 1082, a passenger engine from which the big driving wheels had been removed in order to put journal boxes beneath them. Everything was ready to go. The crew had just raised the locomotive frame with a huge gantry crane when a telephone call came from the Great Northern headquarters in Saint Paul, ordering No. 1082 to the boneyard without further work. The executive office had decided that there was no immediate need for this passenger locomotive.

Olaf took a different view. The idea of wasting the man-hours already invested in getting ready to do the work infuriated him. Since all was in readiness, he took it upon himself to order the necessary work done before the driving wheels were put back under the locomotive and the frame lowered. Next he ordered binders (binding plates) put beneath the journal boxes and the work completed to the extent necessary to keep this phase from having to be redone should the Saint Paul powers have a change of mind about Locomotive 1082.

When word of this got back to Saint Paul, foreman Seltzer received another call, this one rebuking him for countermanding orders. With thinly concealed fury Olaf explained his reasoning and volunteered to resign if headquarters had someone else in mind for the job.

"So long as I'm foreman and I know what's what—and you down there in Saint Paul don't seem to know—that's the way it's going to be," he said in summary.

A Great Northern official wrote to Seltzer apologizing for the interference with his responsibilities. Within thirty days a need developed for No. 1082, and only the finishing touches had to be added before the locomotive could go back into passenger service.

When the war ended and Olaf had time to resume his painting, Mrs. Bryant was still interested in buying. In 1918 he sold her three of his genre paintings, a 7″ × 6″ oil entitled *Man with a Mug*, along with *Birds of a Feather* and *Belgian Drummer Boy*, the last reflecting his preoccupation with war events. He received fifteen dollars for the drummer boy—the first price he recorded.

The year 1919 was a troubled one for Olaf. In spite of his angry threat to resign if his authority in the shops was questioned, Seltzer was still dependent on his pay envelope from the railroad, and there were rumors of a sweeping cutback in railroad-shop employment, now that the war was won. Because he had been concentrating on shop work, he did not have a backlog of pictures, nor had he found additional customers for his work so that he could depend on sales to tide him over. He listed only two paintings sold that year, a 5″ × 6½″ oil he called *Outpost*, depicting the death of a hussar, and one with the pretentious name of *Coloroma Sycophanta*.

The artist turned to another form of creating, signing "Great Falls, Montana, 1919" to a fragment of verse he would use over and over again in the coming years, with slight changes of words, to articulate his sentiments about the changing face of the prairie. He called it *Passe*:

This silent, weird and rugged west
Where trails of men were dim and few
Will soon be but a hazy past:—
For step by step the struggling world
Is slowly pushing into space.

Each feature of the dying west:—
From bloodshot Indian summer moon
Down to the lonely night call of the loon.

Mrs. Bryant bought a 12″ × 9″ genre painting, *Violin Player in White*, from Olaf in 1920. He also

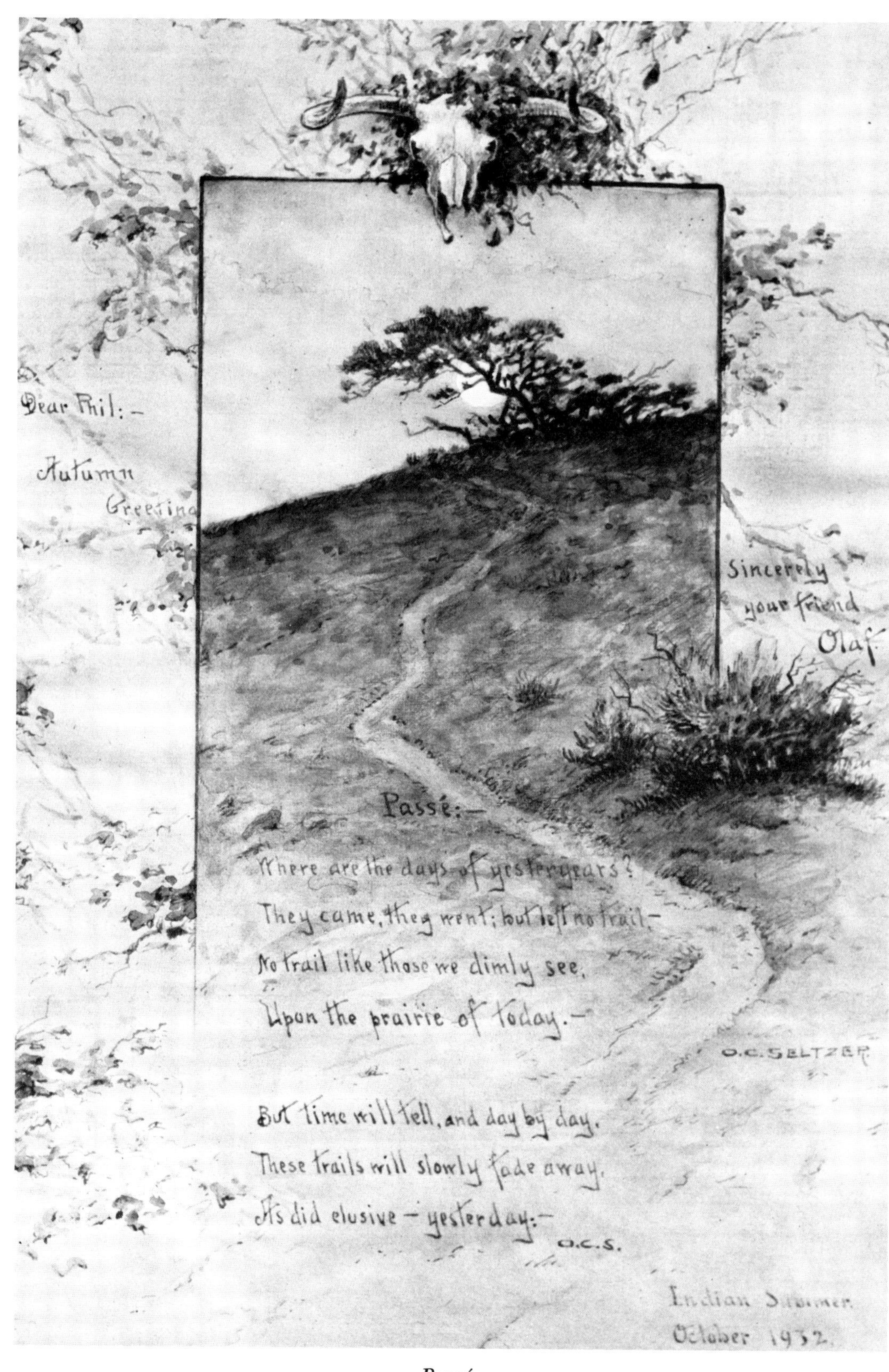


*Passé*
1932
Watercolor, 10″ × 7″

sold a 10″ × 8″ named *Man on Balcony* and a 9″ × 12″, *Chess Players*. *Pandour Outpost*, an 11″ × 14″ oil, was the Bryant purchase noted for 1921. She would continue to be a steady customer throughout the decade.

The postwar period was one of change for the Seltzers, along with the nation. The boys were in their teens; Carl had already outstripped his father in height and weight. Mabel was inclining toward plumpness; her hair was turning white prematurely, but with her sparkling eyes and fastidiousness she kept her good looks. Olaf bought his first car, a locally produced make called the Columbia. But he never enjoyed driving a car and still preferred to travel by train whenever possible. He seemed to mistrust cars, and he operated them in an erratic fashion.

Carl borrowed the family car for a high school dance in 1921. Before he got home, a thunderstorm broke, bringing heavy rainfall and high wind. When he maneuvered the car into the alley, well after midnight, his headlights picked out an irate father waiting on foot just inside the open garage door, worried about his car and "mad as hell" that his son was so late. Olaf ordered Carl out of the driver's seat so that he could put the car in the garage himself. Accelerating too rapidly, he shot through the back wall of the frame garage, causing it to collapse. It was a night not soon forgotten.

A few weeks later Olaf accepted Charlie Russell's long-standing invitation to spend some time with him at the Russell cabin on Lake McDonald in Glacier National Park. Olaf had seen less of Charlie in recent years. The Russells were often away from home, traveling to the West Coast, New York, and Florida. When they were in Great Falls, there was a stream of visitors to their home, drawn by Charlie's fame and charisma and Nancy's sociable nature. At the log-cabin studio Charlie had introduced Olaf to visiting painters such as the California artist Ed Borein and Maynard Dixon, with whom Seltzer felt at home. But he was intimidated by the celebrities Nancy enjoyed entertaining. Like many of Russell's cronies, Olaf felt that Nancy Russell was discouraging friendships from the old days.

In addition to the appropriate timing of the 1921 invitation from Charlie—the locomotive shops were closed down, and there was no sign of an immediate resumption of activity—Olaf was spurred to accompany Charlie by a confidential telephone call from Mrs. Russell. Olaf's relationship with Mrs. Russell was not exactly friendly. In spite of his open admiration for beautiful women, Olaf felt increasingly ill at ease with Nancy as her social contacts extended to include such personages as the Prince of Wales and the Duke of Connaught, whom the Russells had met in Canada, and stage and screen stars William S. Hart, Leo Carrillo, Will Rogers, and Douglas Fairbanks, Sr. With his Old World views, Olaf would have been uncomfortable among the Russells' celebrated friends.

But he was deeply concerned when Nancy Russell shared with him her worry over Charlie's health. She said that he no longer seemed to take an enthusiastic interest in anything, not even his painting. She was at a loss to explain his lassitude. Something seemed to be sapping his vitality; he had gone into a slump.

Since the first year of their marriage Nancy Russell's drive and ambition had continued to open new avenues for her singularly talented husband. It was she who raised the prices on Charlie's paintings, creating more demand for his work as it grew more costly. Now his reputation was at its peak, and he had more commissions than he could handle. Nancy was distraught over the change in his personality.

Some of Nancy's machinations shocked O. C. Seltzer. It was inconceivable to one of his background and pragmatic nature that any contemporary artist's work, even the best, could be worth a five-digit figure.[4] Privately Olaf believed that Mrs. Russell interfered with her husband's business more than was seemly. He would never have permitted Mabel to meddle with his painting career. But he was touched by Mrs. Russell's obvious concern for her husband's health, and he packed his gear for what was to be a seven-week stay on the lake.

The two painters arrived at the Glacier Park Hotel on Thursday, June 9, dining there before taking the local train for the short trip to Belton, where they spent the night. Olaf wrote to his family on Saturday, describing the beauties of the landscape, particularly the overwhelming beauty of the lake itself.

Russell had purchased his site on mile-wide Lake McDonald several years before Congress set aside this pocket of spectacular natural beauty, straddling the Continental Divide, as a national park. His Bull Head Lodge, named after the

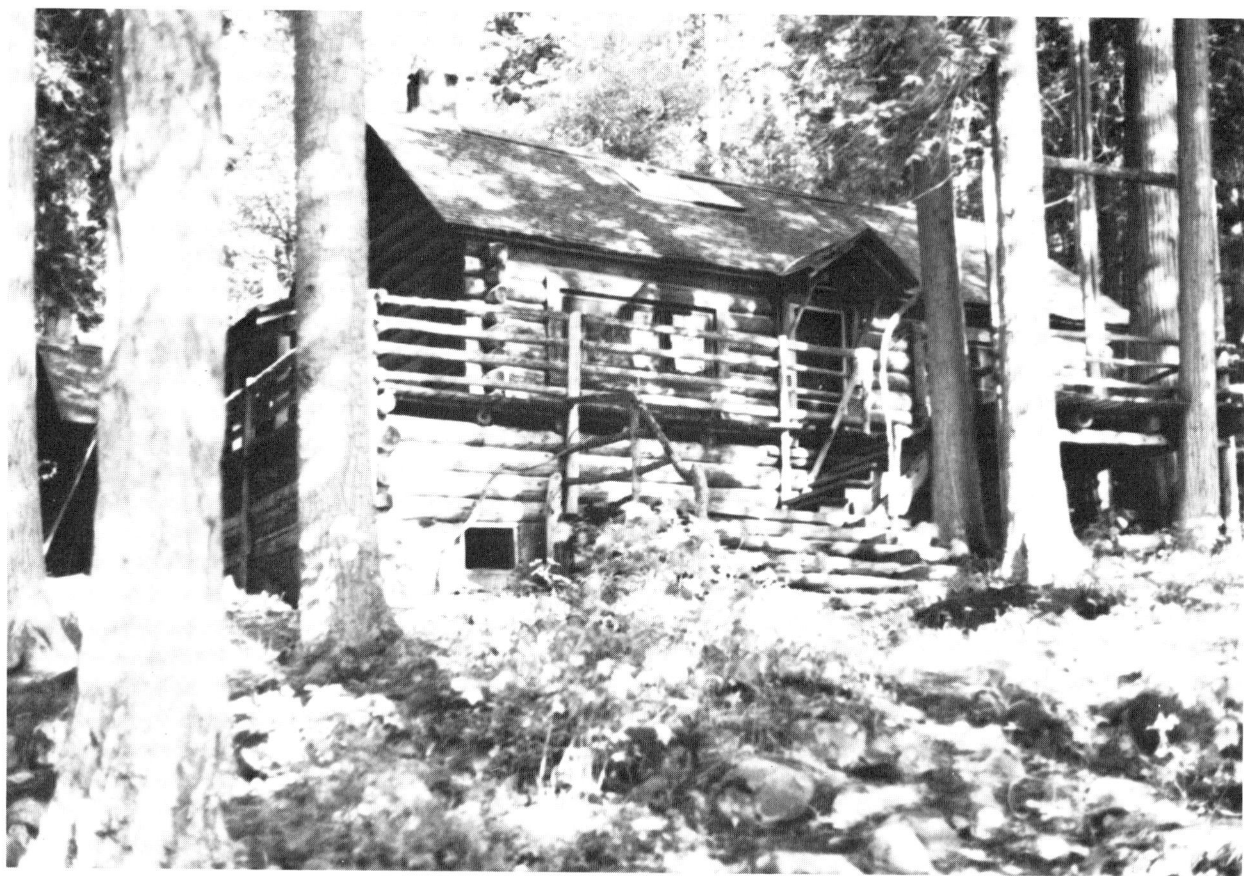

Bull Head Lodge, Lake McDonald, Glacier
National Park.

symbol—the head of a bull buffalo—he used with his signature on all his paintings, was situated in a clearing on a steep slope. It faced the glistening lake on which were reflected snow-capped peaks rising six thousand feet above the lake. In the high altitude and clear atmosphere the effect was breathtaking. Seltzer was enchanted.

On the front of the main cabin was a porch, built around three fir trees that Charlie wanted to preserve. There, on the open terrace of hewed cedar logs, the two painters set up their easels to spend many pleasant hours of concentrated work. The panorama spread before them changed with each passing minute as the sun picked out new formations among the glacier peaks of the incredible "Going to the Sun" country. At times, particularly toward evening, mists would roll across the lake, concealing the landscape as completely as though a stage curtain had obliterated na-

ture's drama. But in the morning the ultimate view in a landscape artist's dreams would reappear, fresh and shining, offering its constantly changing face of mountain beauty.

When Charlie acquired his land from Simon Apgar, the site was in primitive country. Visitors took the "stage," usually a farm wagon, to the log-cabin settlement called Apgar. The stage followed a dirt track that crossed the Flathead River and climbed to the foot of the lake. Ten miles long, McDonald is the largest lake in the park, and the one offering the most scenic beauty in the opinion of many Glacier Park visitors.

From Apgar, Russell would row his guests to a gravel landing where an enormous buffalo skull, made of planks and painted white, was mounted on a ten-foot pole. To guests arriving at night, the effect was eerie.

In spite of the isolation of the camp, it attracted

visitors who traveled many days by rail to gather at the Russells' cabin. Around the octagonal kitchen table spirited poker games took place among such participants as the humorist Irvin S. Cobb and the famous woman aviator Amelia Earhart, with her husband, publisher George P. Putnam.

The original cabin consisted of a single large room with hinged bunks along the walls. The Russells acquired several wood-framed folding screens with panels of unbleached muslin to offer a degree of privacy for their guests. After it became necessary to build guest cabins and to use the main lodge as a living and dining area, the Russells kept the screens as a unique guest register—because friends had begun to autograph the muslin panels. Visiting artists preempted the upper portion of each panel. The top of one bears Olaf Seltzer's contribution: a Rocky Mountain goat set in a circular panel of mountain scenery, dated 1921.

Philip R. Goodwin, an animal illustrator, and William Krieghoff, a portrait painter, decorated the top portions of the two other muslin panels on the same screen. Nancy and Charlie had become friends with both men during New York visits. Goodwin painted an elk head, and Krieghoff sketched remarkable likenesses of his host and hostess on the muslin.[5]

Beneath these outstanding mementos are several Indian cartoons drawn by Joe DeYong, a protégé of Charlie, along with bits of broad humor and inside jokes affixed by artistically less talented guests.

During Olaf's first visit to Bull Head Lodge he and Charlie enjoyed the outdoor life, riding and sketching together as they had been doing for more than twenty years. Russell seemed more relaxed as the weeks passed, but Olaf detected a difference in his normally cheerful attitude. Often they were joined by the Russells' handyman, a Dane who enjoyed visiting with Olaf in their native tongue. The bantering between the two Danes seemed to amuse Russell.

Tucked away in one of Seltzer's books is a scrap of paper on which he noted that "the year 1920 was the start of the finish." He continued: "In 1921 I was with him seven weeks and was able to make personal observations which showed me that he was slipping badly. From then until his death in November, 1926, he was but a hollow husk, a mere shell of his former self, both as a man and an artist."

Olaf later told members of his family that Russell suffered his "first attack" when the two were at the lake cabin alone. Seltzer believed that the attack was a mild stroke. It is doubtful that Olaf reported the incident to Mrs. Russell, since he would have respected his friend's wishes if Charlie had asked him not to mention it.

When Nancy arrived with her household help and two-year-old Jack, the couple's adopted son, Olaf returned to Great Falls loaded down with sketches, watercolors, and a number of oils in various stages of completion. During this working holiday he had begun several of the dozen or more western paintings he sold the following year, including *The Elk Hunter*, purchased by Brown and Bigelow.

In 1922, Olaf began to record the sale of 20″ × 30″ oil paintings. This size would become his favorite size for his preferred medium. Herb Benton, a Great Falls jeweler who invested in Seltzer's work in order to resell it in his shop, bought two such canvases in 1922: *Three Indian Scouts* and *White Man's Fire*. Other local business and professional men—particularly medical men—were beginning to invest in Olaf's work, since his prices were within their reach and his western subjects were similar to Russell's. John G. Brown bought *Mounted Police*; the mortician W. H. George purchased *The Mountain Trail*; and J. W. Butler, *The Horse Thieves* and several Wild Critters. *The Sentinel*, a watercolor, was purchased by a Minneapolis art fancier.

The painting sessions at Lake McDonald and his increased sales had so bolstered Seltzer's self-confidence that by the time the Great Falls city directory for 1923 was published he had changed his occupational listing from "foreman" to "artist." He was also doing some book illustrations, and at long last he could begin to make plans to leave his job in the locomotive shops.

Although Olaf and the boys felt at ease with Charlie Russell, the association never included the painters' wives.[6] Olaf returned again and again to Bull Head Lodge, staying for a few days at a time and still attempting to awaken in Charlie the old spark of enthusiasm for his painting. During these visits Seltzer began to make friends among the local residents and summer folk, including the Russells' neighbors the W. W. Sherwoods. In 1924, Sherwood, an executive of the Royal Milling Company, commissioned Seltzer to do a large (40″ × 64″) painting of Sherwood Lodge. The milling official also permitted Olaf to hang some of his work in the company's executive offices as a means of promoting the artist's sales.

The year 1925 was a landmark one for Olaf. He sold more than fifty pictures for an aggregate sum of well over a thousand dollars. O. C. Seltzer, artist, could bid farewell to the dusty, noisy locomotive shops.

Three of his paintings were 20″ × 30″ oils. *Winter Landscape*, sold to a customer named Cozzens, took a top price of $175. A Dr. Adson paid $150 each for *Rivers of the Prairie* and *The Trail Boss*, which probably represented a special price Olaf made on a package deal. A Mrs. Gergen paid $30 for a small oil of Russell on his favorite horse, Monte.

Eight of Seltzer's watercolors on Indian themes, each 9″ × 13″, were sold to the Como Store. Although becoming more detailed in his record keeping, Olaf failed to note his prices for these, and for the six genre paintings, the four oils of animals, and the Sherwood Lodge oil, all delivered in 1925. He was generally charging twenty-five dollars each for his 11″ × 16″ watercolors at this time.

At the close of a Glacier Park painting vacation in 1925, Olaf crossed the lake to seek permission from John Lewis, owner of the rustic Lake McDonald Hotel, to hang some of his oils and watercolors in the hotel lobby as Russell had done for many years. Lewis agreed without hesitation.

A few weeks later the Danish handyman from Bull Head Lodge made a business trip to Great Falls and came by to see the Seltzers. He told Olaf that none of his work was on display in the hotel lobby.

As soon as he could find the time, Seltzer took a train to Glacier Park to verify his hunch. The paintings had been stored carefully in a closet after Nancy Russell protested their presence.

Olaf was furious. Unable to control his aversion to Nancy, he avoided Charlie after the incident. The Russells by now were spending much of their time in California, where they had plans under way for the erection of their new home in Pasadena. Across the distance Russell sensed Olaf's alienation and seemed to be puzzled by it. He apparently knew nothing of the hotel incident.

Members of Olaf's family were well aware of his deep hurt over the incident. Carl, who was employed by a stationery company but still living at home, recalls arguing that Charlie should not be held accountable for his wife's actions. Gradually the wound healed, and Olaf began to drop in on Charlie once more at the log-cabin studio. The friends were on easy terms once more by the spring of 1926, the last time they would see each other. But Olaf Seltzer never forgave Nancy Russell.

Chapter 6

# Painter Meets Patron

AS THE WINTER OF 1925–26 wore on, Olaf Seltzer quietly laid plans to move to New York City. Free of his daily shift at the locomotive shops, his confidence bolstered by the expanding market for his work, Olaf had begun dreaming of working in a metropolitan center where he could mingle with other painters and visit the galleries.

As he met more of the Russells' artist friends from New York, he became convinced that his work would measure up to the best in landscape painting of the West and that he could make a go of it financially in the city. The episode at Lake McDonald the previous summer chafed him like a bur under the saddle blanket. He would show Nancy Russell that he could hold his own in eastern art circles.

The Seltzers had one strong contact in the metropolitan area, Mabel's close school friend Pearl Webber Hynote. Pearl and her husband had settled in Elmhurst, Long Island, after leaving Great Falls, where Hi had operated the Cream City Saloon and then the Maverick. Pearl had stayed with Mabel and Olaf for some weeks while her husband was arranging for a home for them in Elmhurst; the Hynotes had long been urging the Seltzers to come for an extended visit.

A single link was still to be forged in the chain of associations and events that would move Olaf, Mabel, and their sons to New York in April, 1926. It was supplied in the early spring, when Olaf met Philip Gillett Cole at the home of their mutual friend Dr. W. T. Butler in Helena. It was a singularly successful meeting. Olaf needed a patron to assure him an outlet for his work and a steady income, and Cole needed an artist to translate his dreams to canvas.

Butler, who served as a Montana state veterinary surgeon for nearly thirty-five years, was a fervent admirer of Seltzer's work. He had begun buying from Olaf in the early twenties, at first purchasing animal sketches and watercolors of western scenes and then gradually placing more and more orders for oils. In 1925 he purchased an 11″ × 16″ oil, *White Man's Medicine*, for forty dollars.

Seltzer enjoyed the veterinary surgeon. He always learned from his associations with authorities on animal life.[1] Frequently, when passing through Helena to deliver a canvas, he would call on Butler. No one is sure whether the early spring visit was an impromptu one or whether Butler urged him to come expressly to meet his visitor from New York City. Whatever the arrangement, Dr. Butler took great pride in being the catalyst that brought together his two friends—painter and patron—who grew to mean so much to each other.

Philip Cole's life plan had been to practice medicine in the wide-sky heart of Montana. He had established a practice in Helena before World War I but did not resume it after he returned from service. Because of a fortuitous investment that brought his father great wealth and concomitant responsibility, Phil Cole would live out his years as an industrialist within commuting distance of New York City.

Philip Cole was born in Jacksonville, Illinois, on September 25, 1883, the oldest child of Dr. Charles Knox Cole, a native New Yorker, and his wife, Harriet Gillett, of Illinois. The Coles settled in Montana, where "C. K.," as he was called, became speaker of the Montana Territorial Senate

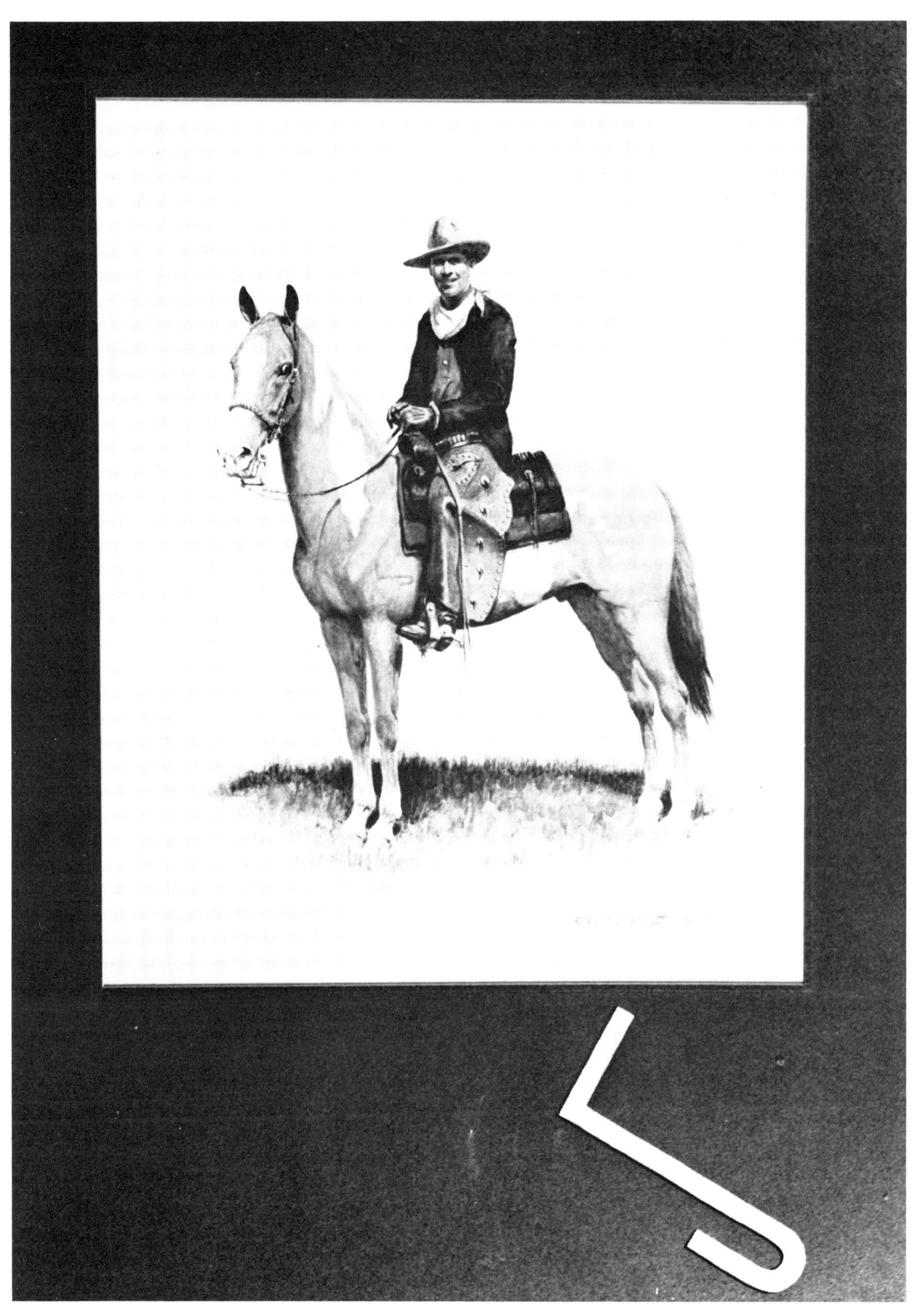

*Owner, PGC*
1927
Western Character sketch

in the 1888–89 session, the last before Montana entered the union as the forty-first state on November 8, 1889. C. K. was an investor and a rancher as well as a physician. He registered the "J Bar" and the "Reverse CK" brands with the territory and then the state of Montana.[2] He built the Helena Hotel. One story has it that it was the trade of this hotel at the turn of the century that took Cole east and launched him on a business career. Another has it that Cole inherited two apartment buildings in New York and sold them early in 1900 for fifteen hundred dollars, the sum he invested in an invention of a tire valve envisioned by a German immigrant named George Schrader. The investment launched C. K. Cole on a second career that brought immense wealth into the family.

Philip studied at Phillips Andover Academy, class of 1902, and went on to Princeton, graduating in 1906. He is remembered by classmates for his "spirit of good fellowship and squareness."[3] He completed his medical studies at the Columbia University College of Physicians and Surgeons in 1910, doing postgraduate work at Bellevue, Harlem, and allied hospitals. He finished his internship as house surgeon for the Harlem Hospital, where he specialized in gynecology. When he prepared to leave for Montana, the newspaper reporters covering the Harlem Hospital district gave a testimonial dinner in appreciation of his "uniform courtesy and his helpful relations with them in the public work of the hospital."[4]

During World War I, Philip, in his early thirties and well established in his medical practice in Helena, enlisted to serve in France as a reserve officer. Upon his return after the 1918 armistice he married Katharine Pyle, the daughter of a prominent Montana family and a talented sculptor. As a wedding gift C. K. Cole presented the couple with the large Russell canvas *The Buffalo Hunt*, dated 1910, which had hung in the elder Cole's suite at the Waldorf Hotel in New York City. Katharine Cole enjoyed telling friends that she was responsible for the start of Philip Cole's collection of western art, since her father-in-law was aware of her interest in art. This painting and several Russell bronzes occupied places of honor in the Cole home.

Phil Cole was faced with having to make an irrevocable decision at the end of the war. By this time his father was principal owner of A. Schrader & Son, Inc., a Brooklyn firm that manufactured

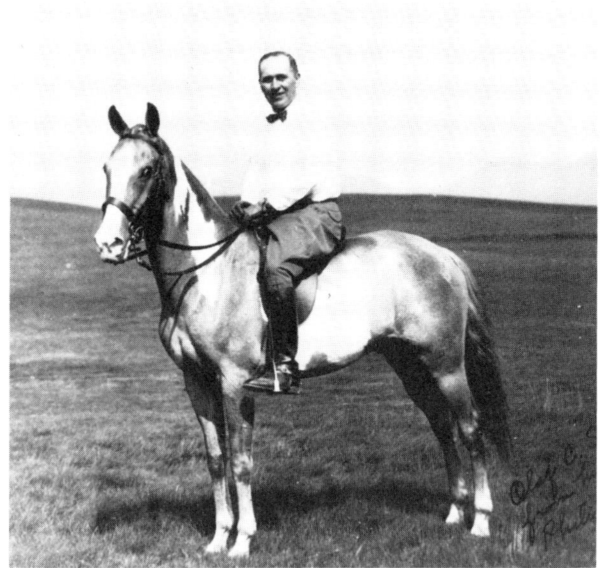

Dr. Philip G. Cole, on a visit to his home state. Courtesy of Carl C. Seltzer.

automotive parts, such as valves and gauges. Its best-known product was the Schrader tire valve, much in demand during the postwar period, when automobile production grew rapidly.

The younger Dr. Cole preferred to live in the bracing atmosphere of the high plains and to practice his chosen profession, but he yielded to his father's wishes and took over management of the company. C. K. Cole died shortly thereafter, and Phil was elected president of the firm. But the transplanted Montanan returned to his home state whenever he had a chance, and he dreamed of the day when he would own a ranch there (since Mrs. Cole did not share his enthusiasm for returning to the isolation of Montana, the "ranch" eventually was established in northern New York State).

In his frustration over sacrificing his plans to live in his beloved homeland, Cole created a western world of his own. He lined the walls of his successive homes in the East with paintings of life in early Montana and filled his bookshelves with folios and historic documents. When he eventually created a replica of a Montana ranch at Lake Placid, New York, he named it Last Chance Ranch after Last Chance Gulch, the original name for Helena and the spot where a group of Georgians discovered gold in 1864 on what later became the C. K. Cole ranch. Cole spared no pains to make his dream come true; he stocked his ranch near the Canadian border with a herd of young antelope flown in from Montana and brought a herd of reindeer from Alaska, along with an Eskimo herder.

Philip Cole had begun to collect western art after he took up residence in the New York area, and he continued to do so until shortly before his death in 1941. His collection would have been outstanding had he never encountered Olaf Seltzer, but with Olaf's contribution the collection became one of the largest and most significant dedicated to the American West, embracing whole areas of western life and bygone customs. It comprises a pictorial record to bring enjoyment and enlightenment to generations yet unborn.

By 1926, when Cole and Seltzer met in the home of Cole's former Helena schoolmate, Philip and Katharine were living in a comfortably large house in Forest Hills, Long Island, with their three children—Philip Gillett, Jr.; Jane; and Katharine, known as "Kay"—and their growing accumulation of western art. Cole had already acquired Joseph Henry Sharp's *Chief "Flat Iron,"* an oil dated 1905, and Frank Tenney Johnson's oil *Indian Lodges*, and watercolor *The Night Wranglers*. He owned Russell's *Where Tracks Spell Meat*, painted in 1916; William R. Leigh's *The Bad Lands at Night;* and Frederick Remington's 1901 canvas, *Missing*.

Albert LeRoy Groll's pastel *Prairie Country* and Ralph Earll Decamp's *The Gate of the Mountains* were owned by Cole, who chose his purchases as much for subject matter and his response to the painting as for the reputation of the artist. The investment aspect—whether or not a painting or sculpture would become more valuable in the future—seemingly never occurred to Cole. He bought solely for his own enjoyment, and the paintings were rarely seen except by his family, guests, and close friends.

Dr. Butler had told his two friends about each other, whetting their curiosity and setting the stage for a companionable session. Neither Cole nor Seltzer was disappointed. In addition to sharing a number of friends, chief of whom was Charlie Russell, they had many personality traits in common. Both were kindly, quiet-mannered, modest, self-effacing. Both were historical buffs, interested in Montana brands, customs, and the minute details of range life, which they enjoyed exploring together as their acquaintance blossomed into a devoted friendship.

In that first meeting Olaf may have learned something about Phil Cole's *modus operandi* in his art buying. Cole usually made his purchases through art dealers—Milch Galleries was a favorite, along with Kennedy—and he never agreed to purchase anything that he had not personally inspected. He was proud of his ability to identify a fake and his objectivity in turning down as many paintings as he bought. He seldom purchased directly from artists—Russell and Seltzer were the exceptions—and he was indifferent to most of the letters he received from aspiring artists of the West who sought to interest him in their work.

He offered to introduce Olaf to some of the dealers specializing in western artists, and also to some of his friends, including the Wall Street brokers Harry Durant and Malcolm S. Mackay, who were interested in western art. If he could do little more, Olaf reasoned from Cole's conversation, there would be some employment for him in New York in restoring damaged paintings and cleaning canvases, work in which there was a scarcity of expertise. Cole backed his talk with the purchase of three 11″ × 16″ watercolors: *Trail Boss, Roping a Maverick*, and *Three Indian Scouts*.

Meeting Cole was the final factor in Olaf's decision to make the move. The family began packing. Shortly after Phil Cole returned to New York, Olaf sent him an illustrated greeting setting forth his personal philosophy. Beneath a watercolor-and-ink drawing of a somber Indian chief, seated on a hide and holding a calumet, Seltzer printed a variation of his early verse:

> This silent, weird and purple vast
> Where trails of men were dim and few,
> Will soon be but a hazy past:—...

Ornamenting each side are beadwork panels, painted with such finesse as to create a textured appearance. Like many of Seltzer's other paintings, this one served as a prototype for a splendid version he would do later on the same theme: *Medicine Man with Beadwork Design*, an 18″ × 12″ watercolor in vibrant colors of orange and bright blue. The beadwork in the upper third of this watercolor is so definitively painted as to lend

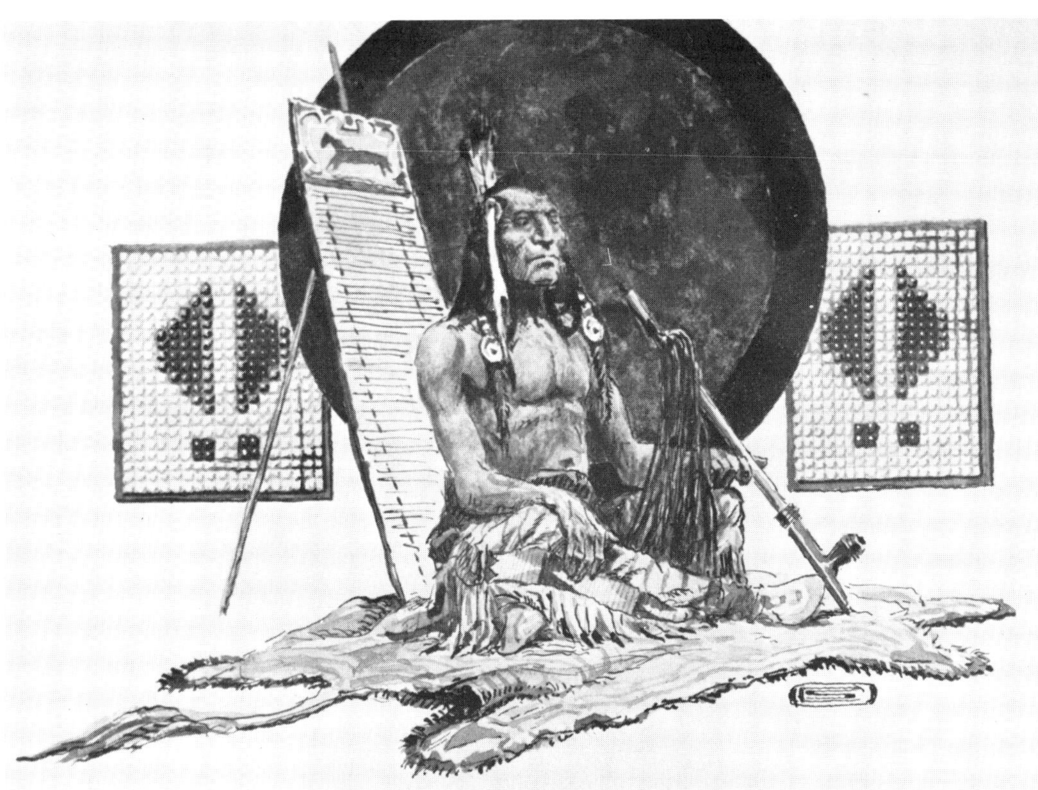


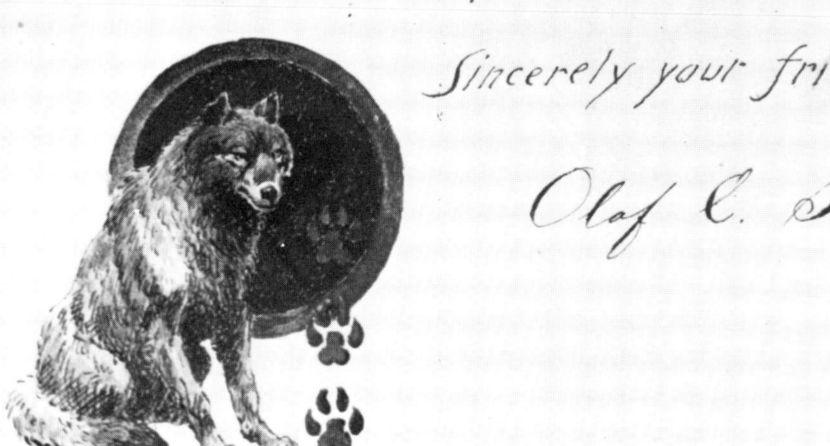

*"This silent, weird, and purple vast"*
1926
Watercolor and ink, 11″ × 6″

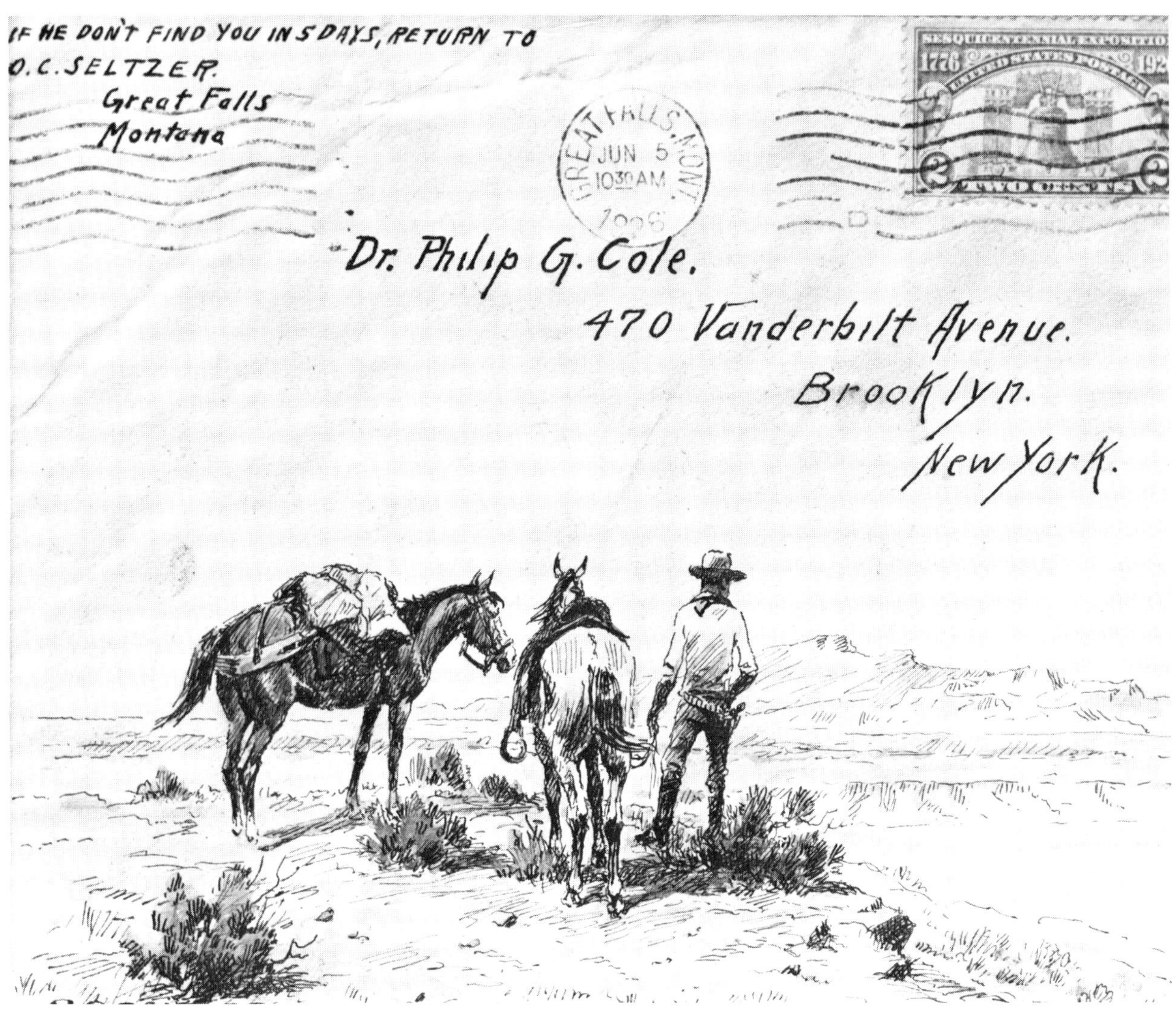

*If He Don't Find You*
1926
Watercolor and ink, 6″ × 6½″

a spatial relationship among the off-white, red, and blue beads, creating a convincing textured effect.

Seltzer's humor surfaces on the 6″ × 5″ envelope in which he sent this greeting. The lower half is ornamented with a detailed drawing of a cowboy standing by his saddle horse and laden packhorse, gazing searchingly over a vast valley with buttes in the distance. The envelope is addressed to Cole's Brooklyn office. In the upper-left-hand corner the sender printed:

IF HE DON'T FIND YOU IN 5 DAYS RETURN TO:
O. C. SELTZER
GREAT FALLS
MONTANA

In May the sender himself would find his way to Vanderbilt Avenue in Brooklyn on the first of many visits. But the intervening period was a frantically busy one for the Seltzers, who viewed the move from Great Falls as a permanent one. They sold most of their furniture, and Mabel stored her prized cut glass and other family mementos. It was late April before the couple was ready to board the train for New York City.

Directly upon their arrival the Seltzers went to Elmhurst to stay with their friends the Hynotes while they looked for a place to live in the neighborhood. After Olaf and Mabel were established in a second-floor apartment on Fifty-first Avenue, the boys set out from Montana in a new Model T Ford that Carl had purchased for the trip. It took them thirteen days of steady driving, much of it through torrential rains, to reach New York—an anxious thirteen days for Mabel.

Carl, who had given up his job as salesman for the McKee Stationery Company in Great Falls, found comparable work in downtown Manhattan. Walt went to work as a clerk in the Oriental art and antiquities section of Wanamaker's Department Store, a job he found fascinating.

Olaf was enchanted with the metropolis. He spent his mornings at the easel and his afternoons visiting the museums. At the Metropolitan Museum of Art he put in hours studying the old masters, particularly Rembrandt. He was also drawn to the heroic work of the nineteenth-century French painter Jean Louis Meissonier. Wandering in the Museum of Natural History, he would lose track of time while studying the wildlife exhibits and the realistic backgrounds against which they were displayed.

He loved to poke around in the shops from which he had so often ordered rare stamps and insect and butterfly specimens. After such expeditions he would return to Elmhurst refreshed.

Before the year ended, Olaf had sold Cole three more watercolors and nine oils, mostly small paintings such as *Medicine Man* (6″ × 9″), *Old Indian Head* (9″ × 7″), and *Pawnee Scout* (6″ × 8″). The largest was the 36″ × 48″ *Prowlers of the Prairie*, a striking painting of a war party of Indians gathered on a bluff from which they command a view of a wide valley. There is a wealth of fine detail, from the beaded trappings on the horses to the horned headdress of the medicine man, who is mounted on a spirited Appaloosa. The light of dawn casts a deep-pink glow that is reflected along the breast and head of the white horse in the lead. The delicacy of lighting alone makes this one of Seltzer's major oils.

Olaf had brought many of these paintings with him from Great Falls. During the summer months, while orienting himself to new circumstances, he also completed twenty-five wild-animal studies for Cole. When he had a few ready for delivery, he would take them to Brooklyn. Cole's personal secretary, a Miss Sansom, was instructed to make immediate payment on any orders if Cole was not in. Olaf always took along a few additional pictures. They usually pleased the collector, and he quickly bought them. Through Phil, Olaf met other admirers of western art. By Christmas he had sold Malcolm Mackay a 9″ × 11″ oil called *The Rear Guard* and a 10″ × 13″, *Crow Scout*, for thirty dollars each.

New York held less fascination for Mabel. She enjoyed the companionship of the Hynotes and occasional gatherings with other Great Falls friends visiting in the East, but she also endured pangs of homesickness. She never expressed envy of Olaf's chances to mingle with wealthy New Yorkers, but she missed her own kind, her bridge foursomes, and the fellowship of the Pythian Sisters.

By autumn the boys were tired of commuting to their jobs in the city. Walt, who was involved in a wreck on an elevated train, remembers the feeling of panic he had when the occupants of the damaged car were squeezed into the one in which he was riding. Carl was restless, too. Gregarious like his mother, he missed the contacts of his sales job back home.

On September 26, Carl started back across the northern brow of the continent, driving alone in the Model T. He arrived in Great Falls on October 6 and immediately began looking for a place for his mother and brother, who returned by train on November 6.

Russell's death on October 24, 1926, brought Cole and Seltzer closer. In the words of his last letter to Philip Cole, Russell had been "trimed" a few months earlier by "the medicine men at Rochester."[5] It was Olaf who conveyed the sad news of Russell's death to Cole's office. On November 5, Phil wrote to thank Olaf and to prod him about some work in progress:

> Thanks very much for your thoughtfulness in letting me know so promptly of the death of Charley Russell. Like you, I was shocked to hear of it. I promptly wrote Nancy.
>
> I am wondering how you are coming along with the two pictures—"Slicker Shy" and the sheep picture. While I do not wish to hurry you in any way, I am, as you will understand, anxious to see them. Am sure you will let me know as soon as you have something to show me. I would even be

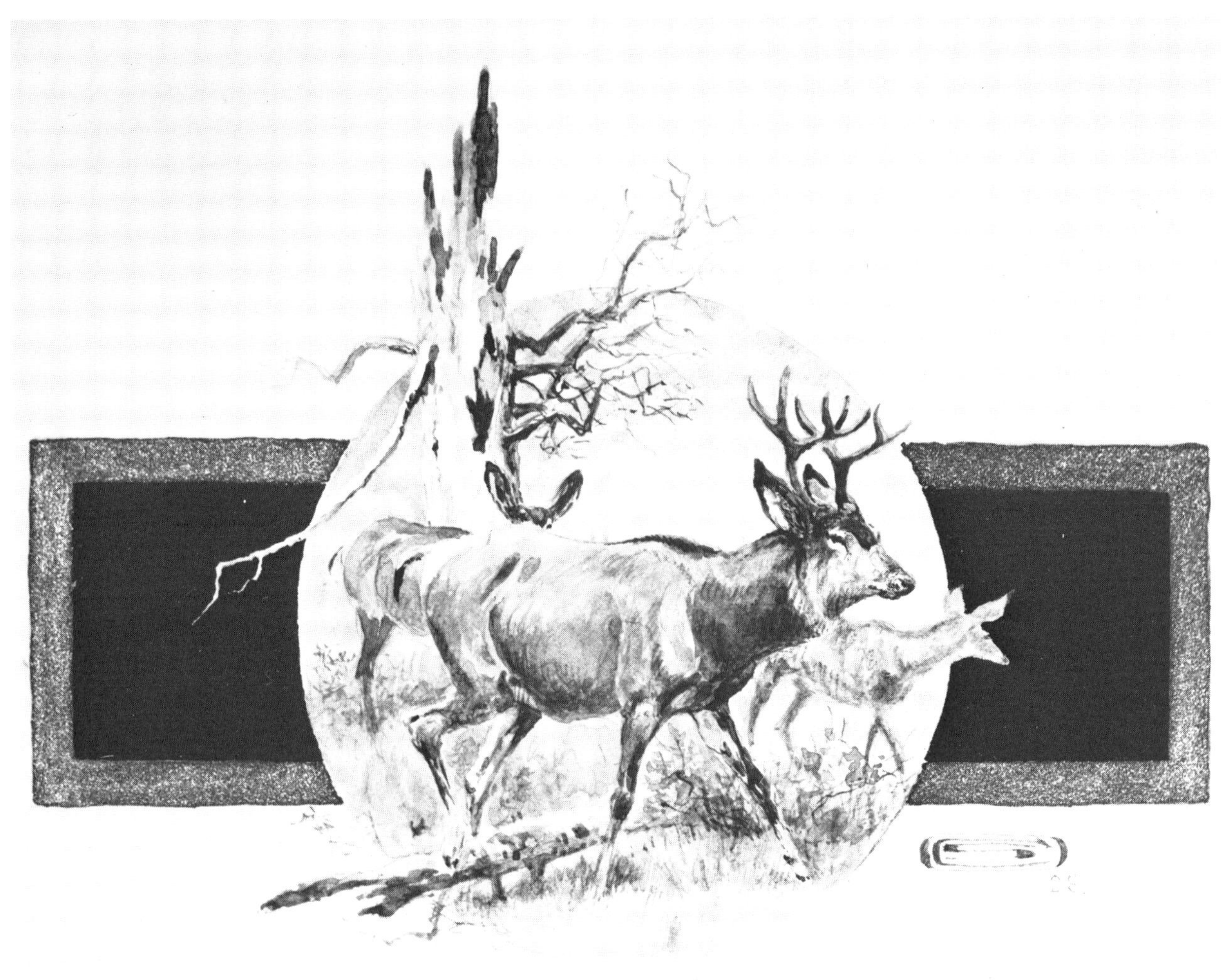

*Three Deer*
1926
Watercolor, 7¾″ × 10″

glad to see them before they are completed, though possibly you would prefer to get them finished up.

When I do see you I want to talk with you about an illustration to cover the book of photographs of my pictures which I am now getting up.

With best regards and every good wish,

Sincerely yours,

Philip G. Cole

Phil Cole's "sheep picture" is a 12″ × 14″ canvas painted in a romantic style. It represented a facet of Montana life not as yet included in his collection. Russell had been prejudiced against sheep ever since a boyhood experience on a Montana sheep ranch, where he grew to despise the muttonheads, and refused to paint them. But Seltzer had no such reluctance. His *Sheep Country* contains a large flock, including the shepherd.

Before Christmas Olaf sent Cole a two-page illustrated letter conceived as a tender memorial to Russell. It is the most elaborate of the many letters Olaf prepared for the pleasure of his patron, and also the longest, featuring at the beginning one of his sketches of Charlie—unruly hair hanging over his eyes, cigarette in hand, colorful garb disheveled.

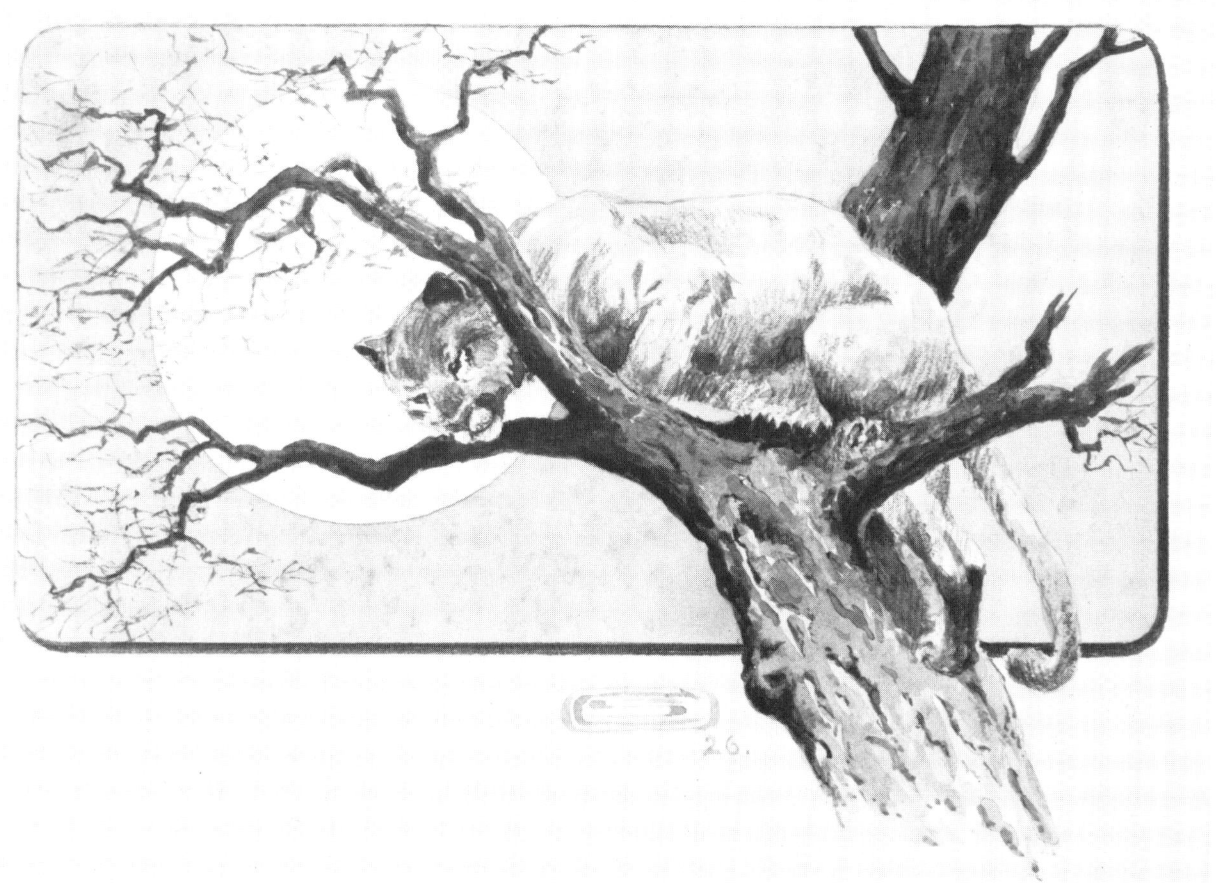

*Cat in a Tree*
1926
Watercolor, 7½″ × 10″

Referring to a previous conversation with Cole about Russell's early days on the range, Seltzer wrote:

I am sure he came out of the Little Belt Mountain about 1882 after living there with old Jake Hoover, the trapper, their stamping grounds in those mountains being around and near old Yogo, later famous for the sapphires mined there. In leaving the Little Belt Mountains Charley dropped down into the upper Judith River country around the old Cow town Utica and the Pig eye Basin, where he struck the N-N Cow Outfit. He was hired by the Trail Boss of this Outfit, Horace Brewster, as horse wrangler, and he was known to N-N in general and Brewster in particular, as "The Buckskin Kid."—due to his straw-coloured hair, and his bleached complexion, and also due to a pair of buckskin seated riding pants. When sometime after that he went north across the Canadian border line, this same pair of pants caused him to be named by the Bloods and Piegans—"Aw-a-Kos"—"The Antelope,"—these Indians figuring in their picturesque, simple way that the rear view of Charley in his riding pants looked like an antelope flagging his danger signal in full retreat. This obscure kid became through evolution an interesting and welknown character throughout the Northwest and even further.

I am now about to pull the old timeworn bromide; but there seems to be but one formula so here goes:—Wishing you, your family and Miss Ralston a merry Christmas and a prosperous New Year, I am,

Sincerely your friend,
Olaf.

In addition to rear-view sketches of Russell and an antelope with *Aw-a-Kos* lettered between, there are five tinted sketches entitled *EVOLU-TION (via the Darwin Route)*. The first features a cup of paint with a broomlike brush poked into it. By the fifth sketch this has become a rear view of the straw-topped Russell, cigarette in hand. Cole's warm letter of appreciation set the stage for the growing comradeship of the two men. Cole wrote on December 22:

Dear Olaf:

I may receive more expensive presents than the one which came to me today from you, but I assure you that nothing that I will receive will give me more pleasure nor touch me more deeply, than the letter from you about Charlie Russell with the charming sketches. Really words fail me in expressing my thanks. You know me well enough to know I am sure without my telling you, that I will always treasure it and that it will have an honored place among my greatest treasures. When I see you possibly I can express myself better.

You ask me to be frank if I have any suggestions to make toward improving it. Yes, I have one thing I would very much like to have you do to it. I would like to have you address the letter itself to me, in your own hand writing: that is, write Dr. Philip G. Cole, Forest Hills Gardens, Long Island, N.Y. at the top before you begin your heading "Dear Doc." I wish you would be kind enough to come in as soon as you can do this, for I want to have the letter photographed, and do not wish to do it until this addition is made. You being a "live one" I do not want to do any forgery on it.

I have one more suggestion to make and that is that you forget that d—— drip about inequalities, appreciating difference in station, etc. You know me too well to feel that I could ever think anything like that. If you ever call me anything but Doc I will have to start calling you Mr. Seltzer. I count you one of my real friends and you can call me any d—— thing you want to; the more familiar it is the more I will know that you return my affection.

Once again, Olaf, thanks for your thoughtfulness as well as for your beautiful gift.

As I told you in the letter which went out this morning before your present arrived, I fear that I will not be able to get my gift of a book to you before Christmas Day, but you will surely have one within a few days after, and it will come to you with the affection of

Your friend,
Doc

Such an expression of friendship following the loss of Russell must have been consoling to Olaf. But the Coles were in California through the winter and early spring of 1927, and Olaf, with his family in faraway Montana, found life in New York less fascinating. When he was not painting, he made the rounds of calendar companies, putting behind him his fears about the loss of color value through reproduction. He sold several paintings to the American Lithograph Company.

Malcolm Mackay, whose father headed the New York Stock Exchange during the 1880's and who operated the family brokerage firm, invited Olaf to his estate in Tenafly, New Jersey, to view his Russell paintings, many of which the artist had not seen before.[6] Mackay wrote adventurous accounts of his hunting experiences in Alaska and British Columbia, some of which were published in the *National Geographic*. Putnam's published his book, *Cow Range and Hunting Trail*, in 1925.

Mackay commissioned Seltzer to paint a 20″ × 30″ oil, *Alaskan Bear Hunt*, based on his most recent hunting trip. For it Seltzer received two hundred dollars. It was to have been used, along with additional paintings Mackay discussed with Olaf, to illustrate a second book the broker was writing.[7] Olaf found Mackay difficult to please; he wrote Mabel, ". . . a good fellow but to me somewhat trying."

One of the irritants in Olaf's relationship with Mackay was that the broker seemed more interested in viewing a Russell canvas, *The Strenuous Life*, which a Great Falls widow, Mrs. Frank Powell, had asked Olaf to sell for her, than he was in getting on with arrangements for the Seltzer illustrations. The Russell painting was purchased by Cole for $4,000 upon his return from California. Ironically, the $300 and $175 in commissions Seltzer gleaned from the sale of Russell's painting made his brokerage fees larger than any single sale of his own paintings during his entire thirteen months in New York.

Being alone in the city gave Olaf a better chance to study his surroundings. Early in 1927 he sent Sylvia Bryant, his earliest steady customer in Great Falls, a charming illustrated letter bearing a sketch in pen, ink, and watercolor of a raffish, mustachioed character with umbrella frames poking out from under his arm. Olaf wrote beneath:

*Who goes?*
*Not King Umberto, well, I guess not. This, you see, is a gr-r-reat americano Signor Pio Angelo Petrinello, one of the six million. Pio lives in Mulberry Street near Fire Station No. 12, during the summer and in the same place all winter, for he don't care about Newport or Florida, no sir, Pio Likes Mulberry Street all year around, with its many odors and noises.*

Mabel received no gaily illustrated letters like those to patrons, but only hastily scratched letters reflecting Olaf's dissatisfaction.

On March 7 he wrote that he was looking for a furnished room because the rent had been raised to sixty dollars a month and that he was "glad to get out from under that hookworm outfit on the third floor, they never seem to go to bed. I was willing to stand for it on account of the cheap rent, but wouldn't pay full fare for the privilege of living under that scrub outfit."

"Now listen," he continued, "I am going to disconnect myself from dear old New York." He gave Mabel instructions about his plans for sending home boxes of paintings. There was a bit of cheerful news: the Louis F. Dow Company, a Saint Paul calendar manufacturing concern, "got ahold of me through Mr. Mackay," he wrote:

*They like my stuff fine and had me loan them two 20 × 30s which they expressed to headquarters for consideration. They had heard of me before and seemed pleased.*
*My efforts with Osborne (calendar company) have been a failure. They high-hatted me in spite of the fact that they had to admit my stuff was good.*

"I haven't made a cent so far this month," he confessed. "This however being the first dull spell since coming here."

Proof of his gloom was the complaint that Pearl and her husband had dropped him completely after Mabel left. This rankled, and it led to a postscript summarizing his bad mood:

*I started out writing a kind of classified letter, but it is pretty rambling by now. If I was a literary light like R this would be a different letter. . . . In conclusion I want to mention that on the 31st of this month a year ago Carl found Fox dead on the lawn. In spite of being a big nuisance he was better company by far than some of these awful good people.*

Fox, a sable-and-white collie, was a favorite pet of Olaf's.

Ten days later, Olaf was preparing to move and his mood was still glum:

*Am damn busy, boxing, putting away stuff, trying at the same time to finish a couple of pictures, etc. This is the worst jam I have been in since coming here and am not in the best of humor about it. All alone trying to cook, paint, wash out a few rags, looking for a place to move to, going over town, ect., ect. It is sure tough on me.*

Part of Olaf's dilemma was that there were now twin skeins to his painting career. Mabel reported from Great Falls about sales and inquiries, including an invitation to take part in a local exhibition of Russell's work, while Olaf painted and continued to make contacts in Elmhurst. He took great pleasure in finding a painting of his that Jim Reid, an assistant to W. W. Sherwood at Royal Milling, had tried unsuccessfully to buy. He wrote Mabel:

*The small 10 × 12 of horses going to waterhole which I got back through trading with Dr. Cole for bigger stuff was very much admired by Jim Reid after Benton bought it from me at the Falls. But Benton wanted to [o] much for it, so Jim didn't buy. I wrote Jim about how I got ahold of it again, from Benton to Yong's Gallery in Chicago where Dr. Cole bought it. I told Jim how I allowed Dr. Cole $25 on it for a larger canvas, and Jim sent the money and is sure pleased with his bargain.*

Commenting on news from home, he wrote, "I'm glad Dr. [E. M.] Larson got the Trigg lion picture. . . . tell Mrs. Larson I'll clean it, retouch it and varnish it as soon as I get back."

By April, Olaf was established in the home of P. J. Byrne:

*A Dublin Irishman, very refined and a designer of women's hats over in Manhattan. They have three boys and one girl from fifteen to eight years,*

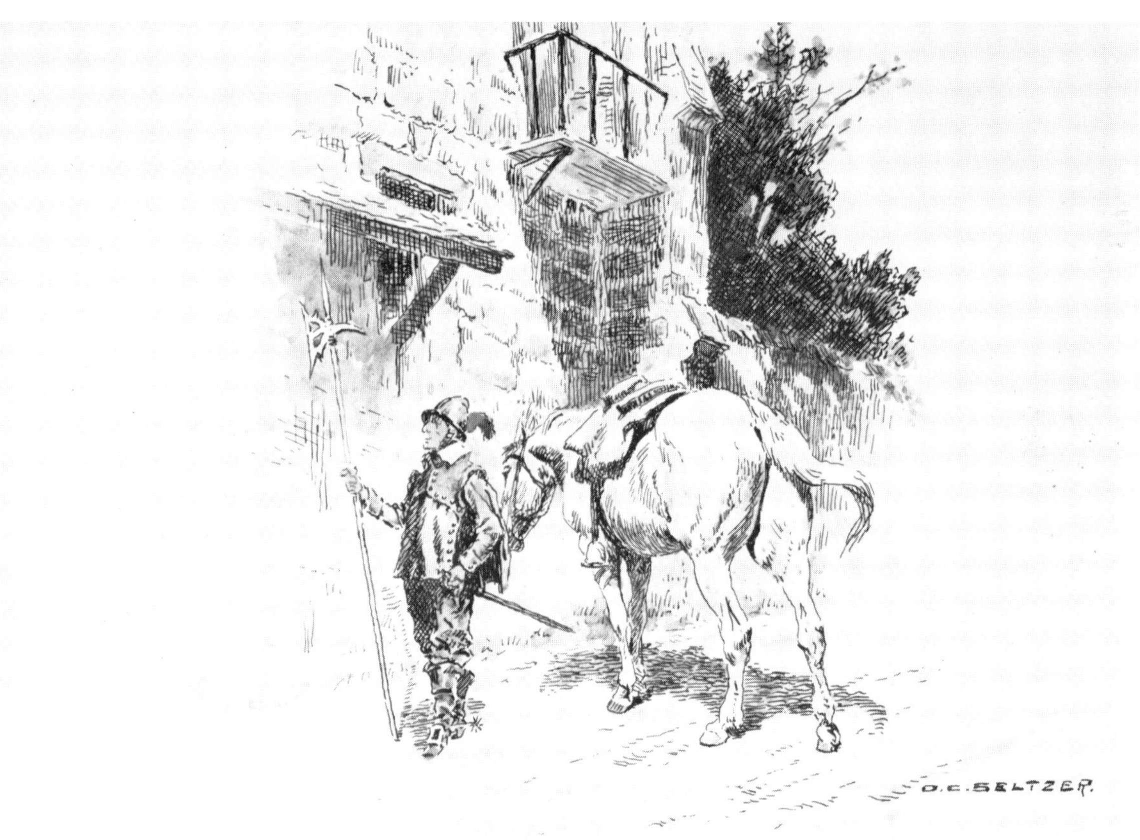



Great Falls, Mont.
June 11th

Dr. Phil. G. Cole
Forest Hills, Long Island, N.Y.

Dear Doc:—
After leaving lil' ol' Noo Yoik this western town seem as ancient and dead as the Hallebardier with his Clydesdale saddle pony weighing about 1350 pounds, in the above sketch. It has been raining since I came here and is very cold, The Missouri and smaller rivers are all overflowing and doing much damage. I have not been able to get out in the hills, as the prairie roads are very bad, but with a little of the famous Montana sunshine They will soon dry up. With kind regards to all I am your friend always.

Olof.



*Hallebardier Letter*
1927
Watercolor and ink, 10″ × 7″

*a nice family and I sure like the Mr. and Mrs. Have a cup of coffee, have some breakfast, have some tea and so forth, real people and goodhearted to a fault and she is a good cook, so I made a dikker with them and am boarding right here, good grub and I am like one of the family. Fine radio music. . . .*

As his depression lifted, Olaf sent his family four books by W. W. Jacobs, including the latest, *Sea Whispers*, commenting that "Walt, the bookworm, will get a kick out of these." But the increased interest in his paintings back in Great Falls and Carl's news of his approaching marriage to a lissome, auburn-haired schoolteacher, Lillian Ruth Zerfoss, of Monarch, Montana, on July 16, outweighed the advantages of Olaf's staying on in New York. By June 11 he had returned home. His relief can be read between the lines of the illustrated letter he sent to Phil Cole, featuring a knight in armor:

Dear Doc:— After leaving li'l ol New York this western town seems as ancient and dead as The Hallebardier with his Clydesdale saddle pony. . . . It has been raining since I came here and very cold. The Missouri and the smaller rivers are all overflowing and doing much damage. I have not been able to get out in the hills, as the prairie roads are very bad, but with a little of the famous Montana sunshine they will soon dry up.

Beneath the message Olaf placed a watercolor sketch of a mounted cowboy leading two pack mules. Under it he printed his favorite sentiment:

I oft times feel a pity and regret;
For those who never knew that wide and
    open space,
Which lies between the sunset and the
    dawn:—
The Prairie.

Olaf Seltzer was home among the undulating prairies rimmed with soft-hued buttes and smoke-shrouded mountains. He would visit New York City many times in the coming years, but he would never again consider changing his residence.

Chapter 7

# Perpetuating the Past

WHEN OLAF SELTZER RETURNED to Great Falls in June, 1927, he had reason to be pleased with his progress during the New York interlude. Doc Cole was bursting with schemes for paintings he wanted Olaf to do. There was a chance for more work with Mackay, to whom he had now sold another small oil. Durant had also made another purchase. Olaf had sold a few other things, including a poster design, and he had made contacts with several galleries.

For the first time Olaf recorded one of his paintings—a 20″ × 30″ oil called *The Range Mother*—as being copyrighted. Benton, the jeweler, bought several oils for resale, and a man named Killinger purchased a 20″ × 30″ called *The White Man's Buffalo* and an 11″ × 16″, *The Boss Mule Skinner*. Dr. Larson paid $50 to add the 11″ × 16″ oil *The Council of Four* to his growing collection, and Sherwood bought a 20″ × 30″, *The Right of Way*. Olaf now charged $200 for his 20″ × 30″ oils and $225 for a 24″ × 36″, such as *A Major Domo of the Prairies*. As a steady customer Cole got a preferential rate of $150 on the 20″ × 30″ oil, *The Crossing*.

A reporter for the *Great Falls Leader* interviewed Olaf in the house at 2815 Second Avenue North, which Mabel and the boys had moved into while Olaf was in New York. The story bore the headline "O. C. Seltzer Gaining National Fame." The content was more modest, quoting Olaf as saying that during the past four years he had devoted much time to painting and was successful "in a small way." The story continued:

*He comes back to build a home studio and to do his work in the country in which he has lived his life. The studio plans are now under consideration, and the place will be located somewhere on "Academy Hill." George Calvert will probably be the builder and Seltzer is arranging to have the kind of a home studio he wants.* [1]

This plan was never carried out, however. The Seltzers eventually bought a modest house on the eastern fringe of Great Falls. The one-story bungalow, at 2715 East Central Avenue, suited Olaf and Mabel's needs now that only Walt remained at home. The large rear bedroom with its north light was earmarked as a studio. With the help of his sons Olaf finished the basement to provide two more bedrooms for the six-room house. The new Seltzer residence was close to a streetcar line— Olaf never overcame his aversion to driving—yet near enough to open areas that he could stroll eastward to the edge of the prairie to enjoy his evening cigar and watch the shifting patterns of light and shadow over the peaks of the Belt Mountains, the backdrop for so many of his paintings.

Olaf spent a good bit of his time in the country-side during the summer of 1927, sketching new scenes to use during the following winter. He drove as far north as Lethbridge, Alberta, where he dropped in on his first sponsor, Fred Downer. The hotelman took Olaf to his home to visit with Mrs. Downer and to view once more his first attempt at working with oils. Olaf carefully scrutinized the still-unnamed painting, a landscape of an Indian war party by the Sun River, and then thanked Downer again for his role in helping him toward his goal of painting in oils.

Within a few weeks after his return Olaf had

64

picked up his old habits. He painted in the mornings, walked to town for supplies and to read in the library during the afternoons, and returned punctually for his evening meal. After supper he and Mabel read and listened to records and the radio.

In September, Phil Cole sent Olaf a copy of the album of photographs of Cole's art treasures. Seltzer had made the pen-and-ink frontispiece illustration for the album. Featuring a cowboy tossing his lariat in the upper-left-hand corner and a shield and coup stick in the lower-right-hand corner, the illustration would become the first piece listed in Cole's elaborate catalogue. Below the title—*Paintings, Bronzes, Etc., of Old Montana from the Collection of Dr. Philip Gillett Cole*—is neatly lettered:

Men in the rough on trails all new-broken—
Those are the friends we remember with tears;
Few are the words that such comrades
    have spoken—
Deeds are their tributes that last through
    the years.

Beneath the formal illustration and lettering Olaf drew a plump prairie rabbit as a whimsical touch.

Cole assembled the record of his treasures in an album sixteen inches long by fifteen inches wide, with stiff pages that would make the album nearly four inches thick by the time it was completed. It has covers of soft suede leather in a rich brown; the photographs are printed in sepia tones.

The collector made several copies for close friends, to whom he would send additional photographs from time to time as his holdings grew. In early October he presented a copy to the Montana State Historical Society in Helena. Included were photos of works by Russell, Joseph Henry Sharp, Remington, Frank Tenney Johnson, Groll, Seltzer, William Robinson Leigh, Borein, DeCamp, Edward W. Deming, Belmore Brown, Charles Schreyvogel, Alexander P. Proctor, J. L. Clark, H. A. McNeil, John Fery, Charles W. Eaton, C. E. Williams, Will James, C. P. Austin, Solon Borglum, Edgar S. Paxson, Colombi, and A. A. Weinman.

Cole employed three secretaries at various times to index the album and to type up the background material accompanying some of the paintings. Dates of execution and the kinds of

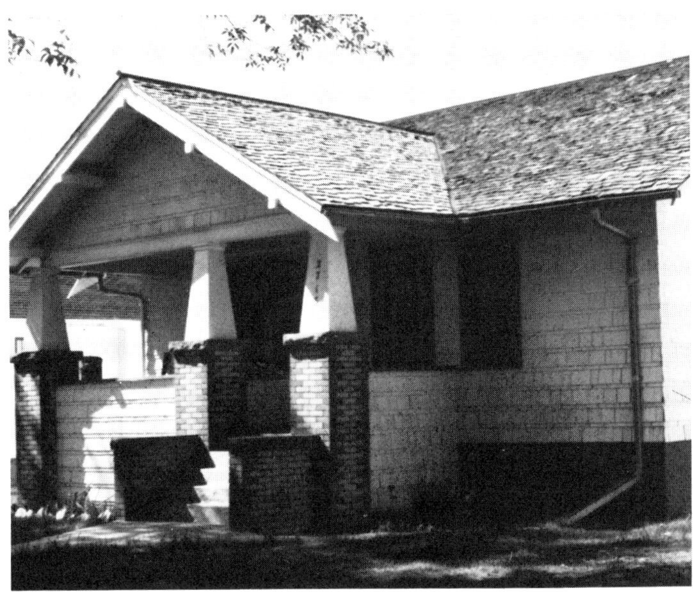

Seltzer home on Central Avenue, Great Falls.
From a recent photo.

media were noted in the index, along with dimensions (sometimes given in reverse). The index would eventually list about 780 paintings, bronzes, letters, cards, envelopes, and miscellaneous items, including a metal fire screen made by Thomas Makinley Wood.[2]

Keeping records on his art collection became an engrossing project for Phil Cole. Knowing that Olaf shared his pleasure in the collection, Cole sent him a copy of the photo album and kept him apprised of additions. Some months after Olaf received the big book, in its custom-made wooden box, Cole wrote to him:

I have recently acquired some new things . . . which I know you will be interested in seeing, a wonderful Sharp portrait of "Chief Joseph," one or two Remingtons, two more of Charley Russell, ("The Bell Mare" and "Before the White Man Came") both excellent things. I will be sending new sheets of all my latest things before long now for your album. . . . I received on approval from Montana and promptly returned two N. G. things of Charley's. Along with other things in the house which I am sure you will be glad to look over are some new (or rather quite old) books on Indians, etc.[3]

Their mutual interest in history was another binding link between Olaf Seltzer and Phil Cole. After reporting on his finds, Dr. Cole continued:

> The library of the early West is rather rapidly developing into a most excellent and unique reference library. I have several books in mind which I am sure would be of value to you and am trying if possible to duplicate them. Whenever I can pick up anything which I think would be of interest to you, it is going to give me lots of pleasure to shoot them on to you. By the way, did you ever get in touch with the Bureau of Ethnology at Washington, or the Field Colombian Museum, to get the valuable books containing both interesting illustrations and valuable data, which they pass out freely?

With all these acquisitions the Cole home now was overflowing with paintings and sculptures, not to mention family, and household staff. The older daughter, Jane, was often sick as a child and needed constant care. The Coles brought from Montana a registered nurse, Alice Ralston, whose brother was married to Mrs. Cole's oldest sister. Phil Cole had met Alice only once before she joined his household, and that was at his wedding. "Aunt Alice" became a permanent member of the household, looking after the children, managing the staff, and assisting Cole with his collection, in which she took a great interest.

It was the crowded condition of the Forest Hills home that led to the most unusual oils Olaf Seltzer ever painted. The four—*The Witch Doctor*, *The Sign Writer*, *A Welcome Guest*, and *Human Wolves*—are identically triangular in shape, each measuring twenty-four inches across the top, thirteen inches along the right side, and twenty-seven and a half inches along the hypotenuse. Neatly framed in gold, these oils may have been designed to hang in a stairwell in the Cole home. Later they were hung among the other western paintings in Dr. Cole's study.

The four triangles are done as painstakingly as any of Seltzer's other works. Each is designed to make the most of its shape. In *The Witch Doctor*, an Indian is seated cross-legged on a bluff. He is making medicine. A steam lodge is shown below and, in the lower angle, a water hole. *The Sign Writer* is a vivid depiction of an Indian hunkered down on the back of his horse to inscribe hieroglyphics on a sandstone rock, and *A Welcome Guest* is a snow scene in which the firelight from a settler's cabin glows warmly, in contrast to the night-shaded snow. *Human Wolves* shows a pair of hunters, disguised under pelts, preparing to shoot arrows into a buffalo herd.

On the first anniversary of Russell's death Olaf sent Dr. Cole a letter headed with a subtly colored watercolor of the boulder used as Charlie Russell's monument in the Great Falls Highland Cemetery. A faded wreath rests against the stone, and a herd of cattle grazes before a background of snow-capped mountains under a cobalt-blue sky. Beneath this peaceful, pastoral scene Olaf wrote:

> *On this night of Oct. 24th just a year ago, our mutual friend, Charles Marion Russell, crossed the great divide.*
>
> In part he sleeps:—
> He'll wake within the whole.

A month later Cole mailed Olaf a brochure distributed at the Memorial Exhibition of the work of Charles Marion Russell, held November 8 to 26 at the Grand Central Art Galleries in New York. "Wish you could have been here to see them all together," Cole wrote in a note attached to the brochure. "Your little grave picture was under a glass case—the only thing not done by Charley himself in the show."

Nancy Russell visited the Coles during this exhibition. Alice Ralston later recalled the long conversations in front of the fireplace after dinner. Cole had purchased some of Russell's work from his widow in the year following his death. Knowing of Cole's admiration for Charlie, Nancy confided to him her concern over the "growing numbers of would-be western artists who were copying her husband's work," according to Miss Ralston. Kindly Dr. Cole was aware of the general sentiment about Russell's later works, painted during his illness. Though sparing Nancy's feelings, he rejected some of the offerings that he felt were not up to Charlie's best.

During the late summer and fall of 1928, Olaf received a series of communications from Dr. Cole about a special confidential chore he wanted undertaken. It was no secret that Charlie Russell was in a deplorable state of health for some years preceding his death, and it was no secret in the Cole household that Olaf Seltzer had to do considerable restoration work on some Russell canvases, including finishing the unsigned *Father DeSmet's First Meeting with the Flathead Indians* (29" × 47").

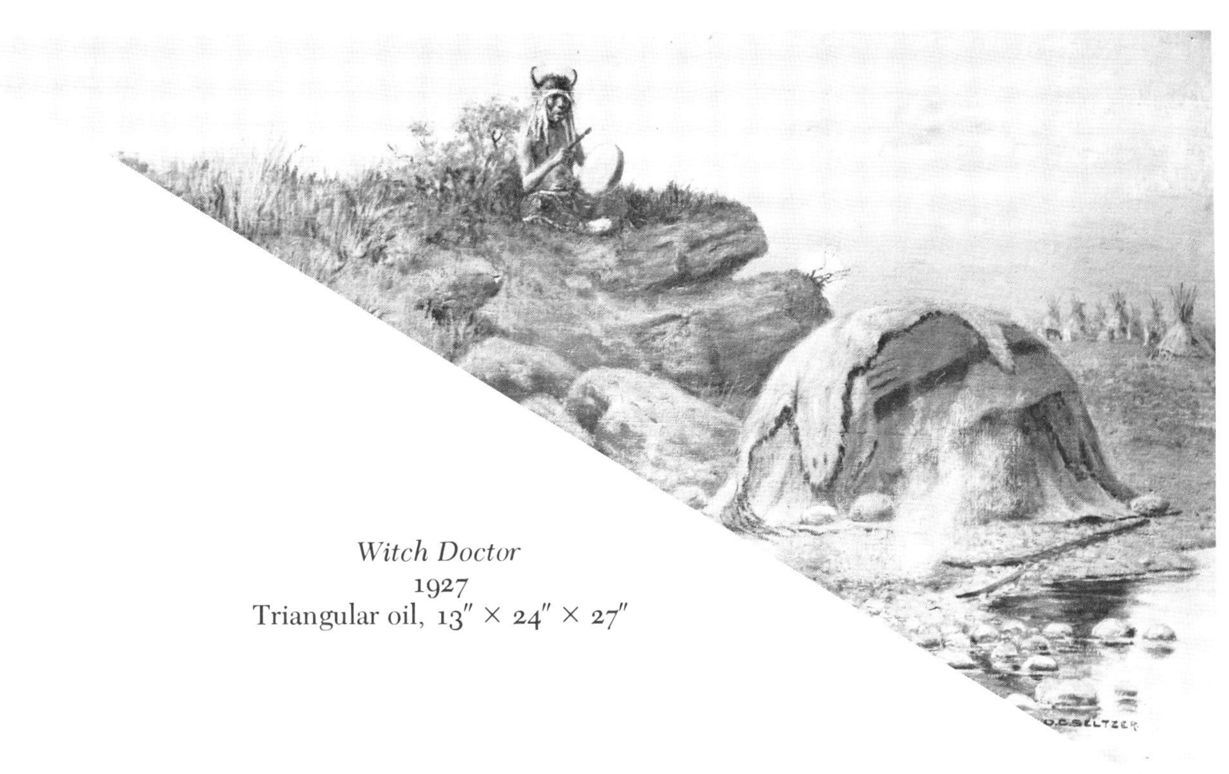

*Witch Doctor*
1927
Triangular oil, 13″ × 24″ × 27″

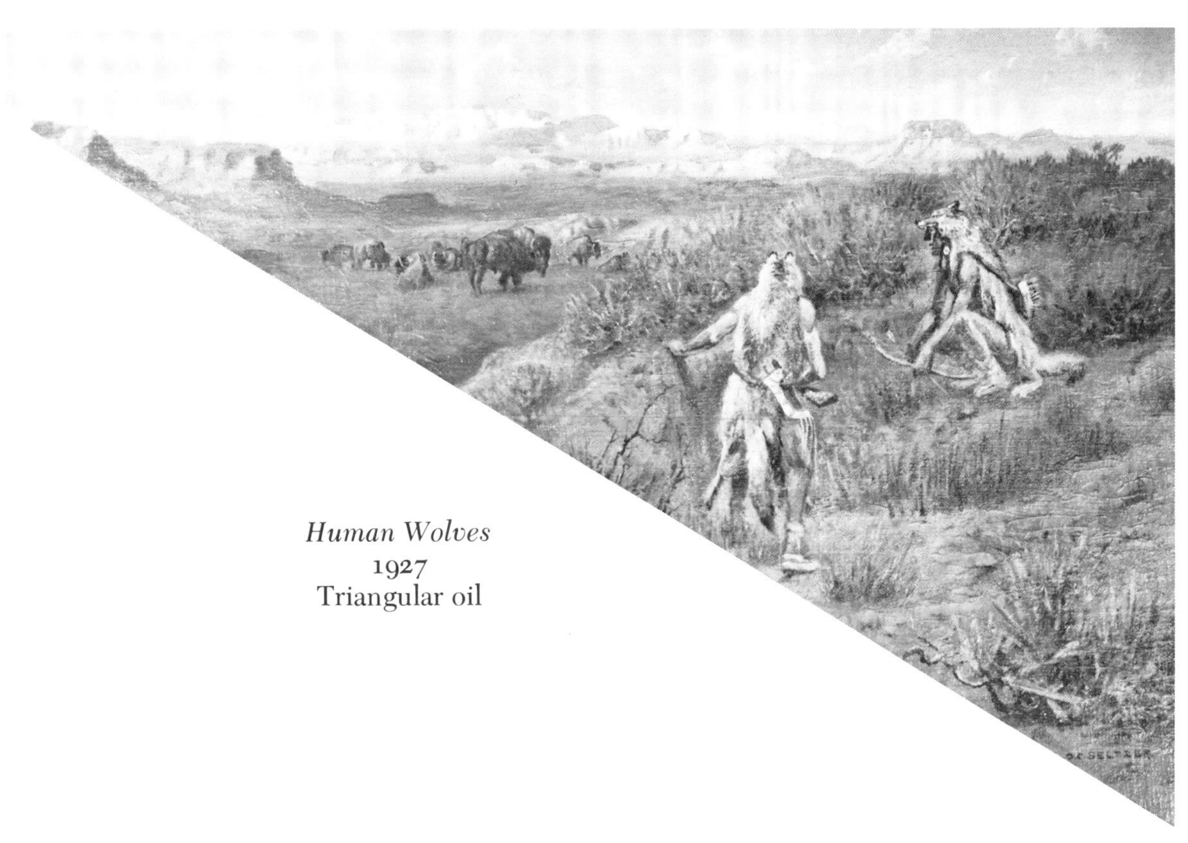

*Human Wolves*
1927
Triangular oil

Cole was unusual among collectors in that the monetary value of a painting meant little to him. He bought for his own pleasure, not for an investment for the future. His earnest concern about putting the DeSmet painting into more presentable shape came from a desire to perpetuate Russell's reputation as a genius among western painters rather than from any crass motive regarding the future of the painting.

In August, 1928, Cole wrote Seltzer from the Lake Placid Club:

> Now as to the more important matter we have so often discussed. You and I agree absolutely on it and *nobody in this world but you* will ever be allowed to do the job—and I want it done this fall. Here again cost does not enter into the problem for I know that your heart is in this as much as mine. Nancy writes me that she is to be in New York for a minor exhibit in October. For reasons obvious to you I feel that it would be better all around to postpone the job until after that time.

Three weeks later he implored Seltzer to clear his calendar so that he could come to New York in November:

> I realize that this may be inconvenient for you. . . . I will do my best to fit my time to yours, but frankly as soon as the opportunity presents I am going to ask you to do this for me *even if you do have to make a sacrifice* for I do not want to take any chances of postponing it any longer. You understand my reason for not doing it right now. I am sure that it is wiser not to unnecessarily stir up trouble from certain sources under the circumstances. On the other hand I do not want to postpone it any longer than necessary because you are the only person in this world who I will allow to do it for me (I might almost say do it for Charley—for I know he would want you to do it and thank you for it). Whatever sacrifice I may put you to when I call upon you I will surely make up to you in other ways.

Cole held back his letter for almost a week before adding a lengthy postscript, which indicates that Nancy Russell had been consulted about the method to be used in finishing the painting:

> Frankly I am torn between two fires whether to get you on and have the work completed before the coming of our friend, or whether it would be more advisable to wait until after her departure, in order to avoid probably hurt feelings. The darn thing is on my mind so that I can with difficulty restrain myself. As you know, I am advised by her as well as by Mrs. Cole, not to have permanent additions made in oil. I might add here that Mrs. Cole, Miss Ralston and I are all in agreement that if this is done in oil it should be touched by no one but yourself. Of course, it is understood that only the cruder unfinished parts of the foreground should be touched and no attempt made to camouflage the fact that it is an unfinished painting of Charley's. It might even be possible that I would get you on here just for a consultation on the matter, though I will appreciate it if you do come armed to do the work. At any rate I am so torn between desires that I had to send you a telegram this morning inquiring whether, if necessary you could hop a train and come on next week in response to a telegram from me, also whether or not I could definitely count on your coming sometime in November. This might all sound rather confused to you, but I believe that you will understand my position. I realize fully, Olaf, that it may be unfair of me to ask you to hop a train and come suddenly. It is a matter very close to my heart. You know that aside from taking care of you properly financially I will endeavor to the best of my ability, make it up to you in other ways, if you will be willing to sacrifice yourself a little to cooperate with me. This is what friends are for, is it not?
>
> As I have told you many times before, you are the only one I would trust with this job and I would be heartbroken should I decide to have it done, to find that I was unable for any unforeseen reason to get you here. . . . My idea has been to pay all your expenses both coming and going, and give you five hundred dollars in addition to cover the job here, you paying your own expenses while you are in the City. If that does not seem entirely proper an amount to you, however, you well know that I am agreeable in every way to doing whatever you think is right in this direction. We have never quarreled over prices and we will not. At any rate I would like a wire from you, sent collect to me here, letting me know whether or not it would be possible, should I send for you, for you to come on at once. Also letting me know whether or not, should it not be best to have you now, I could definitely count on having you come upon receipt of a wire from you some time after the middle of November. In other words let me know definitely how far I can count on you.

Olaf left no written record of his efforts on the Russell paintings save for a brown envelope on

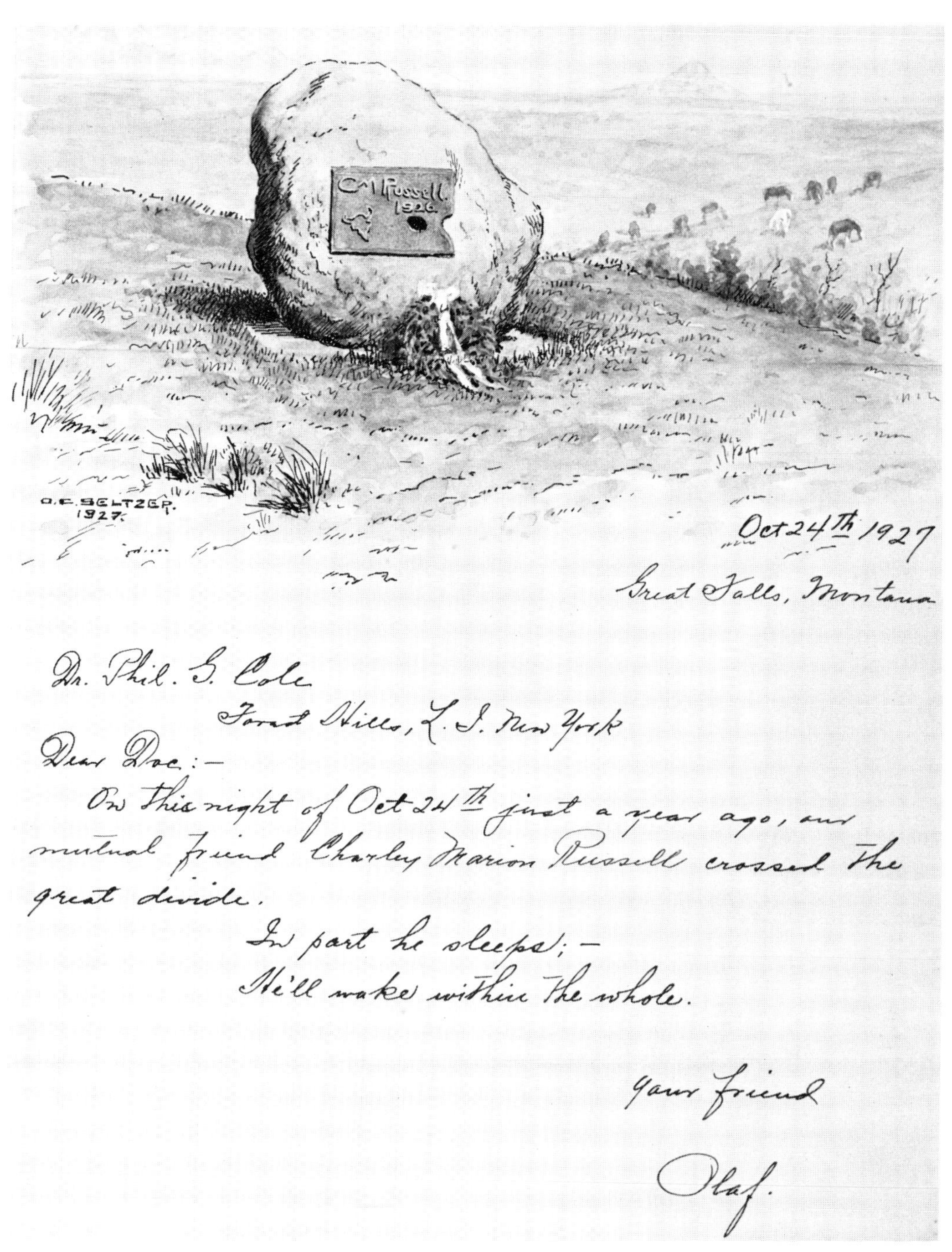


*Russell Memorial Letter*
1927
Watercolor and ink, 9″ × 6″

the back of which he wrote a list of "Recondi-tioned Russell Oils" as follows:

Attack on the Mule Train
Saloon Fight in Moonlight—not dated
Mad Cow Painting (Mrs. Powell)
White Man's Buffalo
Buffalo Hunt (with Bill Cody)
Last Chance Gulch—Helena
The Wagon Boss—(Fort Benton)
The Bull Elk—Winter Scene

The "Mad Cow Painting" was *The Strenuous Life*, for which Olaf had served as broker. The "Buffalo Hunt" listed by him is *Running Buffalo*, the depiction of an 1871 hunt on which Grand Duke Alexis of Russia was escorted by Phil Sheri-dan and Buffalo Bill Cody. Since he thought that few owners of paintings took proper care of them, he may well have simply cleaned and refurbished the paintings without making any changes.

Later in life Olaf Seltzer would often recall Dr. Cole's satisfaction and gratitude when the De-Smet painting was finished. Seltzer's own reac-tion, after overcoming his reluctance to doing any work on Russell's canvas, was summarized in his reply to Phil Cole's thanks: "Charlie would have done it for me."

When Seltzer visited New York City in the autumn of 1927, he and Cole spent many evenings by the hearth in the Forest Hills home discussing ideas for paintings that Cole wanted in his collec-tion. As the winter wore on, Olaf settled in, back in Great Falls, to put some of their ideas on canvas. He also painted four 20″ × 30″ oils for the Great Falls Clinic during early 1928. For the quadruple order Seltzer "made them a price" of six hundred dollars, which covered *The Medicine Man*, *The Rear Guard Buffaloes*, *Cattle Rustlers*, and *The Foothill Nester*.

In 1928, Olaf noted in his records for the first time a group of 9″ × 4″, 12″ × 7″, and 17″ × 12″ watercolors of individual Indian figures—*Standing Squaw*, *Standing Indian*, and *Indian and Squaw*—each bearing "decoration." That was his descriptive term for the small-scale com-plementary motif that was placed either in the lower-right-hand corner or on the matte. The first of these listed is *Buffalo Coat*, a remembrance of the artist's wild night on the driver's seat of Fren-chy's stagecoach.

Two of the early figures, a medicine man and a woman, went to Sylvia Bryant, and four would be sent to Dr. Cole. Most of Olaf's efforts in his patron's direction at this time were oils depicting scenes in which Cole had shown a particular interest. There was no plan behind these at-tempts, as there would be by year's end.

On the crested vellum stationery of the Lake Placid Club, Phil Cole wrote a letter to Olaf on August 31, 1928, urging him to work over a painting on the Vigilante movement and to recon-sider one with Lewis and Clark and their Indian guide, Sacagawea. It was the first time the patron mentioned in writing his hope that the artist would reduce the scale of his work:

I am sorry that I got the wrong slant on the 3-7-77 picture and am glad to be set right on it for I could somehow not figure it out. At that (as you agree) it was not done the best that you can do. I still think that I would like a good little upright one of the same subject (tree, with 3-7-77 sign, rope, etc.)[4] but without the prominent figure in the foreground. Some time when in the mood for it try it again and slip it to me.

I am more than sorry you cannot do a smaller picture for me of Lewis and Clark with York and Sacajawea.[5] I realize that 10 × 15 for this would doubtless be inadequate. I sincerely and honestly like your smaller pictures so much better than your bigger canvasses. Also as you know space is a big item with me. Why don't you work up one for me as small as you can? As you know this picture is very close to my heart and I don't want it to get away. Also I want you to be the one to do it.

Give it a few thoughts anyway, Olaf. As you well know, neither shape nor price cut any ice with me so long *as it is small as consistent and is good.*

I am still clinging to the idea of a series (or collection) of small historical oils by you. I cling to this idea both for my own sake and for yours. I feel that you have your best bet here. If the little ones work out well with me then you can paint them as big as a house if you want to.

In a postscript Cole added: "I had a Russell (very early one) from Butte sent to me on approval but promptly returned it as impossible." Within three weeks Cole wrote Seltzer a four-page, single-spaced letter that he held for nearly a week before adding a three-page postscript. He was exuberant over the first four watercolors in what would become a series of seventy-nine that Selt-zer painted for him.

On September 20, 1928, Cole dictated:

Dear Olaf,

       Yours of the 8th was duly received. Any letter from you is always welcome and interesting. This one was particularly so and I feel that a long answer from me is about to be inflicted upon you.

Last night the four watercolors were received in good shape and I am very, very enthusiastic about them. I am convinced that you are the only person living today equipped in every way to do this great work of perpetuating with paint the bygone days of the great West. This is right along in line with what I so many times harped at you about—that your great opportunity lies along historical lines. Last night I had the opportunity of showing these four water colors to a friend who is a real art critic. He was enthusiastic about them and I am going to show them to some of the art people and dealers here in the City, just to show them what a real "he" man you are at this sort of thing.

Much of the long letter concerned paintings under consideration:

The 9″ × 12″ "3-7-77" sounds good and I am confident I will want it.

I am delighted that you are going ahead with the small Sakakawea (I am glad that you have noted the correct spelling of her name) such details are interesting.

I do hope that you are not going to disappoint me with the small Lewis & Clark with York and Sakakawea oil. Please, even if you yearn to make a big canvas of this some day, make me the smallest size you can of it. As you know, that subject has been very dear to my heart for many years, but it must be small. I suppose, if necessary, I could place it up to 2′ long, though I hope you may get it to be somewhat less. My reasons for wanting the small size are twofold. First, I sincerely feel that your best work is done on the smaller canvas. Second, the amount of space that I can afford to give it in my collection.

Having disposed of these matters, Phil Cole got down to specific proposals for what would become the Western Characters:

The idea of the series of historical figures delights me beyond words. They are great stuff, Olaf. I am, of course, taking the four which you sent me and am enclosing herewith my check for One Hundred Dollars ($100.00) covering—"The Trapper," "The Squaw," "The Broncho Buster" and "The Medicine Man." You have surely not

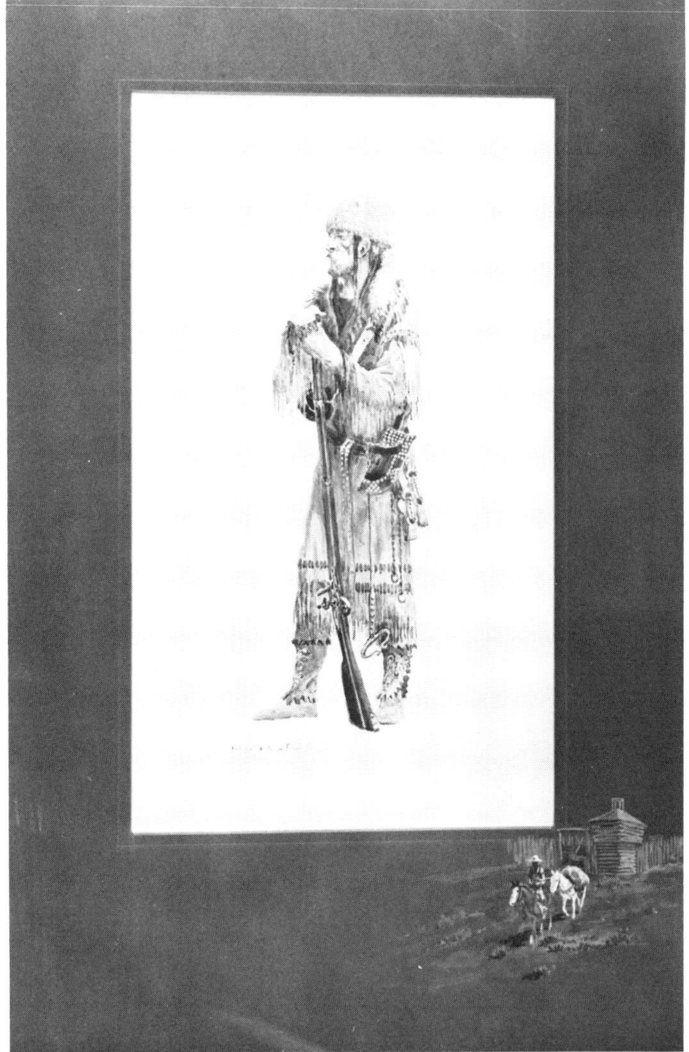

*Trapper*
1928
Western Character watercolor

only executed them beautifully but you have got the characters, the faces, the dress, the accutrements, etc. as I am sure nobody else treading the face of this earth can now do.[6]

"Please go ahead with the rest of them for me," Cole's letter continued:

The Wolfer, The Prospector, The Bull Whacker, The Road Agent, The Warrior, The Buffalo Runner, The Halfbreed, The Sheep Herd-

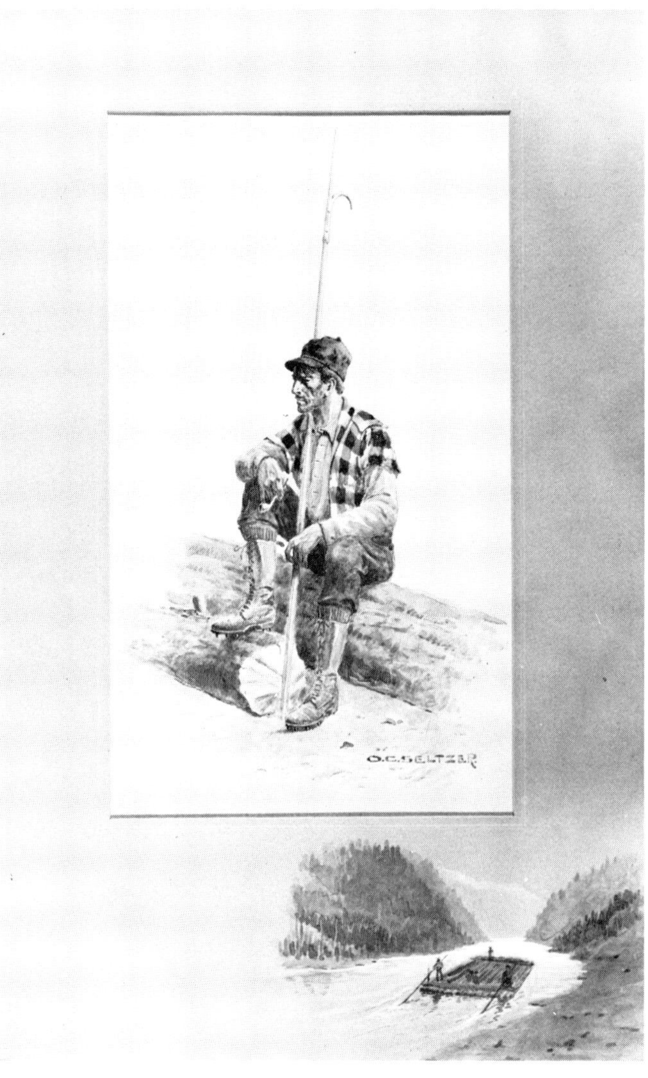

*River Rat*
1928
Western Character watercolor

er, The Round-up Cook, The Stage Driver, and whatever other ones you may have in mind. I can suggest right of[f] the reel a number of others which I would like to have added to the lot you do for my collection:

The Gambler, The Chinaman, The Pioneer Woman, The Papoose, The Vigilanti, The Dance Hall Girl, The Barkeeper, The Surveyor, The Soldier, the Scout, The Indian Police, The Packer (showing Diamond Hitch), The Cattle Rustler, The Explorer, The Railroad Builder, The Greaser, The Texan, The French Canadian, etc., etc.

I have two suggestions I would like to make regarding those for my collection. First, I would like the background not to be plain white. While I may have to mount them for the time being in an album I much prefer to frame and hang them as a separate group belonging to the same collection, and a plain white background is too glaring to permit of this. I think you can use a gray or brown paper. Second, while the vignettes are one of the most interesting, clever and important parts of these pictures and are undoubtedly better placed as you have them on a separate border I sort of wish that in some way they could be incorporated on the main canvas or paper where the figure is. Do not suppose that you can do anything about this, for I must admit that they are more artistic on the mat, yet it does take a large size frame to take the whole thing in, and with a group such as I expect having it is going to take up some space. Incidentally I might add that the vignettes certainly look much better on the gray paper of the mat than they would were they on white.[7]

The ones you do for me I wish you would do on gray paper or at least scuff over the white with some shading colors to take off the curse of the dead white effect. In this connection I would like to send my present four back to you to revise them this way for me if you will say the word.

After this Cole added in his own handwriting: "Or for you to exchange to harmonize with the kind I am asking you to make."

For my own lot I would appreciate it if inconspicuously on each one off in the corner somewhere, you would write in small script "to Philip G. Cole, etc., etc., from his friend Olaf C. Seltzer" or something like that. Incidentally it would mean much to me if you would write something descriptive somewhere on each of them; something like you wrote in your last letter to me—as for instance about the Bronc Rider not registering much above the collar button, the Squaw being the real thing with Umatilla Blanket, not the fancy kind wearing a chicken feather and looking at her own lovely reflection among the lily pads in the sparkling pool, a brief description of the hardware that the Trapper is wearing, a brief description of the medicine man giving his name as Yellow Weasel, what his crook is for, etc., etc.

Phil Cole was not one to give up easily when he had a certain effect in mind. In his long postscript

he returned to the idea for the central figure and
vignette to be all of one piece:

> Incidentally I was looking again at the little
> animal water colors and thinking how nicely the
> vignettes worked in on these—all on one piece of
> paper, though of course, I do not care for the plain
> white background on these as much as I would
> had they colored backgrounds. Would you like
> me to send you an assorted lot of light gray, tan,
> brown, green, orange, yellow, red and blue
> paper for this sort of work? I can possibly make a
> better selection here than you might be able to
> find in Great Falls, and it would be a pleasure for
> me to send some to you to try out.

The Western Character series is probably Seltzer's best-known work.[8] It appeals to a cross
section of viewers, possibly because of the univer-
sal humanity portrayed in the figures. Or perhaps
it is the challenge to the viewer's imagination—
the presentation of each main subject as an inac-
tive character with the action shown in the
vignette—that calls the beholder to fill in part of
the narrative as he studies the drawing.

The *Cattle Rustler*, for instance, is depicted
with a longhorn steer tied for branding and an iron
heating in a small brush fire. The *River Rat* is
shown poling a raft; the *Sheriff* lounges in a door;
in the vignette he is shooting down a rider while
the suspect's horse shies away. A worn-looking
white horse, hitched to a red-wheeled buggy,
waits patiently in the vignette for the *Circuit
Judge*, whose expression from the bench reflects
weary patience.

*L'Voyageur* leans on his paddle; in the
vignette, he strokes through lonely waters. Deer
wait apprehensively in a copse beneath the
*Hunter*.

Nearly a third of the sketches are of Indians.
The vignette for *Story Teller* shows the listeners
seated cross-legged in a semicircle by a campfire.
The *Sun Dancer* bears a stylized sun, Indian
fashion; and the *Beadworker*, a square of blue and
white beading so textured that one can trace flaws
on its surface.

Olaf may have foreseen the fashion for hanging
pictures in matched pairs when he worked on his
characters. He had definite ideas about framing,
and was known to give a purchaser explicit instructions about how to frame a picture and even
where to hang it. After Cole urged him to try

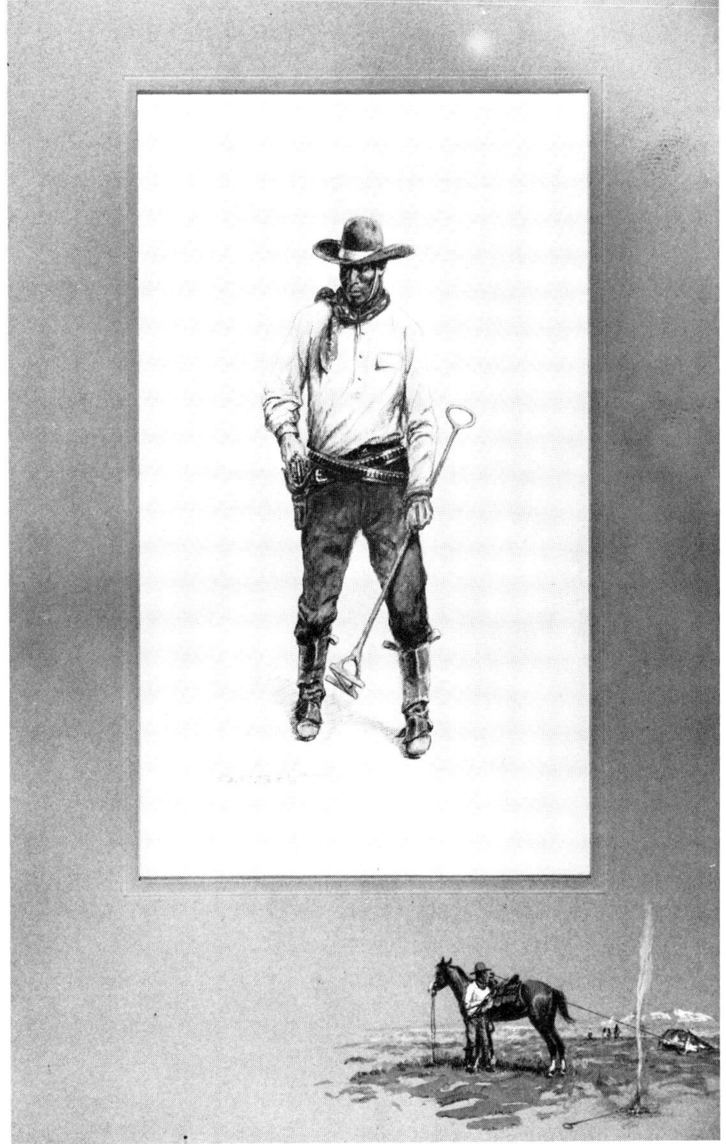

*Cattle Rustler*
1928
Western Character watercolor

darker mats and to tint the backgrounds, he used
ingenuity in pairing without being obvious. The
subtle citron yellows and the gray-green mats of
the *Sun Dancer* and the *Beadworker* make them a
matched pair, as are the more brilliantly colored
*Squaw* and *Reservation Buck*.

The Remington and Russell characters of the

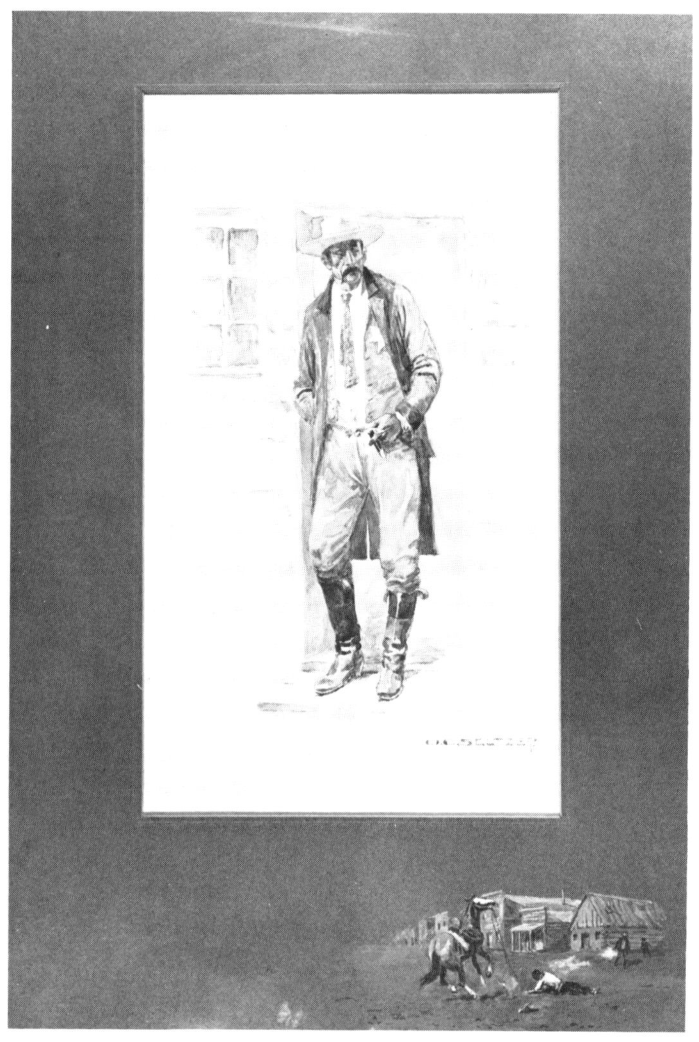

*Sheriff*
1928
Western Character watercolor

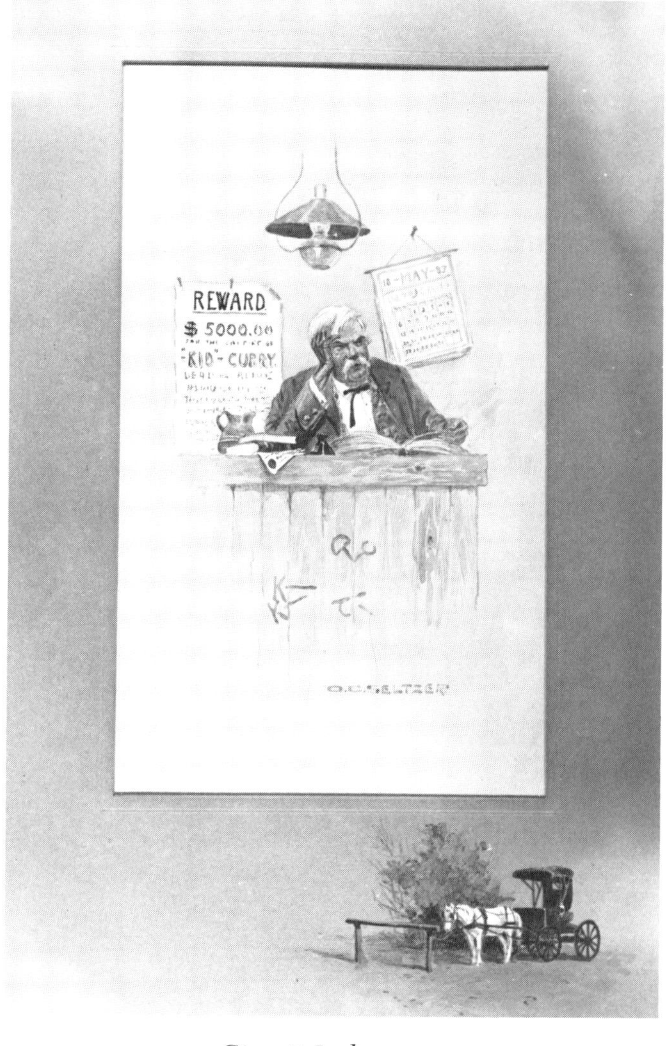

*Circuit Judge*
1928
Western Character watercolor

Old West, while faithfully reproducing characteristic garb and trappings, were in pen-and-ink and lacked the refinements of Seltzer's. Nor did his predecessors exhaust the gamut of possibilities for such drawings. Walt Seltzer has a notebook filled with the definitive pencil sketches his father made for the series before transferring each character to one-sixteenth-inch-thick academy board for the watercolor work. Each of the fifty-eight sketches in rough form in the notebook can be matched in finished condition either from the group in the Cole collection or among the rejects Olaf sold, except for the one Olaf titled *Ranch Girl*. This sketch depicts a graceful young girl whose sunbonnet has slipped from her abundant hair and is hanging on her back. Either the artist never followed through on painting *Ranch Girl* or it is one of only a few of the Western Character sketches in private collections.

The most contemporary character in the group owned by Cole, *Tenderfoot*, looks every bit the part of a naïve easterner in plus fours and knee-

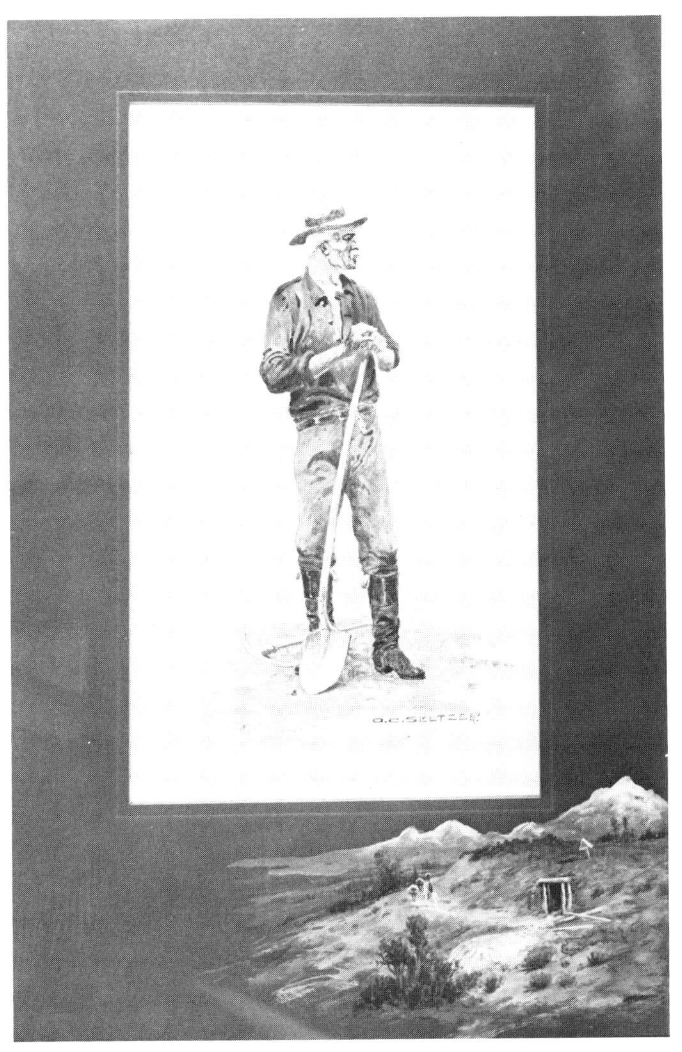

*Prospector*
1929
Western Character watercolor

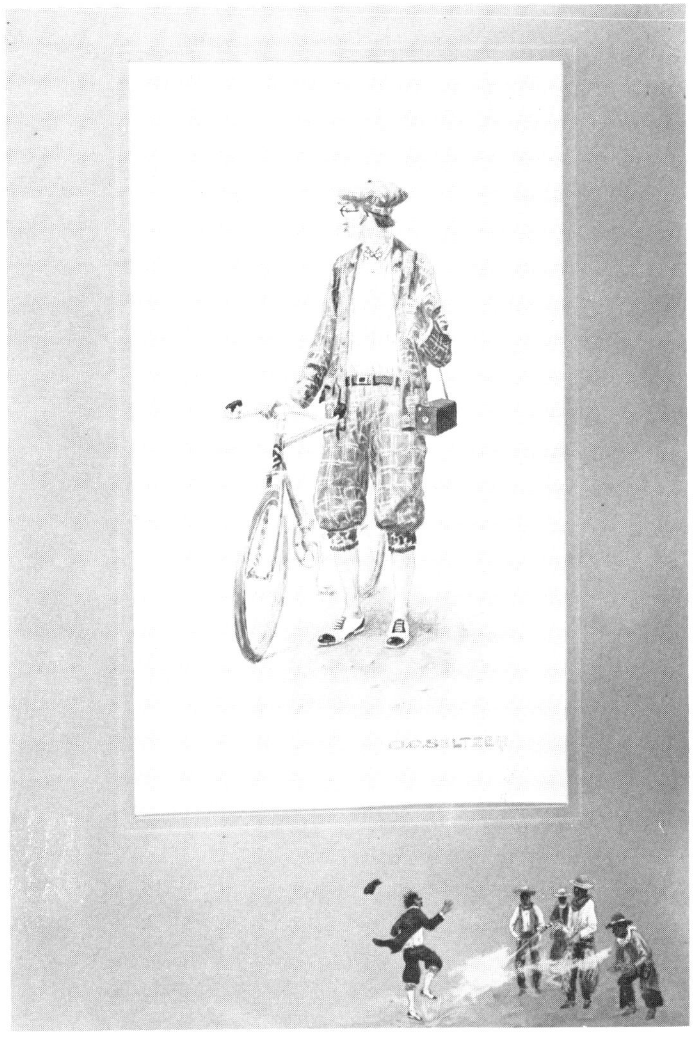

*Tenderfoot*
1929
Western Character watercolor

length socks. Armed with a box camera on a shoulder strap, he leans against his bicycle and holds white gloves. There is a marked resemblance in *Tenderfoot* to illustrations by Norman Rockwell, whose work Olaf admired greatly. The vignette depicts several rough cowhands shooting at the ground to make the harassed "dude" jump.

In Cole's letter he authorized Olaf to proceed with a number of characters the artist had suggested, including the *Road Agent*. A road agent was not included in the seventy-nine characters in the Cole collection but turned up in a collection of similar sketches owned by Dr. E. D. Hitchcock, now in the possession of the Northwestern Bank of Great Falls.[9]

Eighty-five western characters are listed and photographed in Dr. Cole's album, six more than were in his possession. Apparently Cole did not hesitate to reject figures that failed to meet his knowledgeable standards. Since he was reared in Montana, he probably took issue with the artist about some of the details in the watercolors and

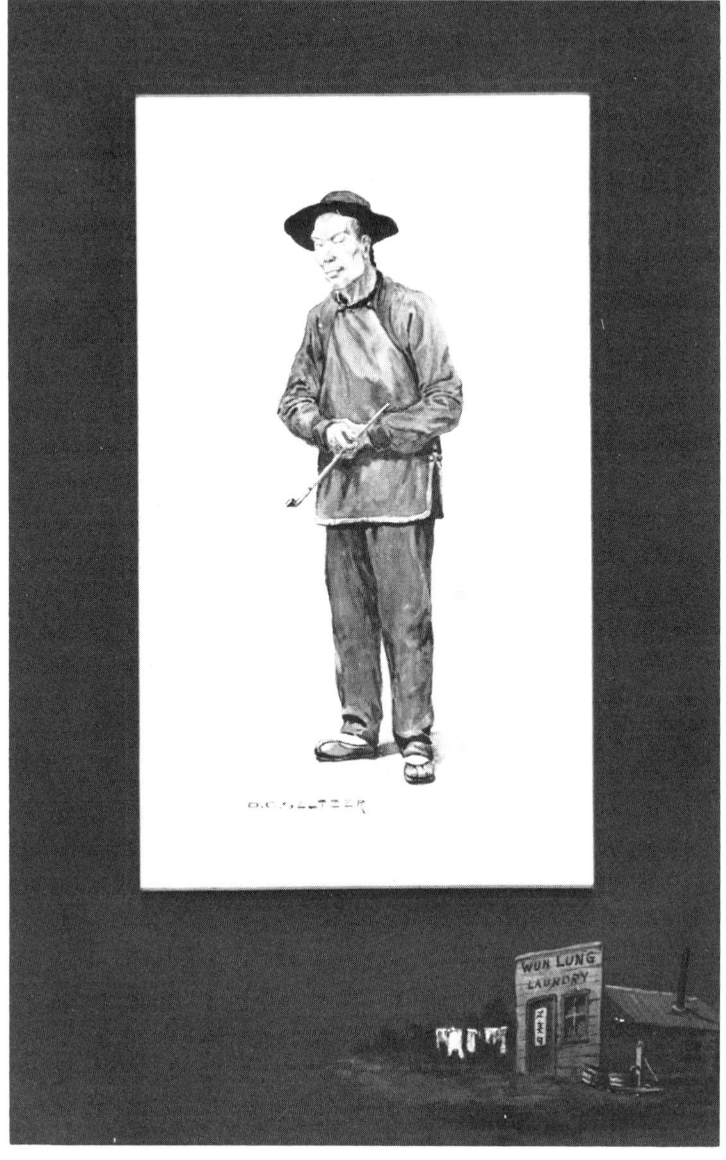



*Chinaman*
1928
Western Character watercolor

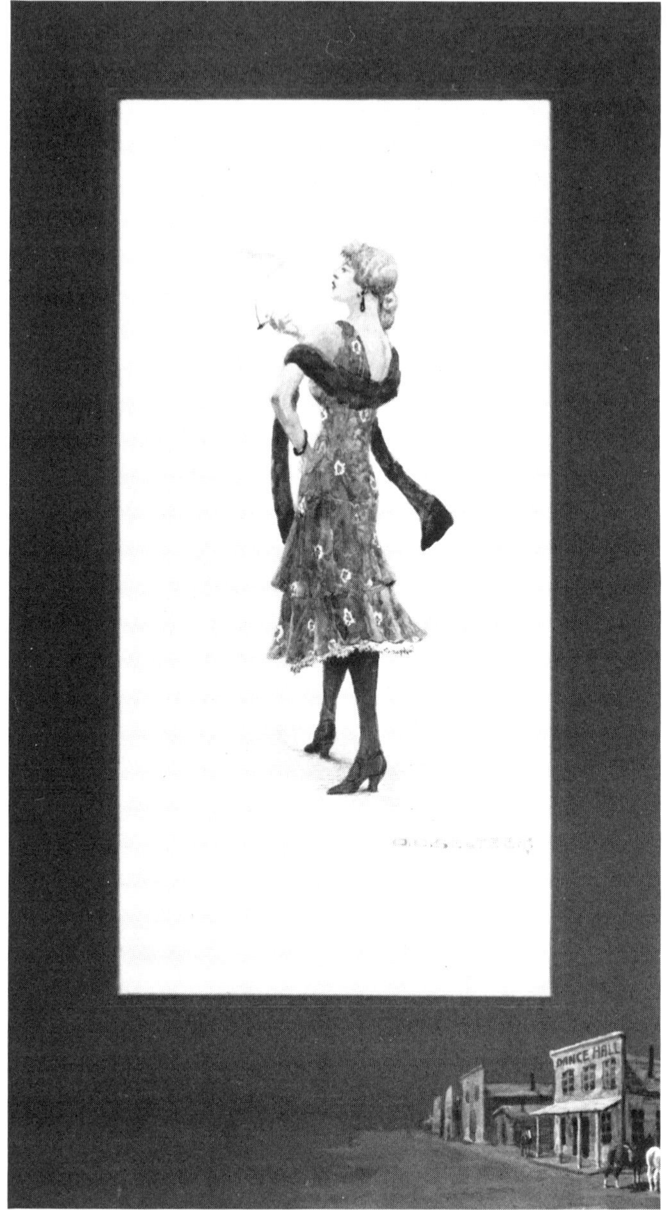



*Dance Hall Girl*
(First version)
1928
Western Character watercolor
Courtesy of Northwestern Bank, Great Falls, Montana.

sent them back for changes, whereupon Olaf did new ones and sold the rejects to Hitchcock for a few dollars.

Each of the six sketches that appeared in photographs but not on Cole's walls has a duplicate— *Barkeep, Dance Hall Girl, Prospector, China- man, Sun Dancer,* and *Owner, PGC*, the last being a drawing of Cole astride his horse Patches. The first *Owner, PGC* is mounted in a mat with

sketches of horses scattered on it. The second bears, as the vignette, the J Bar brand of C. K. Cole's ranch. Phil Cole had made his wishes clear on how he wanted his own sketch finished.

Apparently Cole failed to tell his staff to remove the original photos from the album, enabling the

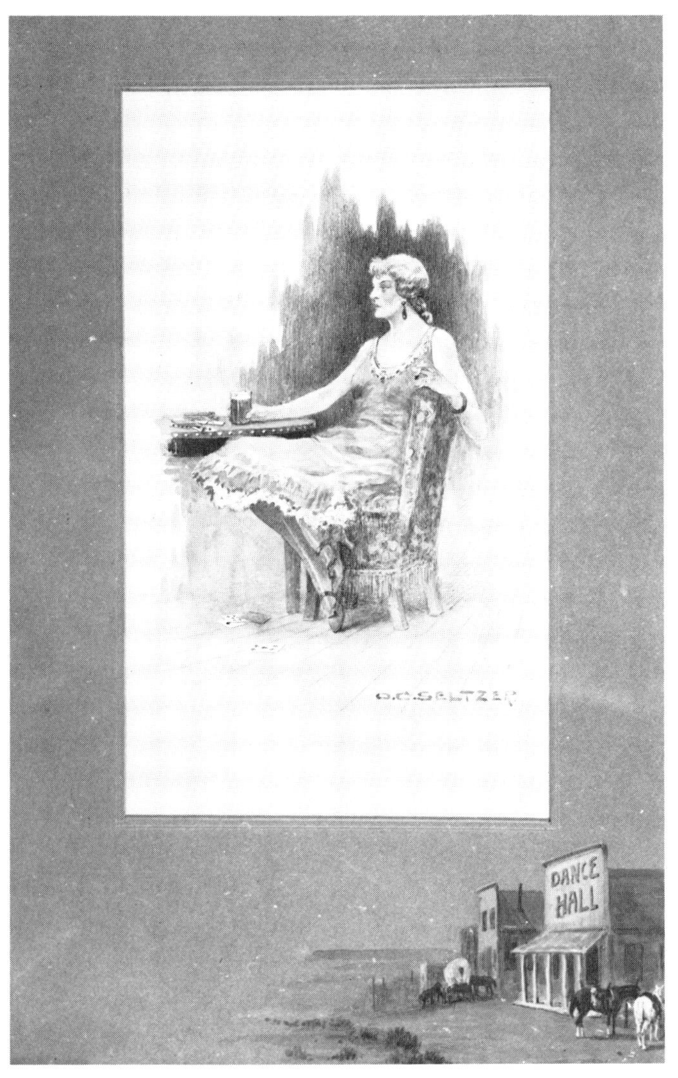

*Dance Hall Girl*
(Second version)
1928
Western Character watercolor

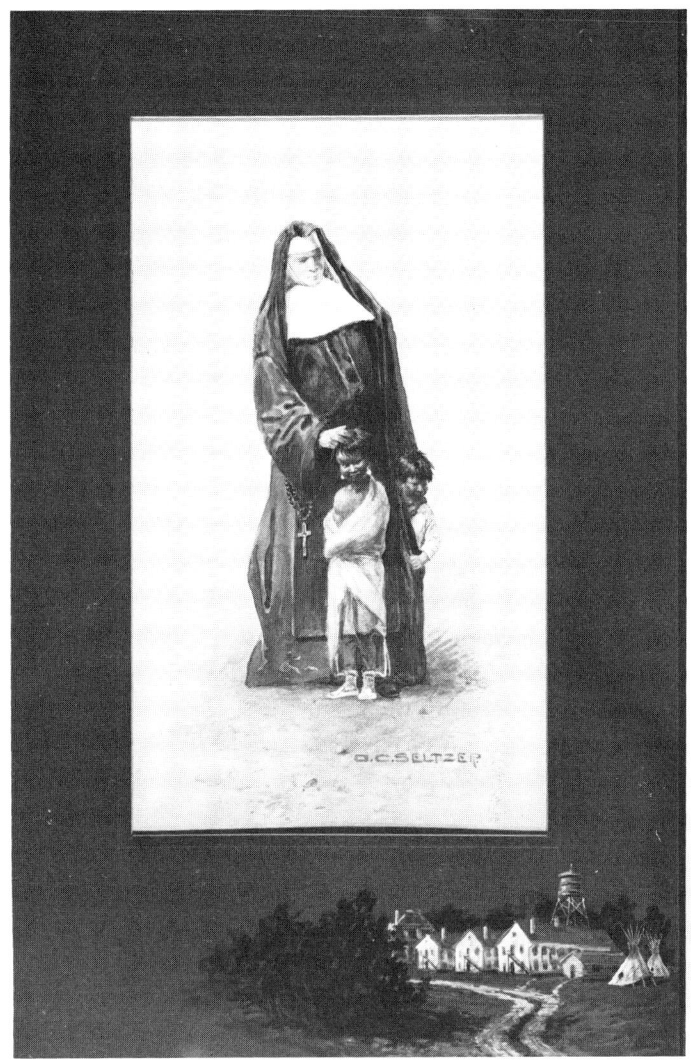

*Sister of Mercy*
(Ursuline nun)
1931
Western Character watercolor

pairs to be compared. From an artistic viewpoint not all of the replacements were improvements. The standing figure of the dance-hall girl owned by the Northwestern Bank is done with a delicacy and provocativeness absent from the heavily rouged *Dance Hall Girl* of the version acceptable to Cole. Dressed in red and slouched at a barroom table, the latter, a rawboned, coarse woman,— must have struck Cole as a more realistic portrayal of a type remembered from his boyhood in the rough gold-mining town Last Chance Gulch.

Olaf expressed disgust at being unable to achieve what he sought when he painted women. Toward the close of the Western Characters series, on January 23, 1931, he reported to Cole:

I am sure pleased to know that this last set of sketches were all to you[r] liking. I worked particularly hard on the Missionary and the Ursuline Nun and am glad I did not fail. I am at this time working on the Pioneer Mother, and when I tell you I am sweating blood, I am putting it mild, for I am surely not a painter of the She-kind of folks.

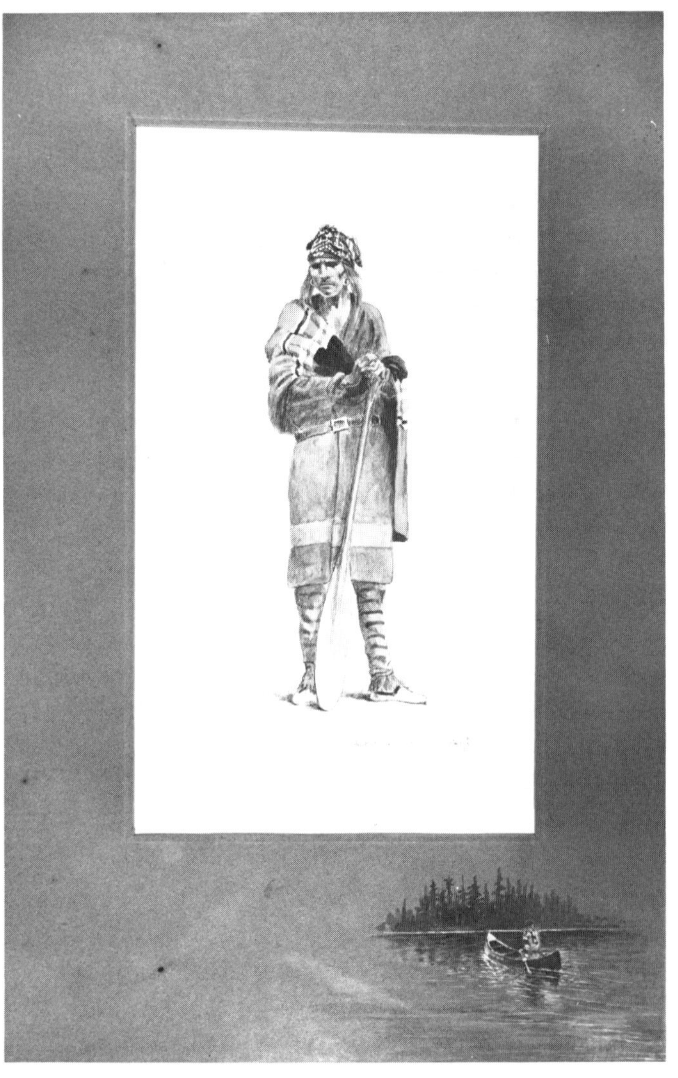

*L'Voyageur*
1929
Western Character watercolor

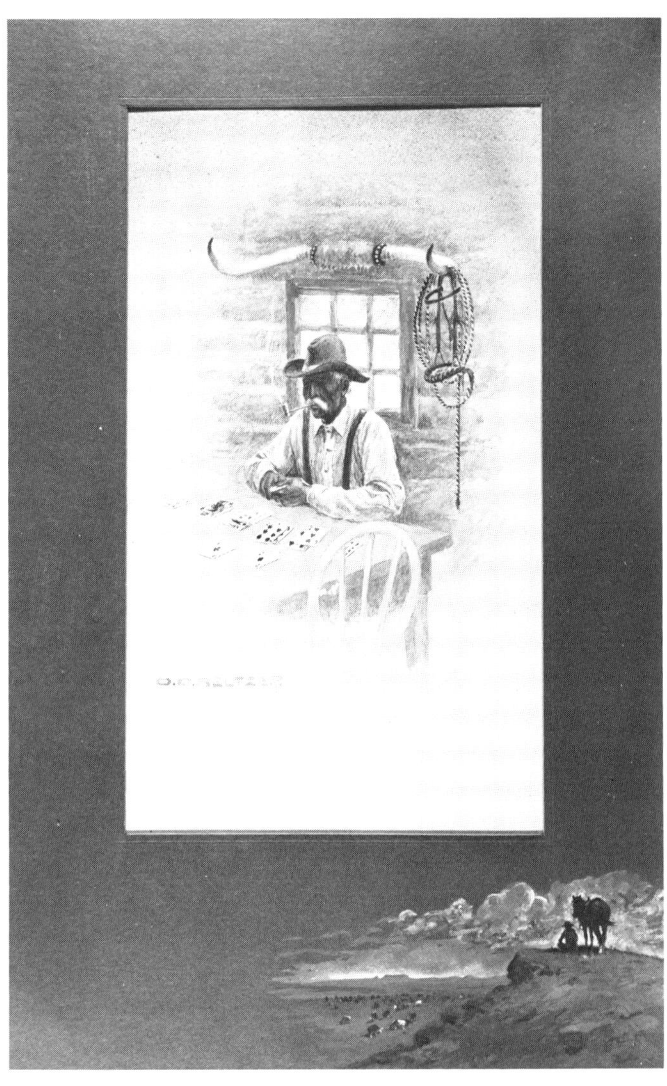

*Foreman*
1930
Western Character watercolor

Seltzer did not feel obliged to follow each of Cole's suggestions. From Cole's list of eighteen characters proposed in the September letter, Olaf failed to paint the Papoose (except for the one peering over the shoulder of the *Squaw*), Soldier, Packer (the Diamond Hitch was used in a later oil), Explorer, Railroad Builder, Greaser, Texan, or French Canadian, at least by these titles. The French Canadian could be *L'Voyageur*. The *Foreman*, depicted as an elderly dignified gen-tleman concentrating on his game of solitaire, could be Seltzer's version of a Texan.

Artist and collector had different concepts of the characters, which Cole referred to as a "series of historical figures." The recognizable figures were in the minority—Cole himself, *A Picture-Builder (C.M.R.)*, the *Gambler* (in reality a Great Falls bartender), the Scots sheriff, the *Stage Coach Driver*, and a few others. The model for a number of the Indian characters could have been

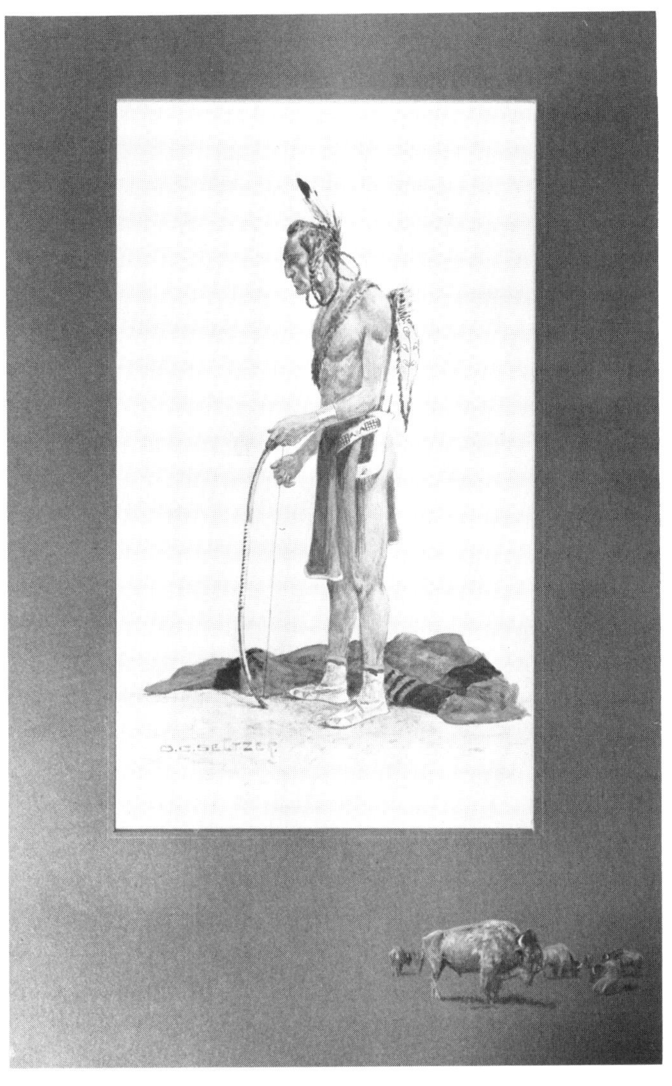

*Buffalo Runner*
1929
Western Character watercolor

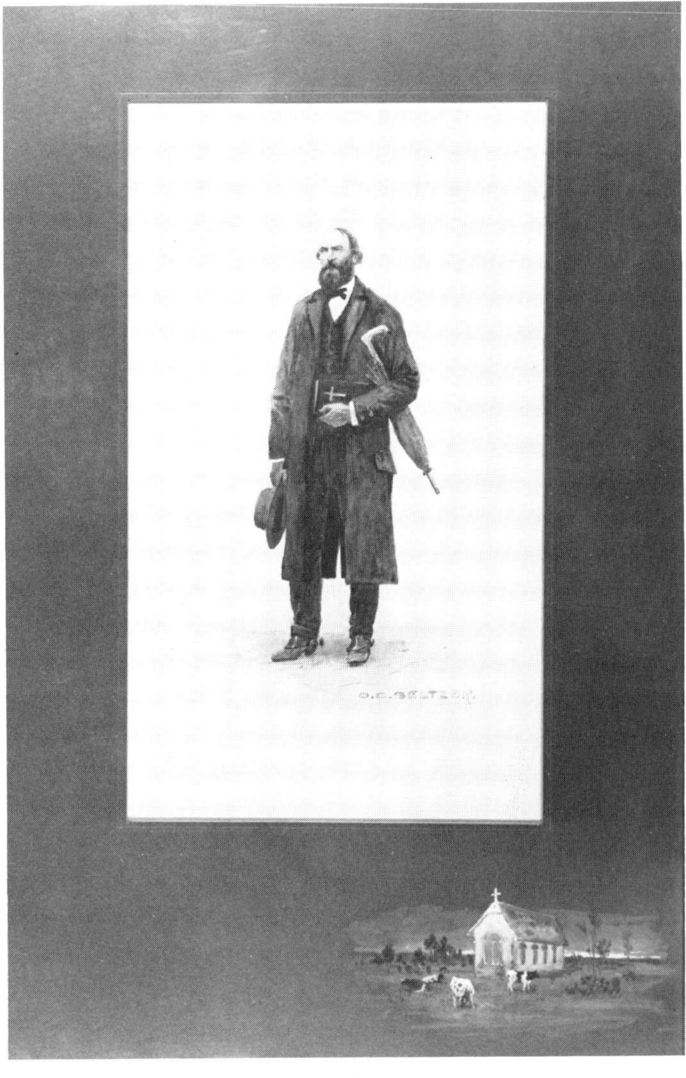

*Circuit Rider*
1929
Western Character watercolor

Young Boy, a Cree who was fascinated by Russell and Seltzer. He liked to hang around while the artists worked, hoping he would be asked to model (he also enjoyed Mabel's cooking).

The artist's conception of his Western Characters was that they would serve to preserve an archetype of each of the many ethnic and occupational groups that comprised the Old West. Some, like the *Squatter* or the *Buffalo Runner*, scratched out a living under the most primitive circumstances. Others, such as the *Sheriff*, the *Circuit Judge* with his damask vest and string tie, and the *Circuit Rider* with furled umbrella and suit of black display a degree of polish and sophistication.

There is pathetic ignorance in the *Village Hag*, frontier self-confidence in the *Horse Wrangler*, quiet pride in the *Beadworker*, and a canniness in the *Cattle Rustler* and the *Gambler*. The combined efforts—and obstructions—of such characters during the last half of the nineteenth century contributed to the color of the settlement of the Northwest.

The painstaking research that went into Olaf Seltzer's characters of the Old West may be lost on the average viewer, but not on Paul A. Rossi and David C. Hunt, coauthors of *The Art of the Old West*, a book based on the Gilcrease collection. Commenting on *L'Voyageur*, they note:

*The hip-length leggings and moccasins worn by this trapper were probably acquired from the Indians of the Great Lakes region and are, perhaps, the handiwork of an Indian wife. The eastern Indian floral designs made of beads and porcupine quills suggest a type universally employed by the trappers before increasing contact with western tribes provided... geometric decorative ideas of the plains variety. The French trade blanket... never gained the popularity among either Indians or trappers as did the later Hudson's Bay trade item.*

*Seltzer carried on exhaustive research into the background of his subjects of American frontier life.... His figure of a French-Canadian trapper of the 1840's called simply* Half-Breed *wears a Hudson's Bay coat common on the northern fringes of settlement throughout the early half of the nineteenth century. He carries a flintlock trade musket that has been sawed off for ease of handling on horseback. The stock is studded with brass typical of many plains Indian firearms of the last century, and his earrings are a combination of European brass rings and Indian shells....*

*The free-roving plains and mountain men were a motley lot. Generally their style of dress was a fur cap, fringed deerskin shirt and leggings, and moccasins of the same material.* [10]

In Remington's version, the voyageur is leaning on an oar and wearing the long-tasseled stocking cap and sash termed typical of the trade, along with a sleeveless vest over a long-sleeved shirt, according to *Harper's Weekly* for February 1, 1890.

According to Rossi and Hunt, the popular notion of the trapper or mountain man is depicted by Seltzer in his *Hudson's Bay Trapper,*

*The skin hat, the long buckskin or elkskin coat with beaded or red flannel trim of plains Indian design, the brass-studded knife sheath, and the wrap-around leggings with separate moccasins*

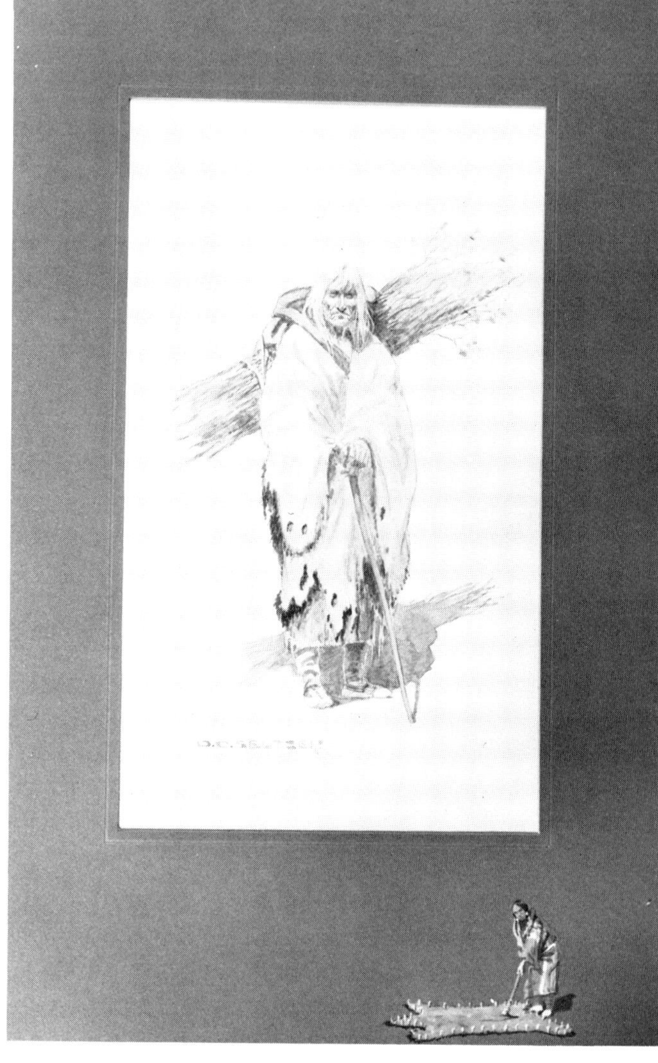

Village Hag
1930
Western Character watercolor

*... were usually manufactured by an Indian wife or several wives scattered throughout the tribes. The long flintlock rifle he carries is of an earlier period than the weapon more often associated with the mountain man, which had a shorter barrel and was of a larger caliber for use against the larger game of the western plains and mountain country. The strike-a-light that Seltzer shows hanging from the trapper's belt is of a variety typical of the period, although the double-spring traps shown suspended from his belt suggest a later period....*

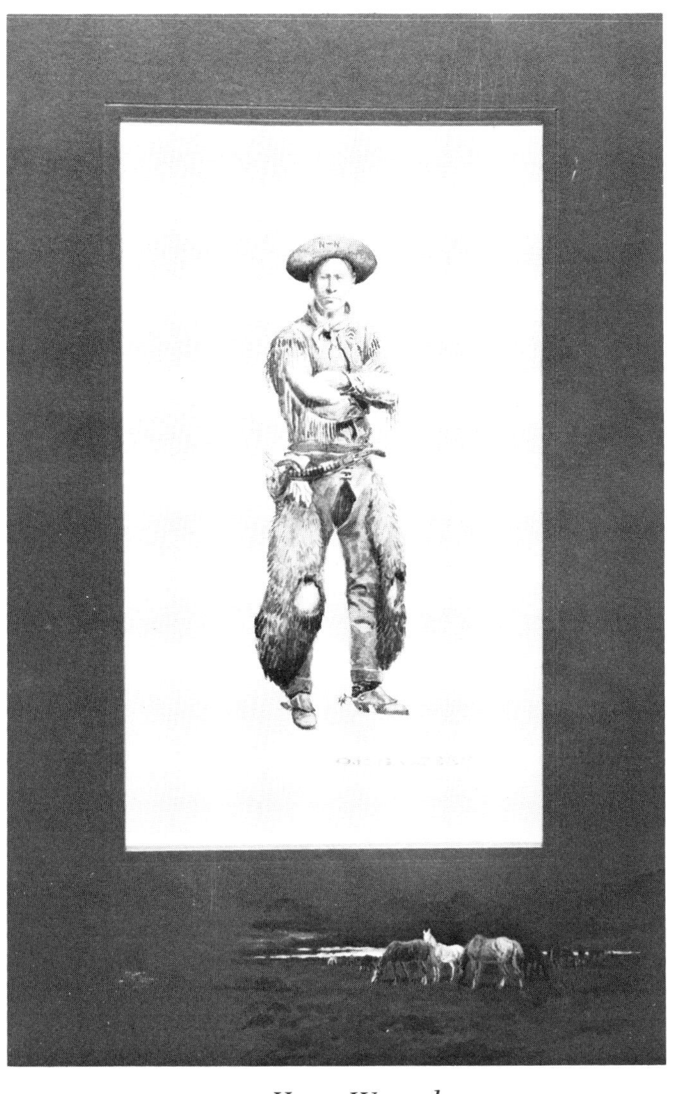

*Horse Wrangler*
1929
Western Character watercolor

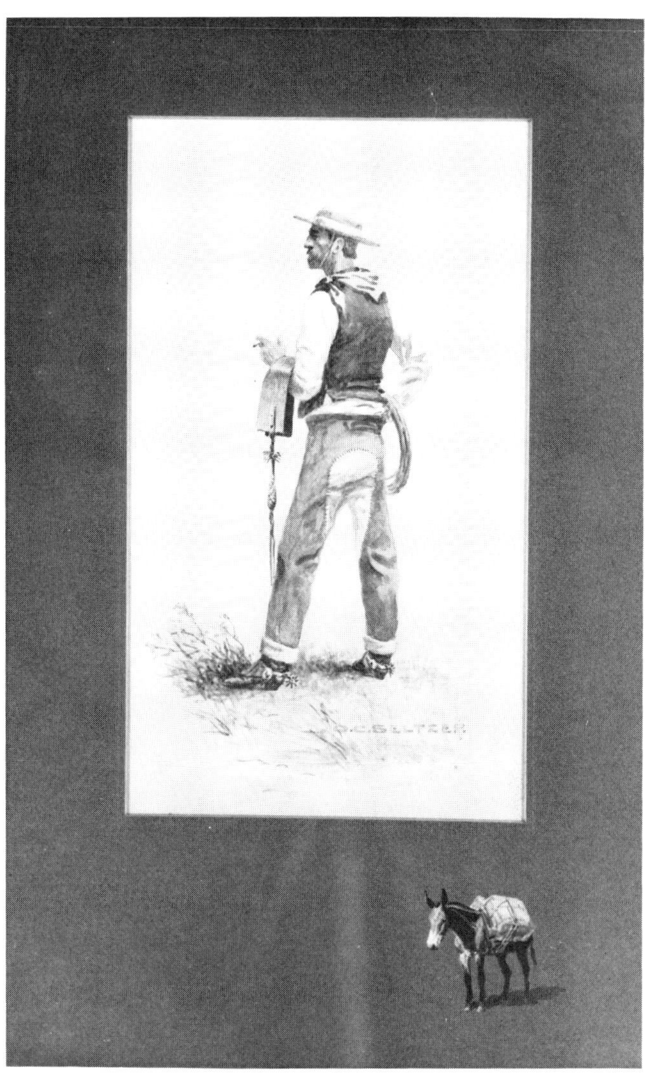

*Mule Skinner*
1930
Western Character watercolor

*Seltzer shows the single powder horn, which was more commonly attached to a bag carryin additional equipment for the trapper's use in the field.* [11]

The artist's expertise is exhibited in more than accouterments. In creating the *Teamster* (listed originally as *Mule-Skinner*) Seltzer

*described a type common to the northern plains; a professional man as opposed to someone simply hired for the job who in most cases was anxious to make his way west however he could with the hopes of reaching the goldfields of Montana, Colorado, or California. Here Seltzer dressed his teamster in the plainest of clothing, which includes heavy woolen pants and square-toed working boots that later gave way to the heavy work shoes of the 1880's. A woolen 'hickory' shirt, plain or checked, and a soft-brimmed hat complete his outfit.* [12]

Philip Cole knew what he wanted, and he usually got it. But Olaf Seltzer also had set ideas.

While meeting Cole's constructive suggestions about shading backgrounds and using darker-toned mats, Seltzer continued to place the vignettes firmly on the mat. If Seltzer did indeed inscribe each sketch according to Cole's request, the inscriptions were so placed on the back of the academy board that the mounting and framing has covered them forever. If the artist ignored this request, he made up for it with a steady flow of delightfully illustrated personal letters and greetings, each bearing Cole's name and address, no matter how informal the message.

It is said that Olaf provided background material on dozens of the sketches, naming his models and telling anecdotes that explained why he dressed them as he did or how he decided upon the material he used. This material was copied into a ledger book that has unfortunately disappeared. Searches for the book have proved fruitless.

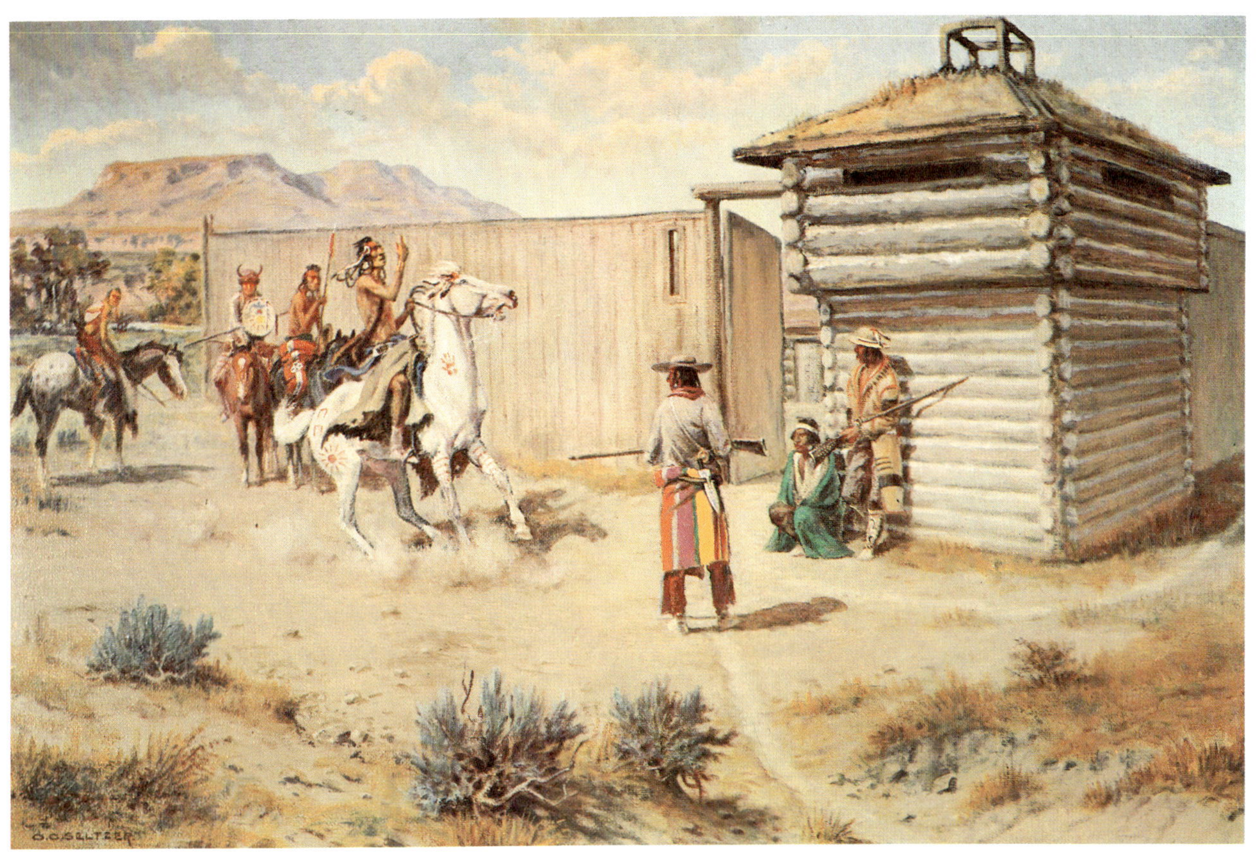

*Herald of the Robe Trade*
1928
Oil, 20″ × 30″

(Unless otherwise noted, all color plates are of paintings in the Gilcrease Collection, Thomas Gilcrease Institute of American History and Art, Tulsa.)

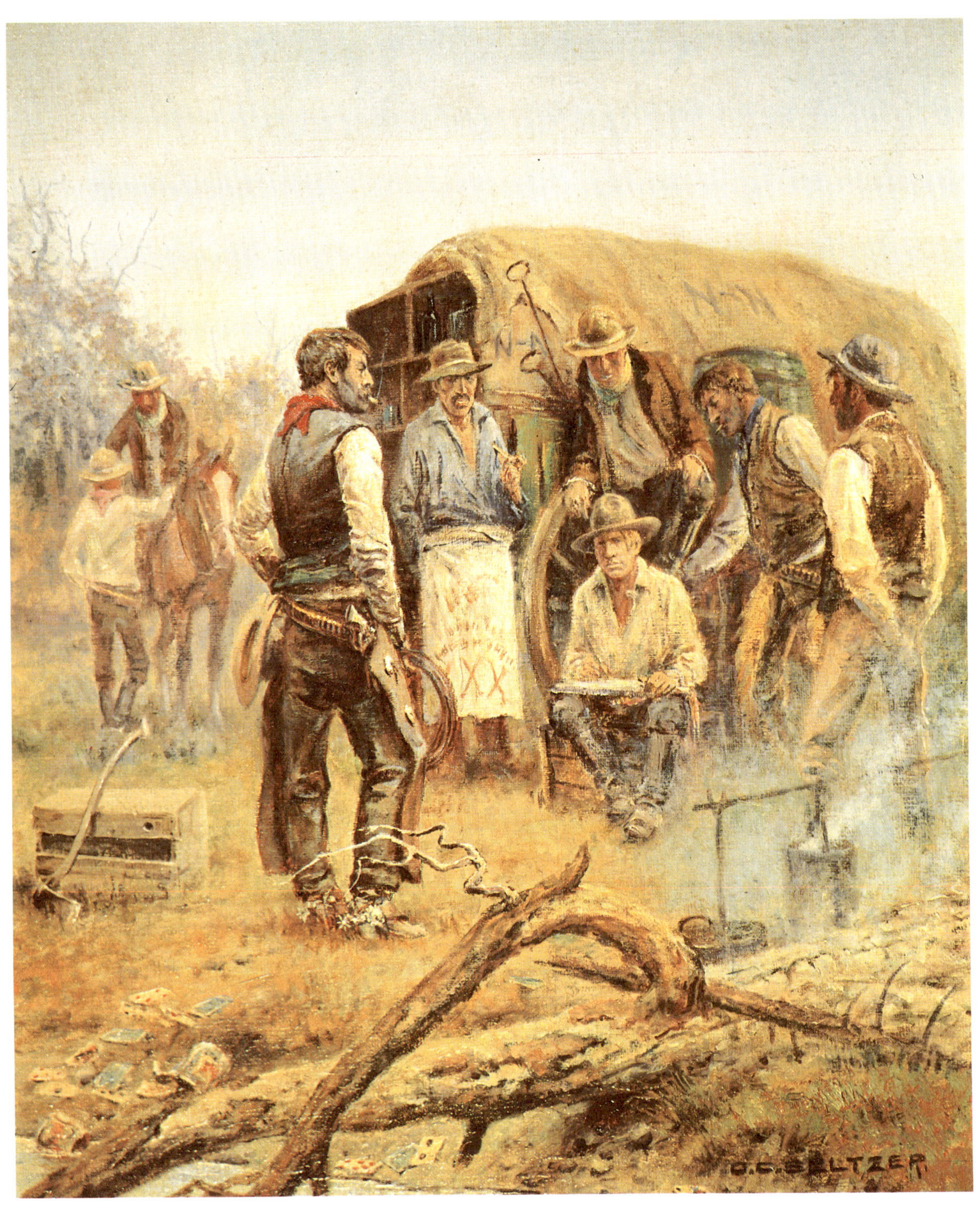

*Charley Russell About 1891 with N-N Outfit*
1927
Oil, 12″ × 10″

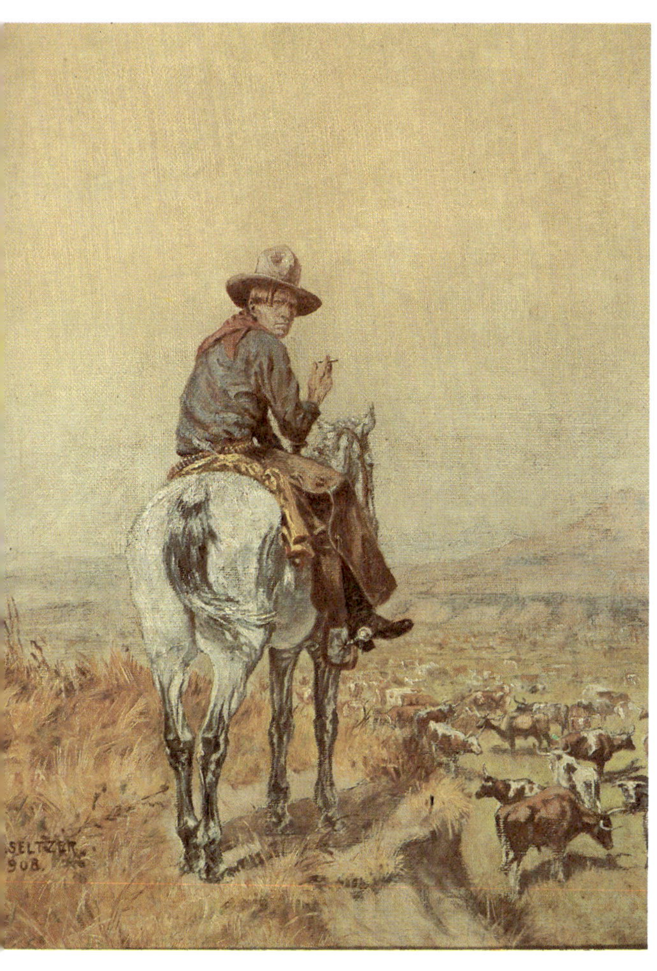

*Portrait of C. M. Russell*
Oil, 12″ × 9½″

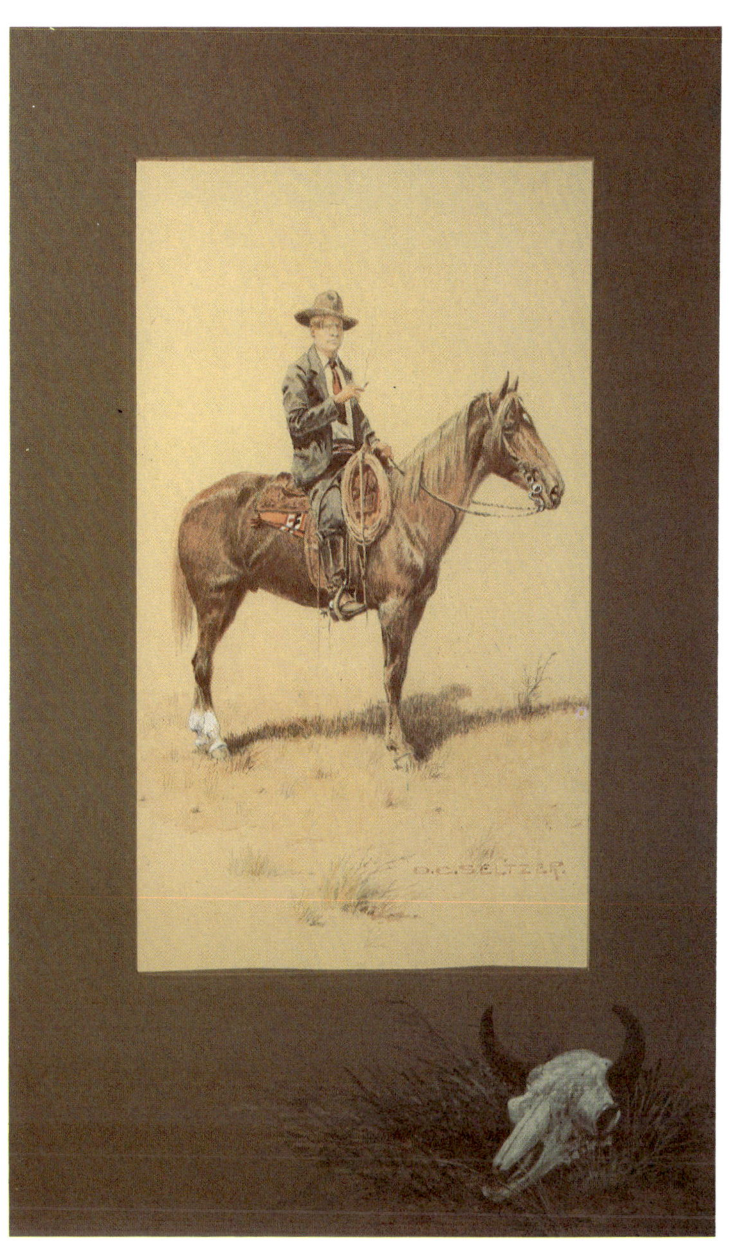

*A Picture Builder (CMR)*
1928
Western Character watercolor, 18″ × 11½″

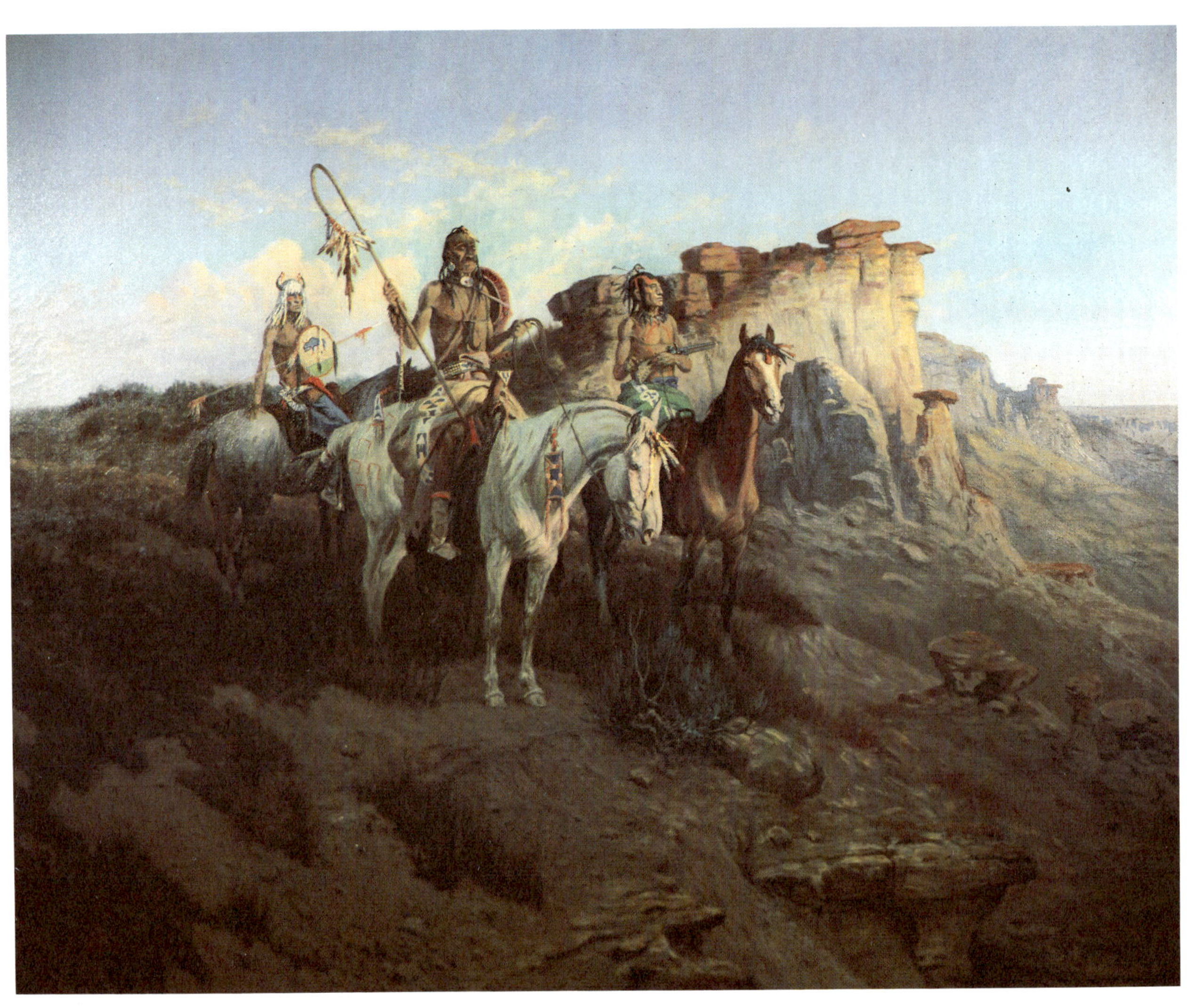

*Prowlers of the Prairie*
1926
Oil, 38″ × 48″

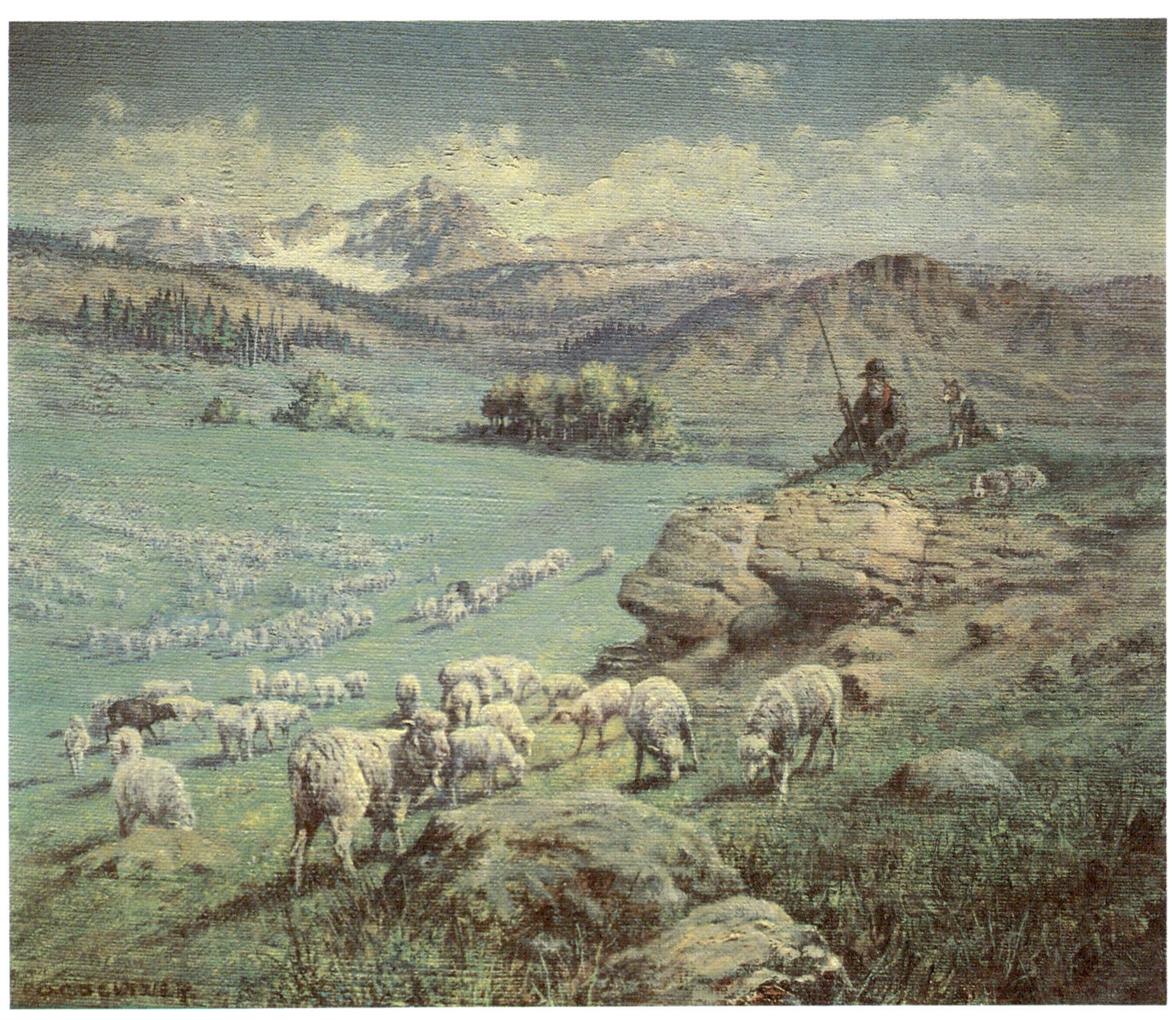

*Sheep Country*
1926
Oil, 12″ × 14″

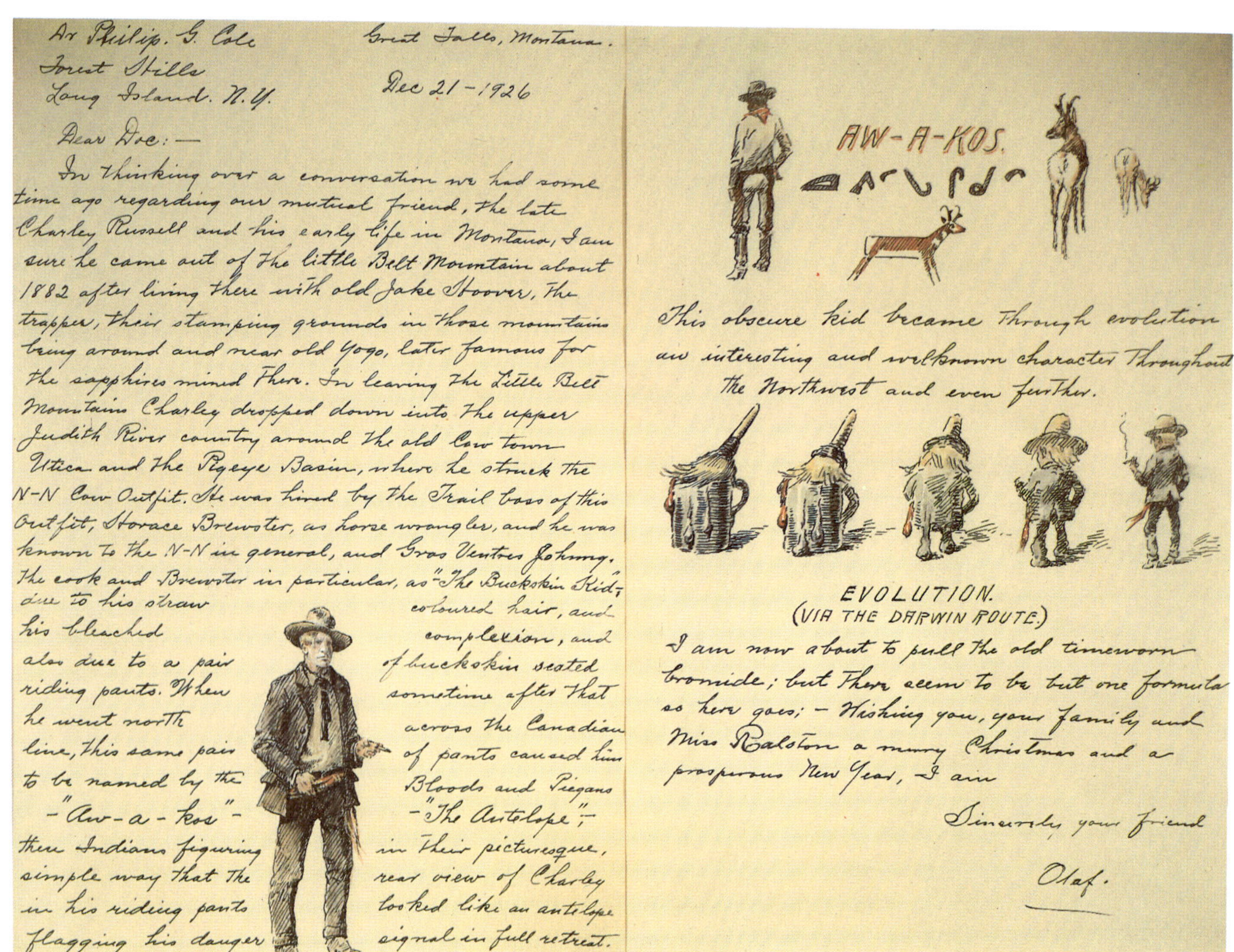



Ar Philip. G. Cole
Forest Hills
Long Island. N.Y.

Great Falls, Montana.
Dec 21 – 1926

Dear Doc: —

In thinking over a conversation we had some time ago regarding our mutual friend, the late Charley Russell and his early life in Montana, I am sure he came out of the little Belt Mountain about 1882 after living there with old Jake Hoover, the trapper, their stamping grounds in those mountains being around and near old Yogo, later famous for the sapphires mined there. In leaving the Little Belt Mountains Charley dropped down into the upper Judith River country around the old Cow town Utica and the Pigeye Basin, where he struck the N-N Cow Outfit. He was hired by the Trail boss of this Outfit, Horace Brewster, as horse wrangler, and he was known to the N-N in general, and Gros Ventres Johnny, the cook and Brewster in particular, as "The Buckskin Kid", due to his straw coloured hair, and his bleached complexion, and also due to a pair of buckskin seated riding pants. When he went north across the Canadian line, this same pair of pants caused him to be named by the Bloods and Piegans — "Aw-a-kos" — "The Antelope"; these Indians figuring in their picturesque, simple way that the rear view of Charley in his riding pants looked like an antelope flagging his danger signal in full retreat.

This obscure kid became through evolution an interesting and welknown character throughout the Northwest and even further.

I am now about to pull the old timeworn bromide; but there seem to be but one formula so here goes; — Wishing you, your family and Miss Ralston a merry Christmas and a prosperous New Year, I am

Sincerely, your friend

Olaf.

*Aw-A-Kos Letter*
1926
Watercolor and ink, 15½″ × 19½″

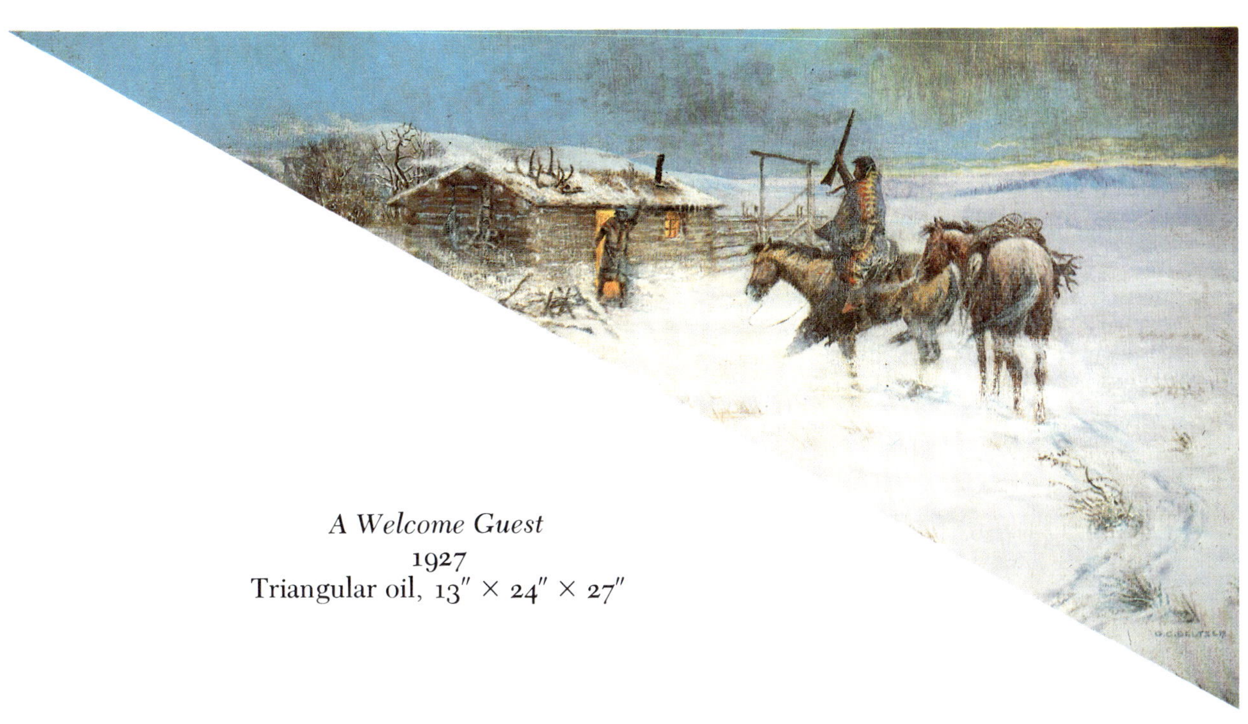

*A Welcome Guest*
1927
Triangular oil, 13″ × 24″ × 27″

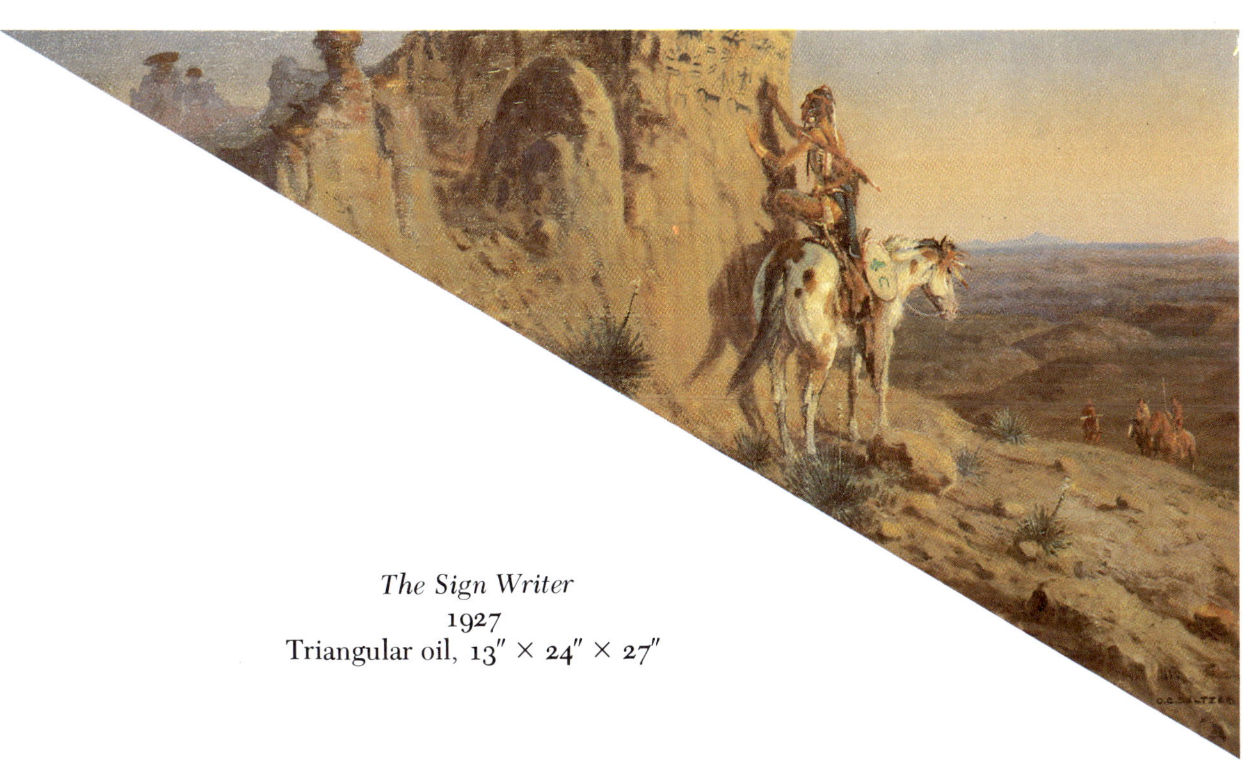

*The Sign Writer*
1927
Triangular oil, 13″ × 24″ × 27″

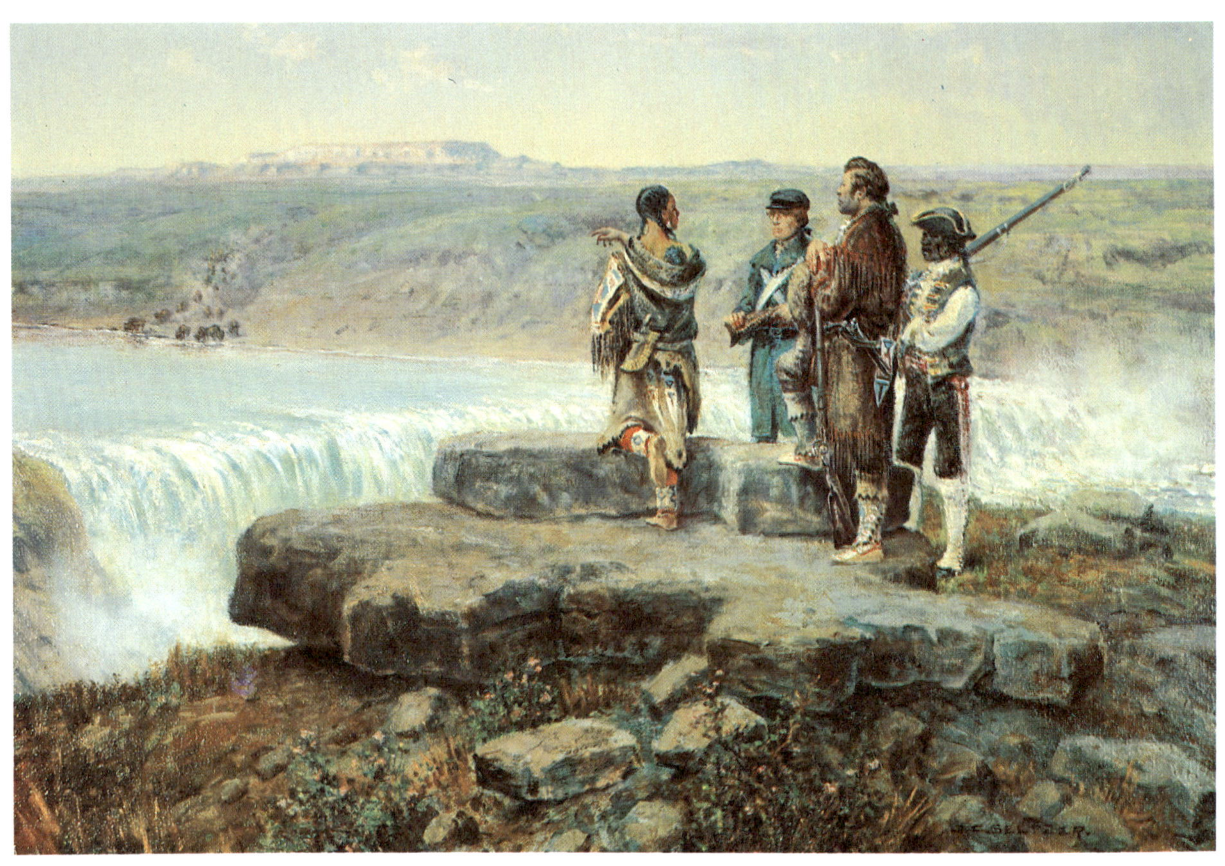

*Lewis and Clark with Sacajawea at the Great Falls of the Missouri, 1804*
1927
Oil, 11″ × 16″

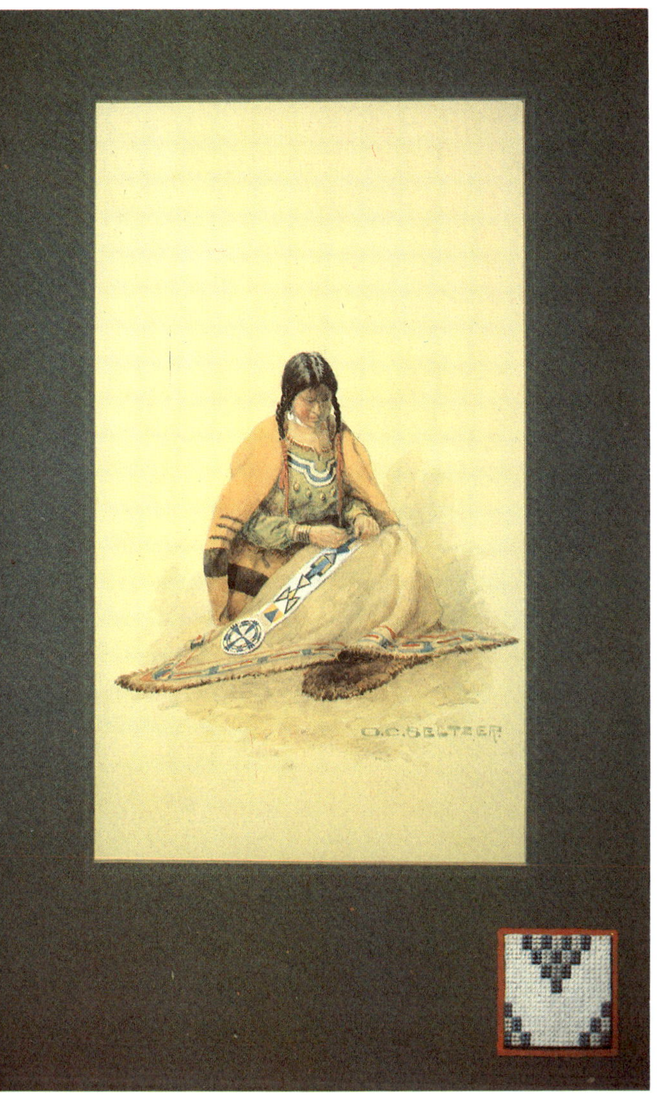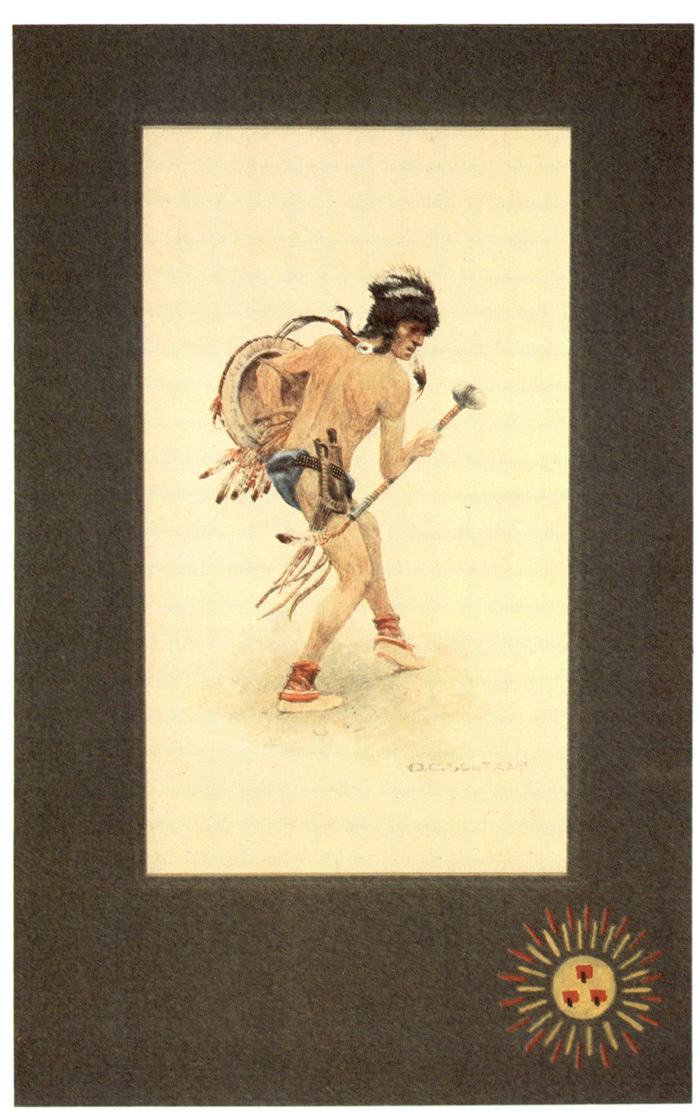

*Beadworker*
1928
Western Character watercolor

*Sun Dancer*
1928
Western Character watercolor

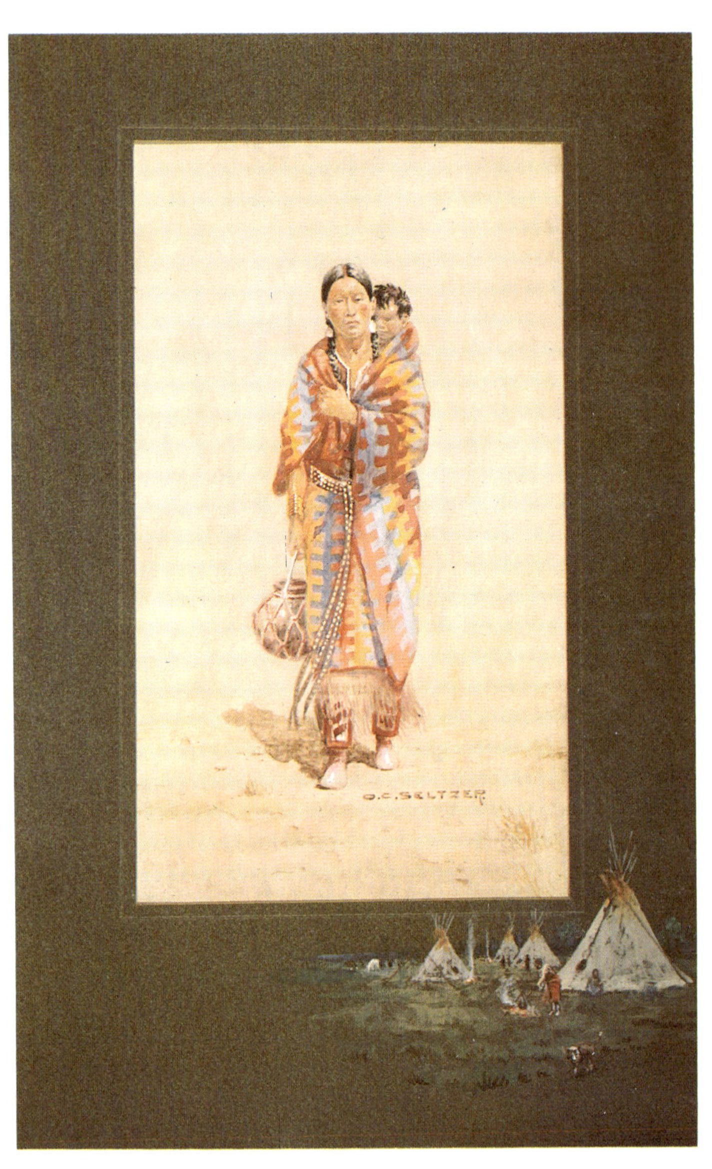

*Squaw*
1928
Western Character watercolor

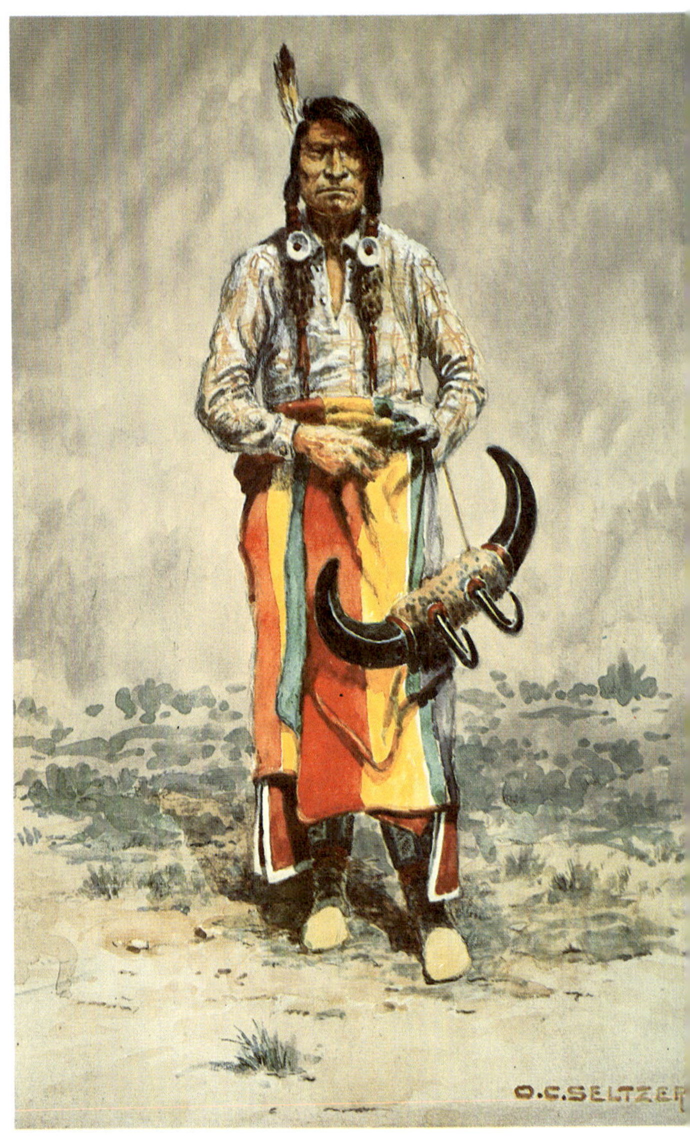

*Reservation Buck*
1928
Western Character watercolor

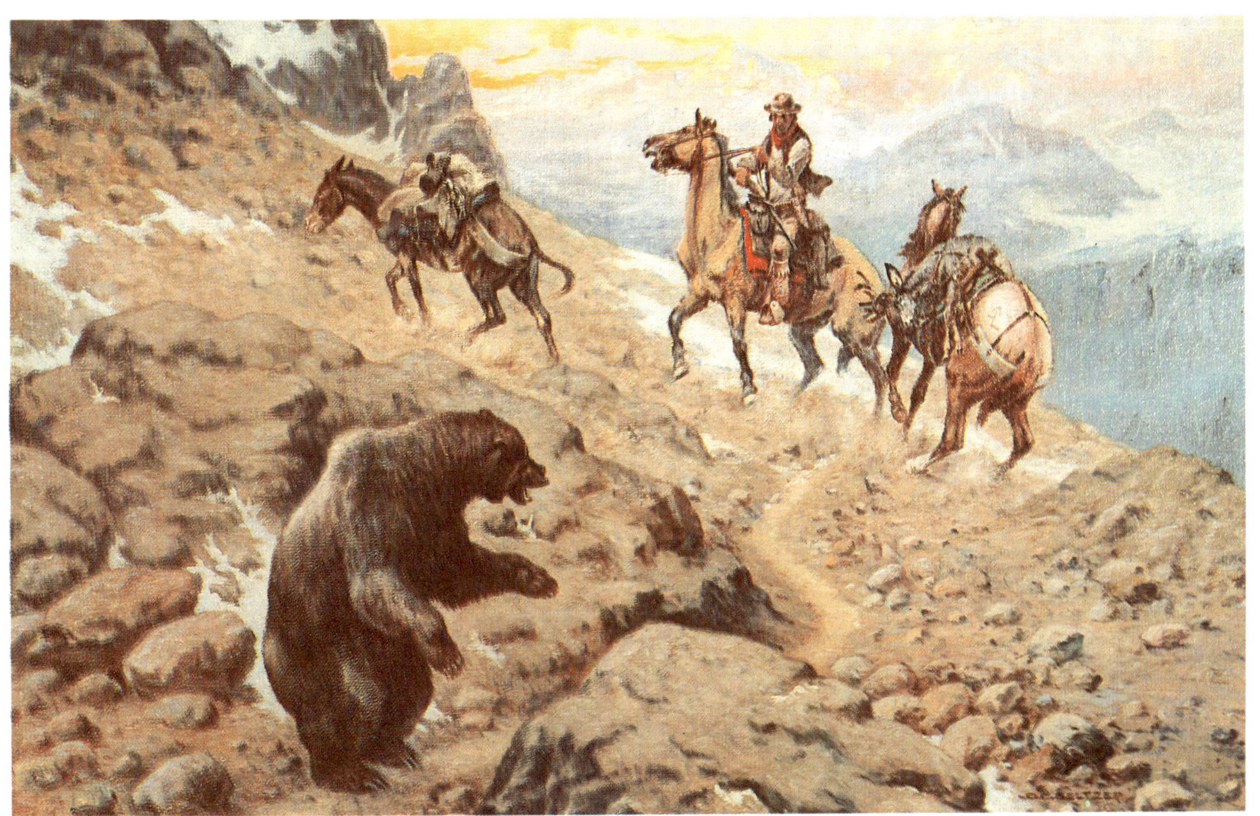

*The Disputed Trail*
1927
Oil, 20″ × 30″

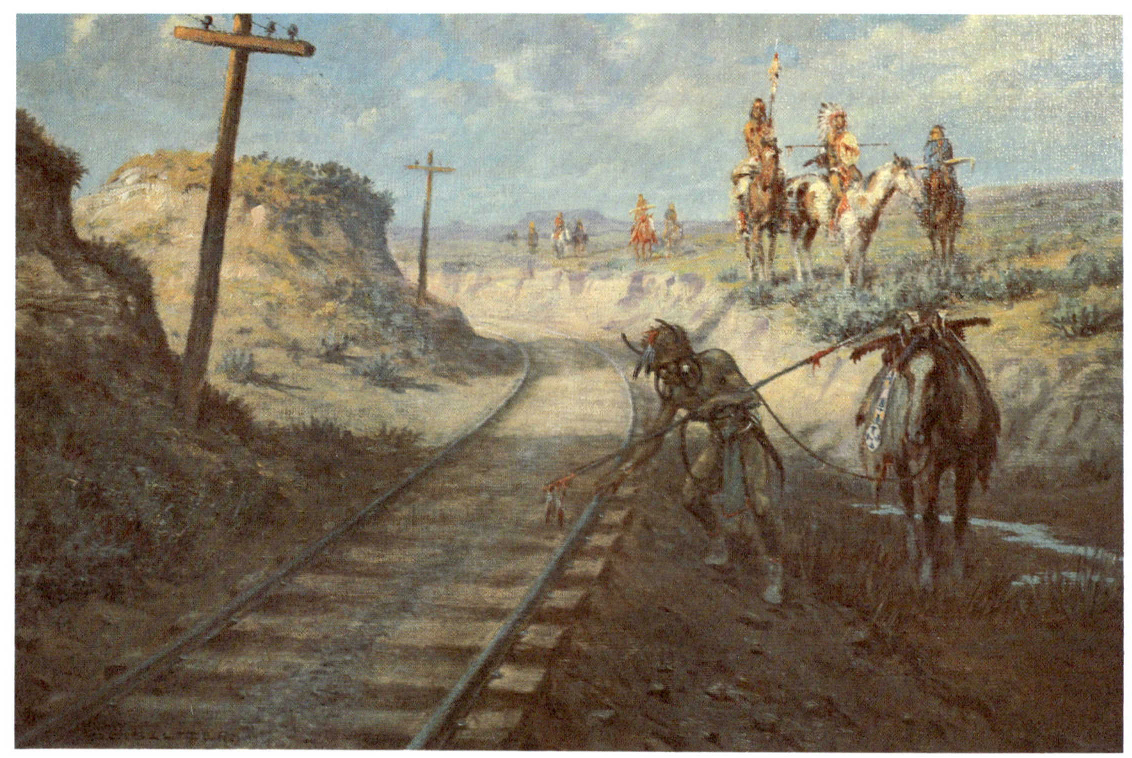

*The Iron Trail*
1931
Early Western Travelogue oil, 11″ × 16″

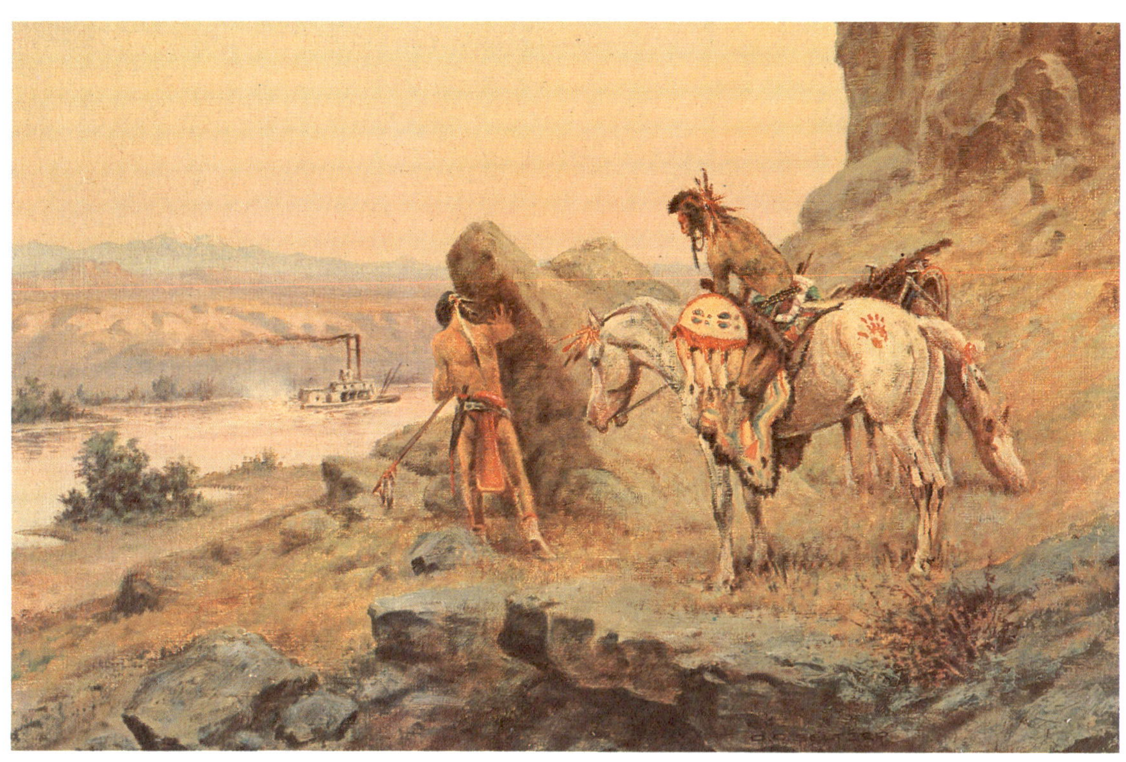

*The Smoke Boat*
1930
Early Western Travelogue oil

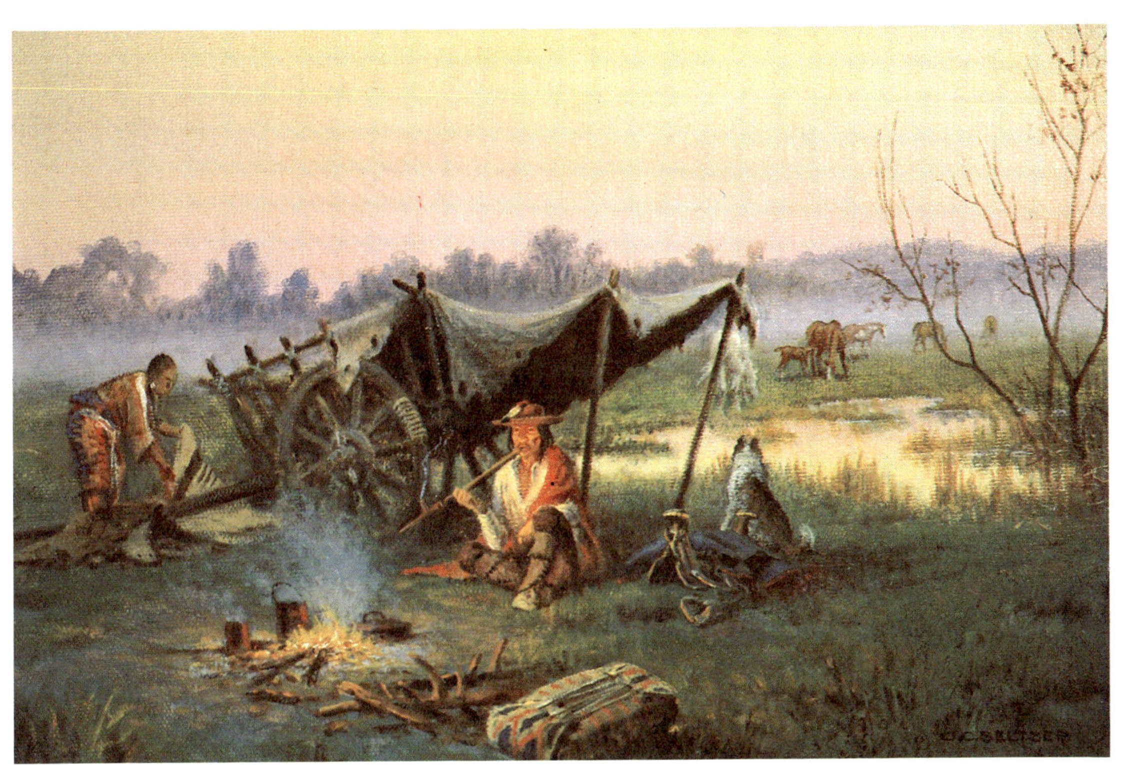

*The Red River Cart*
1932
Early Western Travelogue oil

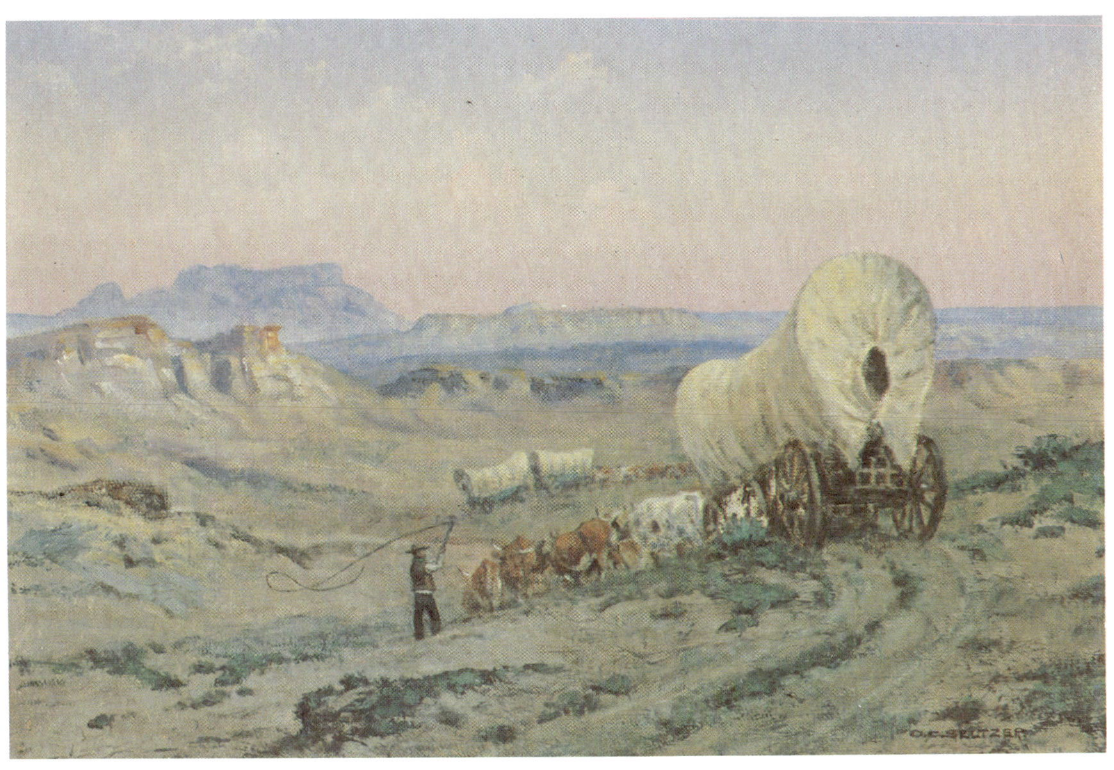

*The Six-Wheeler (Diamond R Mule Outfit)*
1933
Early Western Travelogue oil

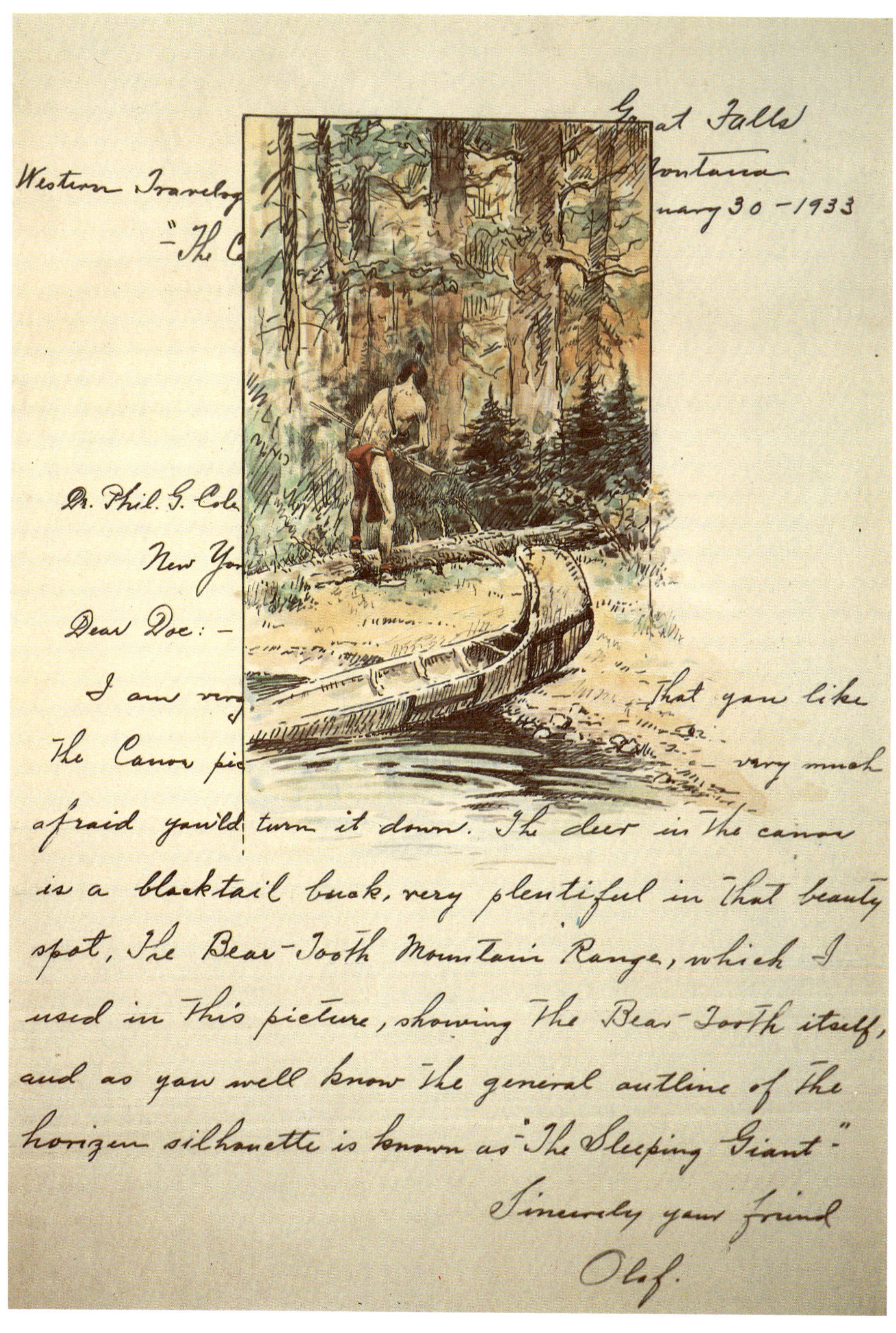



*The Canoe Letter*
1933
Watercolor and ink, 11″ × 8″

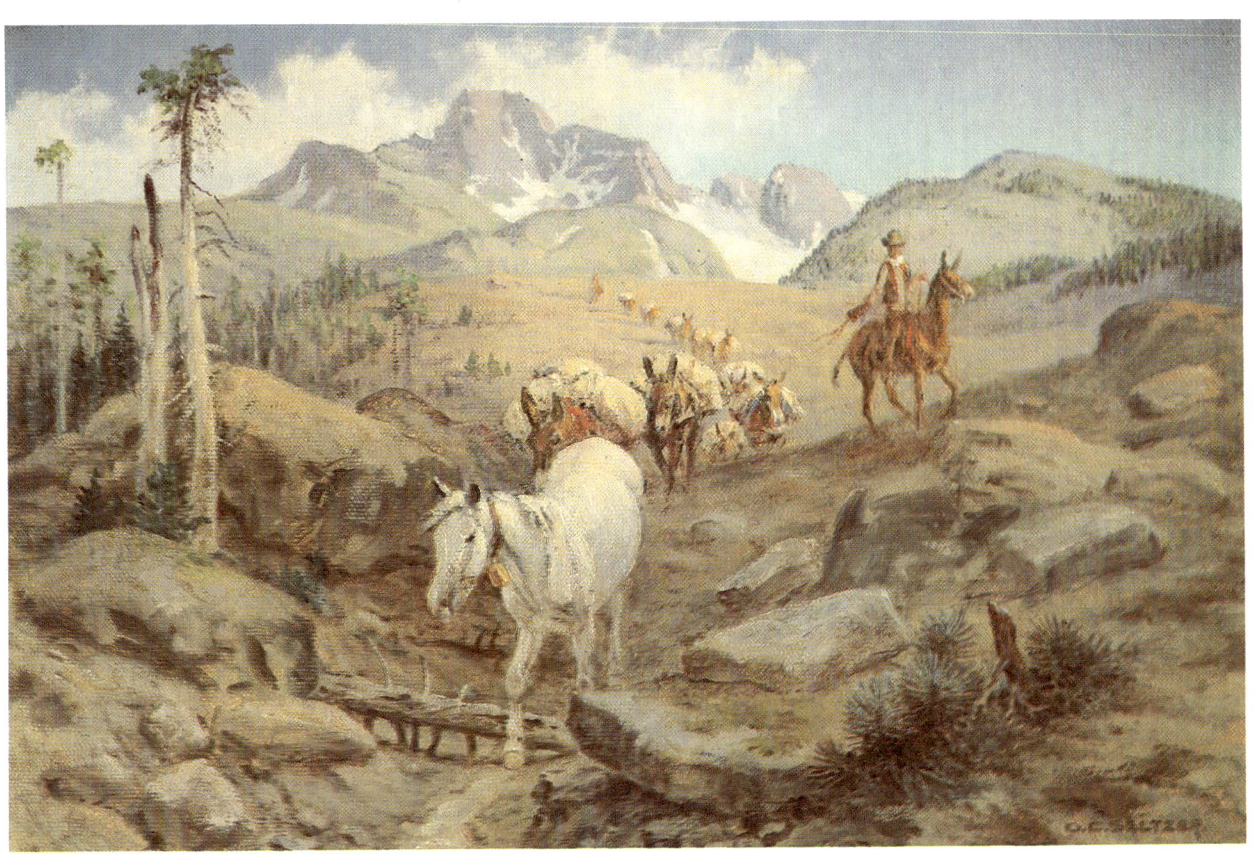

*The Pack Train*
1932
Early Western Travelogue oil

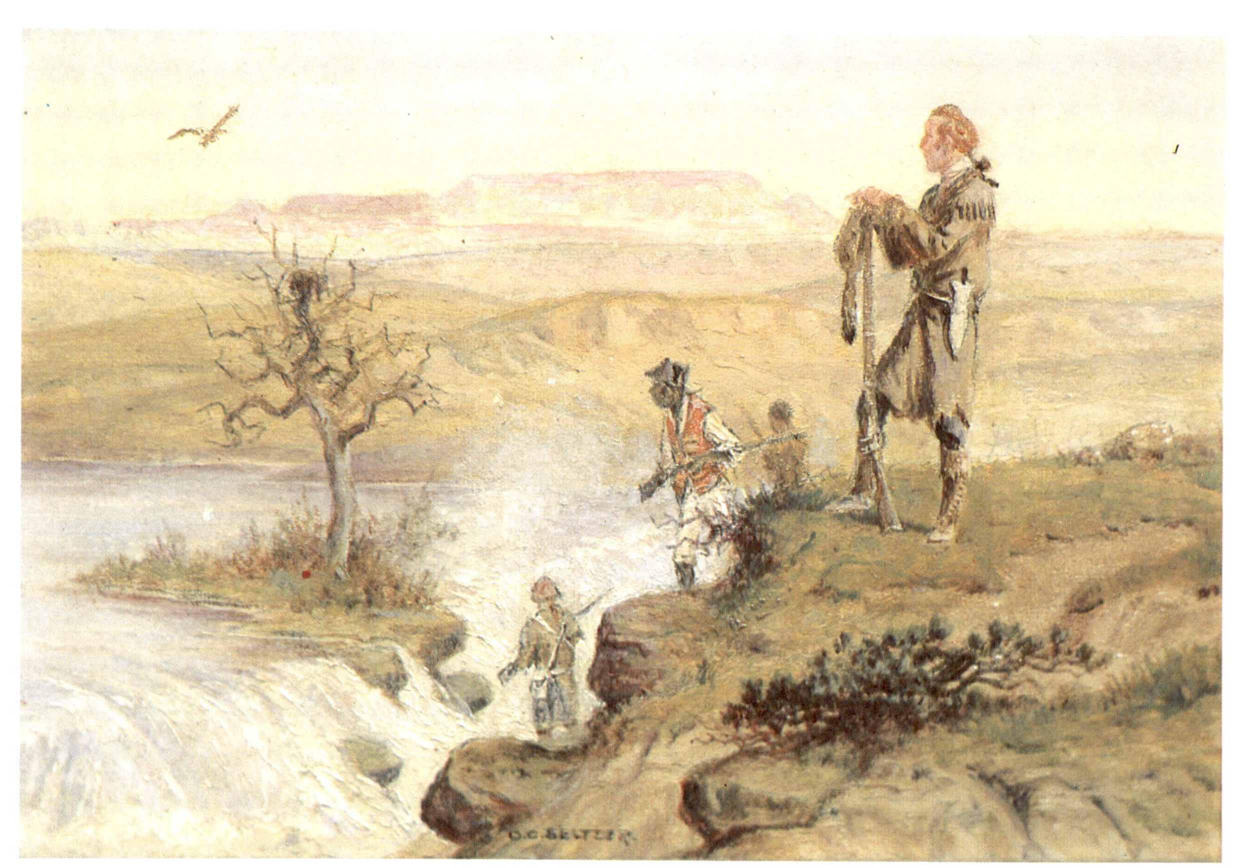

*Lewis at the Black Eagle Falls of the Missouri, 1805*
1933
Miniature oil

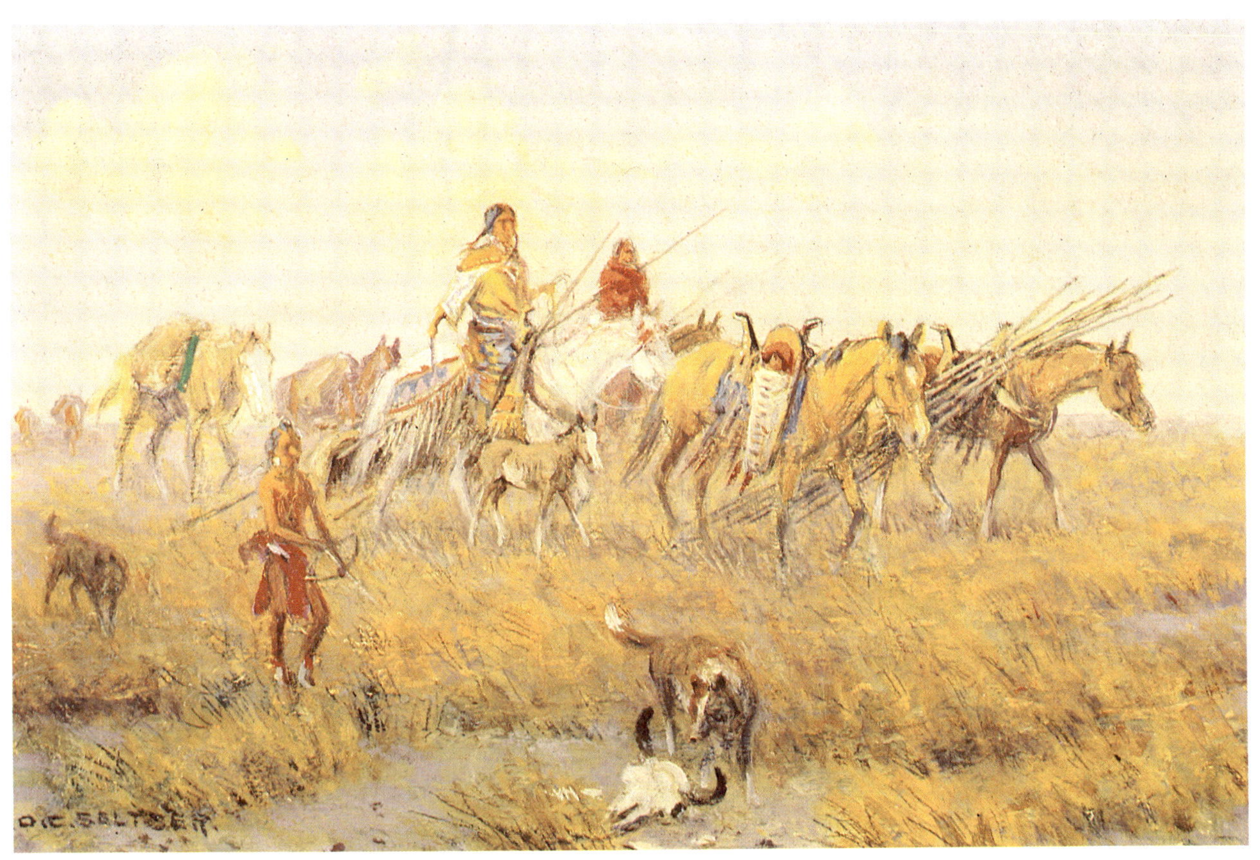

*Moving Camp*
1934
Miniature oil

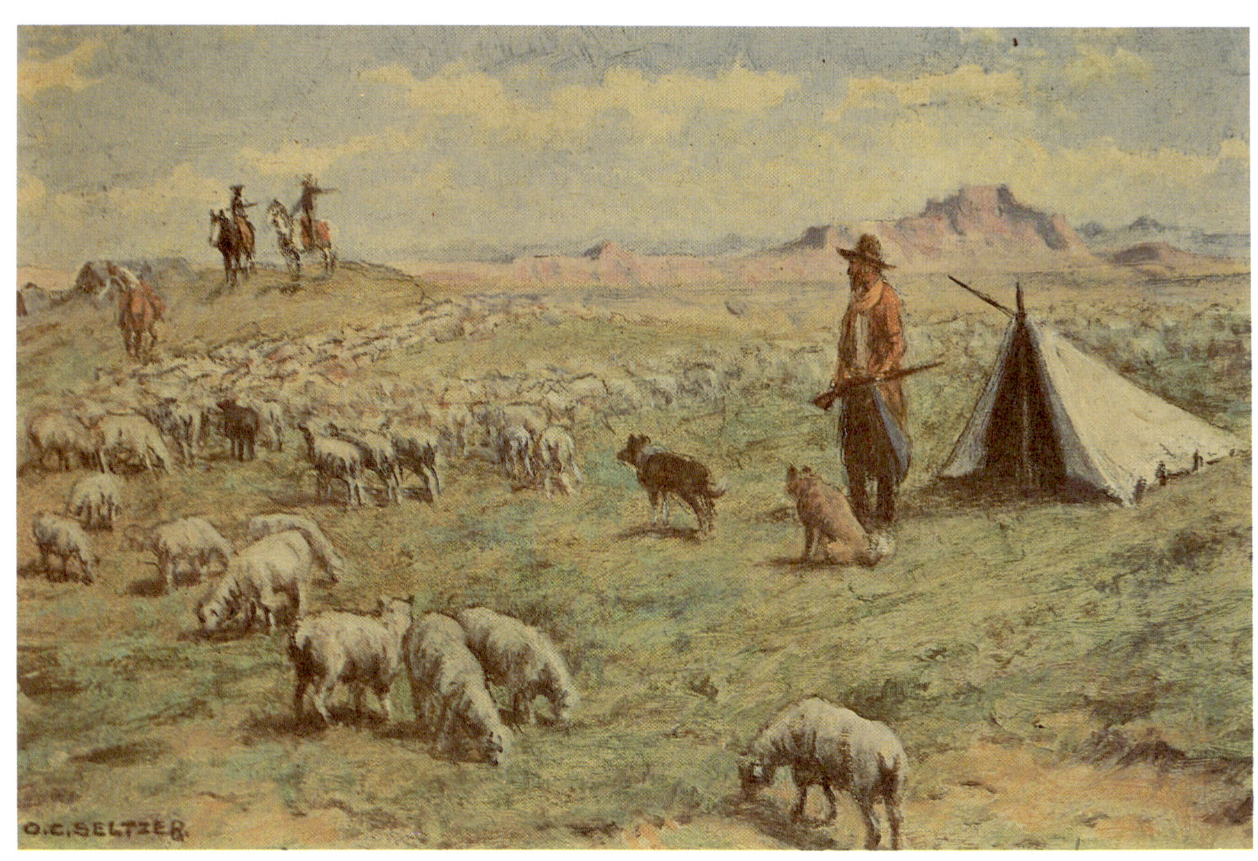

*Sheepmen vs. Cattlemen*
1934
Miniature oil

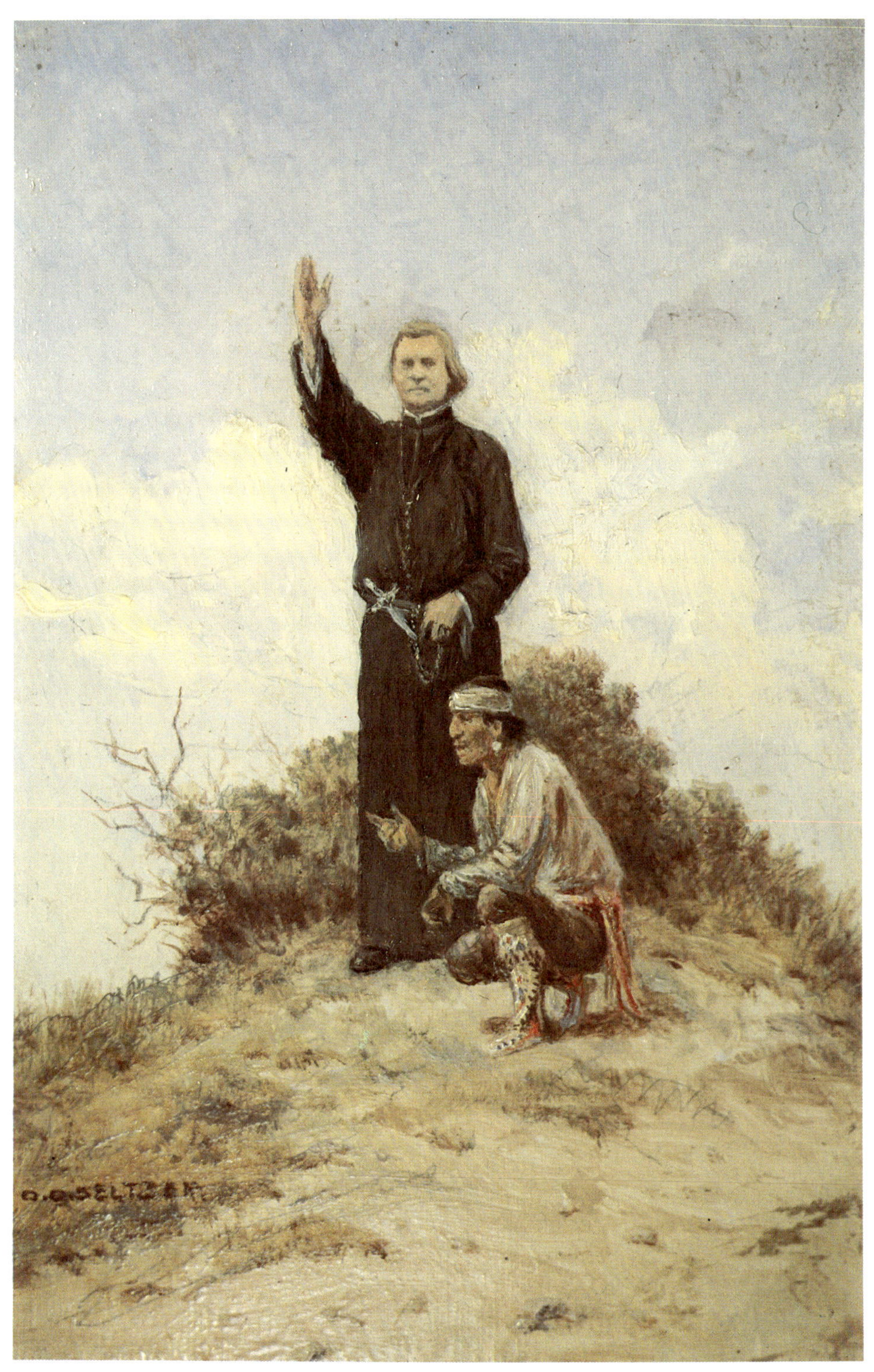

*A Black Robe Pioneer*
(Pierre Jean de Smet)
1934
Miniature oil

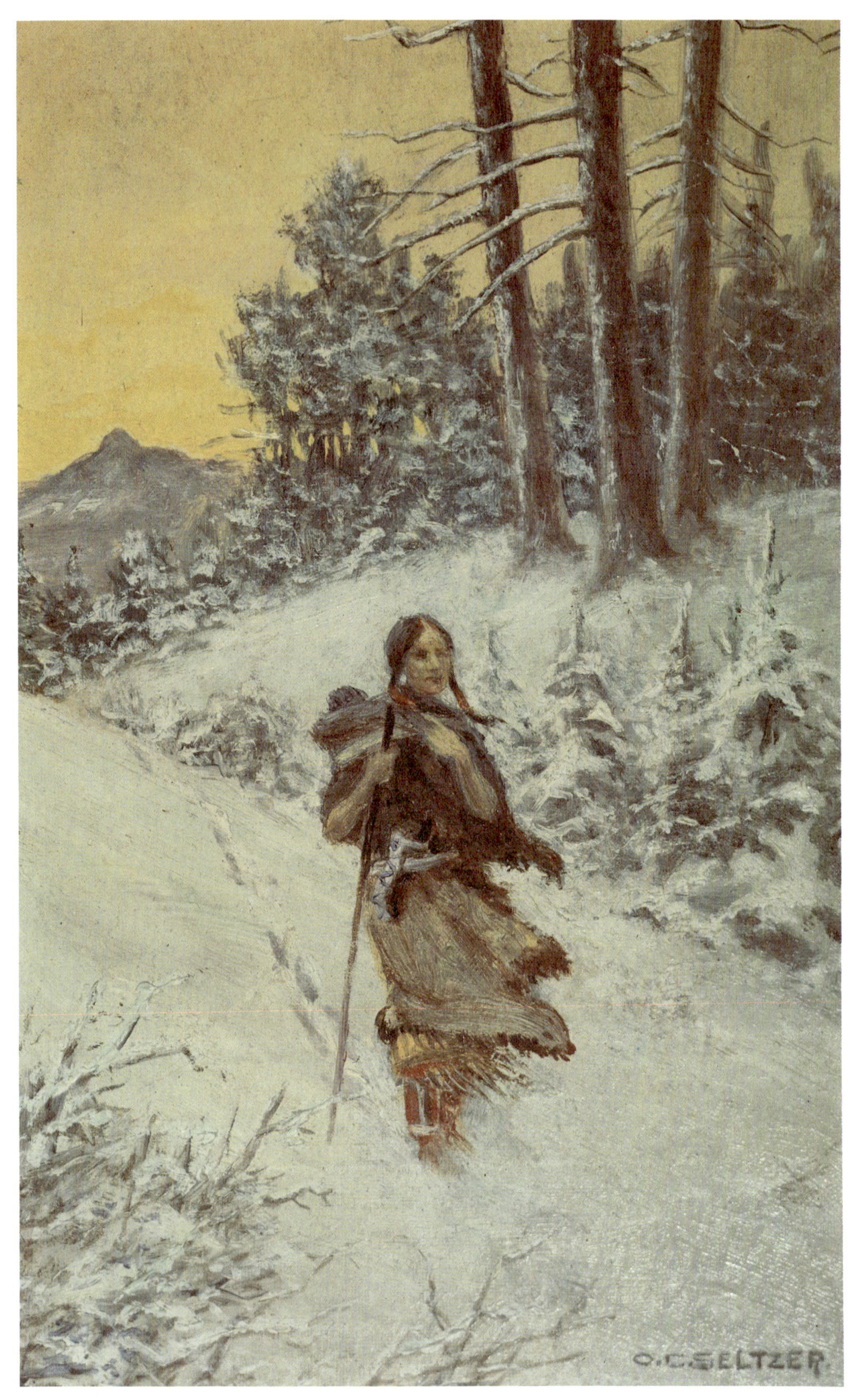

*The Dorian Woman*
1934
Miniature oil

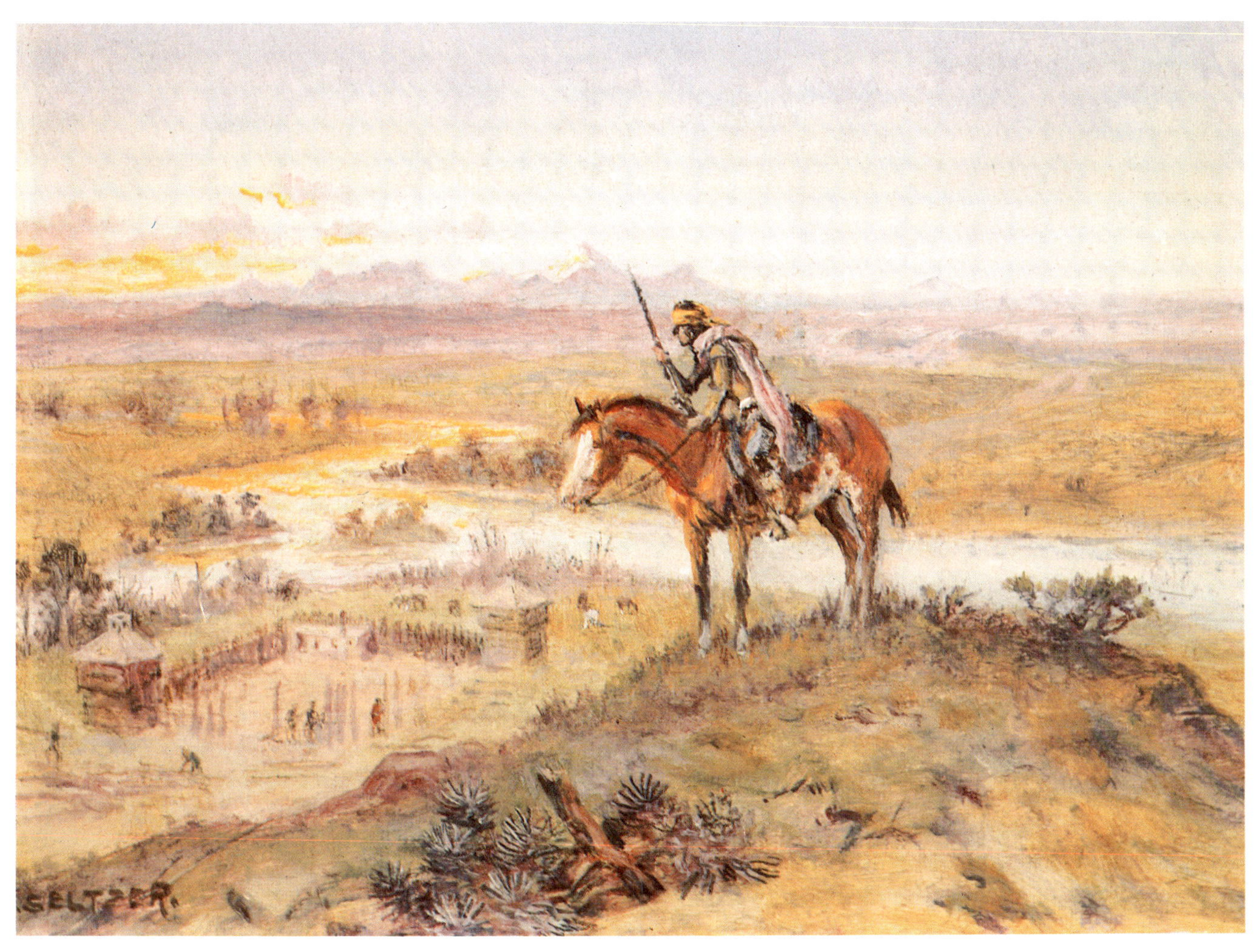

*Manuel Lisa Watching the Construction of Fort Lisa, 1807*
1934
Miniature oil

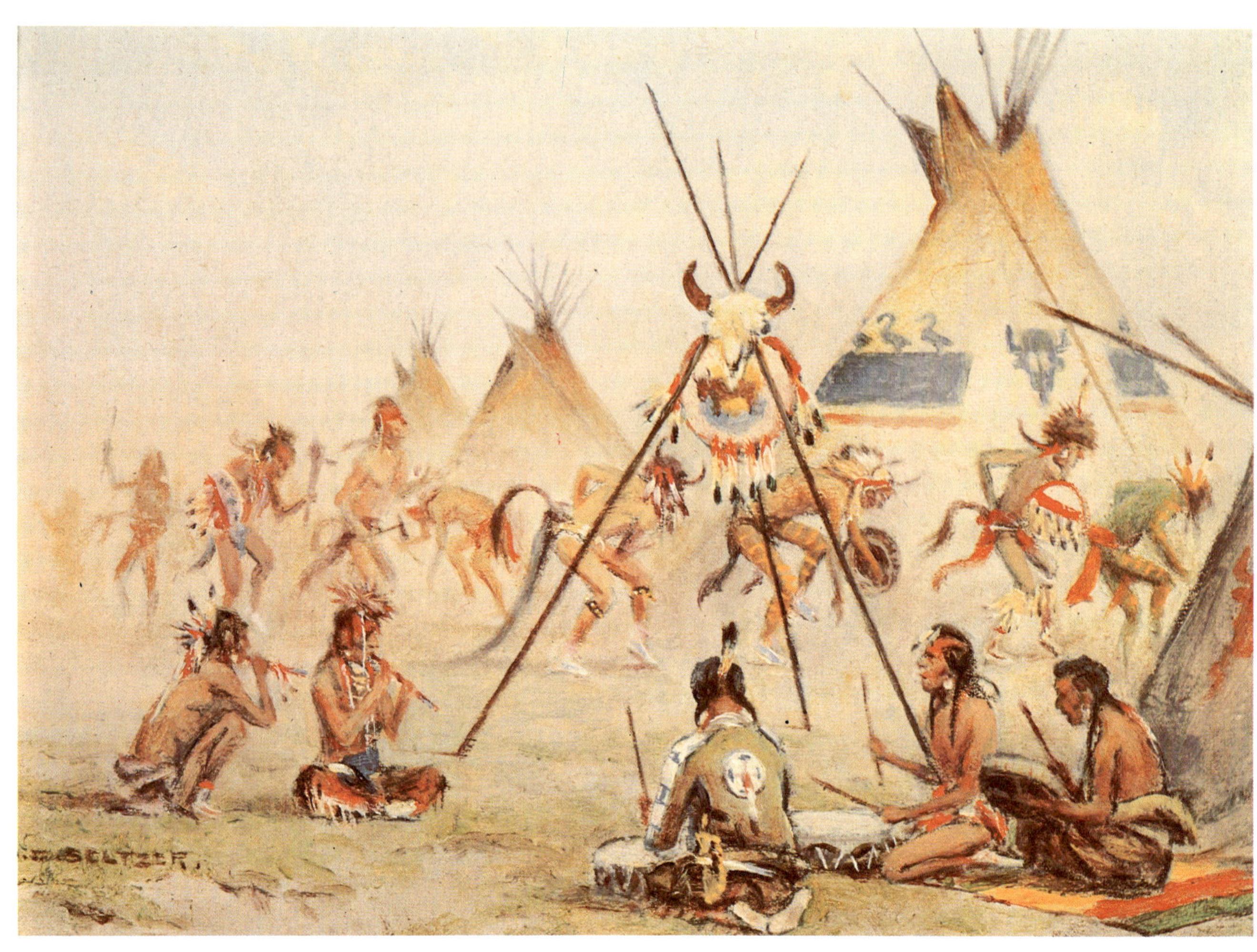

*The Buffalo Dance*
1934
Miniature oil

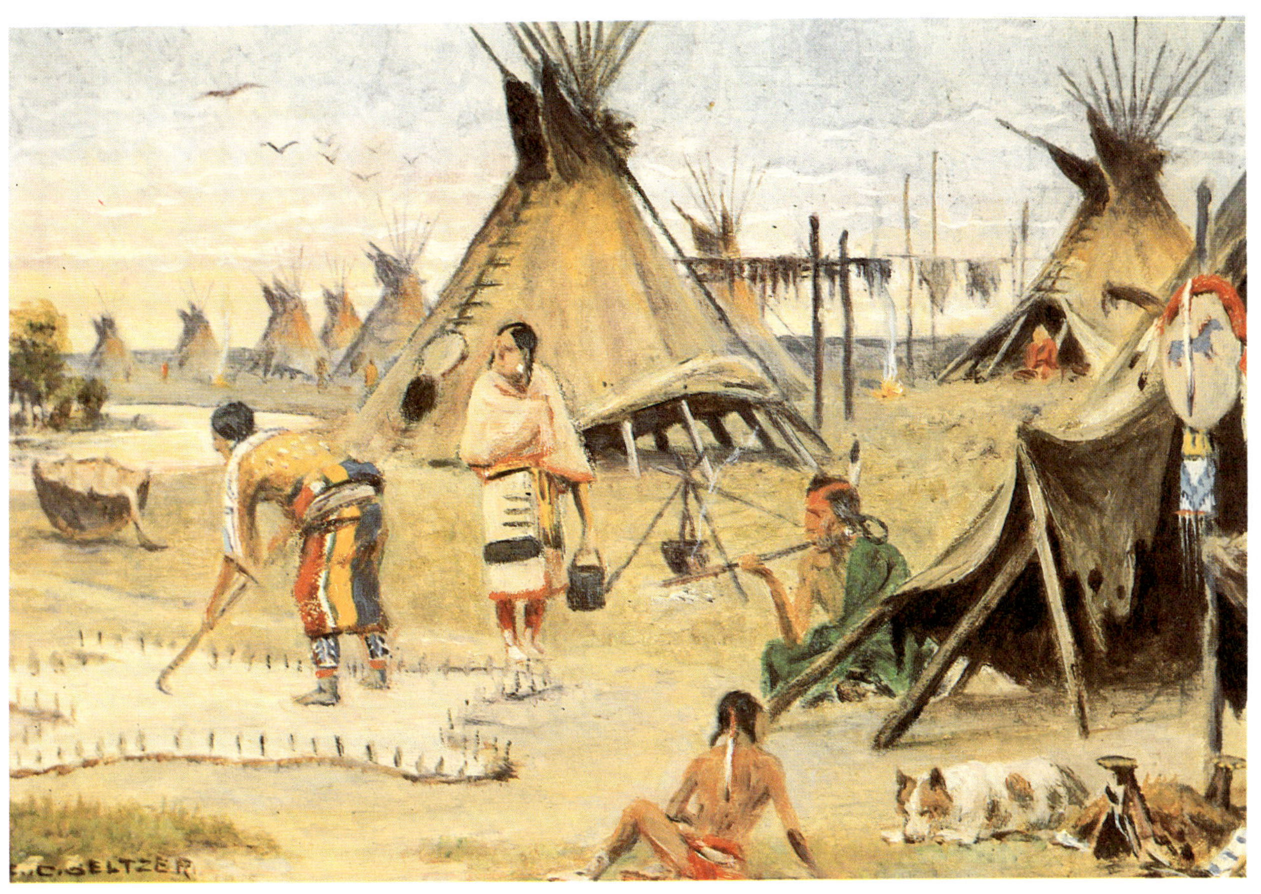

*Parfleching in Blackfoot Village*
1935
Miniature Oil

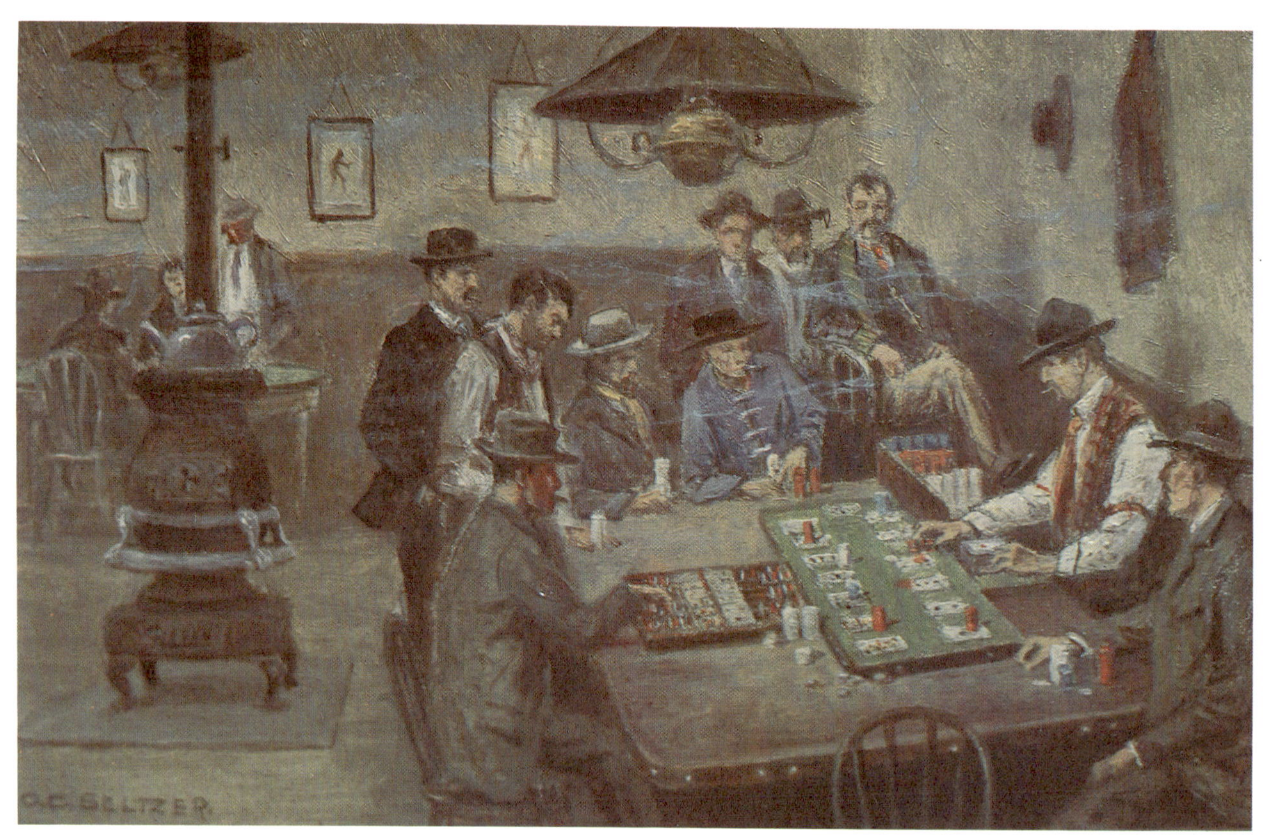

*Faro Layout in the Mint Saloon*
1934
Miniature oil

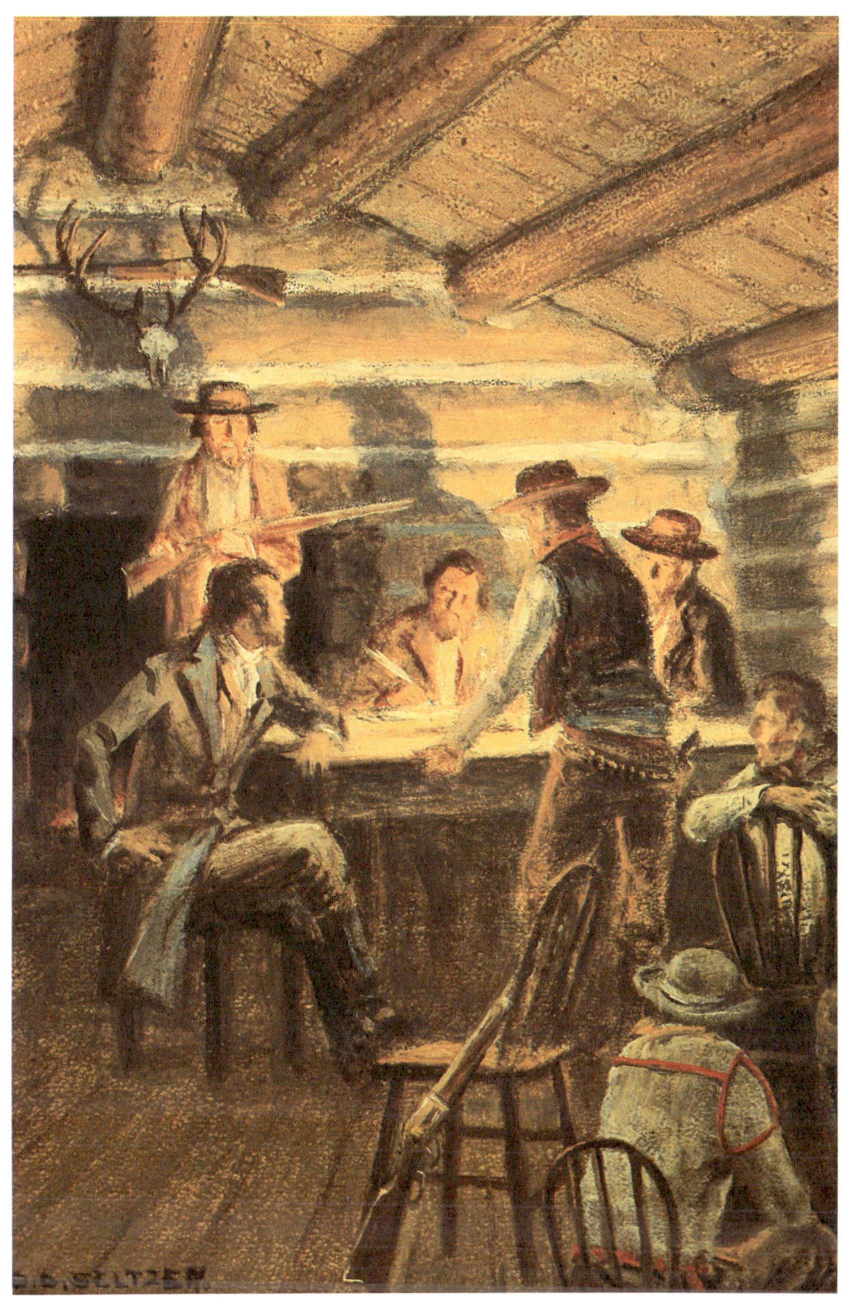

*Vigilantes' oath*
1934
Miniature oil

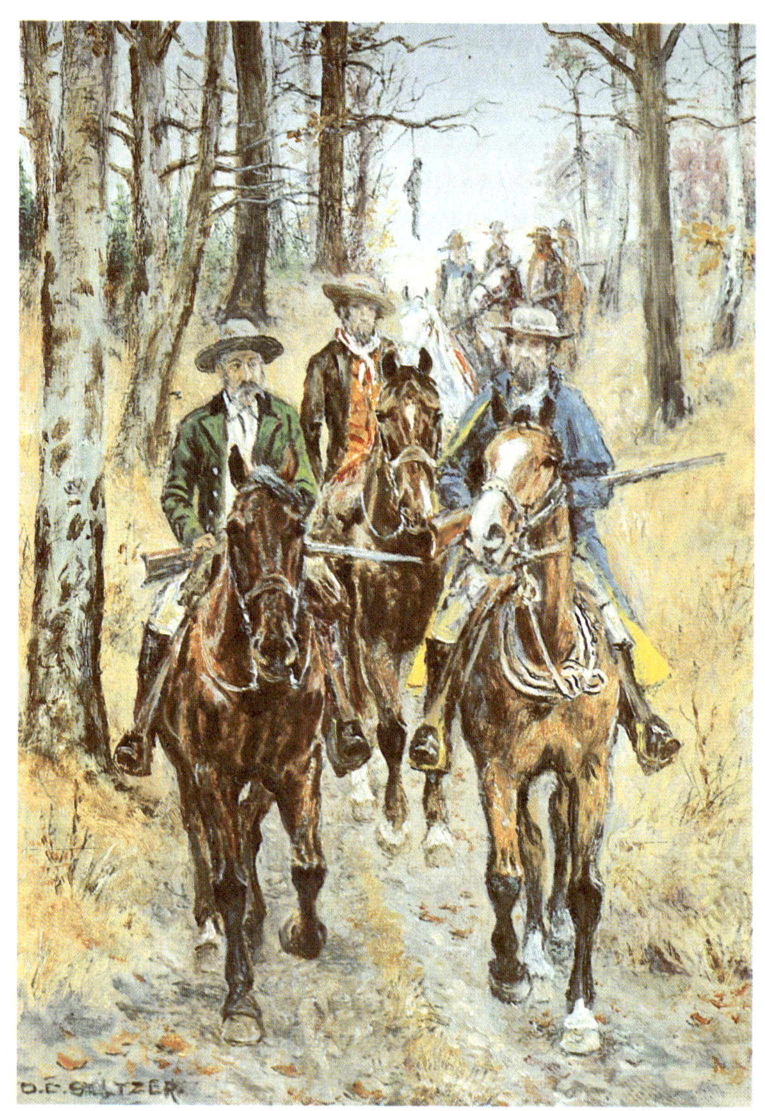

*Vigilante Ways*
1935
Miniature oil

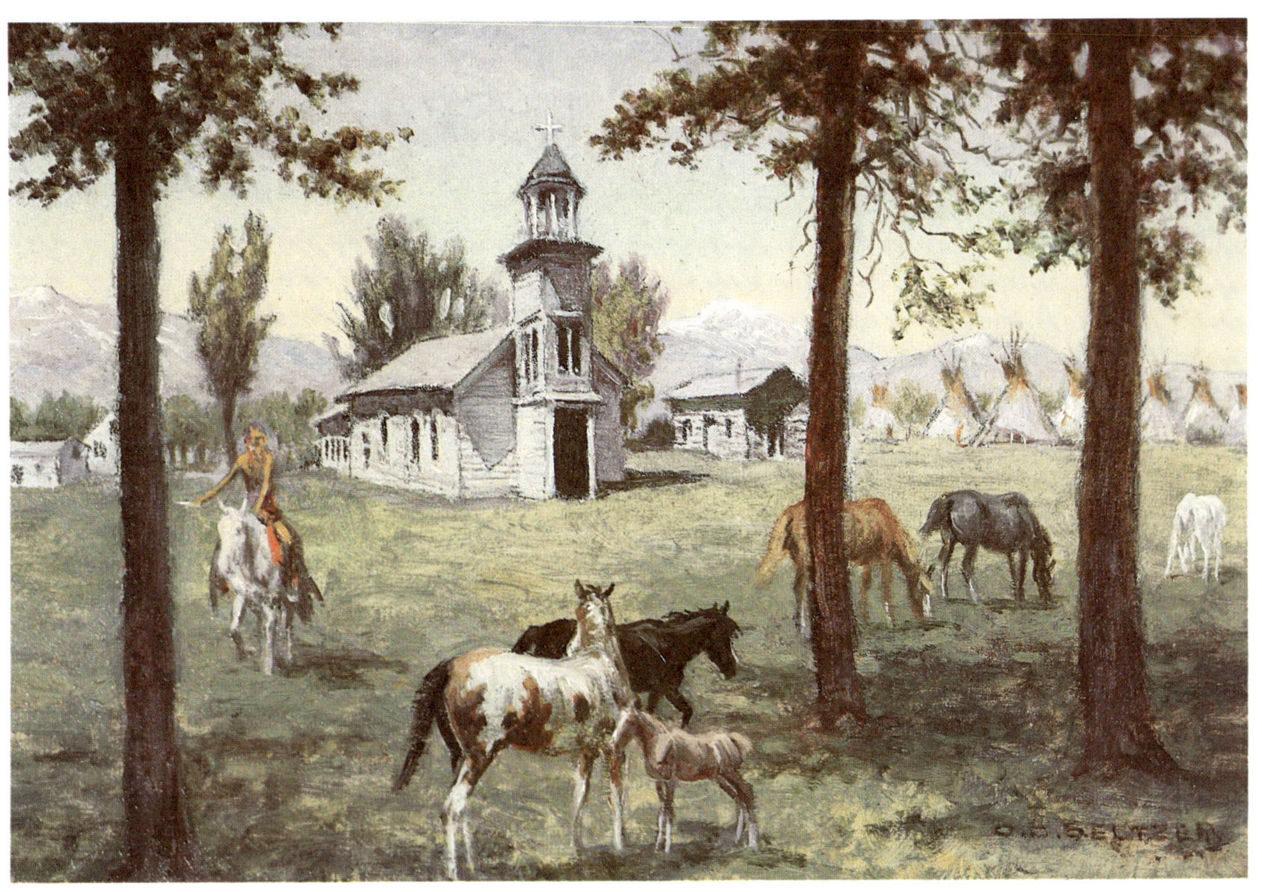

*Saint Mary's Mission*
1935
Miniature oil

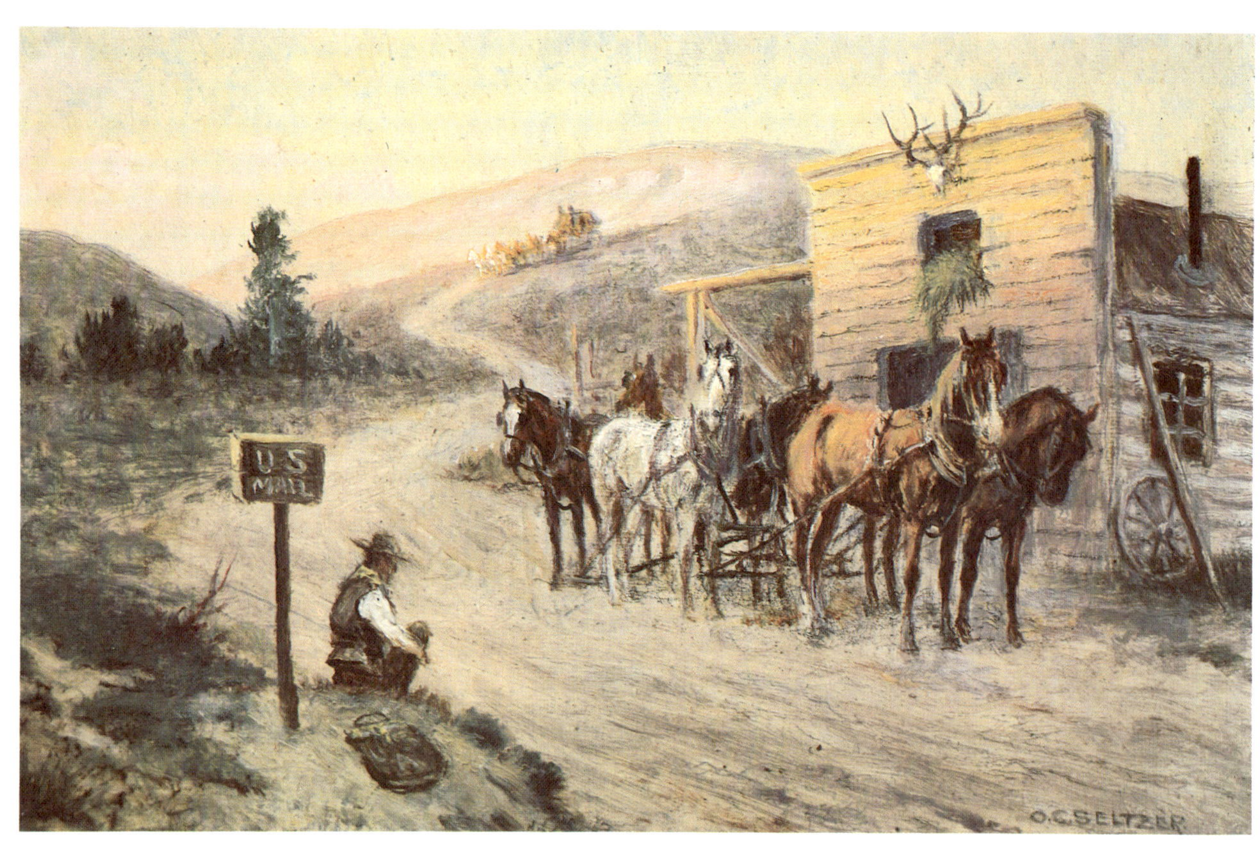

*The Swing Station at Box Elder*
1934
Miniature oil

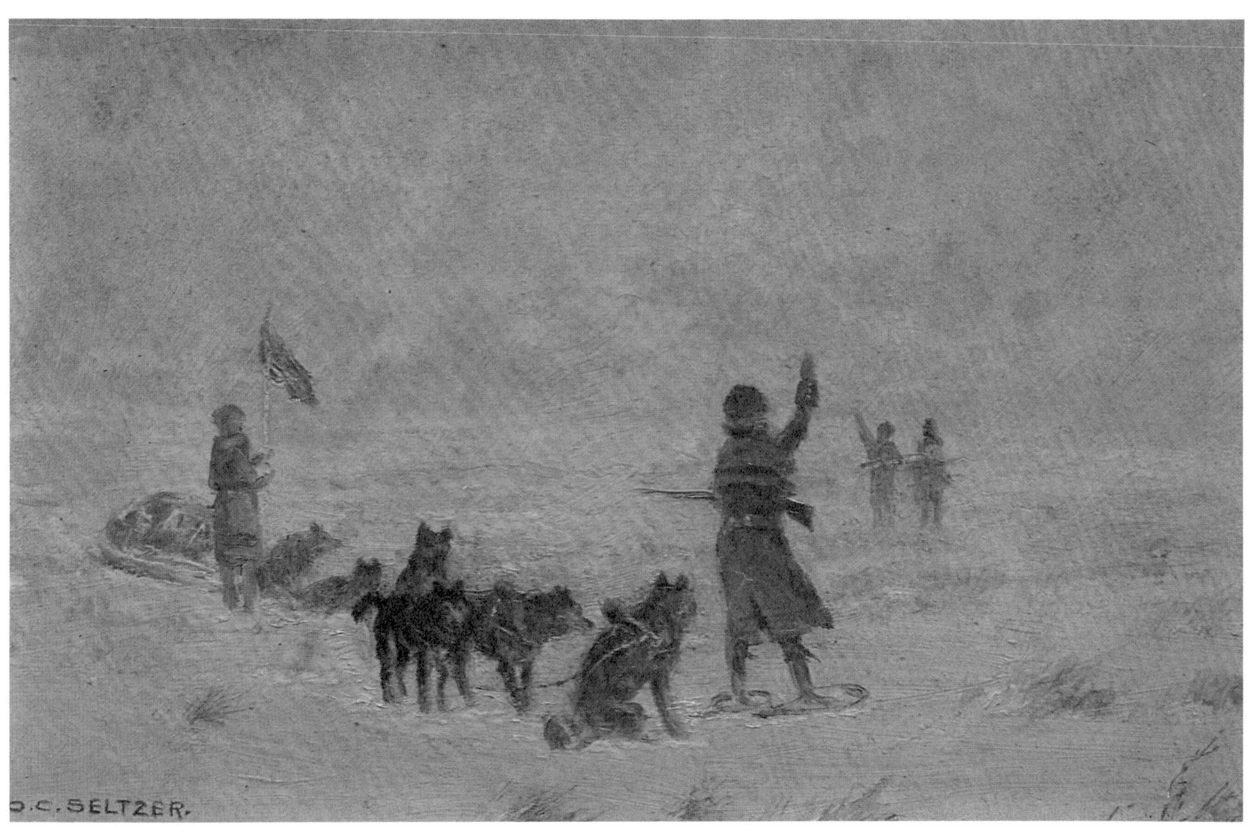


*Kenneth McKenzie*
1934
Miniature oil

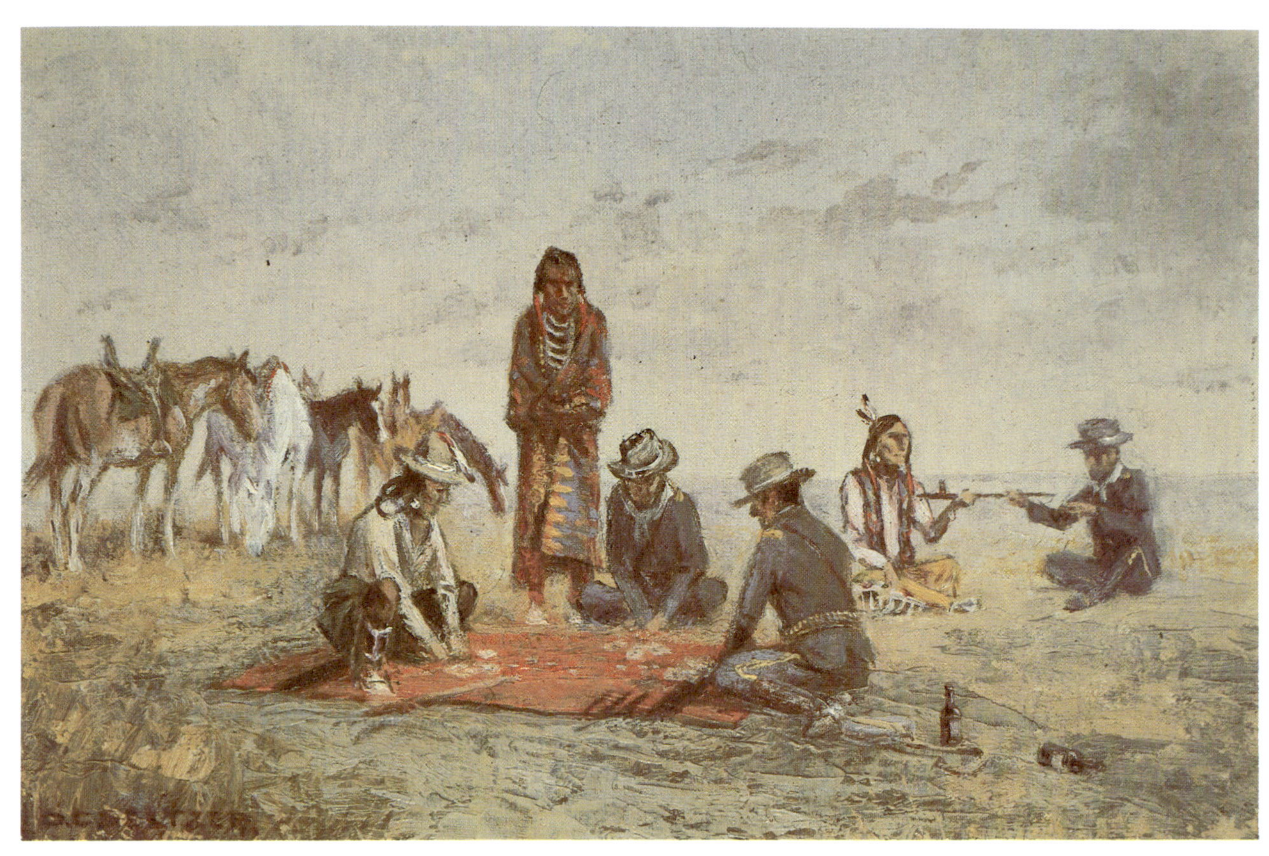

*The Parley*
1935
Miniature oil

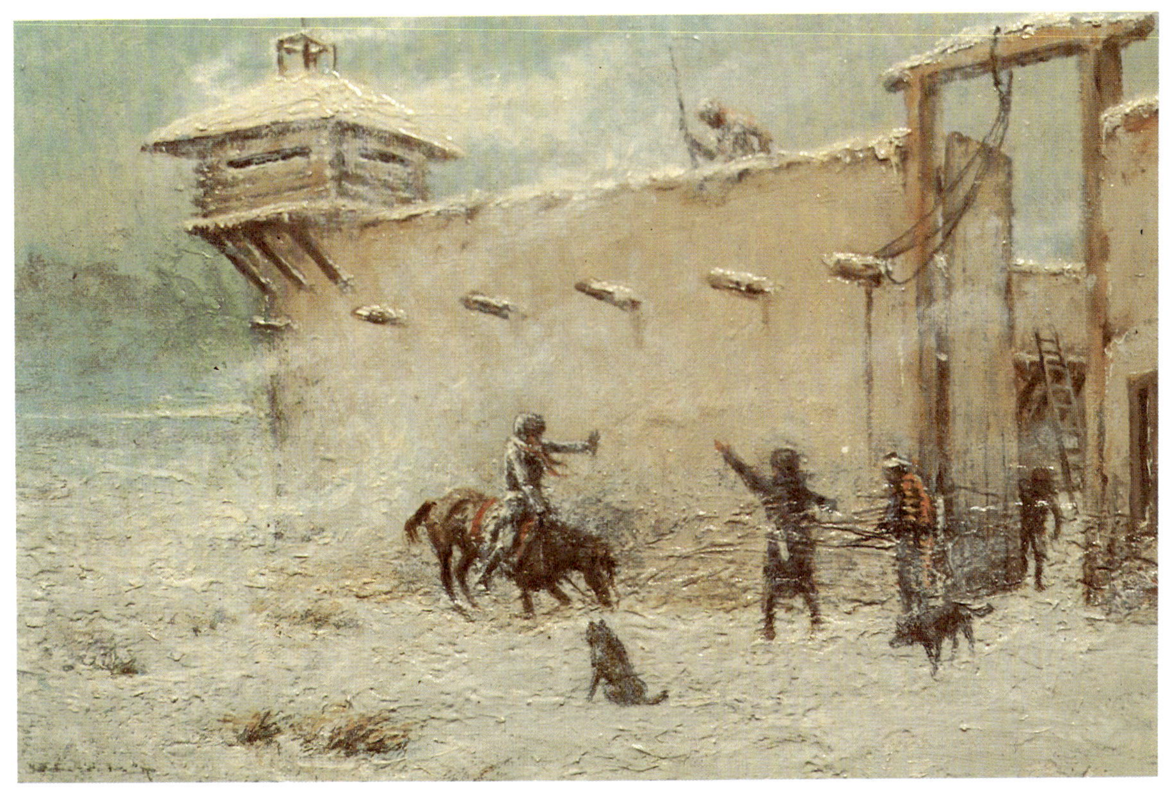

*Portugee Phillips' Arrival*
1934
Miniature oil

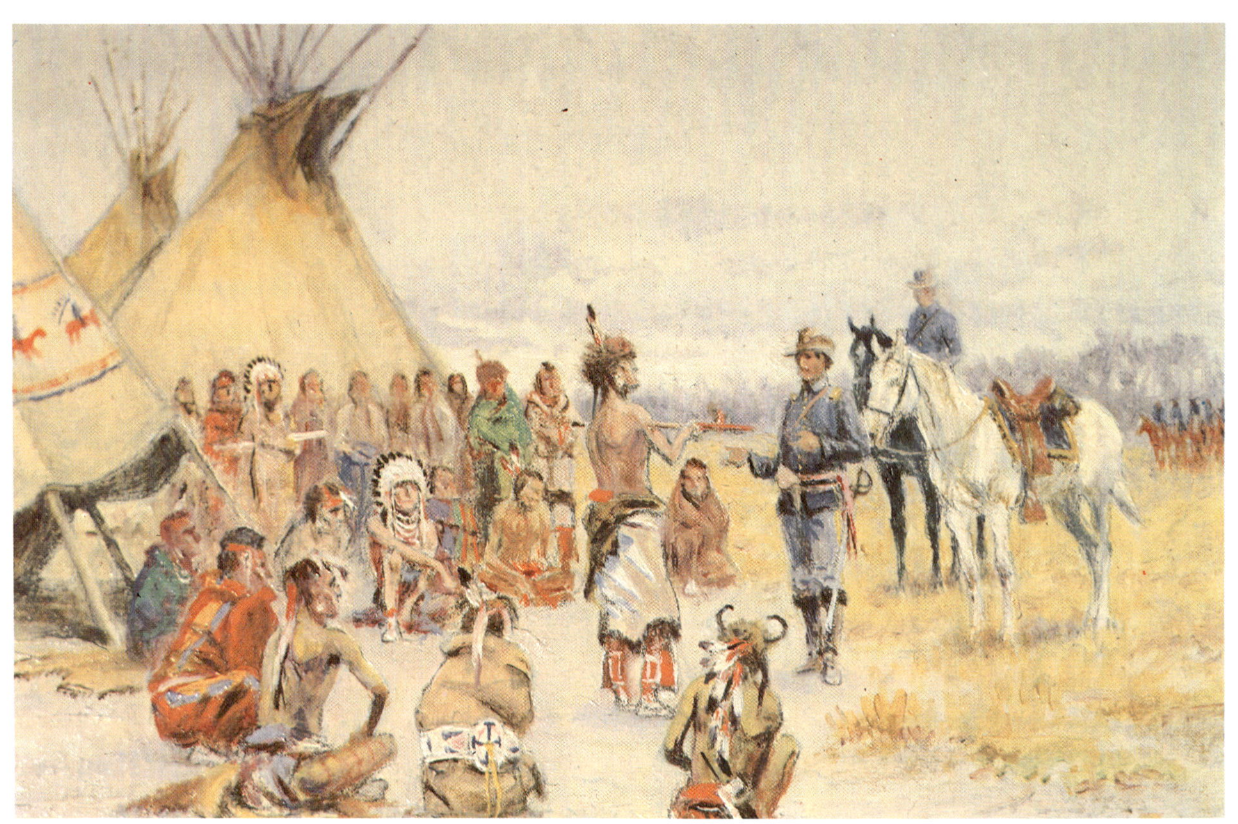

*The Pow-Wow*
1935
Miniature oil

Chapter 8
# Zeeview

While Olaf Seltzer was contentedly working on his Western Characters project in Montana, Phil Cole was making plans for the future housing of his collection, as well as for its expansion. By now, his fortune established, Cole was taking more interest in his acquisitions of western art and his historical documents than he was in his business. At forty-six he was contemplating early retirement to a place with plenty of room for his treasures and for his family. He wanted his son and daughters to have memories of a carefree childhood in the outdoors, a childhood such as he had known.

While he quietly looked around for the proper setting, Cole kept making improvements to the Forest Hills home to enhance the display of his paintings and sculptures. In the postscript to his voluminous letter ("or maybe it had better be called a book") to Olaf, dated September 26, 1928, he made a reference to one such change and spoke of another Seltzer visit:

> You are going to get a great kick out of seeing the new Russell Room which was not completed when you left. It will really almost be worth the trip to New York just to see it, as well as enjoy the library of Western things which is now getting to be quite worth while. For me your trip will be worth while, if nothing more than just for the pleasure of "chewing the fat" with you. . . .
>
> Tex Rickard is putting on a Rodeo at Madison Square Garden next week. It is not like our real Rodeos at home, nevertheless you would be surprised at how good it really is. Wish we could go together to it.

Nancy Russell came to New York that autumn and once again was a guest of the Coles. Phil, the peacemaker, mentioned her visit in a letter he wrote to Olaf on November 21:

> You would be surprised if you could have heard Nancy Russell the other day—she surely had quite a few nice things to say about you. You can be sure that I also repeated to her the fairness with which you always have remarked about her. You know that neither wastes any love on the other, and yet it is good for you both to realize that you are each of you fair to the other when out of hearing.

Cole repeatedly invited Seltzer to New York, usually with the bait of a specific task he wanted him to undertake. That Olaf was making arrangements for such a visit is indicated in a letter he wrote to Dr. Butler a week after Cole's November 21 letter. He informed Butler that he was sending him an oil and a watercolor, *Medicine Man*, with a vignette of "the old sweat-lodge and the Medicine Man driving out the evil spirit with his Tom-Tom." Olaf gently hinted for quick payment:

> Now Doc. I am *not rushing you*. You should know me by this time, but I am cleaning up all my loose ends for I had a letter from Phil yesterday, and may have to jump on a train for New York any day, you know how impulsive he is. As already understood between us, the 20 × 30 is 100.00, the frame 20.00 and the Medicine Man 10.00, making a total of 130.00 which you'll pay some time when it is convenient for you, for your face is good as hell, and I only wish you owed me more.

The proposed trip may have been prompted by the news that the Coles had bought a house from the Whitneys on twenty acres at Irvington-on-

Hudson just below Tarrytown and were planning to move in January.

"There will be a wonderful room for the pictures," Cole wrote excitedly. "All western in one room with 18 ft. ceilings and with Russell separately on the stair landing. You will enjoy seeing it for the pictures will show off much better." He added in jest, "Don't you want to buy the Forest Hills house?"

On December 9 Cole wired Seltzer: "WE ARE MOVING HOME AND PICTURES JANUARY FIRST AND IF POSSIBLE WANT YOU TO COME IMMEDIATELY STOP OTHERWISE ARRIVE HERE NO LATER THAN DECEMBER THIRTIETH STOP WIRE RUSH REPLY STOP WILL WIRE NECESSARY FUNDS ON YOUR ADVICE.—DOC."

Olaf made another preholiday trip to New York City (this was probably the trip, referred to earlier, on which changes were made on the DeSmet painting).

The manor house at Zeeview—the name Phil and Katharine Cole chose for their new home—sits comfortably astride the brow of a bluff overlooking the wide Hudson River and the "Tappan Zee." Spacious hallways link the more than twenty rooms. From the imposing bluff-colored house with its formal terrace, the land dips gently to the east and rises again in a gradual slope to the road. In the hollow lies a landscaped swimming pool. Beyond is a pond large enough for the children's canoes. By the pond Cole had erected an elaborate two-story playhouse for the children. He commissioned N. C. Wyeth to paint a scene over the playhouse mantelpiece (in due time he built a second playhouse especially for the girls).

Across the pond, on a hillside dotted with oaks, pines, and copper beeches, Cole supervised the building of a two-level stone studio with broad casement windows and a skylight. Although it was planned for Mrs. Cole's sculpturing, it would become Olaf Seltzer's haven during his visits to Zeeview. There the artist worked on many of the historical miniatures, changing details, adding finishing touches, and actually painting some of them under Cole's fascinated scrutiny.

Shortly after the move Cole retired to spend more time on his projects at Zeeview. He got out of the stock market to relieve himself of added responsibility and by so doing preserved his fortune against the stock-market crash of 1929.

During the Zeeview years Mrs. Cole enjoyed the Westchester County social whirl and continued her interest in the Broadway theater world. Not so her husband, who became more and more immersed in his own world above the Hudson. Kay Cole Worden, a sculptor like her mother, remembers her father as a shy, unpretentious man "who didn't travel in a 'set,' attended few parties—hated night clubs." She recalls:

*He built Zeeview to be a wonderland for us, and the ranch at Placid because the whole idea of building it fascinated him. Building and collecting were almost—his life.*

*He always told us we were "Montana blood" and reared us to be just "simple Montana folks." None of us had ever been to Montana, though, and living in surroundings somewhat like Buckingham Palace . . . it was difficult to achieve.*

*Living at Zeeview was like living at the Hilton. I never went into the kitchen. I was afraid of the chief cook, but the waitresses were nice to me. Our meals were prepared below and brought up to us in the playroom. Only Mother, Dad, and Aunt Alice [Ralston] ate below in the dining room.*

Mrs. Worden recalls her father's playful way of employing his bronzes for the children's pleasure at Easter: "I remember especially 'Coming Through the Rye' and 'The Stampede.'[1] We were always sure to find jelly beans hidden in the horses' mouths or behind the saddles of the riders on Easter morning when we came downstairs to hunt for Easter eggs."

Miss Ralston recalled how Dr. Cole had come by *Coming Through the Rye*, the famous bronze of four cowboys shooting it up on their way home from a Saturday night in town. He bought it from the Metropolitan Galleries. He found it in the foyer of the men's lavatory, an indication of the regard in which western themes were held at the time he began his collection.[2]

While the Coles were settling in at Zeeview, Olaf continued working in Montana on oils and watercolors for his expanding clientele and developing the Western Character series. Fifteen of the sketches were completed in 1929, along with two 11″ × 16″ oils, *The Smoke Boat* and *The Iron Trail*. These two would be the initial paintings in a new series, which Olaf was quietly planning for Cole, to commemorate modes of transportation.

Frank Leonard, of Butte, became another of Olaf's steady customers in 1929, buying three 20″ × 30″ oils, *Crow Scout*, *Moving Camp*, and *The Trail Boss*, and four smaller oils, three

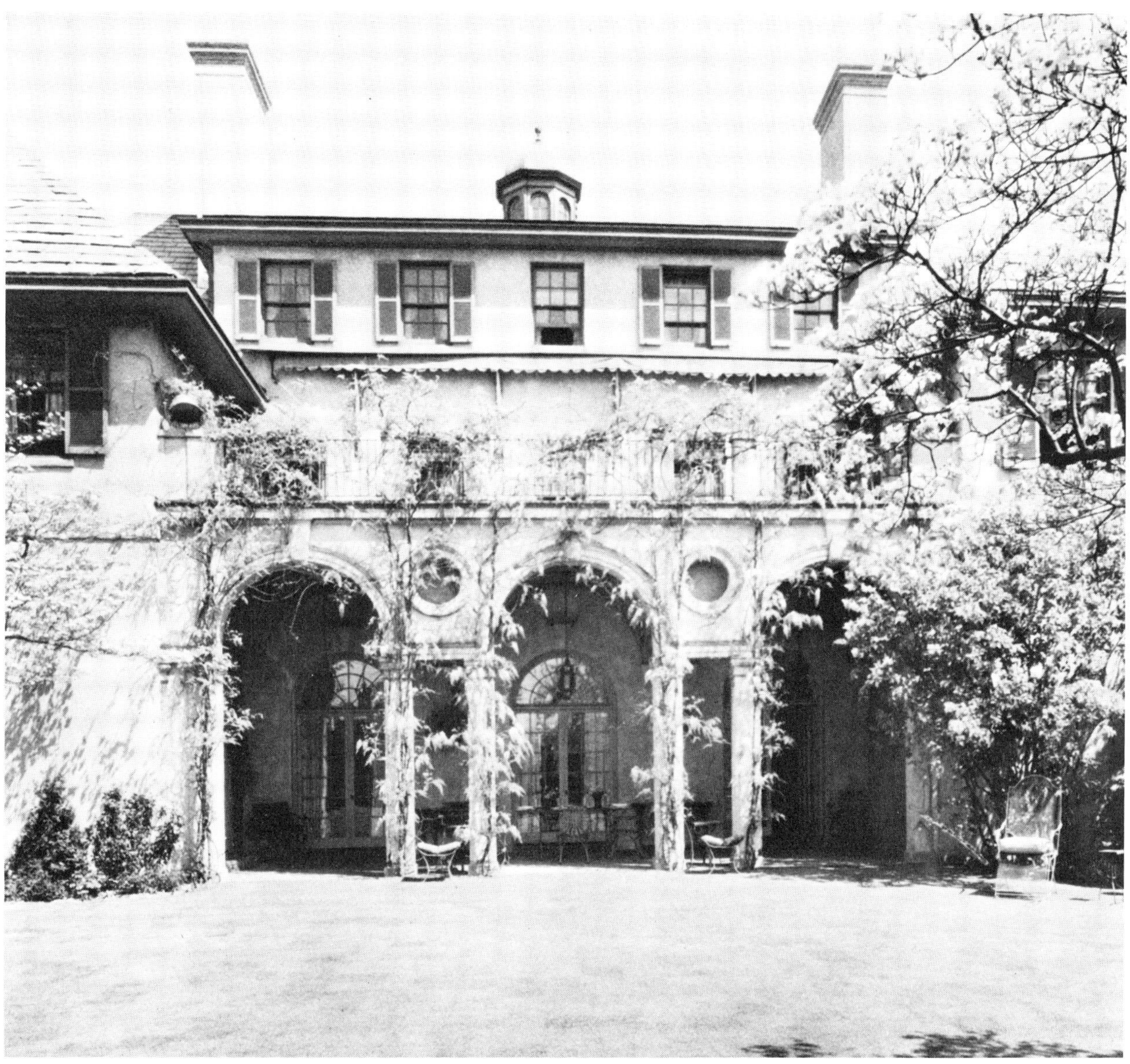

Zeeview, the Cole estate near Tarrytown, New York.
Courtesy of Gilcrease Library, Thomas Gilcrease Institute of American History and Art.

watercolors, and some animal pictures of unspecified medium. Bill Marks, the Seattle insurance broker and Olaf's former pack-trip companion, bought two 20″ × 30″ oils: *A Dangerous Ringtail* and *The Waterhole*, for $100 each (it was typical of Seltzer, for old times' sake, to sell to Marks at less than his price for new customers). The largest oil Olaf sold in 1929 was a 24″ × 36″ called *Mountain Pasture*, painted for W. H. Hoover, of Butte. A man named Meyerdirk paid him $250 for a 24″ × 30″ oil, *Blackfoot Scouts*.

A few months after the Coles moved into their new home, Phil had some additional exciting news to share with Olaf. On April 21, 1929, *The Disputed Trail*, a 20″ × 30″ oil featuring a grizzly bear confronting a pair of horsemen and their pack train on a mountain trail, was printed in full color in the Sunday edition of the *New York World* as

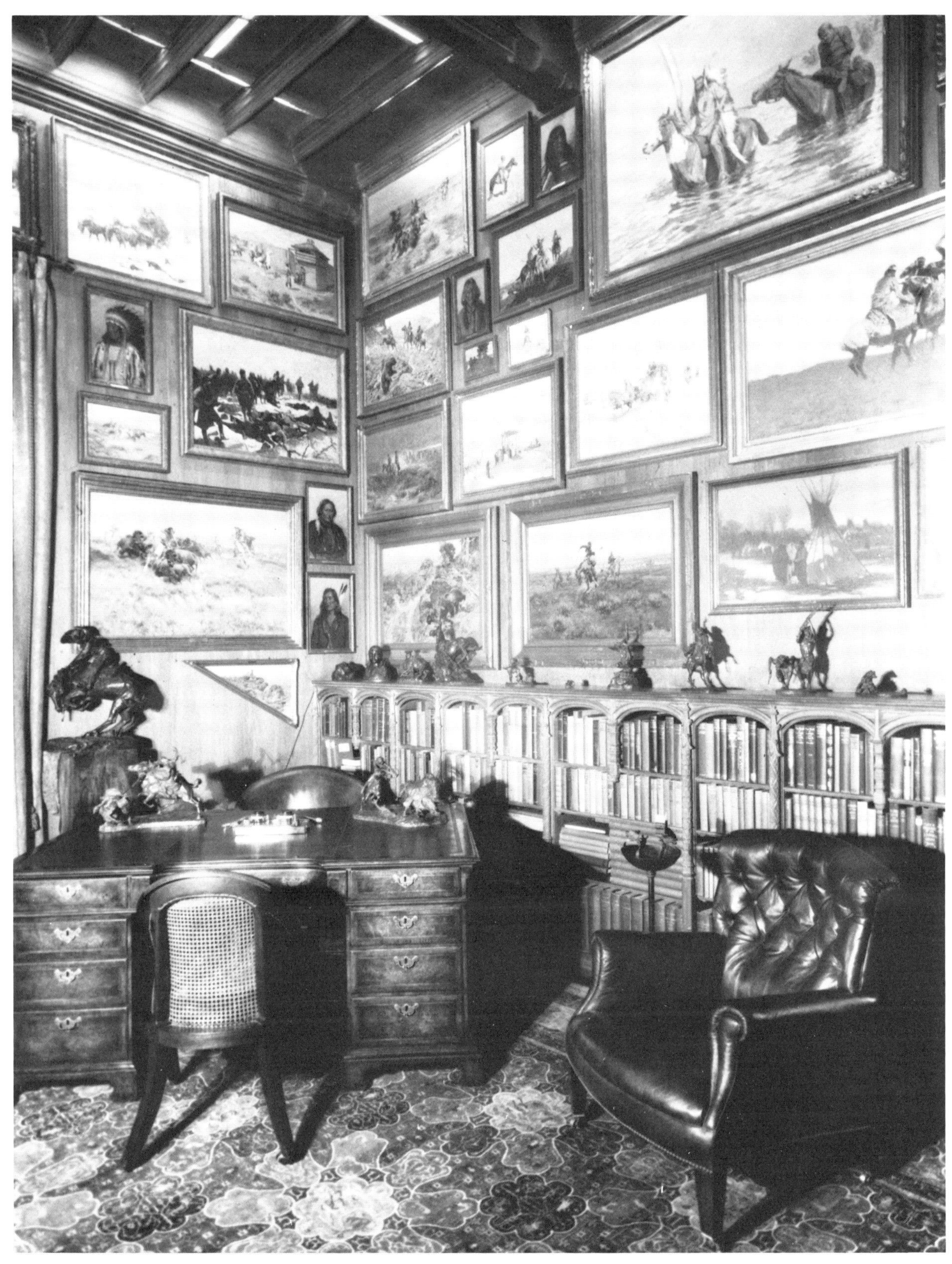

Library, Zeeview.
Courtesy of Gilcrease Library.

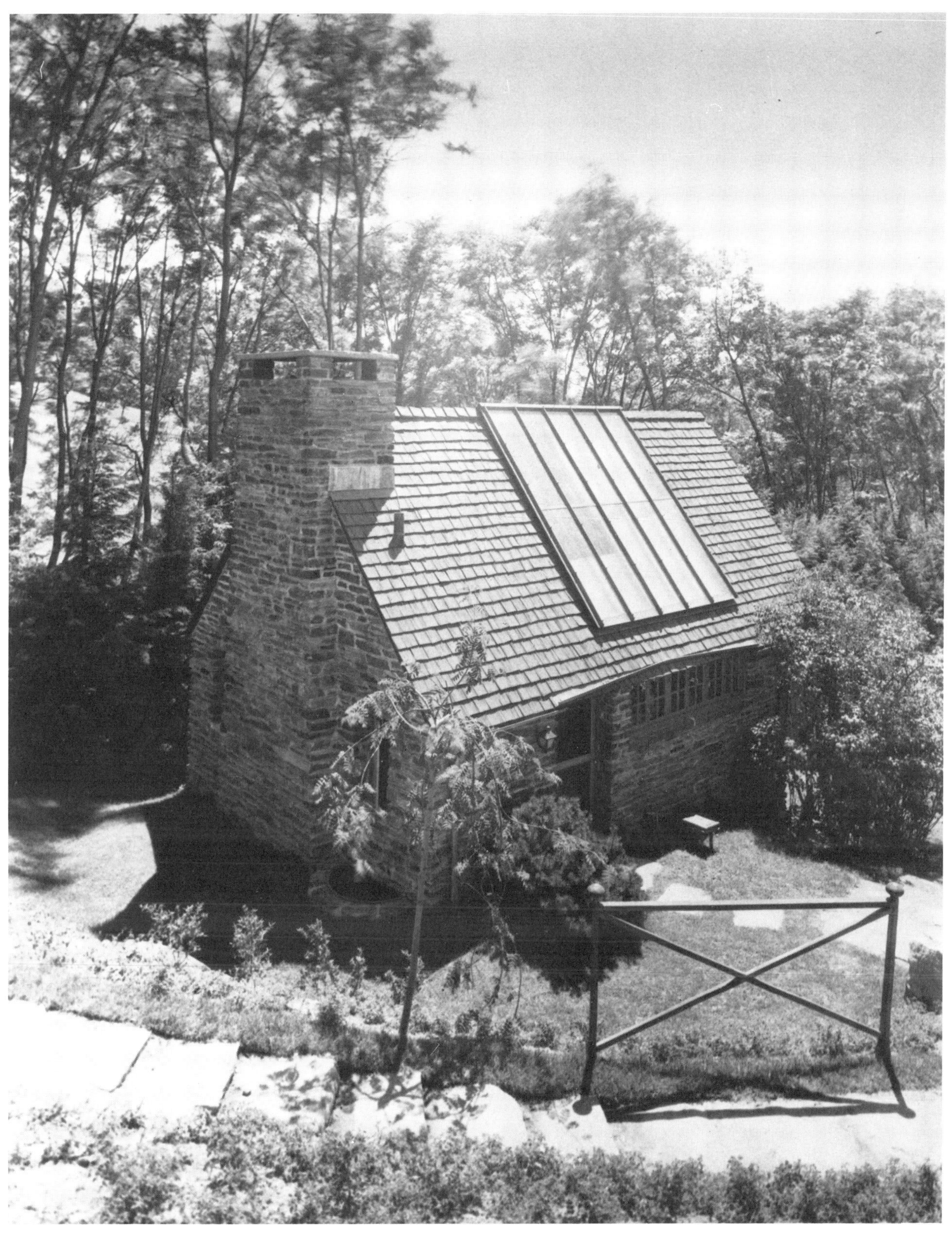

Zeeview studio.
Courtesy of Gilcrease Library.

the eighth in a series of "frontier pictures by famous artists... reproduced from originals in the collection of Dr. Philip G. Cole." The caption beneath the eight-column color reproduction read: "Difference of opinion over the right of way on a narrow path through a mountain range. The grizzly, hitherto the undisputed master of the rocky citadel moves to attack the human invader, whose pack animals start a dash for safety."

Remington's *Pony Express*, Schreyvogel's *The End*, and paintings by Sharp and Russell were included in the group reproduced in the *World* during the spring of 1929. "A good many thousand people are going to see this in color and it will not hurt your reputation at all," the jubilant Cole wrote Olaf. "When the opportunity presents I will again get them to take more of your things. I have already suggested... the little Lewis and Clarke...."

During 1930, Olaf Seltzer recorded for the first time the sale of one of his works, *C. M. Russell and Red Bird*, to S. A. (Sid) Willis for the Mint Saloon. It was not the first Seltzer painting in the Mint's collection; in the early twenties Olaf had painted a mural-sized pair of oils that hung behind the bar, but he had made no record of that unsigned effort. Willis had bought into the Mint in 1908, after ten years as a partner at the Maverick Bar. He had assembled an outstanding collection of western art and artifacts at the Mint, including at least a dozen Seltzer oils. Soon after Russell's death Willis had printed the *Souvenir Illustrated Catalog*, which showed photographs of the Russell paintings and sculptures by Charles A. Beil, but only listed the Seltzer pictures. This omission is partly explained in a brief description under *The Disputed Trail*: "by O. C. Seltzer, another Great Falls product, now located in New York."[3]

Other Seltzers in the Mint collection at the time the catalog was issued were *A U.S. Doughboy in France*, *Roping the Calf*, *The King's Mirror* (depicting a lion drinking), *Indian Scouting Party*, *Disputed Water Hole*, *The Lone Scout*, *On the Lookout*, *Indian Warrior*, *Indian Chief*, and *Chas. M. Russell and His Horse, Monty*.[4] Some of these were purchased by Willis from previous owners rather than from the artist. After the sale of the Mint collection to New York art dealers in 1960, the two paintings behind the bar were sold to Robert F. Rockwell, of Corning, New York, who mounted them in one broad picture, 4½′ × 25′, for permanent display in the Rockwell

Corning Museum. The Mint catalog lists the companion bar paintings as *The Watchers* and *The Herd*, describing the first as "Indians ... watching the Buffalo Herd and ... no doubt laying plans for killing several of them for meat." The second depicts buffalo going to water at sunrise, along with several antelope. A wolf follows, "expecting perhaps to catch a buffalo calf to kill for his dinner."

Twenty-three Western Character sketches for Phil Cole and at least three additional watercolors of Charlie Russell caused Olaf to spend considerable time working in media other than oil in 1930. The Russell portraits he recorded as *The Buckskin Kid, 1886*, *C. M. Russell, 1902*, and *The Cowboy Artist, 1917*. Olaf sold them for fifty dollars each, a fact he duly noted, although neglecting to mention to whom the sales were made.

Doing the portraits of Russell may have inspired Olaf to take time out for an illustrated letter to Doc:

> Dear Doc:—Sometime ago I asked you about your Calico Pinto saddle horse—"Patches"—I am pleased to hear that he still has a good home. In my mind I was comparing his lot with that of the Prairie Cayuse, forwhile the horse of the plains has plenty to eat and drink, still his life is just one damn thing after another. The name—"Philip"—means—A lover of horses and that's you Doc—

Dated June 12, 1930, the letter was decorated in shades of brown, soft green, and yellow, and featured a grazing horse and colt, a dog, rattlesnakes sunning on a rock, and an animal skeleton. The envelope, featuring horses and a nursing colt, is one of the most beautiful that Seltzer painted.

In October, Olaf decorated a letter with a painting of a rope-wielding cowboy and sent it to his patron "to say hello and let you know I am still up and doing." Three weeks later he mailed Cole a heavily decorated letter featuring stylized buffalo tracks, an Indian shield, and other trappings: "Herewith a little decorative stuff," he wrote using one of the main Indian symbols that of the Buffalo... You will also see the coup stick, the Medicine Man's emblem of mysterious authority and power" (while working at Zeeview, Olaf gave Cole two sheets he had covered with details of Indian trappings for use in his paintings. Cole framed them and added them to his collection.)

Olaf prepared an elaborate letter on January 7,

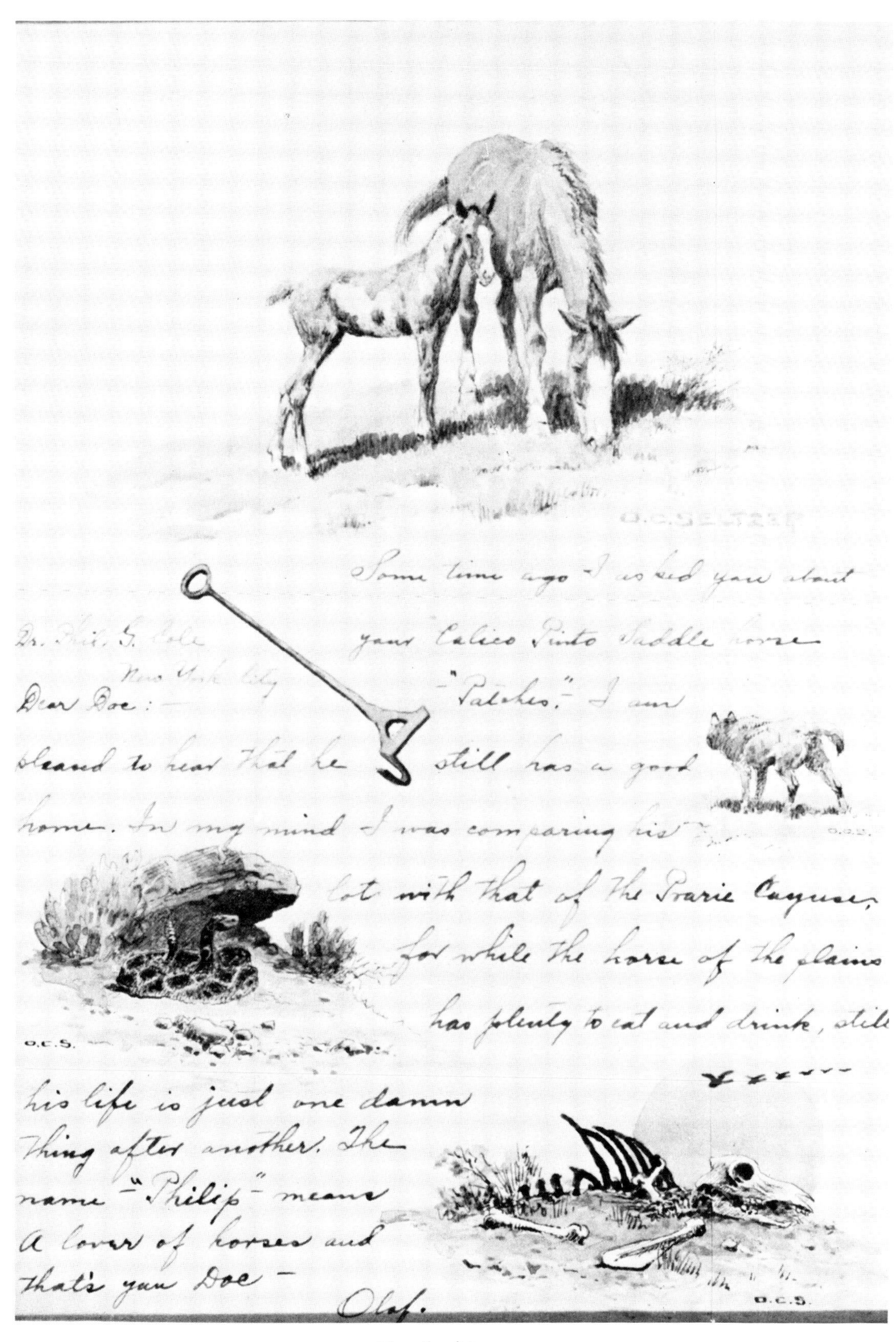


*'Patches' Letter*
1930
Watercolor and ink, 10″ × 7″

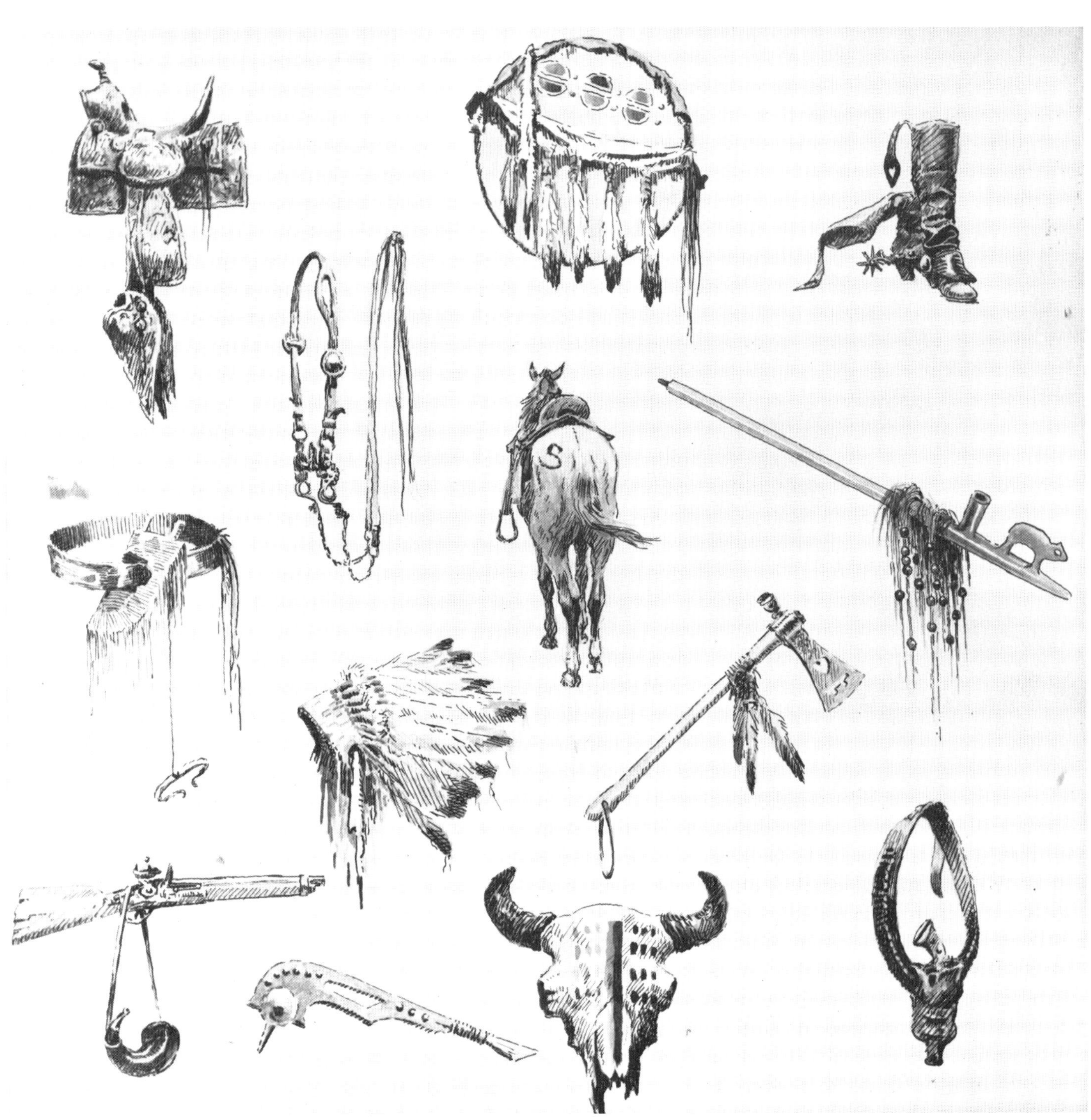

*Indian Trappings*
1930
Watercolor, 11½″ × 11½″

1931, to thank Cole for his Christmas gift, a copy of *Good Medicine*, the collection of C. M. Russell's illustrated letters, including one that Russell, only a month before his death, had written to Cole. In it he extended greetings to Seltzer. In his thank-you letter Olaf again used his poetic statement about the prairie, above a scene showing three Indians surveying the open land. Of the book Olaf wrote, "As a speller, he is not so good, but as a humorist and artist, 'Ah-wah-Kos' is hard to beat." He illustrated the envelope with a mounted Indian holding a shield and coup stick.

Late in April Olaf received a postcard from Doc, who reported on a visit to Spain: "Have taken in two bullfights... also seen some horsemenship stuff by Spanish cowboys in Andalusia what would make some of our Montana punchers open their eyes.... We are bringing home two German dogs and two Spanish burros. You see we travel with our own kind."

Olaf's answer is one of the more strongly colored of his illustrated letters. There is a bullfight scene at the top of the sheet. Below, a señorita with roses in her hair leans from a balcony of elaborate wrought iron. Between the two drawings the artist wrote: "Just a few words to welcome you back to the land of the free? It looks to me that you just got out of Spain in time. The national pastime of Spain is playing the guitar and Bull-fighting while in the U.S. of A. spearing dollars and Bull-peddling are more in vogue." He closed by mentioning that he was at work on the watercolor of Doc, astride Patches, referring to the Western Character sketch *Owner of the PGC*.

Seltzer's notes show a drastic drop in his sales in 1931 and 1932, as the impact of the economic depression was felt nationwide. The leisure time afforded by fewer commissions may have given Olaf the impetus to begin, on May 25, the sixteen illustrated letters that comprise a fascinating record of an artistic work in progress.

Illustrated letters had been in vogue for a hundred years or more before Seltzer's time. Joshua Reynolds and his contemporaries in the late Georgian school sent them. James McNeill Whistler touched up his correspondence with little sketches and frequently signed his letters, as he did some paintings, with a strange-looking butterfly. Van Gogh added rough sketches to his letters to explain what he was working on. The artists of the American West, including Remington, Russell, Borein, Will James, and Joe

Scheuerle, used pen and ink and watercolors to decorate their correspondence and arouse the interest of art buyers.

What puts Seltzer's letters to his patron in a class by themselves is that sixteen of them, in one thirteen-month period, were written on a coordinated theme. For Olaf had a project dear to his heart: he wanted to paint a series of $11'' \times 16''$ oils that would commemorate the role of transportation in opening the West for settlement.

The Early Western Travelogue letters were part sales campaign and part expression of gratitude for a steady flow of orders from Cole during the Depression. In some Olaf worked out details to be incorporated in his scenes; others, sent after completion of a transportation painting, served as commentary on the theme. He referred to each letter as an "opus" and numbered it in relation to the position it held in his survey of transportation development, rather than to the order in which it was painted.

Opus 1 dealt with *The Travaux* (later, Olaf corrected the spelling to *travois*). He depicted an Indian woman and a horse-drawn travois in the largest sketch, with smaller vignettes of a dog pulling a lighter burden and a papoose swaddled in a carrying board.

"This letter is the forerunner of my next small Travelogue oil... depicting a very early mode of Prairie travel," he wrote Doc. "With the Travaux and its broom-tail Indian cayuse are always associated, in my mind, Rawhide Parfleche Bags, dogs with small travaux packed with lodge pegs, and many beady-eyed children."

A month later Olaf sent "Travelogue of the Prairie—'The Iron Trail' (Opus 7)" in appreciation for his patron's earlier purchase of the painting that commemorated the railroads:

*Your purchasing the picture... means "Good Medicine" to me. The Indian in the foreground of the picture giveing the track a careful once over, will sure reverse the Good Medicine verdict when he reports his findings to the wise men waiting in the background, and will sure give a decision on the white man's devil work as "Bad Medicine." Throwing the switch on this little Railroad scene and closing with kind regards....*

The "Last Chance or Bust (Opus 3)" letter, dated only two days later, featured two prairie schooners. Last Chance was the name given the

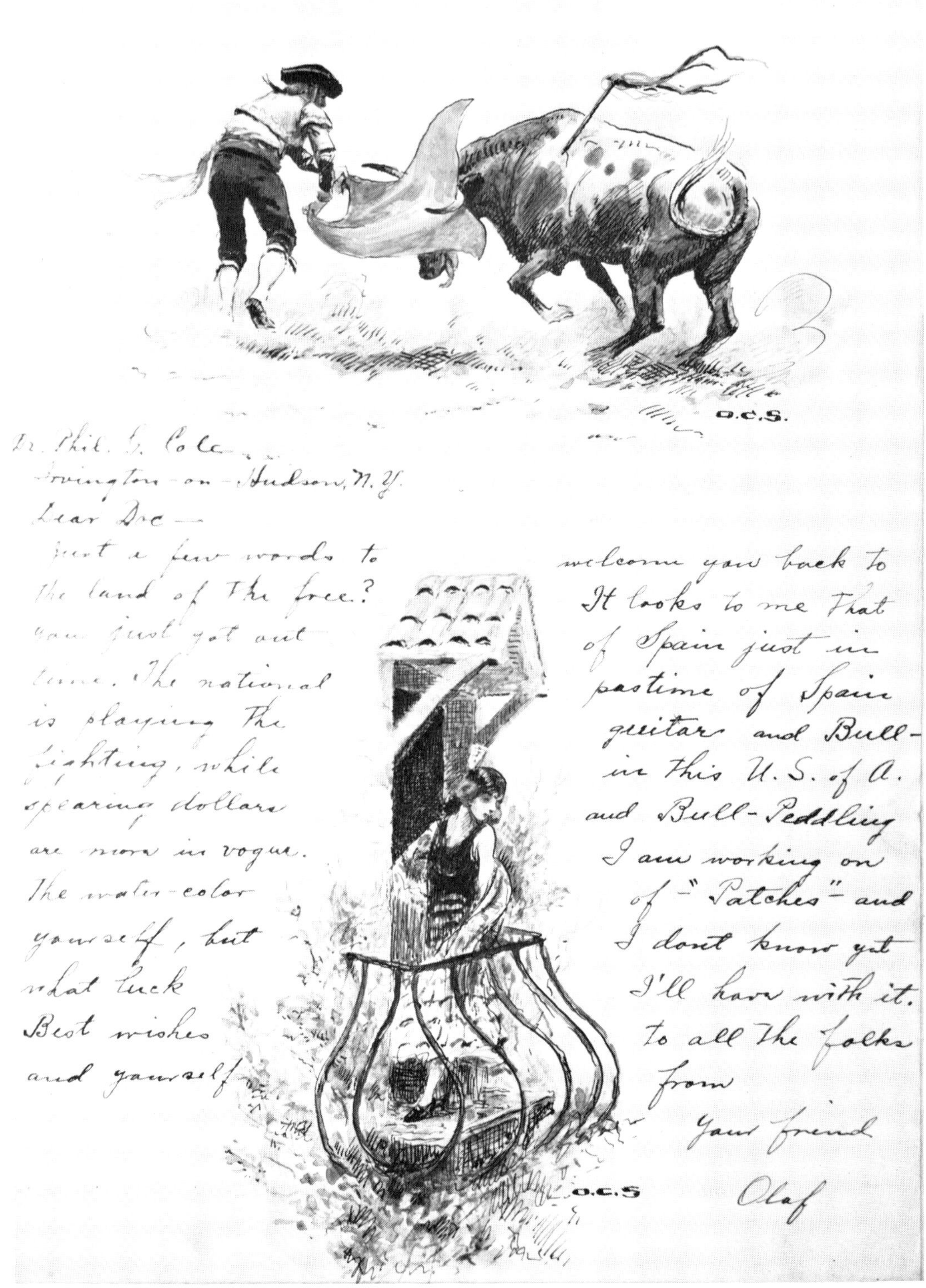


*Letter About Spain*
1931
Watercolor and ink, 11″ × 7″

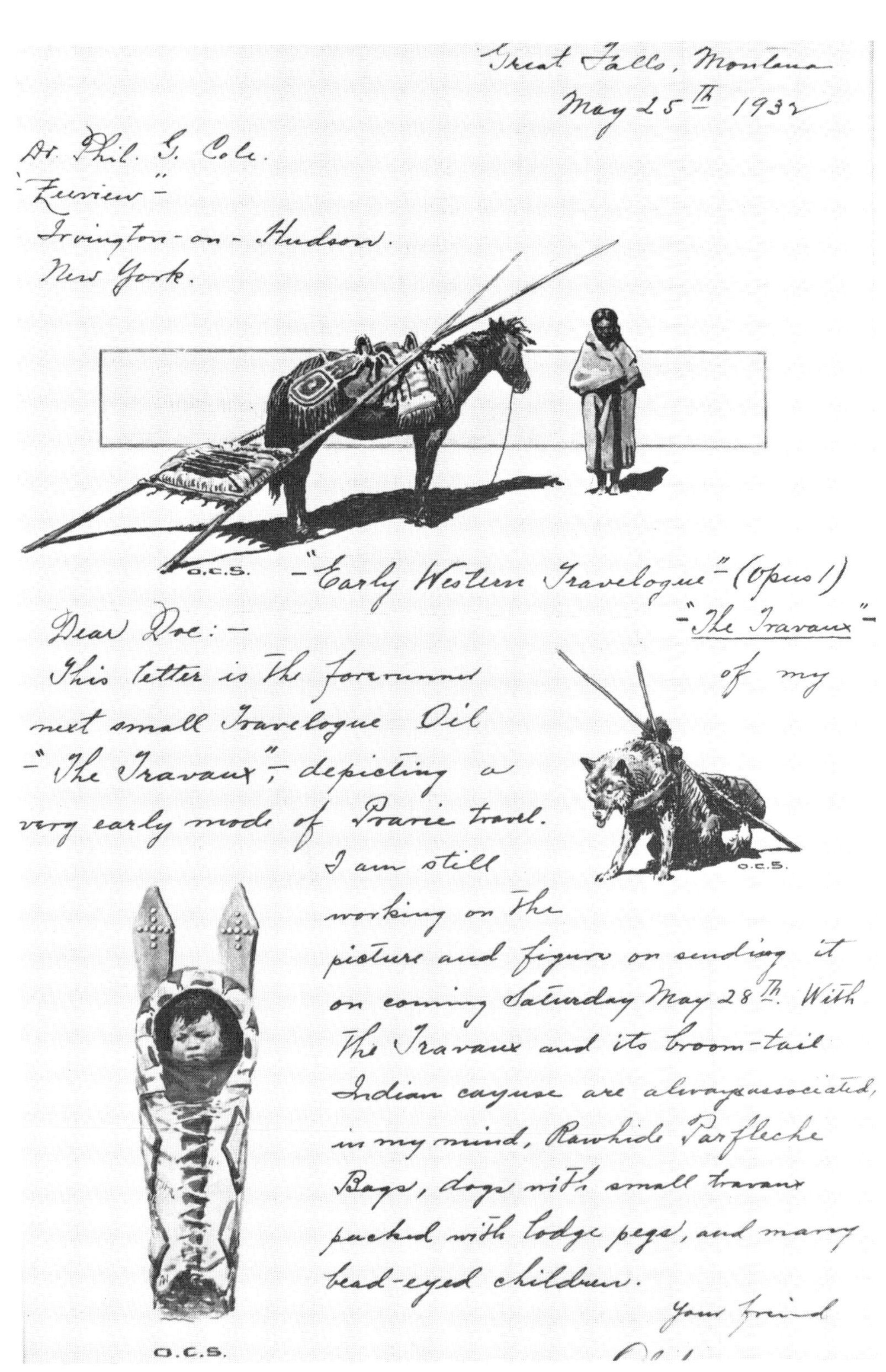


*The "Travaux" Letter*
1932
Watercolor and ink, 10½″ × 7″

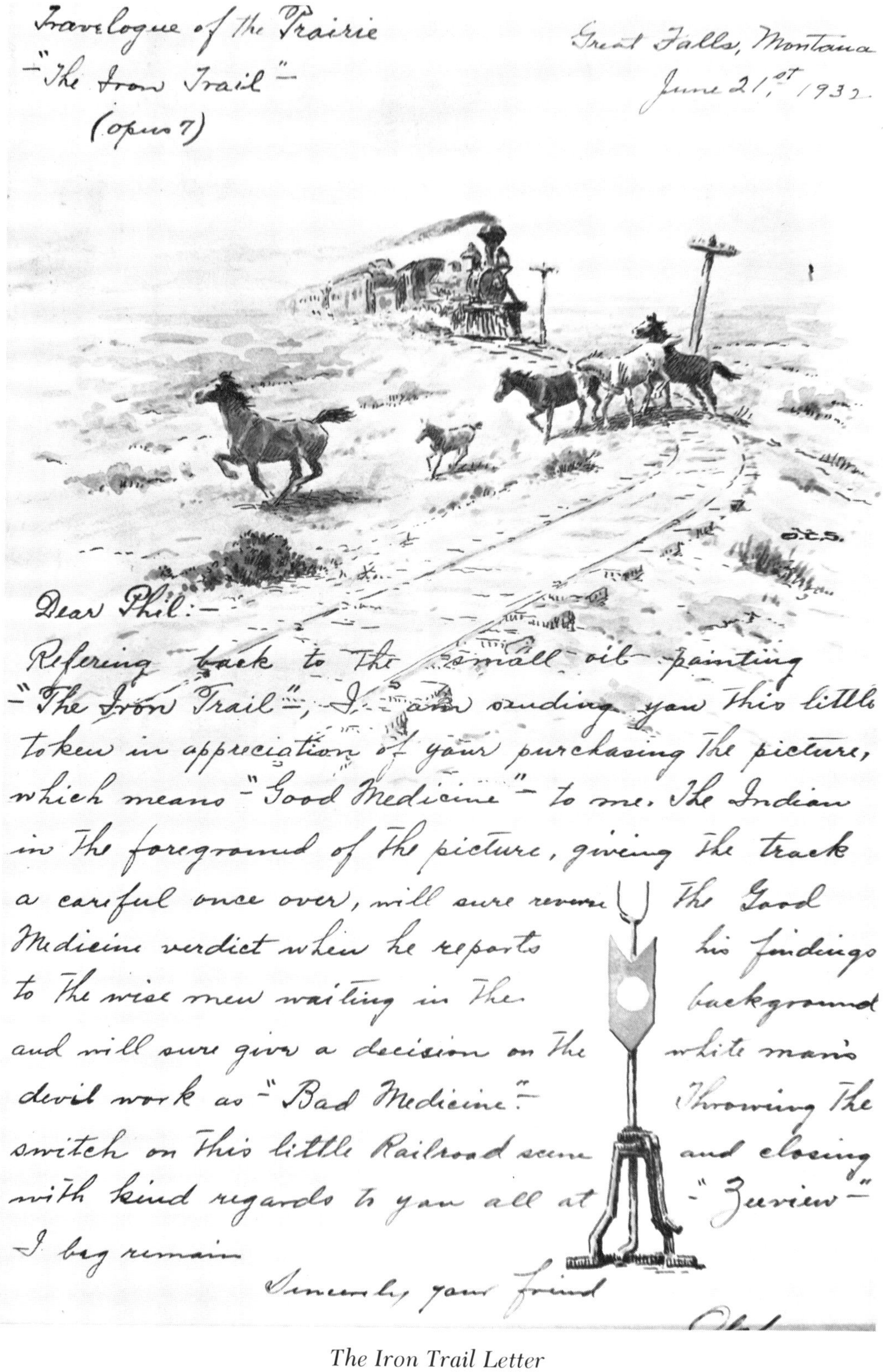

Travelogue of the Prairie
"The Iron Trail"
(opus 7)

Great Falls, Montana
June 21st, 1932

Dear Phil:—

Refering back to the small oil painting "The Iron Trail", I am sending you this little token in appreciation of your purchasing The picture, which means "Good Medicine" to me. The Indian in The foreground of The picture, giving the track a careful once over, will sure reverse The Good Medicine verdict when he reports his findings to The wise men waiting in The background and will sure give a decision on The white man's devil work as "Bad Medicine" Throwing The switch on this little Railroad scene and closing with kind regards to you all at "Zurview" I beg remain

Sincerely your friend

*The Iron Trail Letter*
1932
Watercolor and ink, 10″ × 7″

126

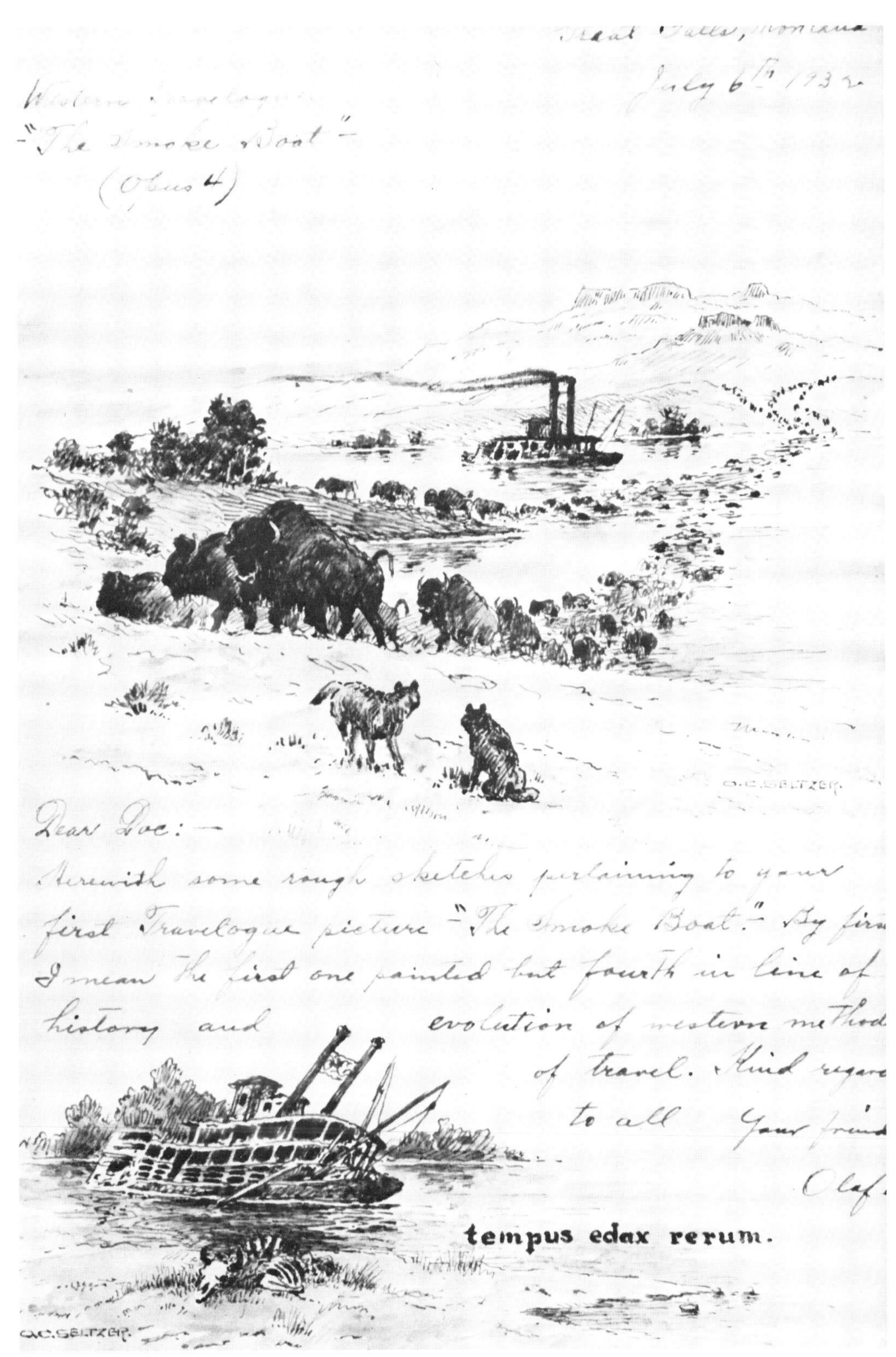


*The Smoke Boat Letter*
1932
Watercolor and ink, 10″ × 7″

127

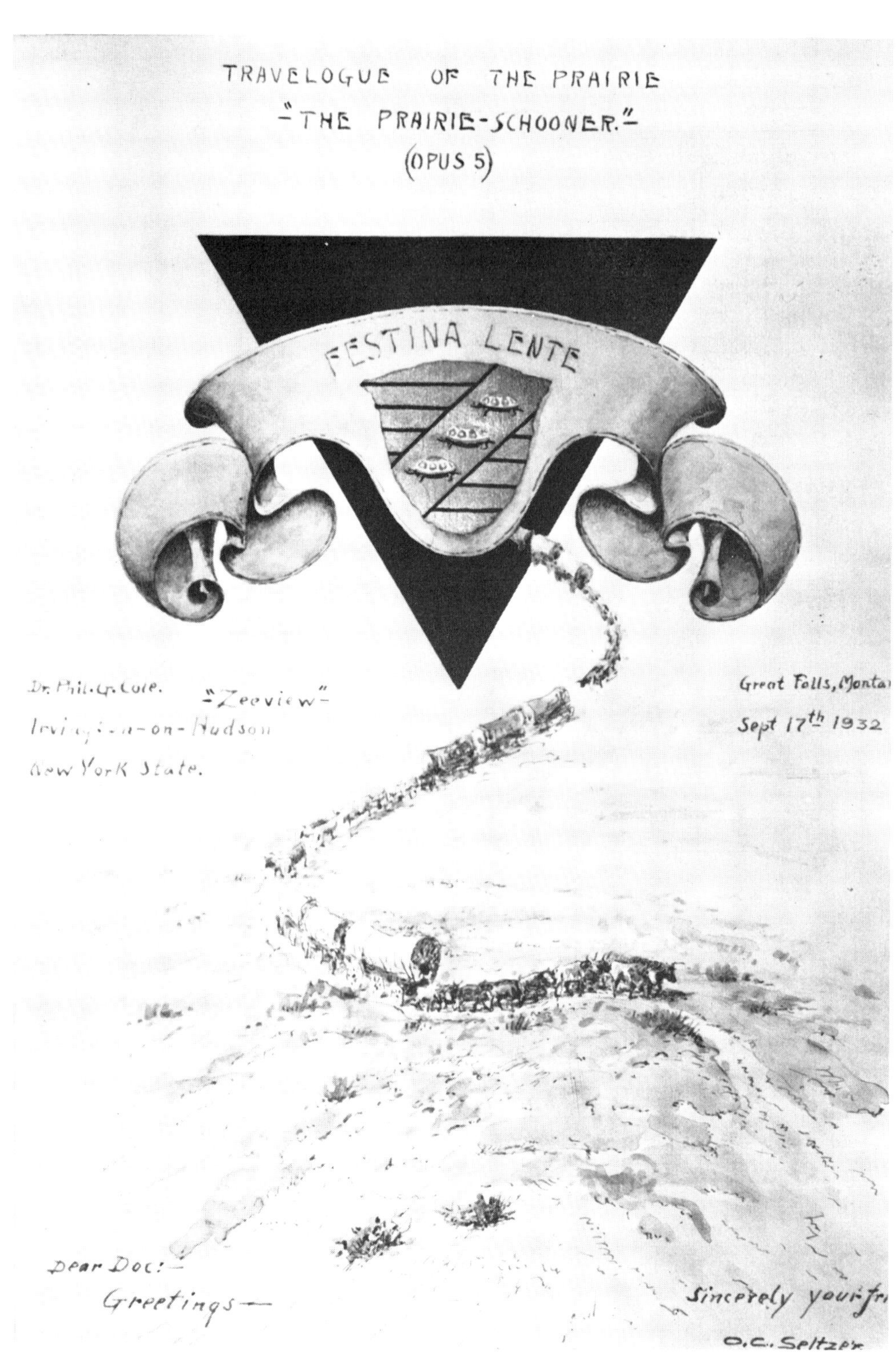


*The Prairie Schooner Letter*
1932
Watercolor and ink, 10½″ × 7″

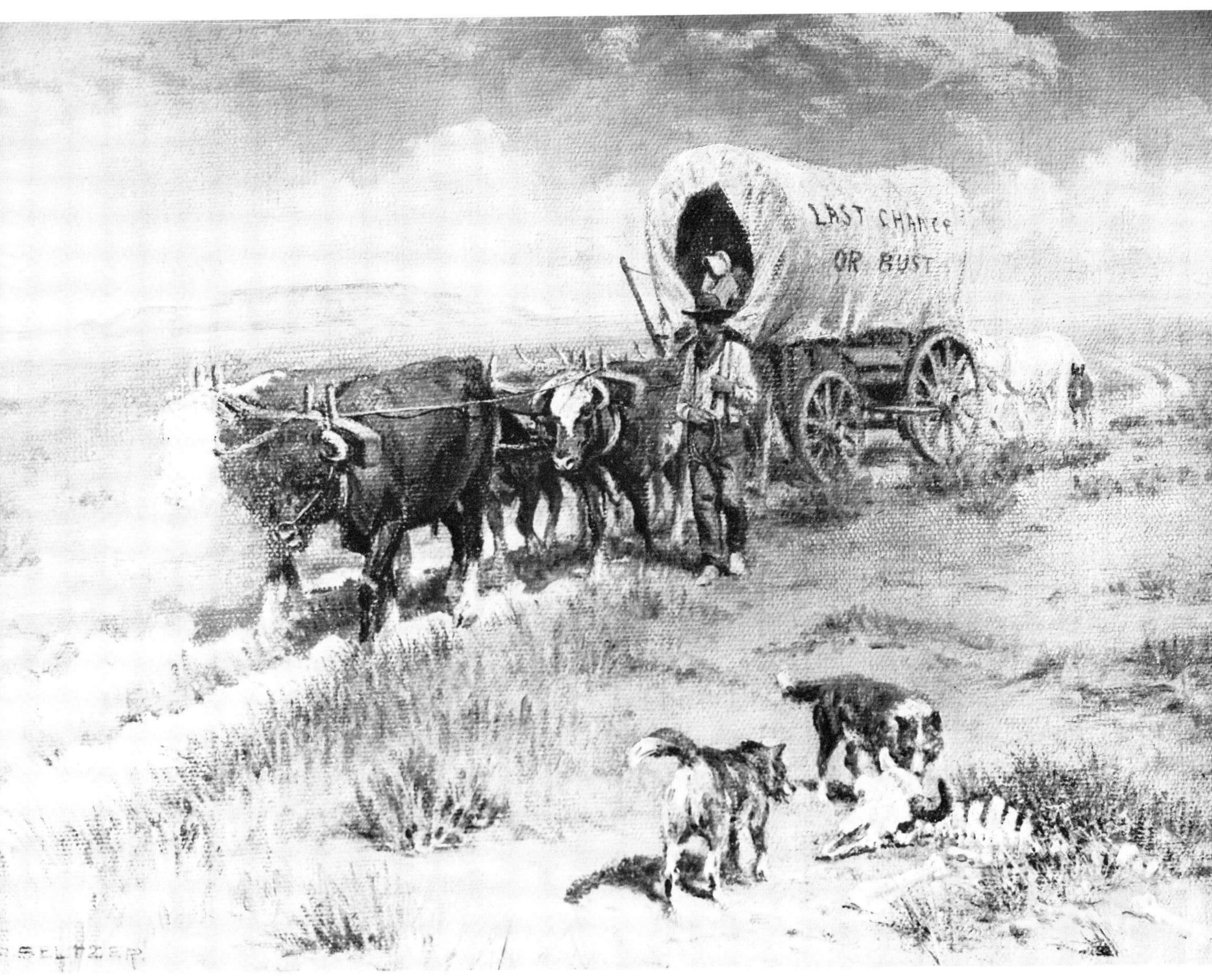


*Prairie Schooner*
1932
Early Western Travelogue oil, 11″ × 16″

gulch where some desperate prospectors struck gold just as they were exhausting their grubstake. It was on the ranch belonging to Phil's father, and subsequently became Helena. Seltzer wrote: "Regarding your close to home picture . . . which must bring you memories of the past . . . I hope you'll enjoy these simple little sketches pertaining to that particular little oil painting." On July 6 he wrote: "Herewith some rough sketches pertaining to your first Travelogue picture—'The Smoke Boat.' By first I mean the first one painted but fourth in line of history and evolution of western methods of travel."

Half of the sheet is covered with a watercolor-and-ink sketch of the kind that Seltzer called a "mezzo-tint," showing a buffalo herd crossing a

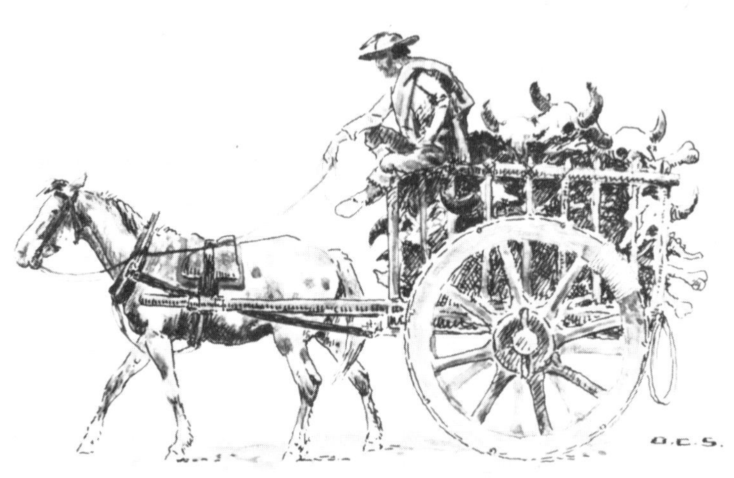



*The Red River Cart Letter*
1932
Watercolor and ink, 10″ × 7″

130

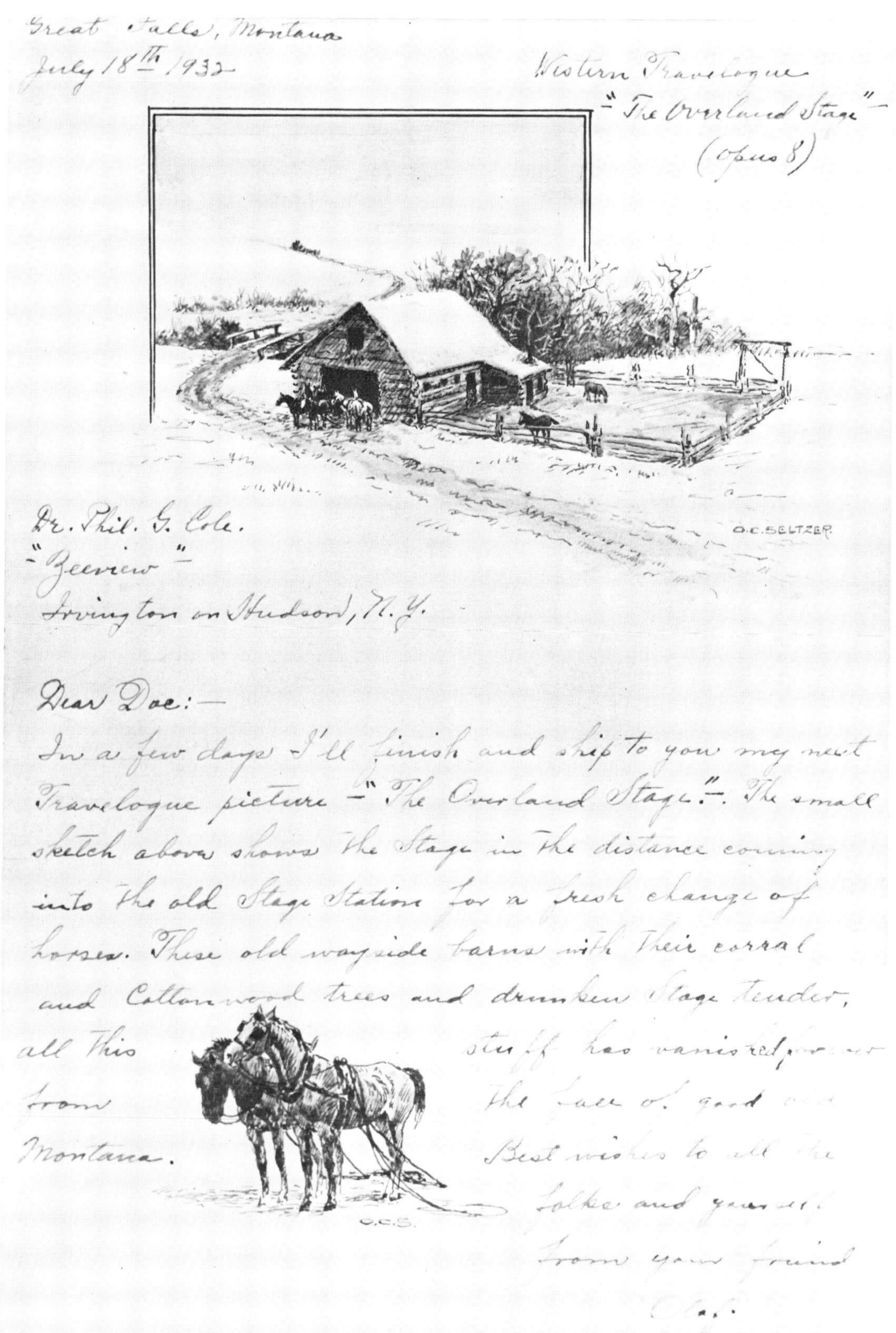



*The Overland Stage Letter*
1932
Watercolor and ink, 10″ × 7″

131

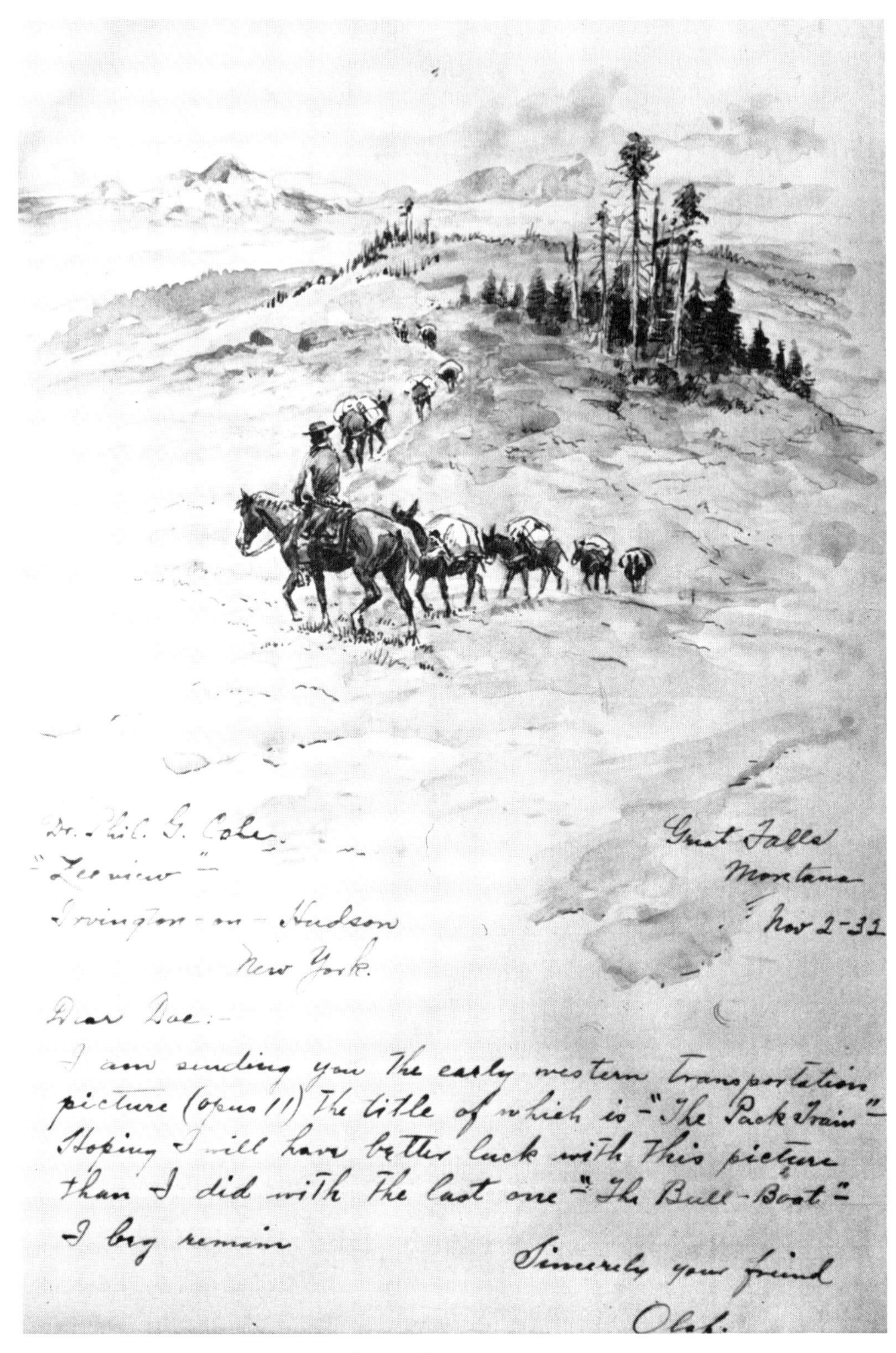


*The Pack Train Letter*
1932
Watercolor and ink, 10″ × 7″

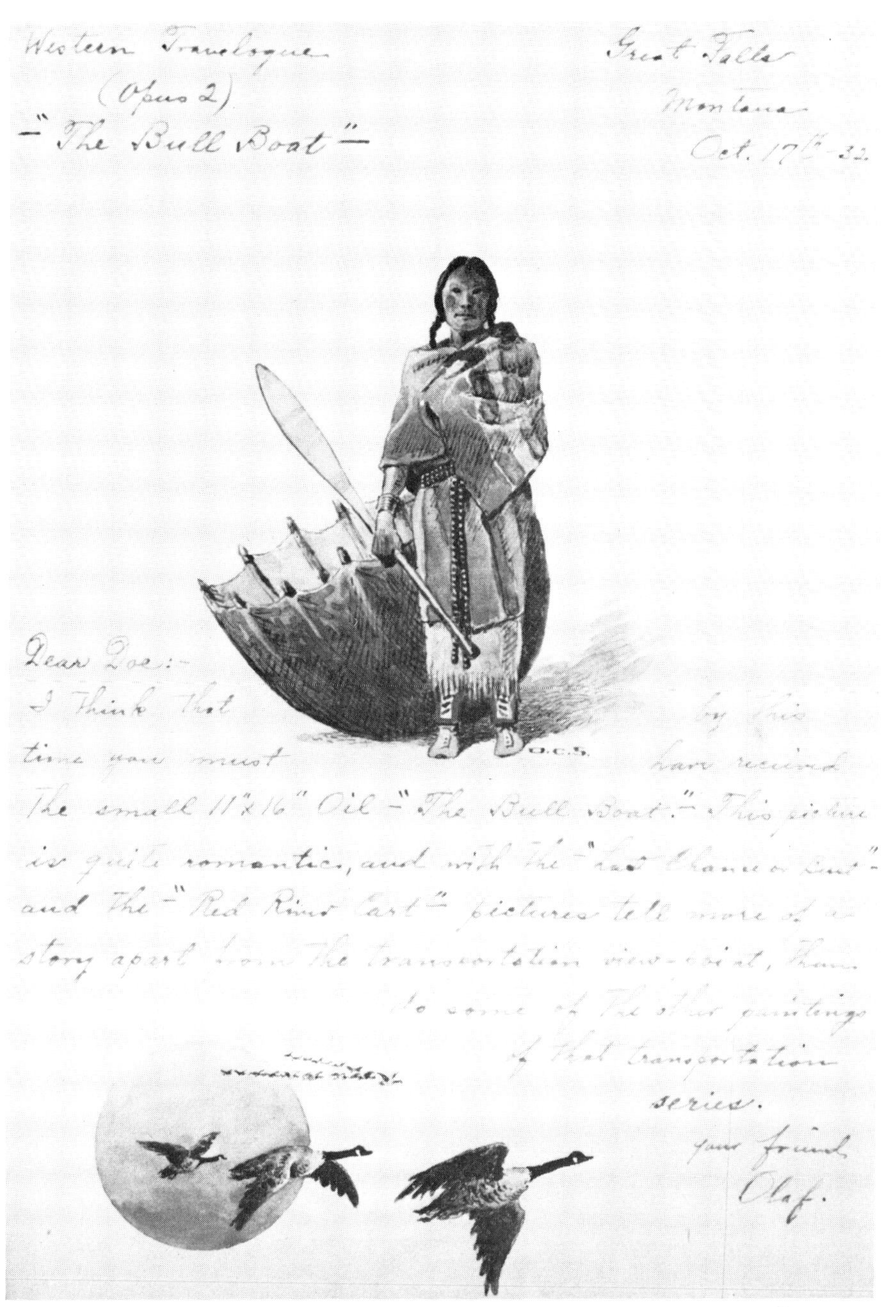

*The Bull Boat Letter*
1932
Watercolor and ink, 10″ × 7″

broad river as a steamboat nears the ford. Beneath, next to a sketch of a deserted, half-sunk vessel, the artist lettered *tempus edax rerum*, ("time the destroyer").

The meagerly educated Olaf enjoyed flaunting Latin phrases before Philip Cole with his Ivy League background. "The Prairie Schooner (Opus 5)" bears a pretentious shield emblazoned with the proverb *Festina Lente* ("make haste slowly"). There are three turtles on the shield, and a long line of prairie schooners snakes down the page beneath it.

Cole responded good-naturedly when Olaf twitted him about his scant knowledge of Latin, although Seltzer's use of Latin was not beyond question. "Latin proverbs, such '*multum in parvo*' is not to your liking I see," wrote the artist on September 22 in a letter showing a confrontation between a bear and a skunk: "It just means Much in Little, or for a broader meaning, "it's the little things that count" . . . Old Bruin is just about to turn a back somersault and be going places, away from there, far away in fact from the little thing with his tail at half mast."

Aware of Phil Cole's insatiable thirst for information about a bygone era, Olaf often passed along colorful bits, such as the common use for the Red River cart:

*As the Buffalo in early days was the most important factor in the necessities of life of the Plains Indians, in fact his whole existence, so has this grand animal . . . in later years and after he vanished from the prairies, through his bleached bones, contributed to the livelihood of the Halfbreed, who gathered and sold these skulls and bones and done his work so well that today you couldn't find a Buffalo skull anywhere on the prairies of Montana.*

Beneath a vignette of the "Diamond R. Mule Outfit (Opus 12)," Seltzer wrote:

*Above you see an important member of the old Diamond R. outfit of years ago. This veteran of the prairie roads of Montana may have been born— "Off Leader"—or perhaps the—"Near Wheeler," but whatever place he filled he was an aristocrat of Spanish blood, and his usefulness as a transportation factor in Montana can not be over-estimated.*

Using a sketch done entirely in shades of tan and brown, except for a pale-blue sky, Olaf explained "The Overland Stage (Opus 8)" as showing the stage "in the distance coming into the old Stage Station for a fresh change of horses. These old wayside barns with their corral and Cottonwood trees and drunken stage tender all this stuff has vanished forever from the face of good old Montana."

"The Chuck Wagon (Opus 9)" was depicted in ink in pale red and black. Branded steers and branding irons enhanced the sketch. "The quarter circle block outfit is bringing up the rear of the round-up cavalcade headed for the next camping ground beyond the stretch of bad-land," Olaf explained.[5] "The four small wiry Jack-Rabbit Mules are pulling hard across this sandy, alkaline sage brush flat, bucking up close to the Remuda ahead. The scene is over the Judith Basin, the Buttes known as the Painted Buttes are over on Painted Rope Creek."

*The Bull Boat* (Opus 2), a painting already shipped to Cole, was in a category with *Last Chance or Bust* and *Red River Cart*, since these pictures "tell more of a story apart from the transportation viewpoint than do some of the other paintings of that transportation series," Seltzer informed his patron in a letter illustrated with a blanketed Indian holding an oar. Apparently Dr. Cole didn't take to the romantic bullboat painting, for in his November 2 letter, "The Pack Train (Opus 11)," Seltzer wrote, "Hoping I have better luck with this picture than I did with the last one—'The Bull Boat.'"

That the Depression had reached Montana is evidenced by what can be deciphered in Olaf's letter concerning *The Canoe*, dated January 30, 1933. The artist was worried that Cole would reject the canoe painting already sent to him; he covered his concern with a watercolor of an Indian by a beached canoe so large that little of the message is readable, except for the comment, "The deer in the canoe is a blacktail buck, very plentiful in that beauty spot, The Bear-Tooth Mountain Range."

Seltzer's next letter, dated Groundhog Day, February 2, concerned "The Pony Express Rider (Opus 10)," a painting already in Doc's hands:

The Express Rider in your 11″ × 16″ oil on that subject is just in the act of spilling the foremost child of the plains, and above the mezzo-tint is a close-up of that same fellow. By mussing up old chief Bacon Rind like that, Uncle Sam no doubt changed the minds of the rest of the herd about

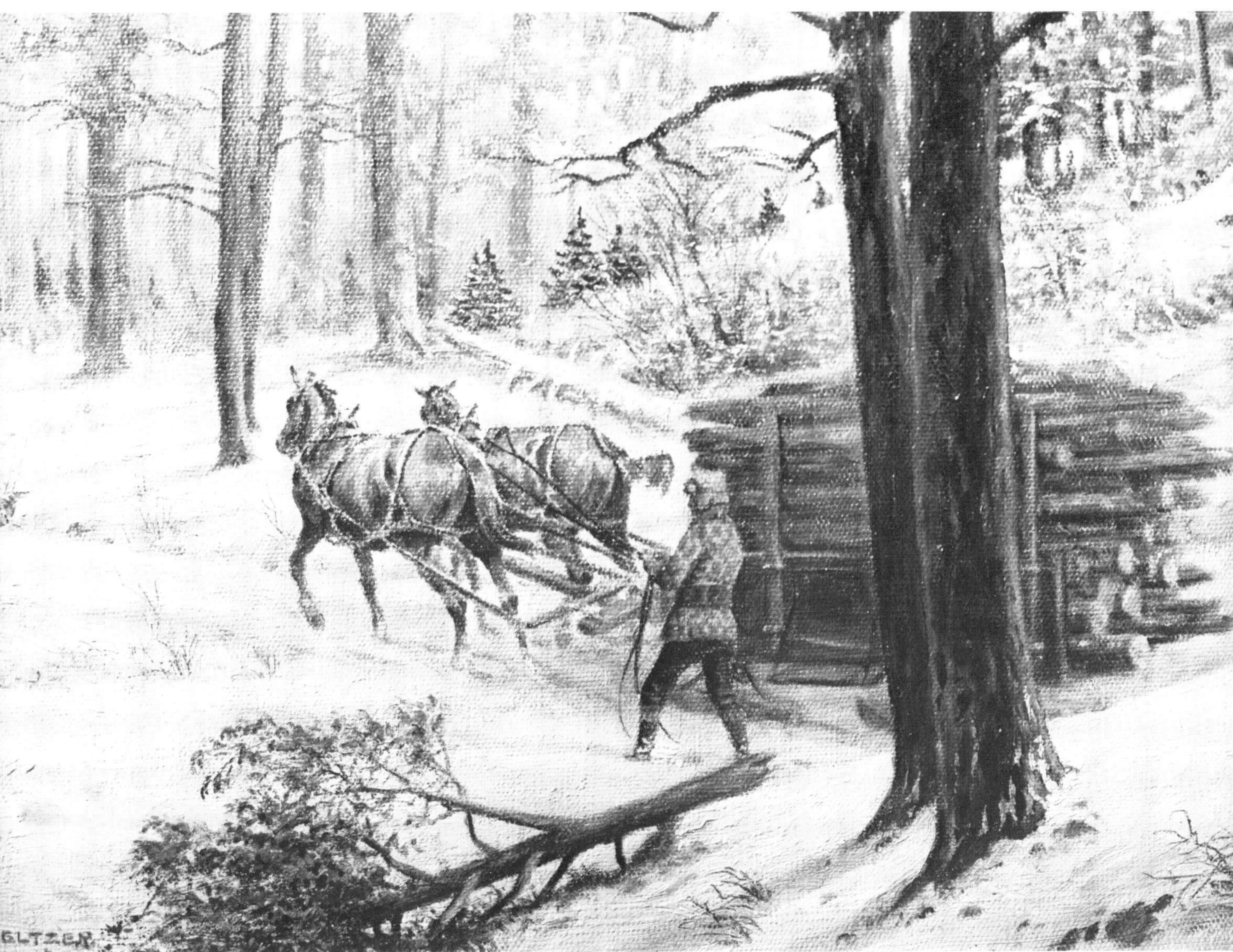

*The Sled (Winter Logging)*
1933
Early Western Travelogue oil

crossing the river, instead of which they would sneak back to their Lava Beds and meditate on the rude ways and means of the white man towards his red brother, and yet they'll have to admit that as a single handed performer and without a rehearsal he's A#1.

Relating to "The Sled (Opus 15)," Seltzer showed a cowboy riding a fence line across snow-covered grasslands:

I herewith depict three main winter pastimes of such cowhands as winter on the big stock ranches, and where they earn their grubstake as Feeders, Fence Riders or Corral Men, sometimes known as Woodchucks. My picture shows a cowhand bringing out corral posts for repairing the various open range corrals against the heavy spring roundup.

On February 27, 1933, under a sketch of an

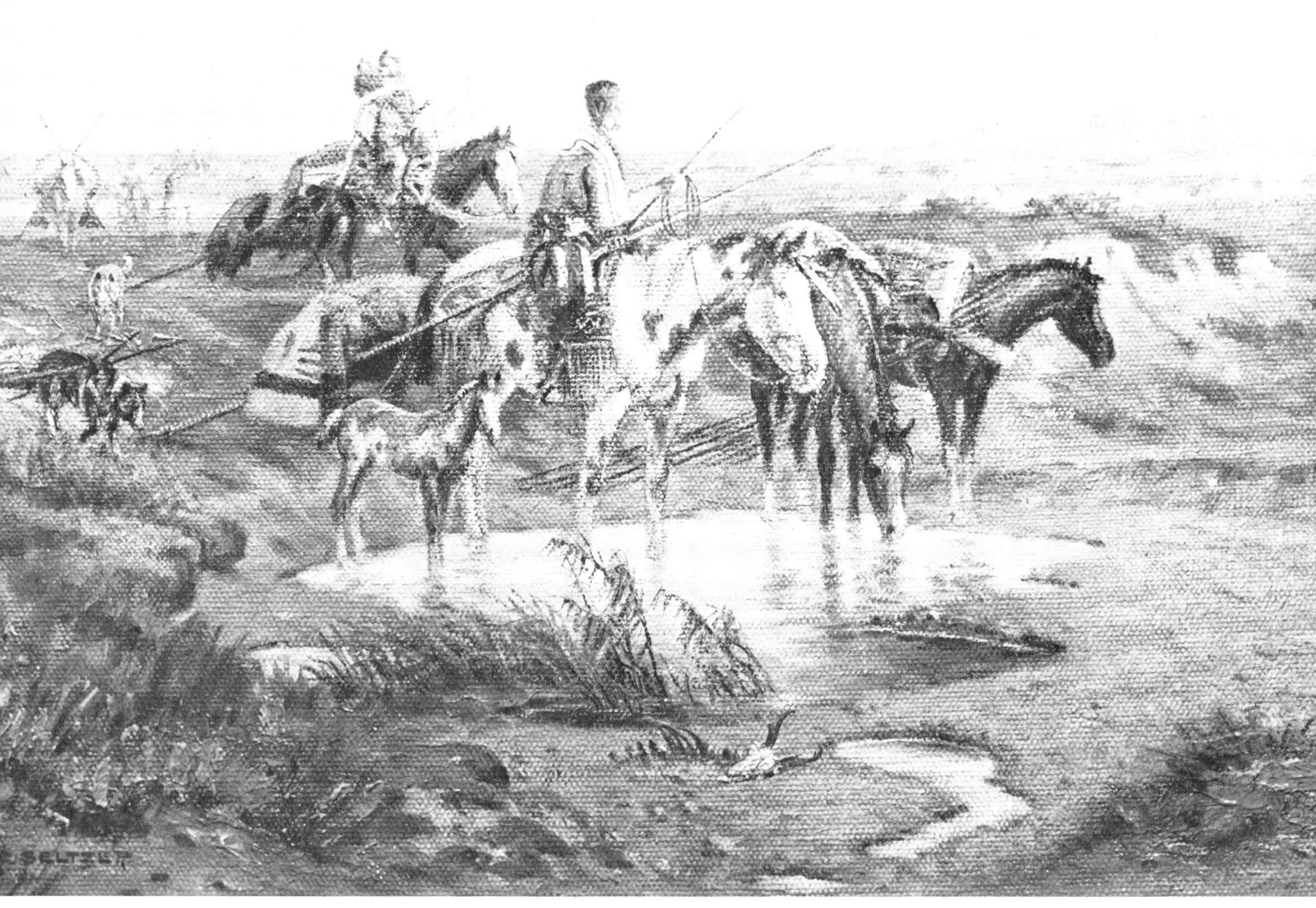

*The Travois*
1932
Early Western Travelogue oil

Indian displaying a blanket, Seltzer announced that he was sending Cole "the last of the series of western travel—'The Dugout Boat'—showing the Robe Traders with their boat load of buffalo skins approaching the old Fort on the river there to dicker with 'the Bourgeois' of the Fort."

The fifteen transportation paintings themselves represent some of Olaf Seltzer's finest work. Jewellike in their depth of color and feeling, they reflect a maturity of style and contain touches that are distinctly Seltzer. In spite of his repeated disavowal of any critical knowledge, the Transportation Series demonstrates Cole's correctness in asserting that someday Olaf would be known for the quality of his smaller paintings.

In most of these 11″ × 16″ oils Seltzer was

working with water—the broad Missouri, a swift-flowing creek, a water-hole pause for the horses. Here also he was at his best with cloud effects, slanted light rays, afterglow reflections, the eerie light that precedes severe storms in the plains country.

In *The Travois* the buckskin-robed squaw riding her Appaloosa is surrounded by packhorses as the moving herd halts for water; her dog travois follows. *The Smoke Boat* features an elegantly ornamented horse, the red hand print clearly marked on his rump. *The Red River Cart* is a sad sociological commentary with its depiction of the half-blood's struggle to eke out a living. The shadow and direct-light effects add interest to *The Iron Trail*, with its line of telegraph poles as a stamp of civilization.

*The Overland Stage*, reproduced as a Christmas card, depicts a stagecoach pushing on through the saffron-colored waning light of a wintry sky, soft snow spraying up in plumes from under the horses' hooves. *The Pony Express* rider has protected the mail with his still-smoking rifle. A white horse leads *The Pack Train* above timberline against a glacial background. *The Sled*, carrying freshly cut poles, is drawn by a team while the woodsman walks. Muted light adds a mystical effect to *The Bull Boat*. *The Dugout* also shows evidence of Seltzer's adroitness in capturing the soft effects of an afterglow. Three of the illustrated letters—those devoted to the pony-express rider, the sled, and the dugout—were awaiting the Coles upon their return from the Mediterranean, by way of Berlin and Paris, in May, 1933.

Now that the halls and galleries of Zeeview were being hung with his paintings to suit his taste, Dr. Cole was eager for his friend to come east to see for himself the improvements on the estate.

In the entry hall was hung the wedding gift from Russell, *The Buffalo Hunt*, flanked by two bronzes on pedestals, James Earl Fraser's *End of the Trail*, and Remington's *Mountain Man*. But most of the western art was displayed in areas off limits to the casual visitor. Cole's big study was hung with oils and watercolors from chair-rail height to ceiling; every bit of wall space was covered, including the offsets along the sides of the fireplace. Twenty-five Seltzer oils and six of his watercolors were hung in the study, among paintings by Leigh, Sharp, Schreyvogel, Johnson, Remington, and Russell. The *Vigilantes' Warning* hung over the wood-paneled arch.

The large Russell paintings were hung on the high walls of the entry hall so that they could be viewed from a balconylike staircase landing. Seltzer's Western Characters occupied three solid rows in the second-floor gallery and a third-floor hall. The framed illustrated letters, envelopes, and greeting cards were also hung in the second-floor gallery. A guest room held seven of Seltzer's pictures.[6]

The best was yet to come. The fermentation of ideas resulting from the camaraderie between painter and patron was still lively. More than a hundred paintings memorializing Montana's past were still to be painted. They alone would perpetuate the name Zeeview.

## Chapter 9
# Montana in Miniature

WHEN OLAF SELTZER SET OUT in 1933 to paint the history of Montana in a group of oils that would not exceed six inches in their longer dimension, he was using a technique seldom employed by the formally educated artists of his day and never by any of the prominent frontier painters of the American West.

Miniature-sized pictures were painted in ancient Egypt. About 2000 B.C. gouache was used with transparent color to illuminate and decorate such manuscripts as the *Book of the Dead* and the *Papyrum of Ani*. The name "miniature" is derived from the Latin word *minium* ("red lead"), the substance used to write initial letters on manuscripts at one stage in their evolution by craftsmen called *miniatores*.

Paintings small enough to be carried around conveniently were popular in the Golden Age of Greece. During the Renaissance decorative borders were added to illuminated initial letters, and designs became extravagant in detail.

Eventually the word *miniature* came to mean "small picture." Portrait miniatures were immensely popular from the seventeenth century until the camera came into general use. Charles Willson Peale and Gilbert Stuart painted portrait miniatures in Colonial America, and dozens of less-accomplished artists copied their portraits of George Washington on ivory miniatures for distribution in England. Cornelis Johnson's seventeenth-century painting of Frances Howard, Duchess of Richmond and Lennox, shows the duchess wearing a miniature of her husband pinned over her heart, a custom of the day.[1]

French artists inclined toward landscape miniatures. Louis Nicholas Van Blarenberghe painted scenes such as *A Promenade in the Park* and the gouache *The Avenue to a Great Palace* with great detail in rectangular areas measuring only $1\frac{1}{8}'' \times 3''$ inches. *A Game of Bowls*, another gouache, is a circular miniature seven inches in diameter.[2] James Arthur O'Connor, the father of modern Irish landscape painting, was known for his exquisite miniature sketches in sepia pen and wash, and occasionally in watercolor, as was his early-nineteenth-century contemporary George Chinnery, the English watercolorist who lived and worked in Dublin for seven years. There were few early American landscape miniatures, except for an occasional ornate scene decorating a case for a portrait miniature.

Seltzer's landscape miniatures fit the definition of a true miniature—one with a maximum measurement of seven inches—as set forth by Cyril Davenport in *Miniatures, Ancient and Modern*. But unlike the placid, stilted depictions of stately palaces favored by the French, the Seltzer miniature paintings are filled with action and peopled with Indians and frontiersmen.

Olaf might have preferred to do the scenes from Montana's past on a larger scale, either his favorite size for oils—$20'' \times 30''$—or the $11'' \times 16''$ he chose, to please his patron, for the Early Western Travelogue series. As early as 1928, Cole was urging Seltzer to work on a smaller scale in executing an oil he had ordered that was to include Lewis and Clark, Clark's black servant, York, and the Indian guide Sacagawea. Cole wrote from Lake Placid:

I sincerely and honestly like your smaller pictures so much better than your big canvasses.

Also as you know space is a big item with me. Why don't you work up one for me as small as you can? As you well know, this picture is very close to my heart. . . . Give it a few thoughts anyway Olaf. As you well know, neither shape nor price cut any ice with me so long as it is as small as consistent and is good.

A few weeks later, expressing his delight with the newly arrived prototypes for the Western Character series, Cole wrote: "The more I see of your works the more firmly I am convinced and the more sincerely I urge upon you the advisability of concentrating on small size things of historic nature. That is where you are in a class by yourself—I am positive of that."

Philip Cole's harping on his dwindling space and his flattery concerning Olaf's ability to portray so much action in a small area had their effect. The historical series was painted on a reduced scale. There are few exceptions to the 4½″ × 6″ or 6″ × 4½″ dimensions, and then the deviations are either 4″ × 6″ or 3½″ × 5½″. Skillful framing has disguised the small differences in size.

Olaf's enjoyment in ornamenting his Western Character sketches with individual teacup-sized vignettes in watercolor started his trend toward miniatures. Two of his letters to Phil Cole are illegible, except for random words, because the artist was carried away by his enthusiasm for the sketch painted over the script. One, featuring an Indian launching a canoe, has only a narrow border of handwriting on each vertical margin. The message, which appears to be concerned only with the weather and the usual amenities, apparently was not important enough for the artist to recopy his words.

Such indications of Seltzer's interest in smaller paintings and of his obvious ability in executing them, at least in watercolor, were not lost on his ever-planning patron. With forty years of painting experience behind him, Olaf was now able to transfer his ability for fine-line work to illustration board, to paint in oil the more than one hundred historic scenes for a demanding collector who was running out of wall space in his personal galleries.[3]

Olaf had always enjoyed doing his genre paintings in sizes that exceeded the classic definition of a miniature by only a few inches. Now, spurred by the delight of his patron, he found it a challenge to depict in restricted spatial areas subjects that would be worthy of treatment in murals: Indian

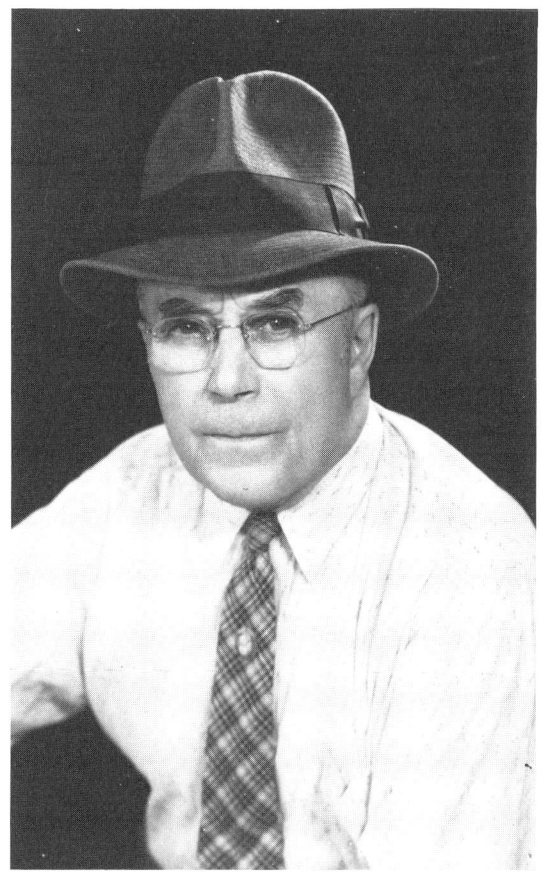

Seltzer in 1933, at the age of fifty-six. Courtesy of Carl C. Seltzer.

battles, such as *The Wagon-Box Fight* and *Battle of the Big Hole,* and natural disasters, such as *The Blizzard of 1886–87* and *Buffalo Fleeing Before Forest Fire.*

Phil Cole knew full well that the series of small oils would comprise a unique record of a bygone era. The two men would discuss many of the events covered in the series over after-dinner drinks at Zeeview. Upon his return to Great Falls, Olaf would research material in the reference section of the public library to learn as much as he could about historical events or customs in which Doc had shown an interest.

Such was the impression of Alice Ralston, whose knowledge of her home state and interest in her employer's collections often drew her into discussions with the two men; she knew more about the genesis of the historical paintings than

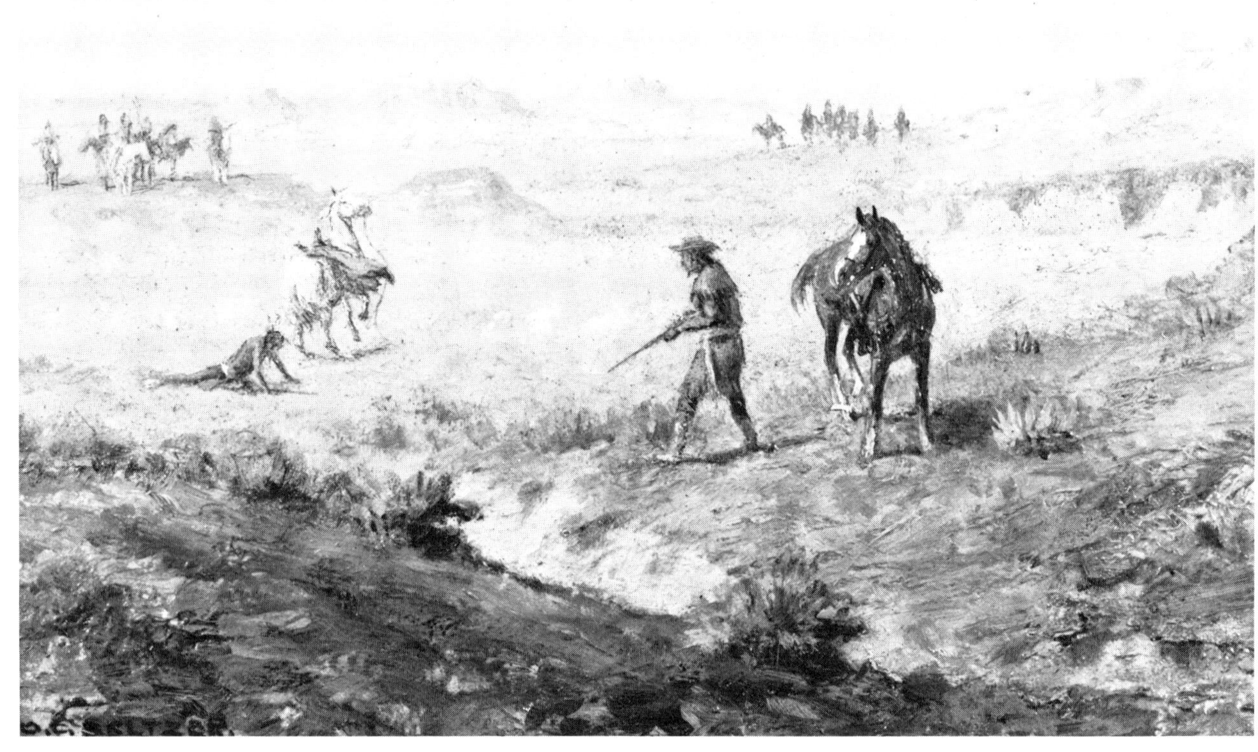

*Buffalo Bill's Duel with Yellow Hand*
1933
Miniature oil
(*Originally painted as Killing Yellow Hand in Duel with Buffalo Bill, 4″ × 6″ watercolor*)

any other member of the Cole household except Cole himself. In a 1966 interview, only months before her death in Bozeman, Montana, Miss Ralston said that she believed that "Seltzer himself determined for the most part what specific scenes or events he would represent," although the "idea for creating the miniature series was Cole's." After Olaf started work, "He and Dr. Cole compiled most of the commentary to go with each of these pictures."

She credits Seltzer, the immigrant, with a thorough knowledge of the history of Montana "and also the history of a lot of Russell's paintings. . . . His interests were a little wider ranging than Russell's."[4]

Cole spent countless hours checking and double-checking the research material that Olaf

prepared and sent with each miniature. While the artist checked the accuracy of details in the Great Falls Public library, Cole studied his personal acquisitions of journals and eyewitness accounts of Montana happenings. Word of the project spread among old-timers who had known the Coles in Helena. Three pages of descriptive material on the *modus operandi* and trappings of a bullwhacker were sent to Cole in New York in February, 1935, by John R. Barrows, of San Diego, California, who remembered the collector as "Doctor Cole's little boy." By then the detail on *Calamity Jane* and her team was complete, but Olaf was known to revise in an attempt at perfection.

After Cole decided on a description that suited him, one of his three secretaries would type sev-

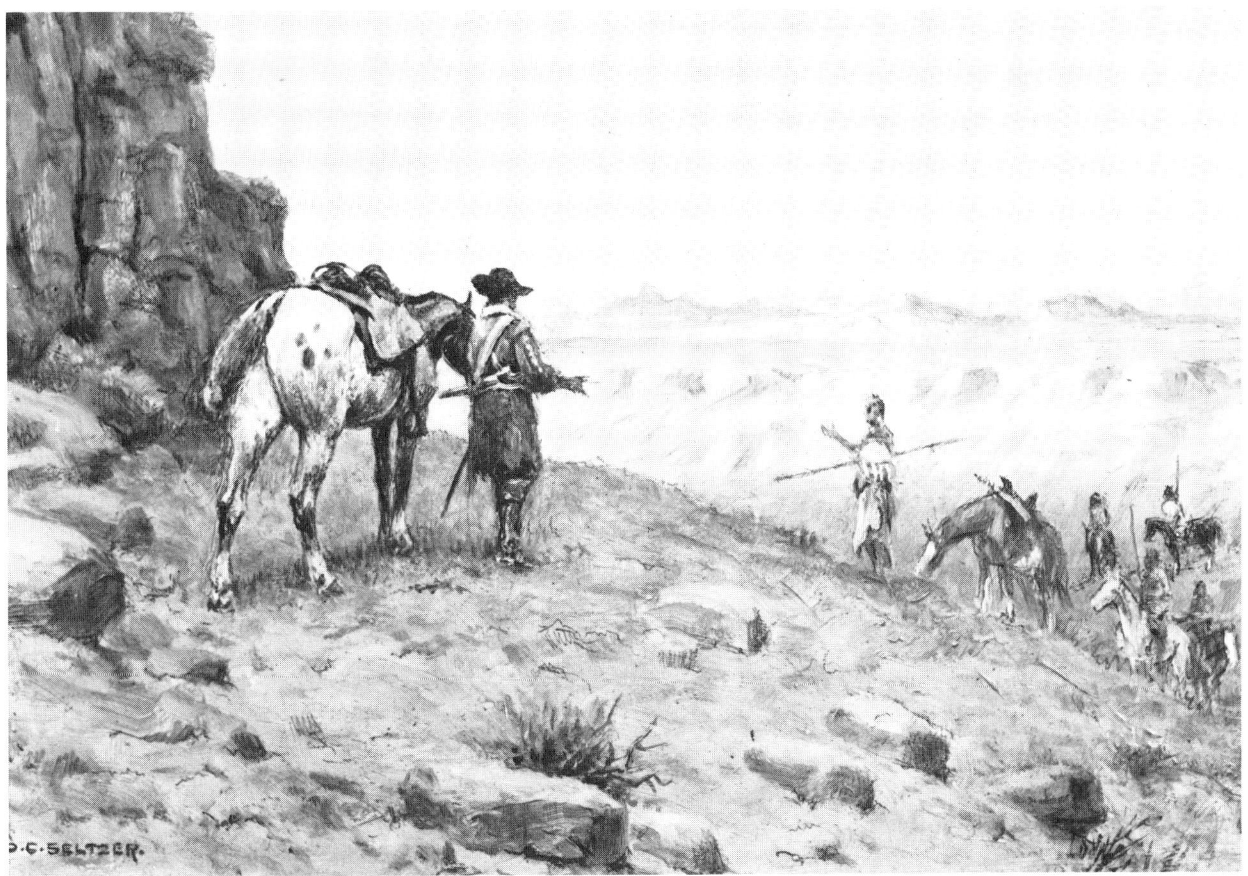

*Chevalier Verandrye's First Sight of the Big Horn Mountains, 1743*
1933
Miniature oil

eral copies. One was glued to the back of each framed miniature (these descriptions are still intact). A second copy was placed beneath a photograph of each miniature so that a photostatic catalogue could eventually be made.

But such details lay a few years ahead when the first miniature, a 4″ × 6″ watercolor entitled *Killing Yellow Hand in Duel with Buffalo Bill*, was received from Seltzer in the spring of 1933. Apparently the two men had not as yet determined the medium in which the historical series was to be done.

*Chevalier Verandrye's First Sight of the Big Horn Mountains—May 2, 1743* and *Lewis at the Black Eagle Falls of the Missouri*, both 4½″ × 6″, were the first two oil miniatures catalogued, indicating a chronological approach to the project at least at the outset. The last one, catalogued in late November, 1935, is *Mike Fink—Double Crosser*, a depiction of a murder during a William Tell–type incident along the Yellowstone River in 1822. By the time this painting arrived on the Hudson, the Zeeview staircase must have been overflowing, for this last entry and two odd-sized miniatures—*The Deluge at Colter Falls*, measuring 5½″ × 4″, and *The Wolfer*, 3½″ × 5½″ —were moved to a guest room.

The text concerning Verandrye, shown standing by his horse greeting a dismounted Indian at the head of a small scouting party, is typical:

*Pierre Gautier de Varennes de la Varendrye was born at Three Rivers, Que., in 1686 and died in 1749. He was a well-educated Canadian and a natural born rover and explorer. After having experienced military service in France, he returned to the west shores of Lake Superior in 1731 and in 1732 erected Fort St. Charles on the Lake of the Woods. Pushing still further west he established Fort de la Reine on the site of Portage la Prairie. His roving nature carried him as far west as the Rocky Mountains where in 1743 he had his first glimpse of them when he viewed the Big Horn range from somewhere in what is now Montana. In 1749 he built Fort Dauphin on the Saskatchewan River.*

To judge from the first nineteen miniatures recorded in Cole's album, there was no particular scheme for producing the little paintings. The chronological order was short-lived. Verandrye's brief biography, with its illustration of a milestone event in the explorer's career, is followed by the colorful *Curley Bringing News of the Custer Massacre to the Steamer 'Far West'—June 26, 1876*, and this in turn is followed by *Wrecked River Boat 'Chippewa' Found by Crow War Party on the Missouri River*, an event that transpired in the autumn of 1861.

The first group of miniatures to be painted included an interesting portrayal of "Smoky" Wilson, a black man who joined the Crow tribe. Another memoir of outlawry,—*Kid Curry Killing Pike Landusky in Jew Jake's Saloon, Landusky, Mont.—1885*, is among the early entries, along with *Chief Joseph's Surrender* (celebrating an event that took place in 1877), *Custer's Last Stand, Buffalo Bill's Duel with Yellow Hand* (substantially the same scene as the trial-run watercolor), and *Yellowstone Kelly About 1869*. The last, another biographical account, depicts a famous scout as Seltzer thought he would have looked on the trail in 1869. Luther Sage Kelly died in 1928, only a few years before the series was undertaken.

When Olaf began the historical chronicle in oil, he was in his mid-fifties and at the peak of his artistic competence. The nation was in the midst of a gripping economic depression. In spite of his trips east, the artist had not developed the market that he knew his paintings merited. Doc, Bill Marks, and a few of their friends on both coasts, plus his Montana customers, provided a slow, steady demand, but all his efforts to develop new contacts seemed to come to nothing.

Most disappointing to Olaf was that he had not received the recognition of Montanans, who continued to mourn their lost cowboy artist. Russell had been gone for more than five years, but time had not dimmed the luster of his image. Olaf had hoped that some of the appreciation bestowed on C. M. R.'s work would eventually come his way. His was a rare talent, he knew, and he had developed it well. But Montanans were loyal to the painter who, along with Will Rogers, had done so much to create the cowboy mystique. They all but deified their hero. Olaf was asked to make talks about his departed colleague, to provide paintings for memorial brochures, to advise on exhibitions, and to authenticate Russell works. He suffered in silent frustration, patience giving way to an increasing testiness as the myth displaced the man.

Seltzer held his tongue, but his disappointment surfaced at times in his letters to Mabel or in the notes he wrote on scraps of paper to ease his tension. Sometimes it manifested itself in a brusque, even cantankerous attitude toward visitors who sought him out on the pretext of wanting to see his work, when often their motive was to learn about Charlie and his painting methods. J. Kenneth Ralston, of Billings, Montana, a contemporary Montana artist who painted the murals at the Custer Battlefield and in the Centenary Arch at Saint Louis, was warned of Seltzer's irritability but refused to let it deter him. He visited Olaf, and, after the ice was broken and the older artist recognized that young Ralston was a serious painter, the two formed a friendship that lasted until Seltzer's death.

Olaf's disappointment in his seemingly stalled career was alleviated by the pleasure he derived from his family. Of particular joy were two additions: granddaughters Ruth Lillian, born on her mother's twenty-seventh birthday, June 2, 1931, and Sue Carla, who arrived on October 16, 1933. While the girls were toddlers, the Carl Seltzers lived almost next door to the new grandparents' home on Central Avenue, and Olaf saw his granddaughters every day. When the girls were older, their parents built a home in the next block; Olaf watched with great pleasure as his "little devils" grew.

Such was Olaf's personal milieu in 1933, the year in which he actually set to work to put Cole's ideas on canvas. Enthusiastic as he was about the series, Cole never hurried or pressured Olaf to get on with it. Instead, he expressed his wishes through encouragement and compliments and was unremitting in his efforts to interest others in

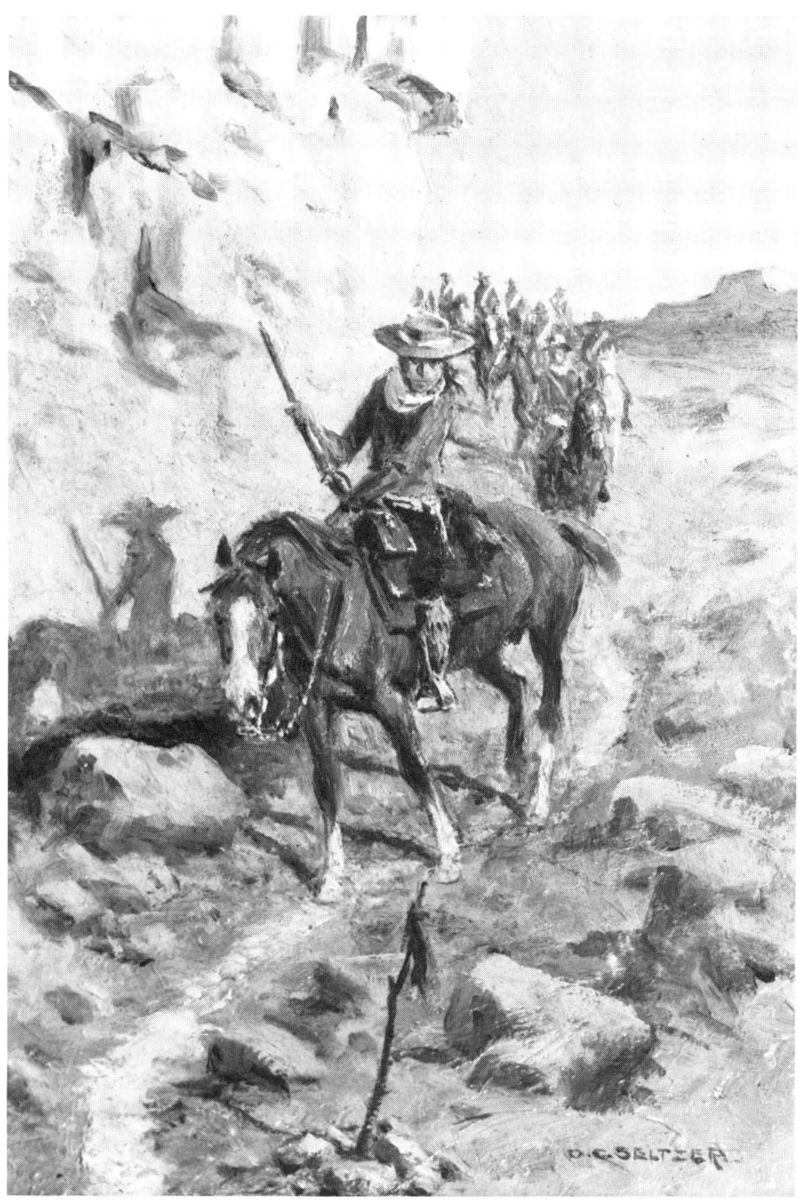

*Yellowstone Kelly*
1933
Miniature oil

Seltzer's work, never failing to pass on compliments from those who viewed his collection.

Early in 1933, Phil asked the artist to send an illustrated letter to a couple who had admired his paintings at Zeeview. Olaf complied and received a warmly worded acknowledgment from the famed woman pilot Amelia Earhart on her behalf and that of her husband, publisher George Palmer Putnam.

From Rye, New York, she wrote on March 28, 1933:

My dear Mr. Seltzer:

Your lovely "letter" came the other day and I know it is one of the most interesting pieces of mail I ever received. Thank you indeed for sending it.

Mr. Putnam and I dined with Dr. Cole shortly before he left for Europe. At that time he showed

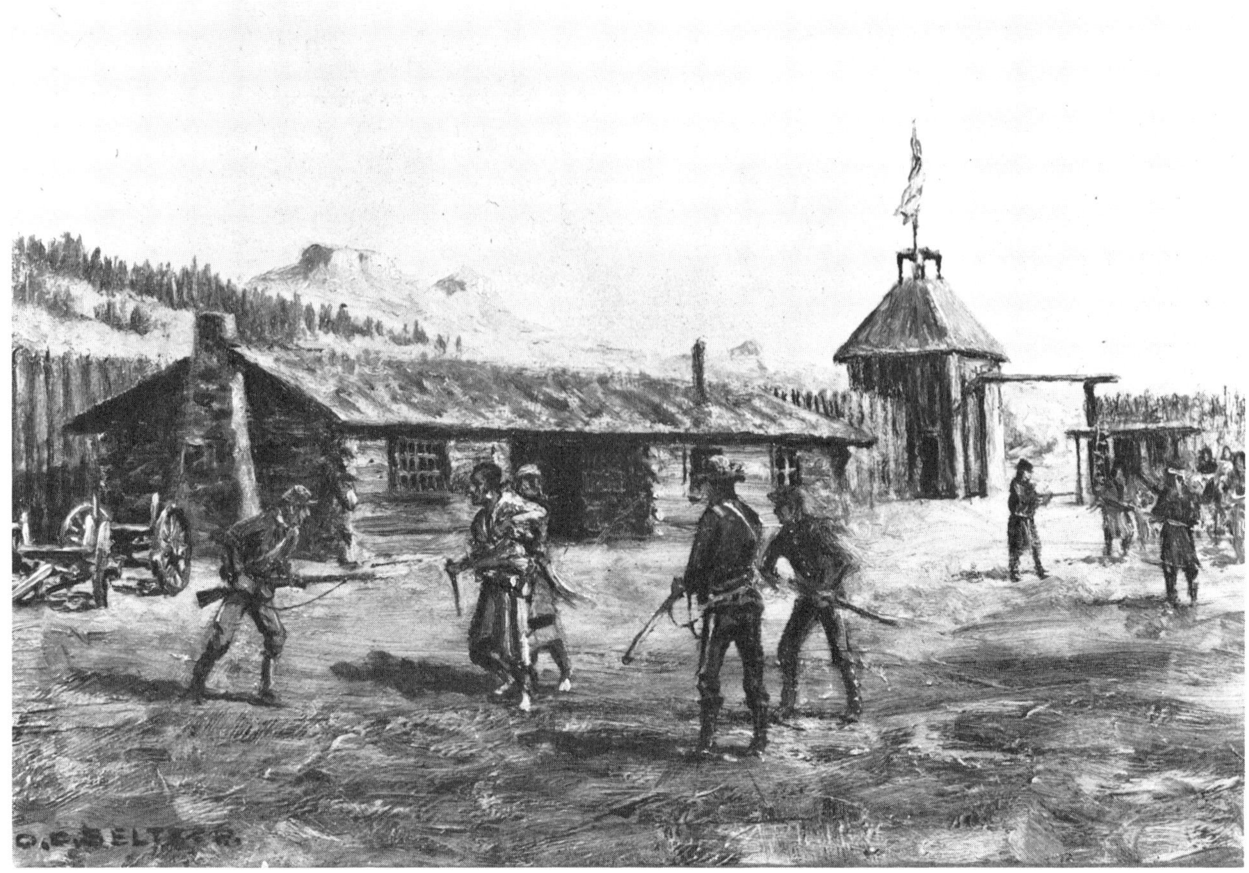

*The Stabbing of Crazy Horse—1877*
1935
Miniature oil

us a number of your drawings and promised that he would ask you to send me a sample. You were very gracious to respond so promptly.

I do hope I shall have the opportunity of seeing more of your work. If I fly out your way, I shall plan to stop over, if you care to have visitors.

Sincerely yours,
Amelia Earhart

More than a year elapsed before the artist heard from the Putnams again. In the interim he was hard at work on historical scenes such as *The Stabbing of Crazy Horse* at the Spotted Tail Agency, the *Fort McKenzie Massacre* of 1842, the 1835 *Duel between Kit Carson and Captain Shunan* on the banks of the Green River, and the action-filled *Killing of John M. Bozeman*.

On August 2, 1934, Putnam wrote to Olaf from New York City:

You remember, perhaps, that through Dr. Cole we had the pleasure of "meeting" you a year or so ago.

I am venturing this letter because I am just today back from Wyoming. I found myself rather unexpectedly some seventy-five miles to the south of Cody and I wired New York to find your address. We wanted so much to see you. But when we discovered you were not in Great Falls we had to give up the prospect of meeting you again because we were obliged to return east via the southern route.

Miss Earhart and I visited my old friend, Carl Dunrud, who has a ranch in the back of Sunshine. We like it so much there is just a chance we may

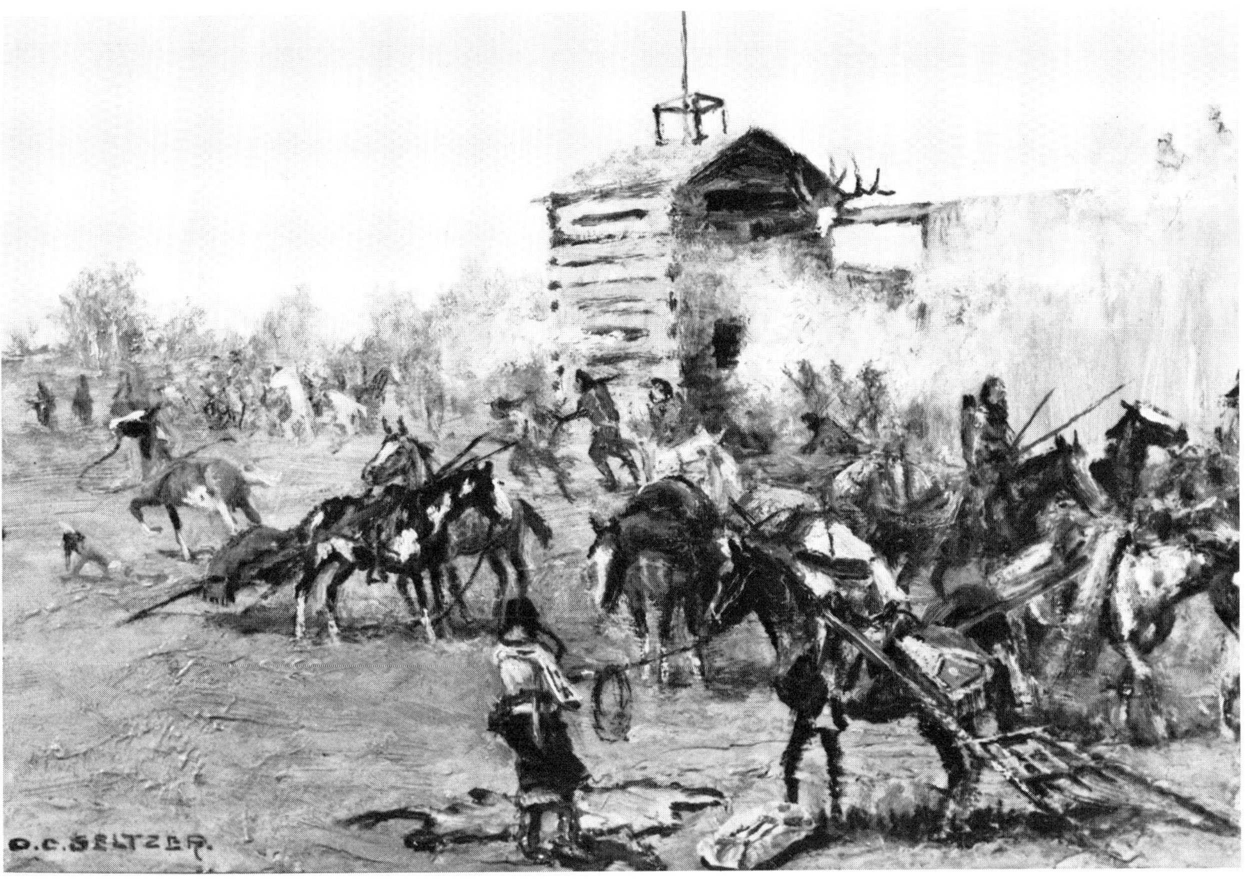


*The Fort McKenzie Massacre—1842*
1934
Miniature oil

have just a cabin there to spend our vacation time hereafter. If so, we certainly look forward to seeing you. I want you to know of our real enthusiasm for your drawings. There is a lot about them, and their possibilities, I would enjoy talking over with you when opportunity offers.

I just found that Dr. Cole is away from New York until September. If you have the time you might drop me a line telling me whether there is any remotest chance of you being east this winter, or what your general plans are.

Putnam's letter reached Olaf in Pocatello, Idaho, during a long painting trip the artist made through southern Montana, western Wyoming, and southeastern Idaho in the company of Bill Marks, who enjoyed taking Olaf along with him on business calls connected with his four-state insur-

ance brokerage firm. On such trips Olaf filled sketch pads and rolls with backgrounds he could put to use in his paintings, particularly as locales for the historical miniatures.

Seltzer answered Putnam's letter immediately, promising a more interesting (meaning illustrated) letter upon his return to Great Falls. He told Putnam that Phil Cole, then at Lake Placid, was considering coming to Montana so that the two of them could go "all over the Custer Battlefield country in order to get regular historical data with the proper setting of country."

In late September, Olaf mailed the promised illustrated letter, addressed simply to "Miss A. E., Rye, New York." It was delivered without delay. At the time Miss Earhart was in her mid-thirties, a casually pretty woman who resembled

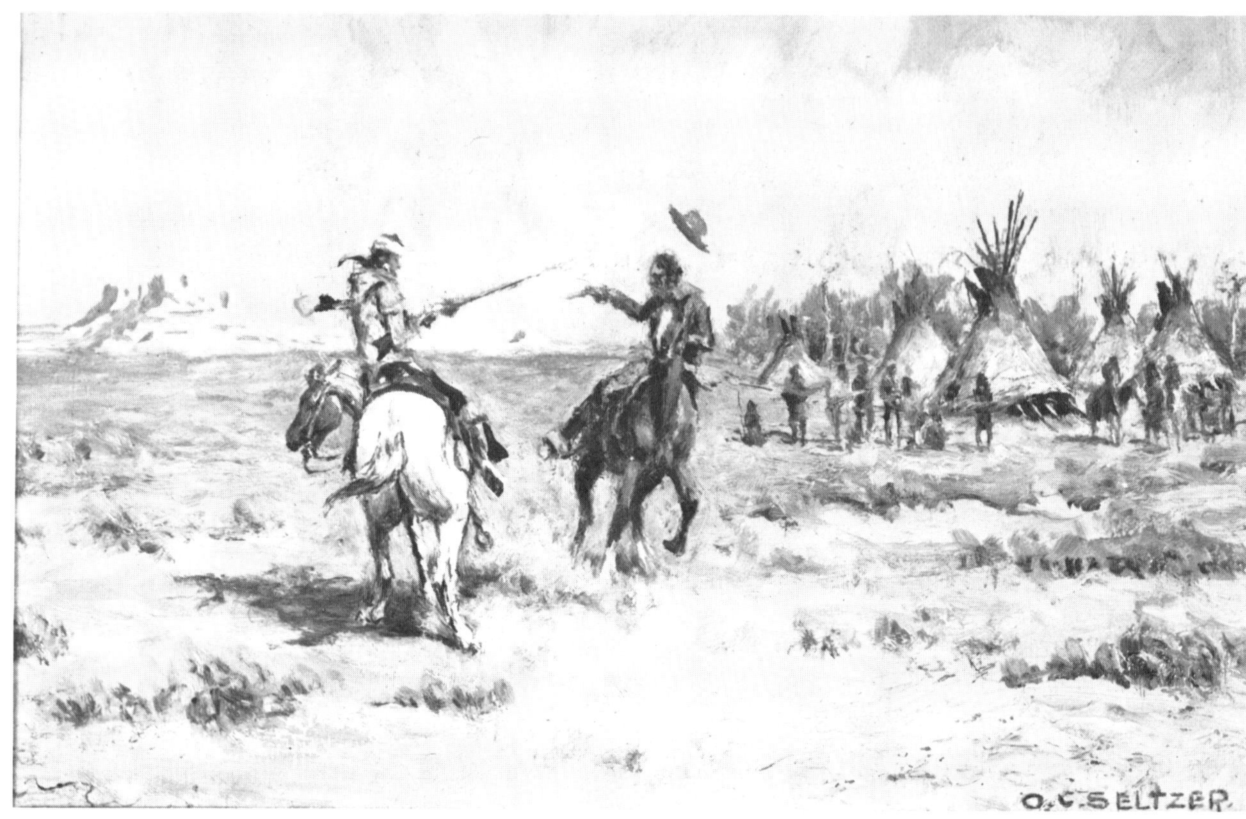

*Duel Between Kit Carson and Capt. Shunan—1835*
1934
Miniature oil

the hero of aviation Charles Lindbergh. Daring and independent, "Miss A. E." nevertheless had about her a feminine air and a gracious way of expressing herself. A World War I nurse and former Boston social worker, she had written a book about her experiences as the first woman passenger on a transatlantic flight (Newfoundland to Wales in 1928). She married her publisher and in 1932 became the first woman to fly the Atlantic alone.

The Putnams had in mind a unique commission for Olaf. Delighted with the little watercolor scenes with which he ornamented the three or four square inches at the left of the address on a business envelope, they had decided that he should design first-day covers for airmail envelopes Miss Earhart wanted to carry on her proposed solo flight from Honolulu to Oakland. She was in hopes of setting another record for women flyers.

Twenty-five different covers were needed, Putnam explained in a letter, dated October 1, 1934. He urged Olaf to "start knocking them out now":

It seems to me the one you did for Miss Earhart is just about right, so far as space is concerned. I suggest that some be made with the circle and others in varying design so that there be a variety.

It will be proper, in connection with this batch, to have a few of them indicate a tropical starting point. That is, palm trees and that sort of thing can be a motif. One or two could have a volcano. The arrival point will be the United States. Also perhaps a few could concern trans-continental crossings, of which she has made so many. . . . The Mississippi below or the Rocky Mountains, or a bank of sheep, packtrain, railroad train, prairie schooners, and the like. Her plane is a single engine, high wing monoplane Lockheed. It is red with a gold stripe. You will note that the number NR 965 Y is painted on the tail. The same number appears on the lower side of the left wing and the upper side of the right wing. Not, understand, that I am expecting any portraits of the plane, but all this may help a bit.

Now another matter. I dropped over to Dr. Cole's Sunday and refreshed my memory of the things of yours he has there. And, I might add, my enthusiasm. I wish at your leisure you would send me on some data. First, you might write me a letter pretty deliberately couched a bit in the vernacular, in which you give me the highlights of your own history—the sort of letter I could quote. Or perhaps, if you indulge in any illustrations, photograph bits of it. And in another letter, which just make routine, give me any stuff you can about yourself and your own experience, and especially your work with and memories of Charley Russell, and some odds and ends about Russell. I want to use this material to supplement what I have in this personality sketch about you I plan to write. As I see it now, the first one would be built primarily around your envelopes and your letters—not only those addressed to Miss Earhart and myself, but some selection of the most graphic of those which Dr. Cole has. I think, and he agrees, that this little article can be made a very interesting opening gun in what we may call a "Seltzer top-of-the-heap Campaign."

Two days later, Putnam notified Olaf that he was sending him pictures and sketches to develop ideas for the airmail envelopes:

Several steamers, hotels, etc., are included for sound reasons. Anyway, perhaps these will be helpful in working out a few suggestions. As you realize, this all has to do with the Hawaiian Islands. Miss Earhart has just accepted an invitation to go there later this winter. She is interested in inspecting the air line which operates between the several islands which has just secured an air mail contract.

On October 13, Amelia wrote to Seltzer from Michigan, Indiana, to tell him, in answer to an inquiry Putnam had forwarded to her, that she came under the zodiac sign Leo. As to the card she came "under" (heart, diamond, club, or spade), she wrote in her spidery script: "I haven't the foggiest idea what card—how does one find out?" Typically, Olaf offered to redo any of the covers

Putnam or Amelia did not like when he sent the publisher the first eight in mid-October. Putnam answered:

I see no reason why you should put in any more time on them. Each in its field is just about right.

One query. The one involving the air mail stamps is extremely clever and very attractive to the eye. But I have a sneaky suspicion that we may get in trouble. One isn't allowed to reproduce stamps even as generically as this. So I wouldn't do any more like that.

In short, I like them all. For the immediate problem at hand my hunch is that if you get a few more directly tied up with Hawaii, it will be helpful. The gang out there I am sure will fall for them. And they are the people in pleasing whom I am most interested.

You are very prompt and efficient. It is a pleasure to work with you.

In his eagerness to please Amelia and G. P. Putnam with his work on the envelopes, in which as a philatelist he took an inordinate interest, it is unlikely that Olaf followed through on the publisher's suggestion for a letter in the vernacular. He was not publicity-conscious, preferring to let his work speak for itself.

In early November, 1934, Olaf arrived in Tarrytown, New York, where he stayed at the YMCA for a number of weeks while working on the historical miniatures in Mrs. Cole's hillside studio at Zeeview. He brought along additional miniatures in various stages of completion, including *George Ives—Road Agent*, one of three dealing with that notorious outlaw; *The Killing of Chief Lame Deer*, an 1877 scene packed with action; and *Moving Camp*, another rendition of the Crow squaw. The legend accompanying the latter read:

*. . . "moving camp" in typical manner. The bucks have gone on ahead while the squaws and children are making their way to the new camp. The old sorrel horse dragging the lodge poles; the buckskin with the papoose slung at the side of the high-horned squaw saddle; the old white cayuse mare with the squaw all decked out in her finery, the travois, the bald-faced white bellied colt, the fancy rigging on the old mare, the pack horses bringing up the rear and the boy on foot with his dogs and his bow and arrow ready for any small game such as birds or prairie dogs that may jump up—all these are characteristic of this part of "Moving Camp."*

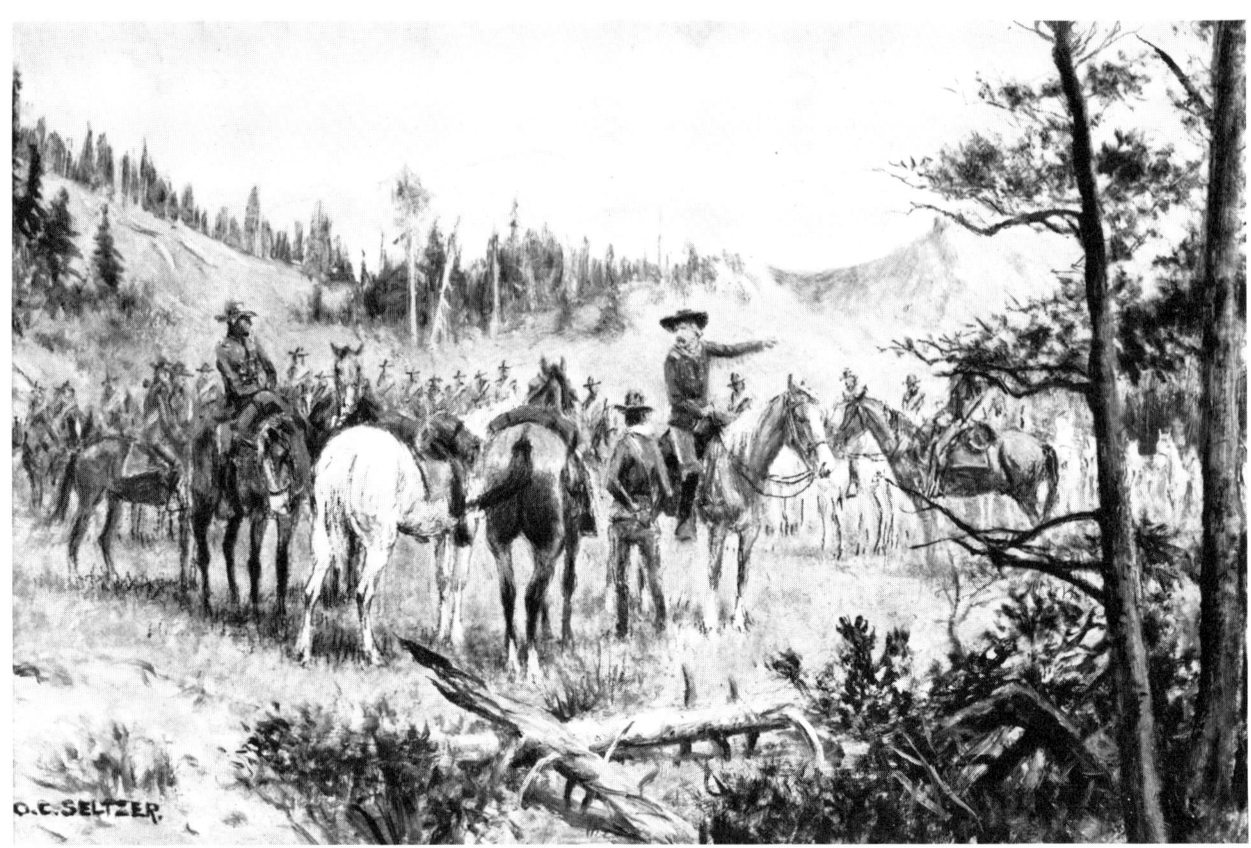

*Custer, Reno, and Benteen*
1934
Miniature oil

But the 1934 visit to New York was not all work. At last Olaf met the Putnams in person. Throughout his six- or seven-week visit he saw a lot of the publisher. Amelia was out of town most of the time. Phil Cole and G. P. Putnam took Olaf to the Madison Square Garden Horse Show. Later Olaf told an interviewer in Tarrytown that it took him back to those Sundays before the turn of the century when he would visit friends at the Lethbridge barracks of the Canadian Royal Mounted Police, partly to admire the sleek, well-trained horses and partly because of his high regard for the officers as men and horse handlers. He also recounted a conversation he had with a woman who he later learned was Mrs. Ogden Mills Reid, a name meaningless to him until his escorts explained her connection with the *New York Herald Tribune.* On November 15 the *Tribune* carried a five-column layout entitled An Artist's Impression of the Last Night of the National Horse Show," with sketches of Mrs. John Hay Whitney's Kinprillis, a French jumper, a pinto, and the Squadron A guidon bearer. Each sketch was initialed O. C. S. According to the copy:

*Olaf C. Seltzer, the Montana artist who specializes in drawing horses and western scenes, enjoyed his first experience at the National Horse Show at its final session. . . . He was so enthusiastic over the color and charm of the general scene and so impressed by the performance of the French army officers in the international jumping class, as well as with the showing of the horses in other classes, that he reached for a pencil and drawing pad and recorded some of his impressions.*

Olaf sent home some clippings, commenting, "As you can see, I am mixing with the face cards." Doc had ten copies of the *Tribune* sent to Olaf's room at the "Y." "These people treat me something wonderful," he concluded his letter to Mabel, enclosing his press badge for Carl.

Putnam was preparing to leave for the West Coast, which Olaf said he would not regret, since the publisher had begun to make him nervous, "wildgoose chasing around with no particular point in mind." Before Putnam's departure the two men had an evening on the town, including dinner in a Japanese restaurant. "Saki wine served hot, oh boy, it will knock you silly," Olaf wrote to the teetotaling Mabel. "I wish Carl could have been there."

Before leaving, Putnam wrote to Olaf, urging him to get in touch with Mr. Jed Fiske, at the Pan Pacific Press Bureau, who

> knows all about the bully covers you have made for us and is, indeed, a very great admirer of your work. He is keen to meet you. . . .
>
> I think he would like to get some stuff written about you and arrange, perhaps, for some pictures. . . . what he can do for you may be of very real helpfulness. So please don't fail to contact him.

Scarcely a week later, on December 13, 1934, Putnam wrote from Hollywood:

> I want you to send a swell envelope addressed to Louis D. Lighton, Paramount Studios, Hollywood.
>
> Lighton is an important executive here, who is a great friend of Miss Earhart's and mine. He has a big ranch down south of here. He is a fine horseman and loves everything that has to do with horses and the West. He would get a great kick out of one of your envelopes. I have a hunch for instance that he will be wanting a little painting later on. For the envelope itself, I suggest some western scene with horses.

Olaf complied with the request for the producer of *Captains Courageous, A Tree Grows in Brooklyn, A Bell for Adano,* and *Anna and the King of Siam* and corresponded with Lighton until 1959, when the ailing producer sold his ranch in Prescott, Arizona, and retired to Majorca. In the interval Lighton launched his own collection of Seltzer's western paintings.[5]

It is doubtful whether the publicity-shy Seltzer ever followed through on Putnam's suggestion that he get in touch with Fiske, for he never mentioned the publicist in his letters home from New York or kept any clippings or photos to indicate personal promotion during this period. It would have been characteristic of Olaf's fatalistic nature not to base any hopes on the expectation of publicity. He was at his happiest while working at his easel to please a friend like Phil Cole, particularly in the pleasant setting of Zeeview in late autumn. Dry oak leaves tumbled in heaps of copper across the still-green slopes of the estate as Seltzer applied himself to the task at hand—the historical miniatures. To rest his eyes, he could shift from the miniscule snow scene or battlefield he was working on to the peaceful view of the Hudson River through leaf-thinned trees.

During his sessions at Zeeview Olaf worked on miniatures in which Cole had a particular interest. At least two Custer-related events were done close to Cole's extensive collection of records pertaining to the Custer battle. In *Custer, Reno, and Benteen,* Custer, on the eve of his annihilation, is pointing in the direction in which he will send his disliked subordinate, Benteen. A number of cavalrymen and horses are in the background. *Lieut. Bradley's Discovery of Custer's Massacre* is a far less cluttered scene, emphasizing the openness of the country.

*The Discovery of Gold in Last Chance Gulch by John Cowan in 1864* was also done while Seltzer was "in residence" at Zeeview. It bears the only personal reference in the entire series. Writing in the first person, Cole begins the description: "The site of this picture showing Mount Helena in the background is evidently a part of the Ranch formerly owned by my father, Dr. Charles K. Cole."

Although he missed his family, the artist thoroughly enjoyed his stays in Tarrytown. His daily routine began with breakfast in the Main Cafe and an exchange of the news of the day with the proprietors, Ethel and Iz Cohen. By daybreak he would be on the suburban bus bound for Zeeview, where he would go directly to the studio, not continuing up the drive to the house. After lunch with the Coles and Miss Ralston, Olaf would go back to the studio to review his morning's work, often in the company of Dr.

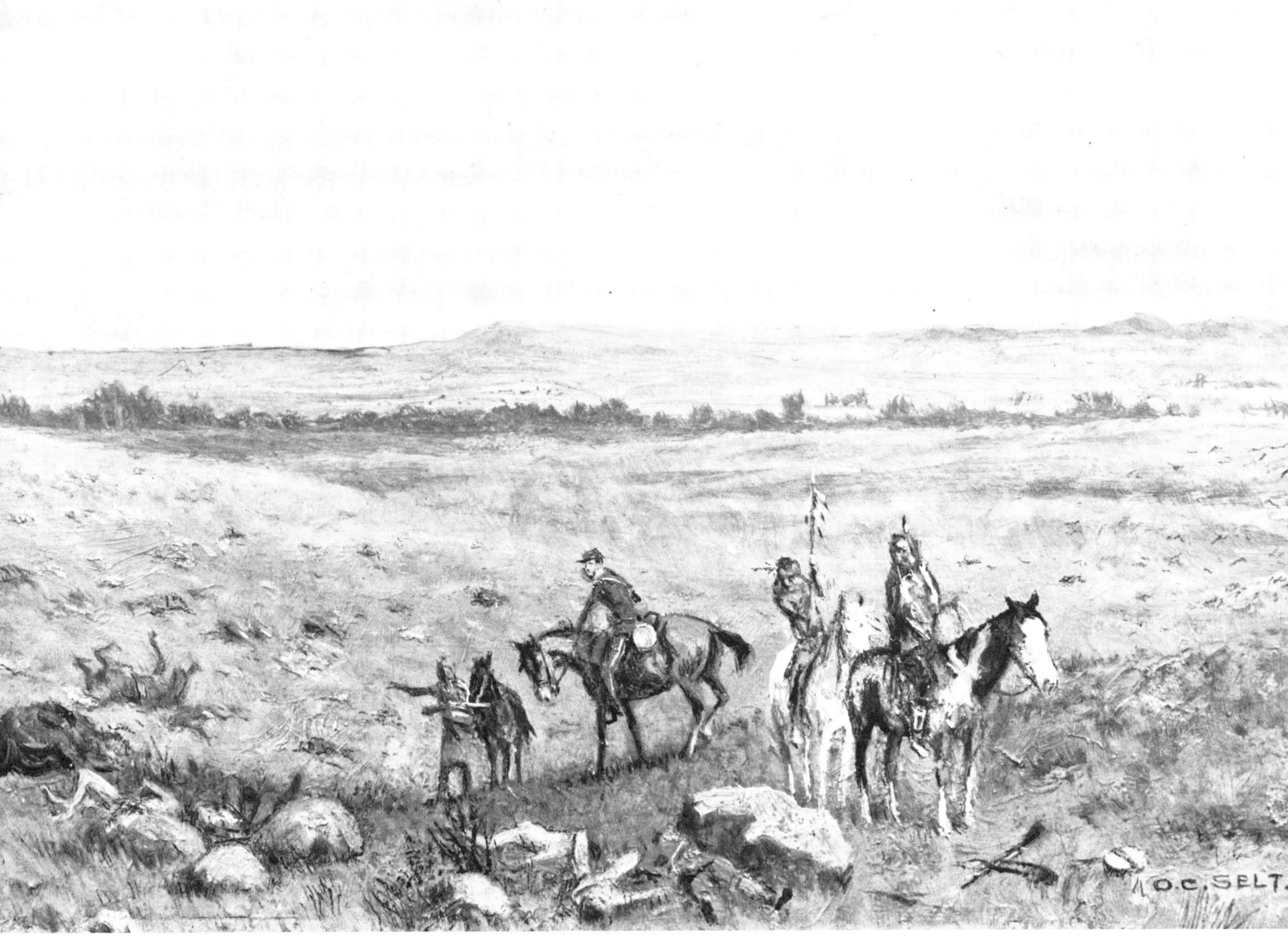

*Lieut. Bradley's Discovery of Custer's Massacre—1876*
1934
Miniature oil

Cole, who knew precisely what he wanted in the series and thoroughly enjoyed going over the minutest details with Seltzer. Later Olaf would read and do research in the western-documents collection in Cole's study. If Phil and Katharine Cole were dining at home, Olaf was usually invited to join them. After dinner he and Doc would sit for hours in the study, discussing fine points of frontier history and coming up with new ideas, or perhaps going over Cole's excellent stamp collection.[6] Before midnight Cole would have Olaf driven back to the YMCA.

Olaf took to the opulence of what he jokingly referred to as "Cole's Palace" as though he had been reared to such luxury. Once in a while his unsophisticated background tripped him up. Alice Ralston remembered vividly the performance of Oskar Straus's *Great Waltz*, for which Mrs. Cole had prominent orchestra seats. Dr. Cole decided not to go, and Olaf was invited to escort Mrs. Cole and Miss Ralston. Having had several drinks before dinner and being unaccustomed to the scanty costumes of the chorus line, Olaf nearly fell out of his seat when the curtain rose.

"Jesus Christ, Alice, look at that!" he exclaimed, stealing the first chuckle of the evening away from the stage.

On occasion Olaf would go into the city to visit such of his favorite haunts as the Museum of Natural History, the Metropolitan Museum of Art, the Bronx Zoo, the Aquarium, and the Brooklyn Museum. He also enjoyed the conviviality of Manhattan's cocktail lounges. Sometimes Miss Ralston was called upon to drive into the city and bring back the inebriated artist. One such excursion was etched on her memory. Copying one of Dr. Cole's enthusiasms, Olaf had started still another collection—tiny, delicate hand-blown glass animals whose translucent colors and whimsical shapes tickled his fancy. On the day of the Sawmill River Parkway incident, Seltzer had had a number of drinks while "stalking" glass animals in Manhattan curio shops, and was forced to call for help in getting back to Tarrytown.

Driving along the parkway during the rush hour was taxing Alice Ralston's nervous stamina even before a tipsy Seltzer decided to "liberate" some of his glass beasts. No sooner had he sailed a couple of them out of the car window than he regretted his rash act and demanded to be let out of the moving car. It was a ride the Montana nurse never forgot.

Olaf's "morning-after" embarrassment was acute. Several months later, after he had returned to Great Falls, he sent Miss Ralston an illustrated letter featuring a big-game hunter taking aim on a procession of blue elephants that was emerging from a narrow street among towering skyscrapers. He wrote:

Dear Alice: Having some time ago concluded a very successful hunting season in the Jungles of Manhattoes, particularly in that wild and isolated country known as Madison Avenue, Lewis & Conger, Kinzy's Pet Shop and the Curio Shoppe of Radio Center, I find myself once again midst the silence and solitude of the Prairie, surrounded by my many Trophies of the Chase, running the gamut from Green Elephants, Pink Penguins and silver-plated flamingoes up to Angle Fish and Chinese Calico Dragon Eyes, the last two items, however, being very much alive and not belonging to the Glass Blower's Art.

In the upper-left-hand corner Olaf wrote: "Rejoice when you hear the Dummy speak." Beneath the text the artist depicts himself in cartoon fashion, smoking a cigar in his easy chair, surrounded by a fishbowl, aquarium, penguins, seals, and similar glass creatures. The envelope bears a flamingo on a pedestal.[7]

Whenever he returned to Montana, Olaf felt nostalgic about Tarrytown. After his 1934 visit he sent the Cohens an illustrated letter. A New Year's card went to Patrolman Charles Schneider, although Olaf did not know the name of the officer, who was always followed by a little yellow dog. Seltzer enclosed the card in an envelope bearing only a sketch of the policeman and the dog. It was delivered without question.

At fifty-eight Olaf was no longer the stylishly dressed dandy he once had been. His hairline had receded so far that he could be described as bald. He wore rimless glasses, and he had a formal, old-fashioned manner. Kay Cole Worden remembers him from her girlhood as "short in stature, somewhat shabby" in his working clothes. She was impressed by his kindliness but at the time never thought of him as an artist. "The artists painted the pictures which filled the walls," she said. "And then there was Mr. Seltzer, who seemed to be always there—he was like a member of the family."[8]

Back in Great Falls in the early months of 1935, Olaf once more immersed himself in the historical project. He and Cole had discussed several additional mining subjects, *First Sluicing for Gold in Montana* and *Hydraulic Mining at Last Chance Gulch*, as well as *The Vigilante's Oath, A Quintuple Hanging*, and *Twin Cottonwoods on Stinking River*, the last three concerned with efforts to bring law to the Montana frontier. Some of the miniatures had been started at Zeeview and were now being completed. *The Sheep Eaters*, for which Olaf asked his son Walt to do some research while the artist was working in New York, was completed in Montana.

Amelia Earhart made her Honolulu-to-Oakland flight in mid-January, 1935. President Franklin D. Roosevelt and Postmaster James A. Farley were among the celebrities to whom she mailed, as souvenirs, the Seltzer-decorated envelopes. Despite the limited number, Miss Earhart sent one of them back to Olaf. It featured winged Mercury, god of travel and commerce, poised atop the world. Seven planes of windswept design are in formation flight, left to right. There

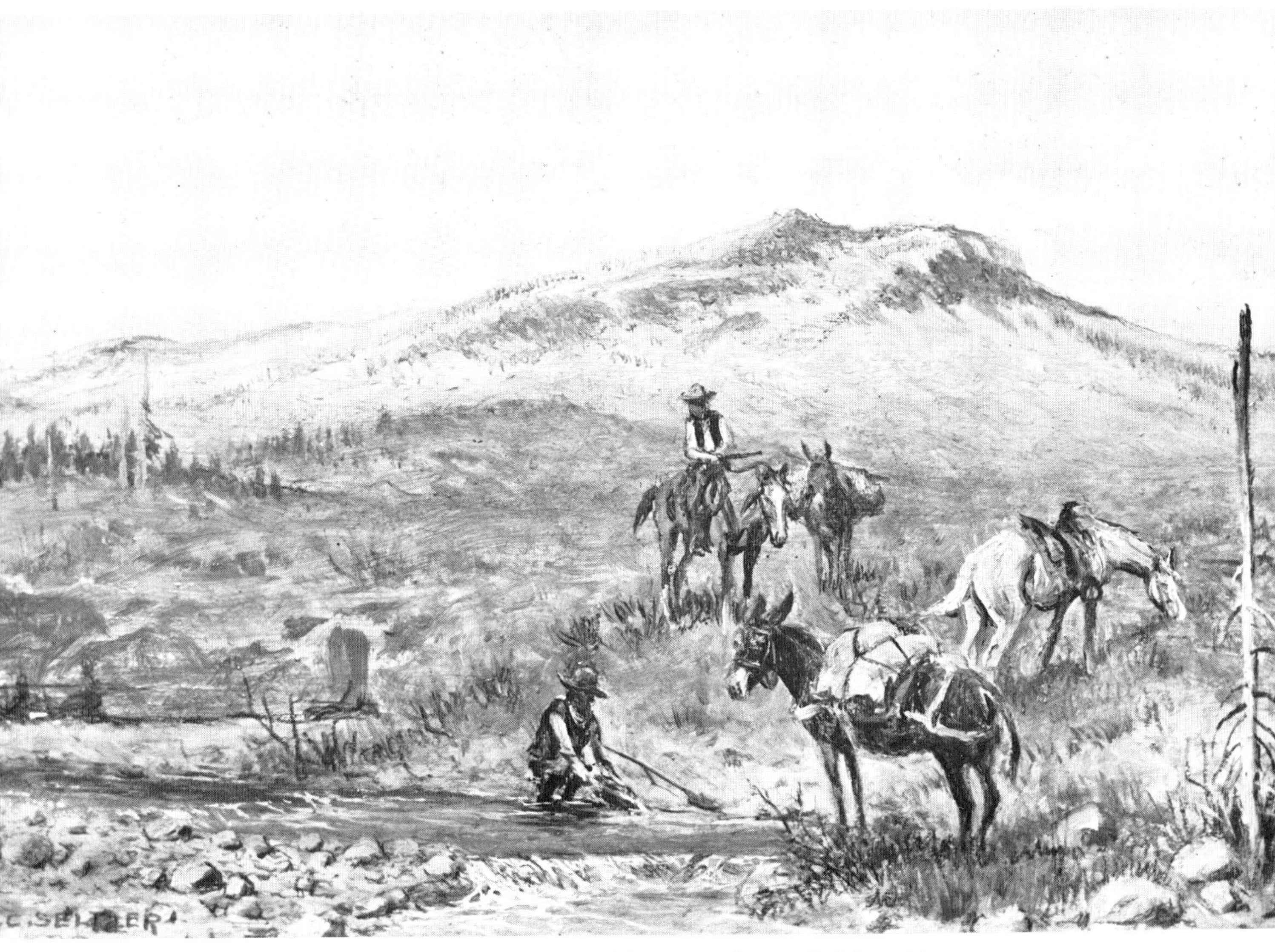

*Discovery of Gold in Last Chance Gulch—1864*
1934
Miniature oil

are background panels of loden green and black. To the left Miss Earhart wrote, "Carried by air, Honolulu, Oakland, January 11–12, 1935." Olaf Seltzer, philatelist, numbered this envelope among his prized possessions.

The following spring Phil Cole remarked in a letter to Olaf that he was glad the artist had been given an order from "G.P.P.," although he had not seen either of the Putnams for some time. The order was for *The Fallen Monarch*, a 24″ × 30″ scene of a hunting party with pack train riding out of the Absaroka Mountains in Wyoming. Putnam commissioned it after he lost some paintings in a fire. He wanted it for his wife, as a remembrance of their Wyoming hunting experiences. Olaf worked on the commission during 1935, but heard from the Putnams less following the Honolulu-to-Oakland flight. Nothing ever came of the proposed article involving the illustrated letters. The "Seltzer top-of-the-heap Campaign" fizzled out.

By late February, 1935, Dr. Cole had eighty-

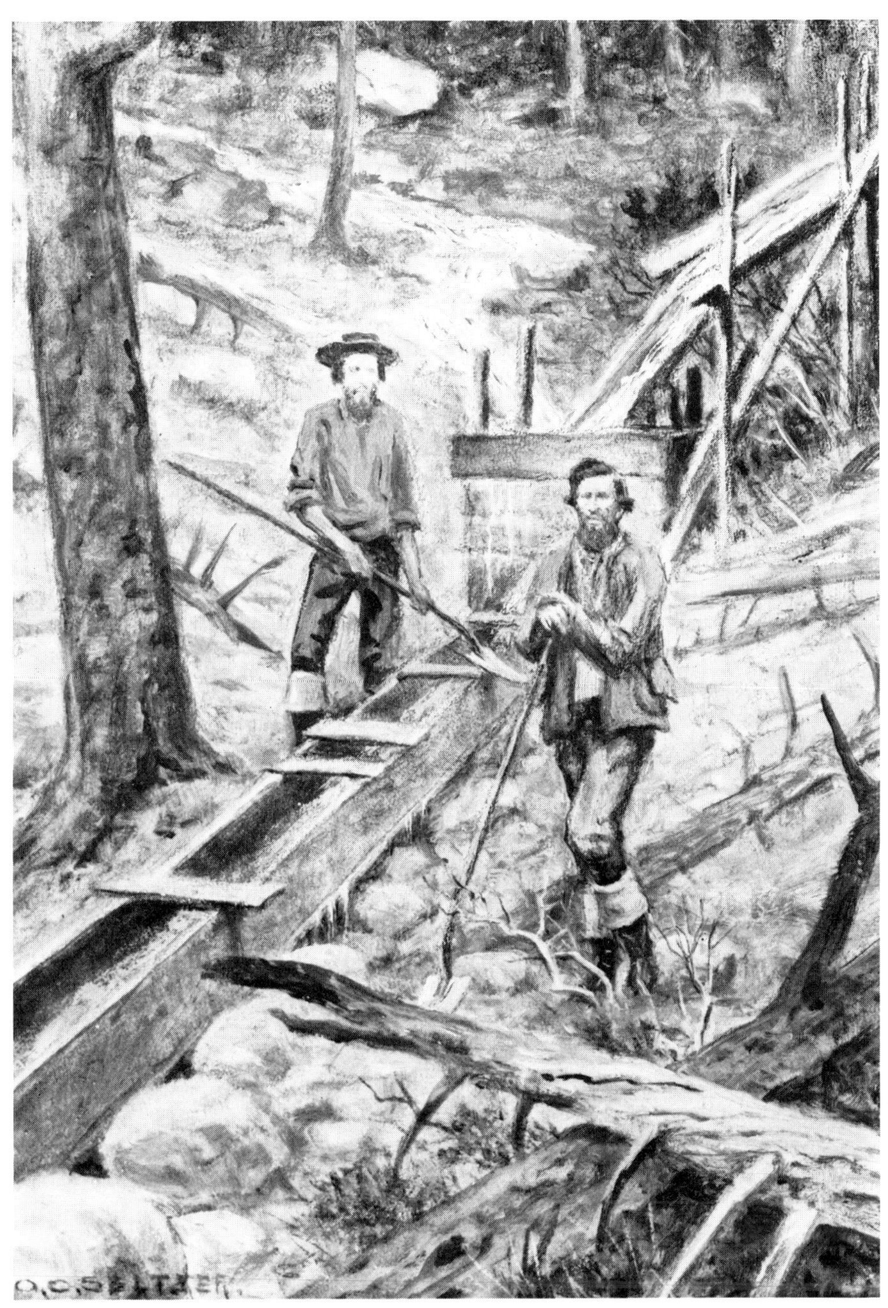

*First Sluicing for Gold in Montana*
1935
Miniature oil

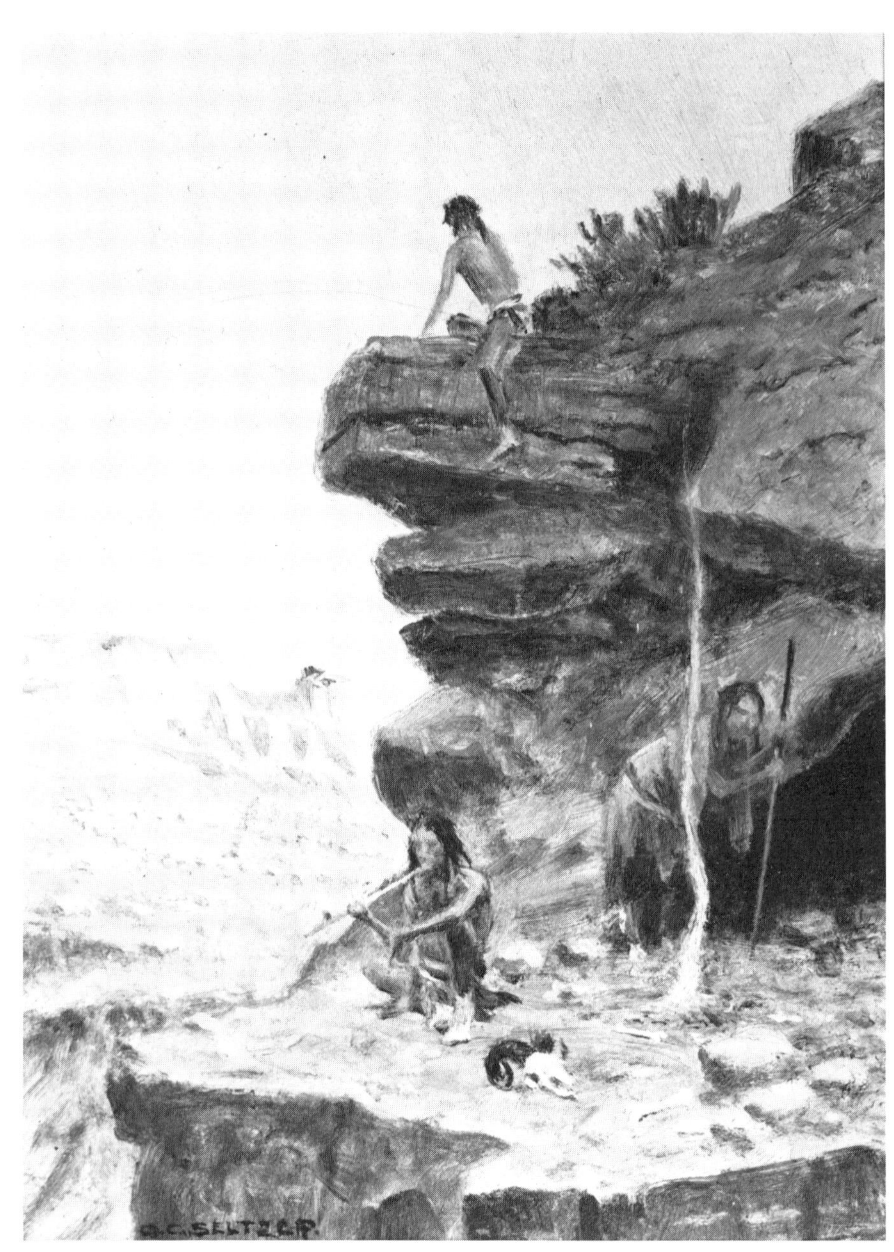

*Sheep Eaters*
1935
Miniature oil

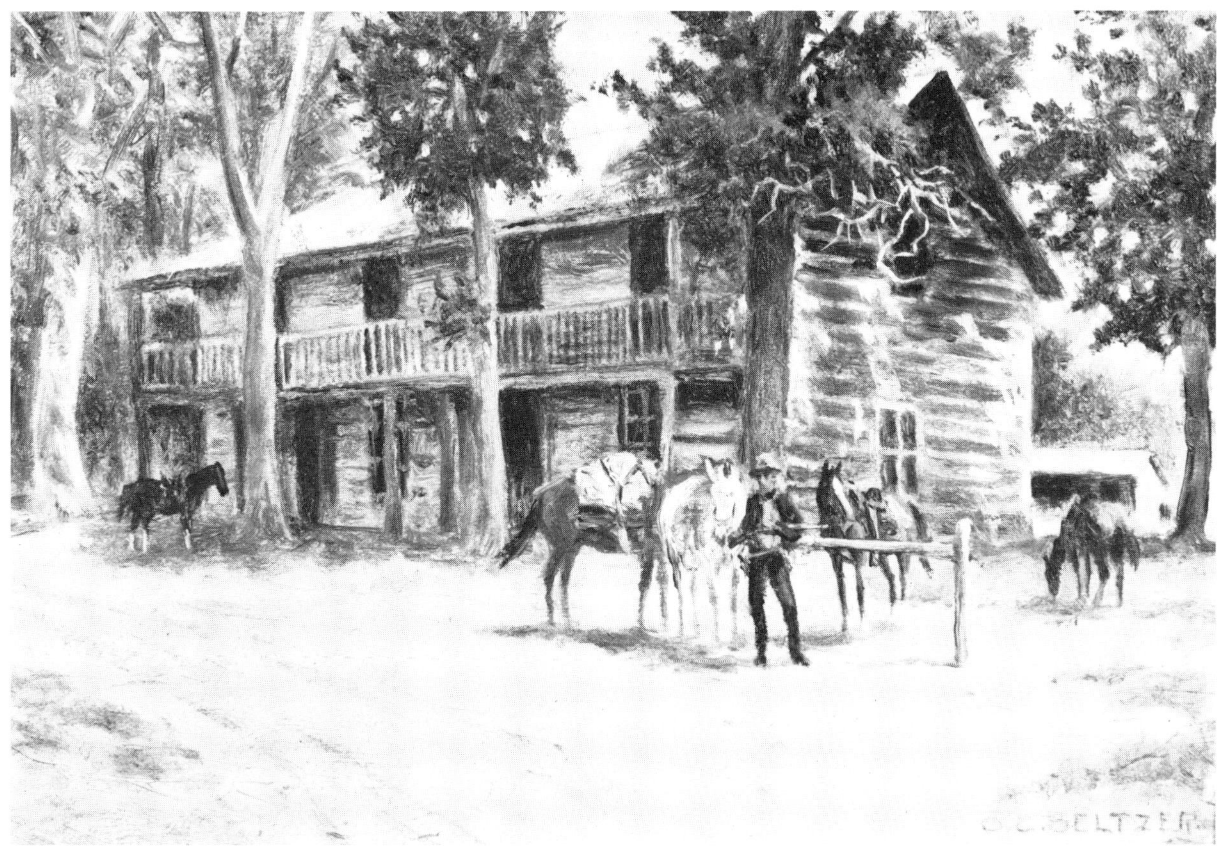

*Robbers' Roost*
1935
Miniature oil

four of the miniatures in his possession, including some new arrivals, such as *Sheep Men vs. Cattle Men*, *Robber's Roost* (the rendezvous of the Plummer gang of road agents), *Freighting at Fort Benton*, and *Sir Alexander Mackenzie*, shown standing in his canoe on the Peace River in 1793.

Seltzer broke his concentrated effort on the historical project only to represent Cole in the purchase of another Russell painting. Cole asked the artist to inspect a 24″ × 18″ oil, *Through the Alkali*, which Dr. George M. McCole in Great Falls had offered to sell to the collector.

Cole sent Olaf a copy of his answer to Dr. McCole, dated February 26:

> From your description it sounds very interesting.
>
> You make no mention of what date this picture was painted. Also, while you mention it having a

$2,000.00 value but that you will take less money for it, you do not tell me what you will take.

I suggest that if you have a photograph of it or could have one taken and send me a copy, at the same time letting me know its date, etc., it would help me a great deal in telling you whether or not I am interested. I am, as you doubtless have been told, interested in Russell, Remington and other western paintings but I am acquiring them only when they can not only be picked up at a truly reasonable price consistent with these days rather than the good old days when Charlie's paintings brought such fabulous sums, but also when they are good enough to raise the standard of my collection rather than be suspended by it.

I mention all this about price because it is pretty shocking the price at which paintings can be picked up today. I will however be glad to hear from you along the lines I have suggested.

You undoubtedly know Olaf C. Seltzer. . . . It

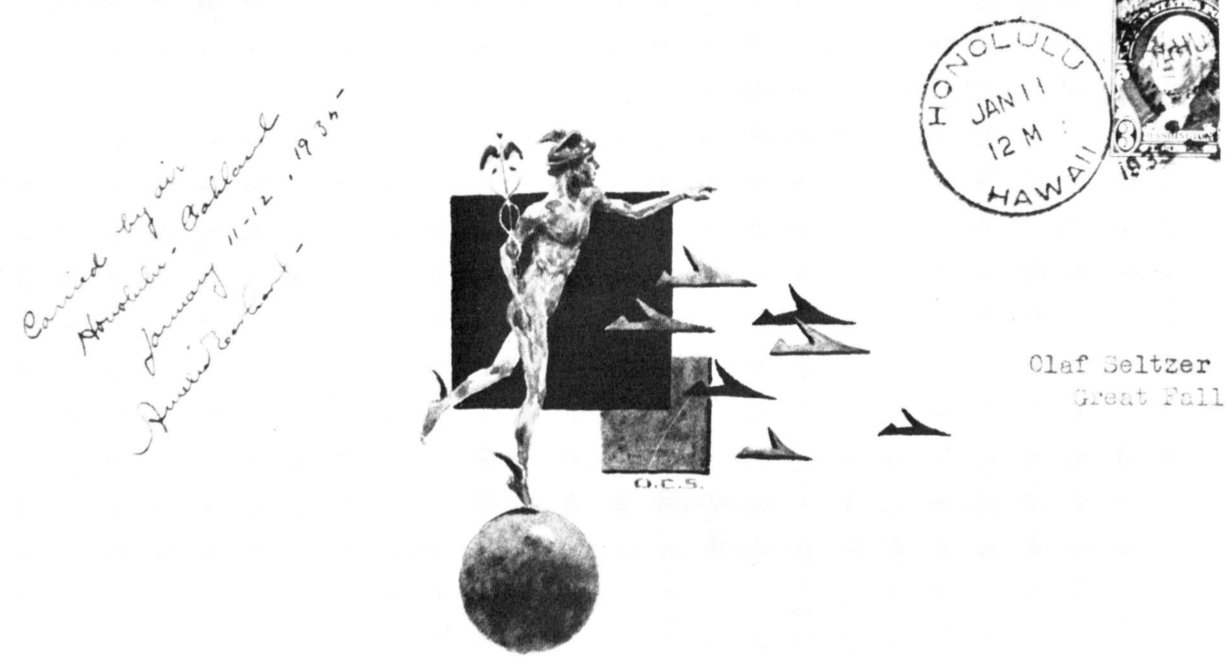

*First Day Envelope*
1934
Watercolor and ink, 4″ × 6″
Courtesy of Carl C. Seltzer.

might not be a bad idea for you to get in touch with him. He knows my ideas along these lines pretty well.

To Olaf, Doc wrote:

> I wish you would look into this for me and give me the real lowdown on it. I mentioned your name to him because I want you to be sure to see the painting. It sounds like a good subject and it is an upright which is somewhat helpful. I am paying no attention of course to the $2,000.00 value price he mentions. I will as you know, only be interested if it is a *real bargain* and would build up the collection. As you know the space in my home is so filled that to add one picture now means removing from the walls something else. You know the whole story too well for me to have to repeat it to you and I know that you will give me the real lowdown as well as tip him off as to what prices really are today.

Olaf dropped everything to fulfill Doc's request, and *Through the Alkali* was in Cole's hands by March 7.

On Olaf's recommendation regarding quality and interesting subject matter Cole bought the painting, mailing his check for $1,000, the price agreed upon, on March 13 and asking McCole to furnish him with

> a bill of sale for my records and insurance purposes, also a little note telling me what you can of the history of this painting, when you acquired it, from whom, who previous owners may have been, what Charlie Russell said about the painting, and anything else you can think of which might be of interest. The painting is indeed a lovely one and I am proud to have it in the collection.

At the same time, Phil wrote to Olaf:

> I agree with you that this is a good example of Charlie's work and that it also tells an interesting story of why and how the cowpuncher's necker-

chief or bandanna is used. As a matter of fact, I really don't consider $1,000.00 a very cheap price . . . and I damn near didn't take it at that. However as I have said I not only like the painting but more or less felt that I ought to take it after the courtesies extended by Dr. McCole and yourself.

I am going very easy on paintings from now on and really only going to pick up a new one when a real gem comes along at a real bargain. Incidentally I think the collection calls for Remingtons now rather than Russells. The reason for slowing down is twofold. In the first place to add a painting means removing one from the walls of the house for the walls are not elastic and as you know every inch of space is already filled. Also, believe it or not, I can't afford it like I used to could.

Cole's March 13 letter to Seltzer continued:

I am looking forward to the arrival of the next lot of miniatures. I haven't been able to hang the last two verticals yet because the horizontal ones have to be placed first on the wall.

I am going away on the 20th and will be back on the 30th, but don't let that hold you back from sending on whatever you have as I have arranged with the office to take care of sending you a check if anything arrives during my absence. Please try to have some things here for me so that I can hang them immediately upon my return home.

Olaf's assistance on *Through the Alkali* turned out to be only the first of several Russell-related chores Doc called upon Olaf to undertake for him in 1935. General W. A. Allen, of Billings, wrote Cole in May offering the collector some Russell watercolors along with some photographs he had taken after Custer's debacle when, according to his letter, he was "on the battlefield when the soldiers all lay dead." Once again Phil Cole forwarded for Olaf's information a copy of his answer to General Allen:

I am delighted to hear from you particularly as I am very much interested in anything having to do with the Custer Fight, and even more so from anyone who was on the ground as soon after the Fight as you were.

The Russell watercolors I am quite sure I would not be interested in as my collection of Russell's is mostly restricted to his oil paintings done somewhere after about 1908 or later.

The photographs you took on the Custer Battlefield sound very interesting and if they are good it might well be that I would be interested in acquiring some from you.

May I suggest that you get in touch . . . with my friend Olaf C. Seltzer. . . . He is a personal friend of mine and knows the type of thing in which I am interested. I am sure he would be glad to run over to see what you have and report to me.

In forwarding a copy of his letter to General Allen, Cole also acknowledged a note from Seltzer telling Cole of the prospective arrival of two more miniatures, *Fort Piegan* and *Saint Mary's Mission*. "Many many thanks for the written data on these two subjects," Cole continued. "This helps a lot. . . .

"I am glad you like the Texas longhorn idea." This upright miniature was accompanied by a long description of the cattle herds and the "Run-Five men, riding double rig saddles with saddle pockets and trapaderos, using Hackamore headstalls with braided horsehair McCarty instead of the split-ear headstall and spade bit."

Olaf still had seventeen subjects to document in the historical series after he finished the Texas longhorns. Most of these dealt with Indian customs and frontier practices, but the dramatic *Battle of the Big Hole* and *The Stabbing of Crazy Horse* were also in this last group.

The miniatures can be divided into three categories: historical events, personal histories of prominent western personalities, and the graphic portrayal of customs that were rapidly becoming archaic. The personality pictures differ in format from the Western Character watercolors, which have little or no background detail, depending on the vignette to tell the story. All but two of the Western Characters represent stereotypes, the exceptions being *A Picture Builder, C.M.R.* and *Owner, P.G.C.*, the latter a sketch of Cole on his favorite horse. The figures commemorated in the miniatures are, by contrast, identifiable and are frequently celebrated persons, such as *Jim Bridger on the Powder River in 1830* and *Kenneth McKenzie*, first emissary of the American Fur Company, portrayed in his characteristic red coat and accompanied by his dog team. *A Black Robe Pioneer* (Father John Peter DeSmet) shares the spotlight with his faithful Iroquois guide Ignace, who helped him with his work among the Flathead Indians.

*"Smoky" Wilson* is clearly a personality study. Seltzer depicts the black man dressed as an Indian, and standing before a tipi, rifle in hand, his cayuse on a lead. Wilson, son of slaves, went up the Missouri River to Helena in 1866. At the time the painting was made, Smoky was still living

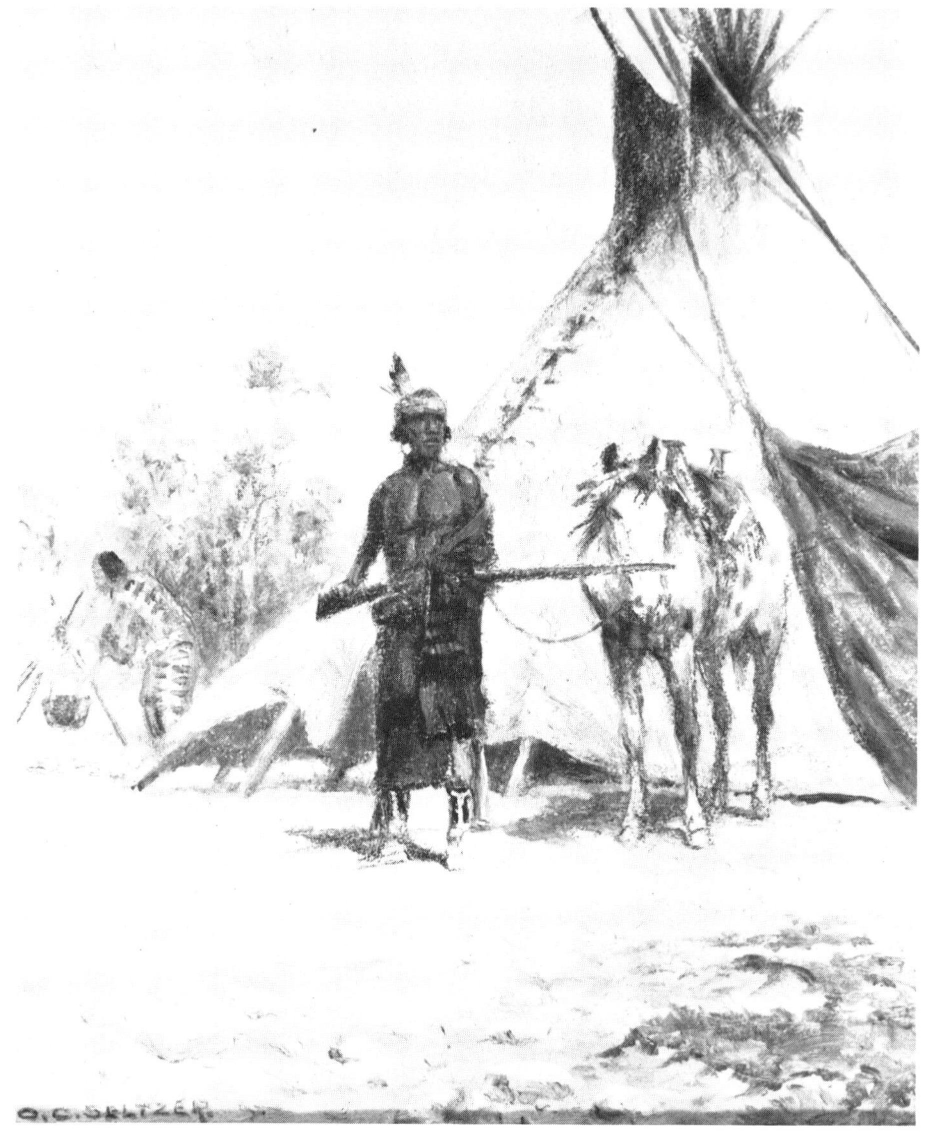

*Smoky Wilson*
1933
Miniature oil

among the Crows. According to the accompanying text:

> For awhile he worked . . . in Bozeman, breaking horses and riding the range. He came in close contact with the Crow Indians, learning their language and often serving as interpreter between them and the Whites. Gradually he drifted into living with the Crows by whom he was finally adopted as a member of the tribe.

Wilson went on war expeditions with the Crows against the Sioux, Piegans, and other enemies for sixty years, according to the description, but never fought the whites.

Despite Seltzer's feeling of incompetence in painting "she-kind of people," his treatment of *The Dorian Woman*, a western personality whose bravery was legendary, is marked with tenderness and unabashed admiration.

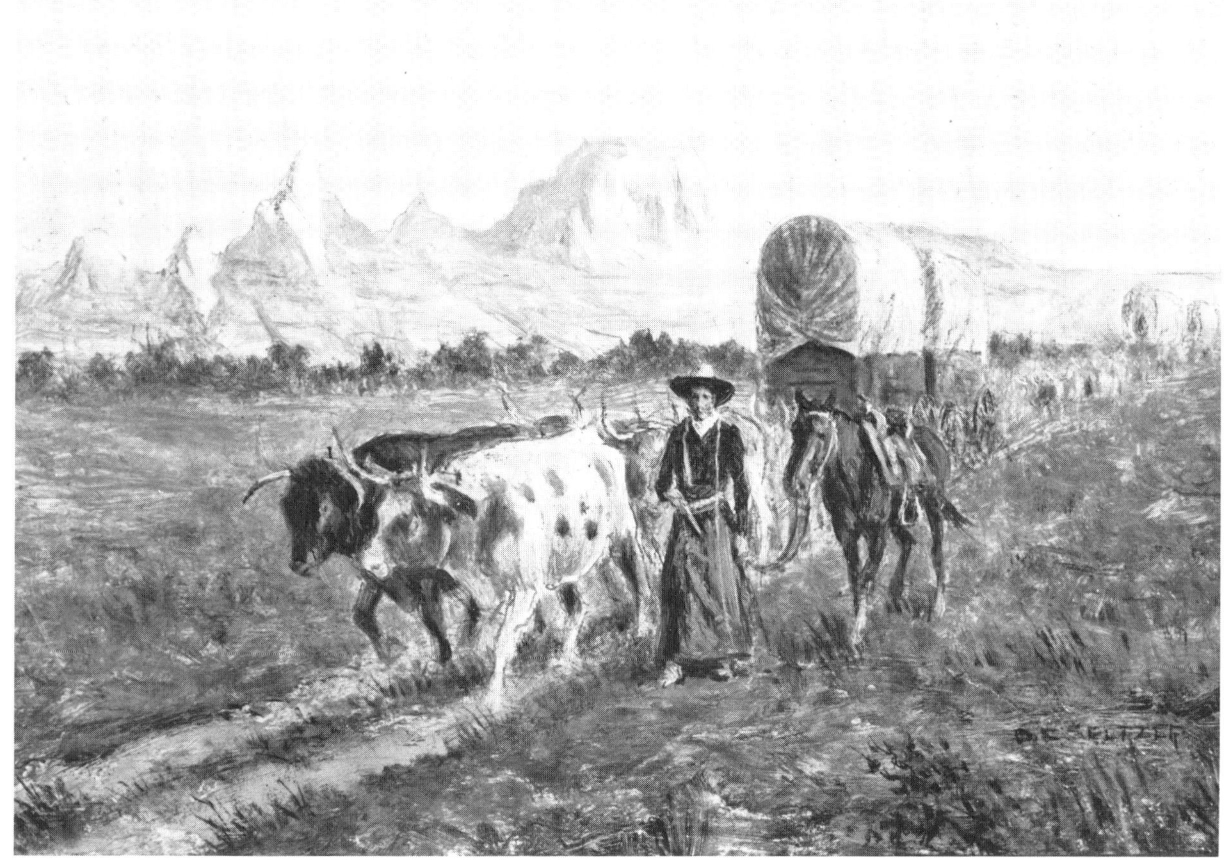

*Calamity Jane*
1934
Miniature oil

"History of the early days of the Pacific Northwest is replete with acts of bravery and amazing experiences but none can surpass the heroism and incredible adventure of the Dorian Woman," begins the *Montana in Miniature* narration of the Sioux woman's ordeal. The property wife of a drunken, abusive Yankton Sioux named Pierre Dorian, her nightmarish story began on New Year's Day in 1804:

*. . . A friendly Indian warned her that a band of Dog Ribs (a tribe of the Athabaskans) had burned their camp . . . and that her husband was in great danger. By means of a horse to whose back she was tied lest she fall from it, she succeeded in reaching her husband only to find him dead. Tying to the back of her horse her own two boys*

*she . . . escape[d] in the dead of winter through the country of the hostile Snakes.*

*For many months she lived in a tiny wiki-up, subsisting on berries and occasional squirrels which she was able to catch in a mesh made from her horse's tail hair. Eventually after the death of her horse she attempted to continue her journey with her papoose strapped to her back. At one time she became stone blind and on regaining her sight she found herself staring into the eyes of a wolf. Finally she hid her boys under a rock and she succeeded in reaching a camp of friendly Walla Wallas with her papoose Baptiste still alive on her back.*

Seltzer painted her as he imagined she looked, leaning on a sturdy stick, making her way through

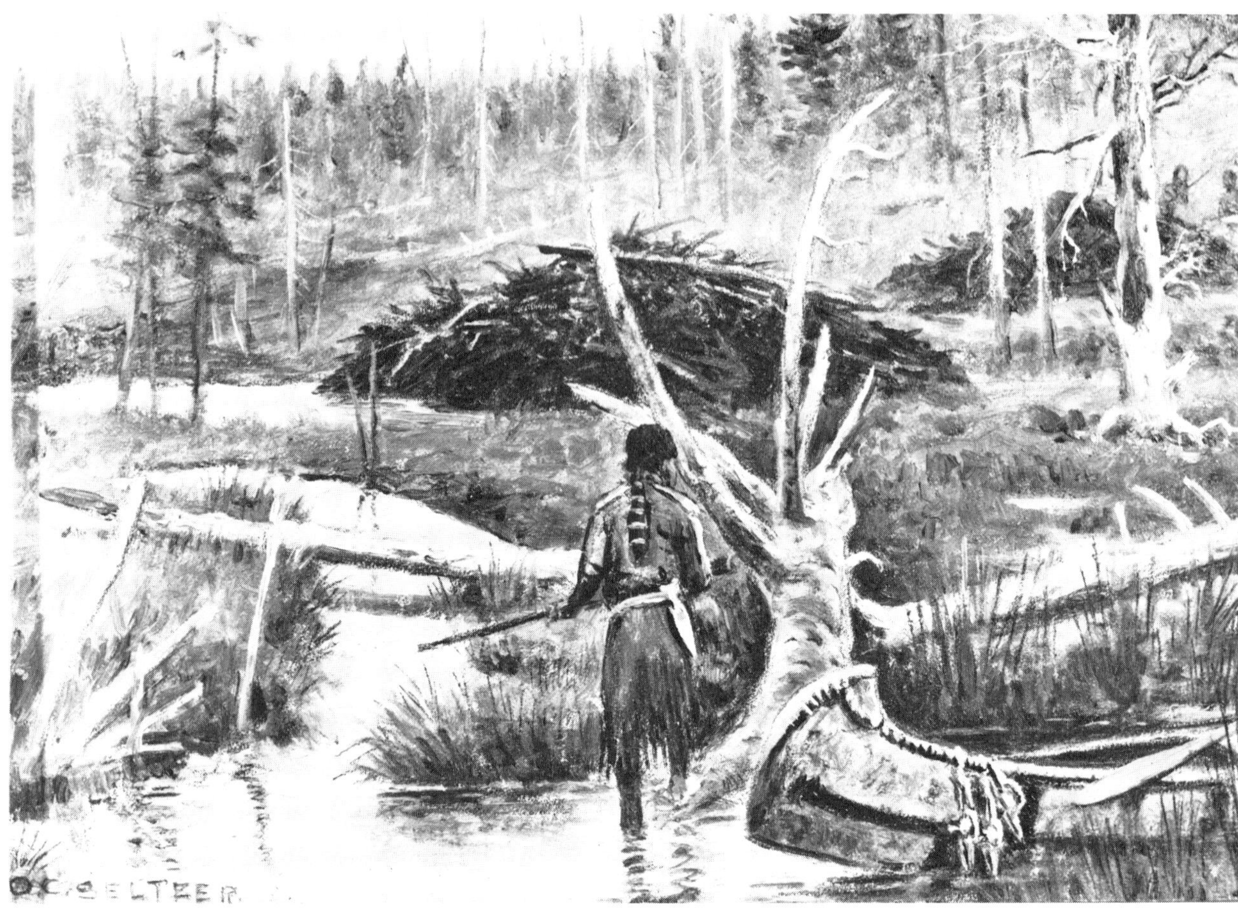

*Thomas Fitzpatrick About 1824*
1934
Miniature oil

several inches of newly fallen snow. Her arms are bare beneath the shawl that she has wrapped around the infant and across her back; the wind blows her fringed, hide robe forward, and snow covers her footprints. It is a picture of desolation, touchingly treated.

Another female personality is portrayed in *Calamity Jane (Bullwhacking in the Neighborhood of Townsend, Montana)*. On foot at the head of her oxen team, with her riding horse on a lead, she is described as "a hard riding, hard drinking, hard working and hard playing woman whose affections could easily be momentarily gained but whose dislikes could not be disregarded with safety." Nonetheless, Seltzer had added a certain femininity to her figure in its long riding skirt, and a romantic softness pervades the coloring of the scene.

A second group of personal histories has the subjects reduced in size against a more elaborate background that fixes the significance of each personality in the context of a memorable scene. *Manuel Lisa—1807 (Watching the Construction of Fort Lisa)* is portrayed on horseback as the central figure in a scene that shows work going on at one of his trading posts a half mile or so below. Lisa, a member of the Lewis and Clark Expedition, established his first trading post in 1806 near the site of Mandan, North Dakota.

Do Seltzer's depictions impart the facts about

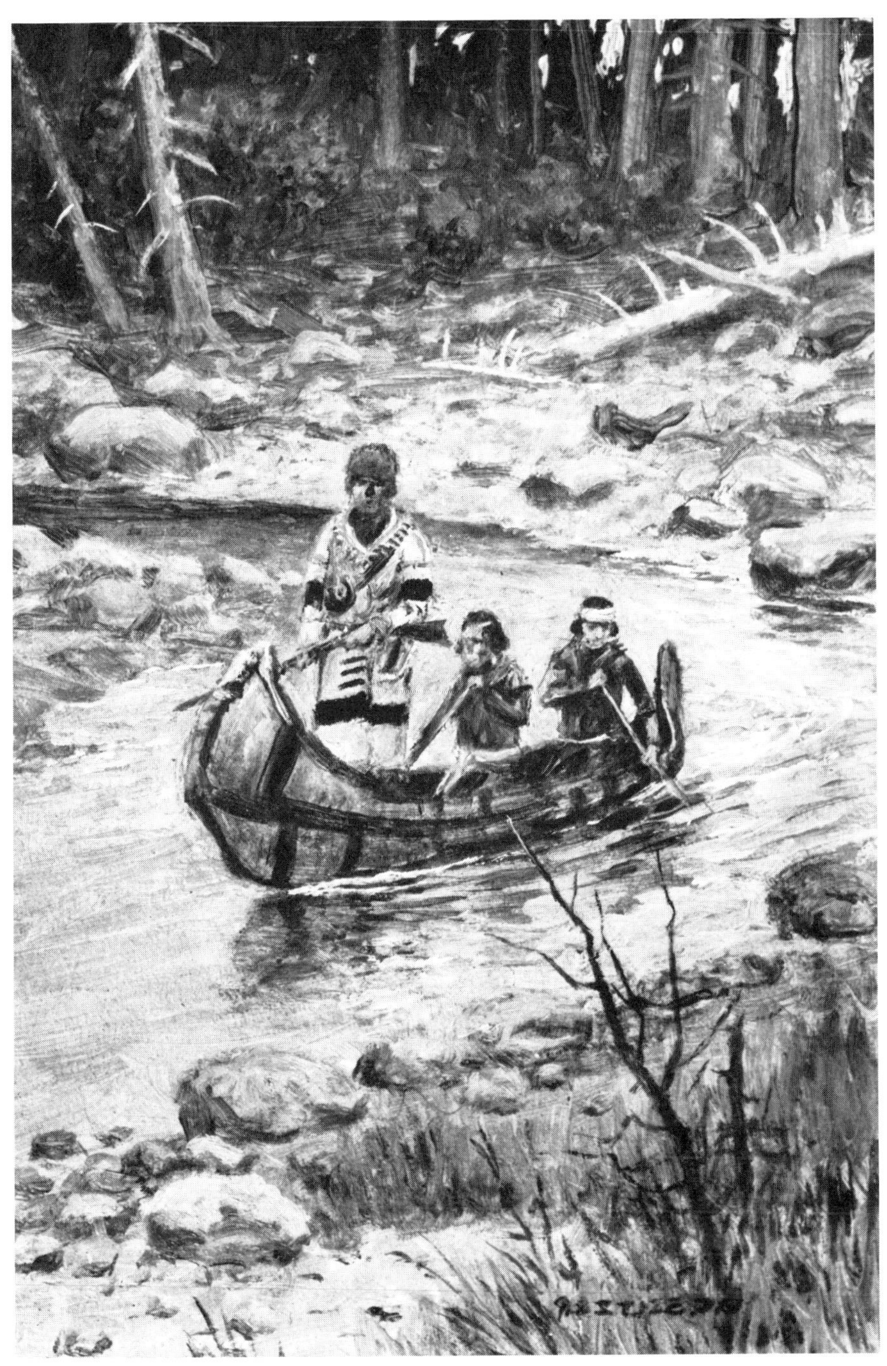

*Sir Alexander Mackenzie*
1935
Miniature oil

western historymakers? In *The Art of the Old West* the miniature of Manuel Lisa is cited for its historical and pictorial significance:

*Lisa remains one of the most controversial figures involved in the American fur trade, some contemporaries and later historians describing him as a villain, others as a noble character. Hated by his rivals in the Upper Missouri trade, he was hardly better liked by his own men or those whom he persuaded to back his many ventures. Olaf Seltzer has pictured Manuel Lisa . . . as he might have appeared overlooking the construction of his first fort along the Yellowstone . . . Seltzer's miniatures do not lend themselves to the depiction of more specific details, but the artist presents a fine graphic sense of place and time in this portrayal.* [9]

Olaf painted Lisa as an unpretentious man with a touch of the savage. His head is tied with a band in the manner of the southwestern Indians; he leans forward, low over his horse's neck. There is nothing in his bearing in this depiction to indicate that he was a man of wealth and importance.

*Thomas Fitzpatrick about 1824* shows the head of the Rocky Mountain Fur Company trapping for beaver, "a silent game best played solo," on Rock Creek in the Little Belt Mountains. Fitzpatrick, who "almost epitomizes the fur trading industry," was one of the discoverers of the South Pass, the future gateway to Oregon. The authors of *The Art of the Old West* go along with the trapper's garb and gear but contend that the canoe was introduced by the French for use along the Upper Missouri beaver haunts and was not usually seen farther west (Seltzer planned no portrait depiction here; he painted the famous trapper from the rear view).

Another famous explorer in the fur trade, Sir Alexander MacKenzie, is painted standing in the prow of his canoe on the Peace River in 1793, dressed as a voyageur.

Included in the series are several milestone events in the adventures of the Lewis and Clark Expedition, usually featuring Captain Lewis as the central figure. *Lewis' First Glimpse of the Rockies* brings the captain's figure into a close-up range, while the oft-reprinted *Lewis at the Black Eagle Falls* also features Clark's servant, York, wearing the tattered remains of a Continental uniform. [10] Sacagawea has a recurring appeal for the artist. She is painted in a number of the

scenes, and one of the longest commentaries accompanies *Sacajawea at Sulphur Spring*. It tells of her convalescence beside the healing waters in 1805. Lewis is by her side, and Clark is shown indistinctly in the background, approaching on horseback from a scouting mission.

Captain William Clark is the featured figure in *The Deluge at Colter Falls*, one of the last miniatures to be painted. He is shown thigh-deep in swirling water as he pushes Sacagawea and her child up a riverbank, where York and Charbonneau, her husband, assist them to safety. Other renditions dealing with the expedition are *Lewis on the Marias*, the scene of an 1806 skirmish with the Indians, and *The Lolo Pass*, showing expedition members in a pack train ascending the trail that seventy years later would be an escape route for Chief Joseph.

Seltzer highlighted his miniatures on Indian life with colorful details. The most beautifully detailed of these is *The Buffalo Dance*, showing the Assiniboine musicians in the foreground while the dancers perform against a backdrop of lodges. Four singers with drums and several pipers using whistles made from the wingbones of eagles provide accompaniment. The longest of the background descriptions is provided for *Parfleching in a Blackfeet Village*, which shows a squaw working over a hide staked out on the ground with pegs scraping away the fragments of tissue and fat. The dressing of skins "was not only woman's work, but her worth and virtue were estimated by her output." According to the commentary:

*Soles of moccasins, parfleche and other bags are made of stiff rawhide, the product of one of the simplest and perhaps most primitive methods of treating skins . . .*

*The task was laborious and unpleasant, requiring more brute strength than skill. The skin was . . . worked down to an even thickness by scraping with an adzlike tool. The hide was then turned and the hair removed in the same manner. After fleshing and scraping, the soft tan finish is obtained by rubbing the surface over with an oily compound composed of brains and fat mixed with liver. The hide was placed in the sun and rubbed with a smooth stone until dry, then saturated with warm water, rolled in a bundle to dry again, after which it was rubbed with a rough edged stone until it presented a grained appearance.*

*Note in this picture the poles of the Blackfeet*

*tipi, long and slender usually of pine or spruce, carefully selected, peeled and seasoned. . . . The Blackfeet tipi is made and owned by the woman. . . . Among the Blackfeet, the door faces East, perhaps because the winds are usually from the West, although there is a mystic reason.*

*Note the shield, quiver and medicine bag hanging on the post in front of the lodge, also the buck's saddle (squaw's saddle has a higher fork) and in the saddle is a piece of buffalo or beaver robe with beaded border and fringed, called "pishamore," used to lay across the seat of the saddle, as an Indian saddle is just a skeleton affair.*

There is a Dakota Sioux *Picture Writer*, and there is a group of Blackfeet *Horse Thieves* driving back to their own country a herd captured from the Crows or Sioux. According to the text: "Horse stealing was . . . one of the main reasons for the almost continuous wars among the different tribes of the horseback riding Plains Indians. . . . They took horses from their enemies by stratagem. This for them was a legitimate prerogative of war and captured horses were the legitimate spoils of war." Describing horses as "the only property that could be carried off," the text concludes, "To the pioneers of the West, horse stealing signified almost the depth of depravity; it was to the Indian an honorable evidence of prowess."

Many of the miniatures, such as the previously described *Grub Pile* of the N–N outfit and the *Faro Layout in the Mint Saloon, Great Falls, Montana,* depict persons identified in the text. The latter, Seltzer, contended, "is a true reproduction of the oldtime Faro layout." The commentary continues:

*Note Miles Henderson, the picturesque early day Faro dealer for Jack Enright when that gambling lord was at his height, wearing his loud-checked vest, his scarlet sleeve supporters and his hat which he always wore, and the toothpick that was usually in his face. The lookout with the walrus mustache is old Bill Marks.[11] He is true to type, sitting in his high chair and wearing his fancy smoking jacket with silk lapels and cuffs of gay colors. Note the case keeper on the opposite side of the table from the dealer. Note also the oldtime potbellied stove with its ever-present kettle of water for hot drinks, and the pictures on the wall of John L. Fitzsimmons and the other old-*

*time prize fighters. The ventilation was not part of a Faro layout as is shown by the smoke laden room.*

The faro layout is replete with incredibly fine detail, from the bright green of Marks's cuffs to the red dice cups and the playing cards lying face up, a deuce of spades in the foreground. Careful scrutiny of this miniature shows why Olaf Seltzer used brushes from which he had plucked all but one sable hair and, before the series was finished, employed high-powered magnifying glasses for this work.

Notes were detailed to help future generations understand how it was in frontier saloons such as the Mint:

*Gambling halls, where the ceiling was the limit as to the amount one could bet on the turning of a card were one of the few places of diversion where one might find sociability as well as give free rein to the gambling spirit with which most of the early comers were so thoroughly endowed. . . . The professional gambler was one of the most respected men in the community. His honesty was unquestioned and his nerve was that of iron. The odds were known to be somewhat in his favor but he was on the level.*

Nearly a dozen paintings in the series are concerned with life on the range. *The Cattle Stampede,* reminiscent of Remington's *Stampeded by Lightning,* shows a cowpuncher, with coiled rope held high, riding madly alongside the pelting cattle. The description explains that by "slapping their coiled ropes against their stiff slickers" the cowhands "endeavor with hideous noises to get the cows milling in a circle rather than allow them to scatter in a mad straightaway dash."

*Roping a Maverick* tells the story of Sam Maverick, of Texas, whose name came to mean an unbranded critter. *Cattle Rustlers' Stand* provides detail on the practice of altering brands. *The Wolfer* describes the activities of a dog trainer, once employed to protect cattle ranges. *The Remuda,* a scene depicting a nighthawk taking out a herd of beautiful horses, adds to the panorama of range activities.

Seltzer's compassion for animals adds pathos to his paintings *The Blizzard of 1886—87* and *The Hide Hunters,* both scenes of fallen carcasses in the snow. The leaden skies of the hunting scene

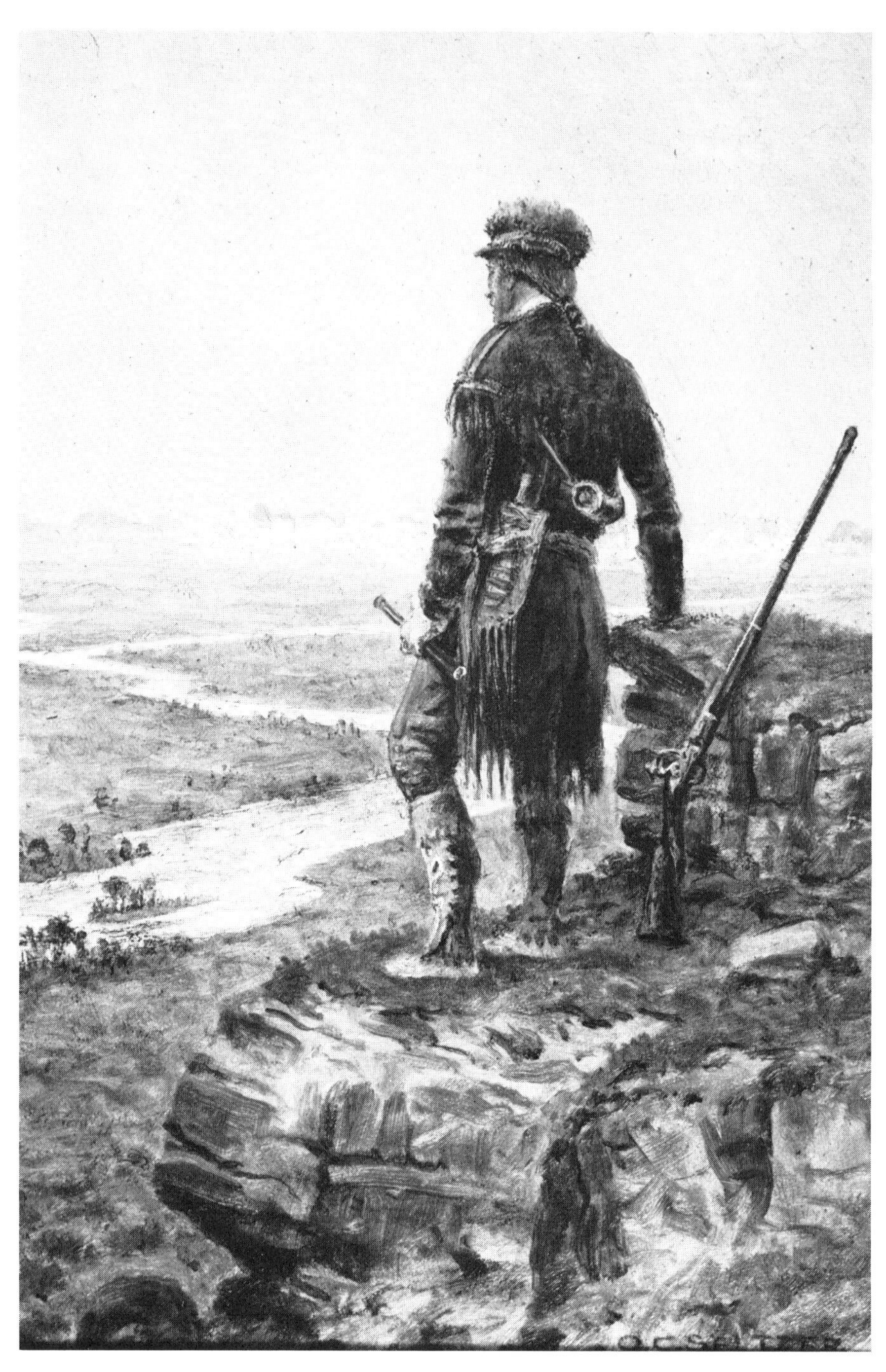

*Lewis' First Glimpse of the Rockies*
1934
Miniature oil

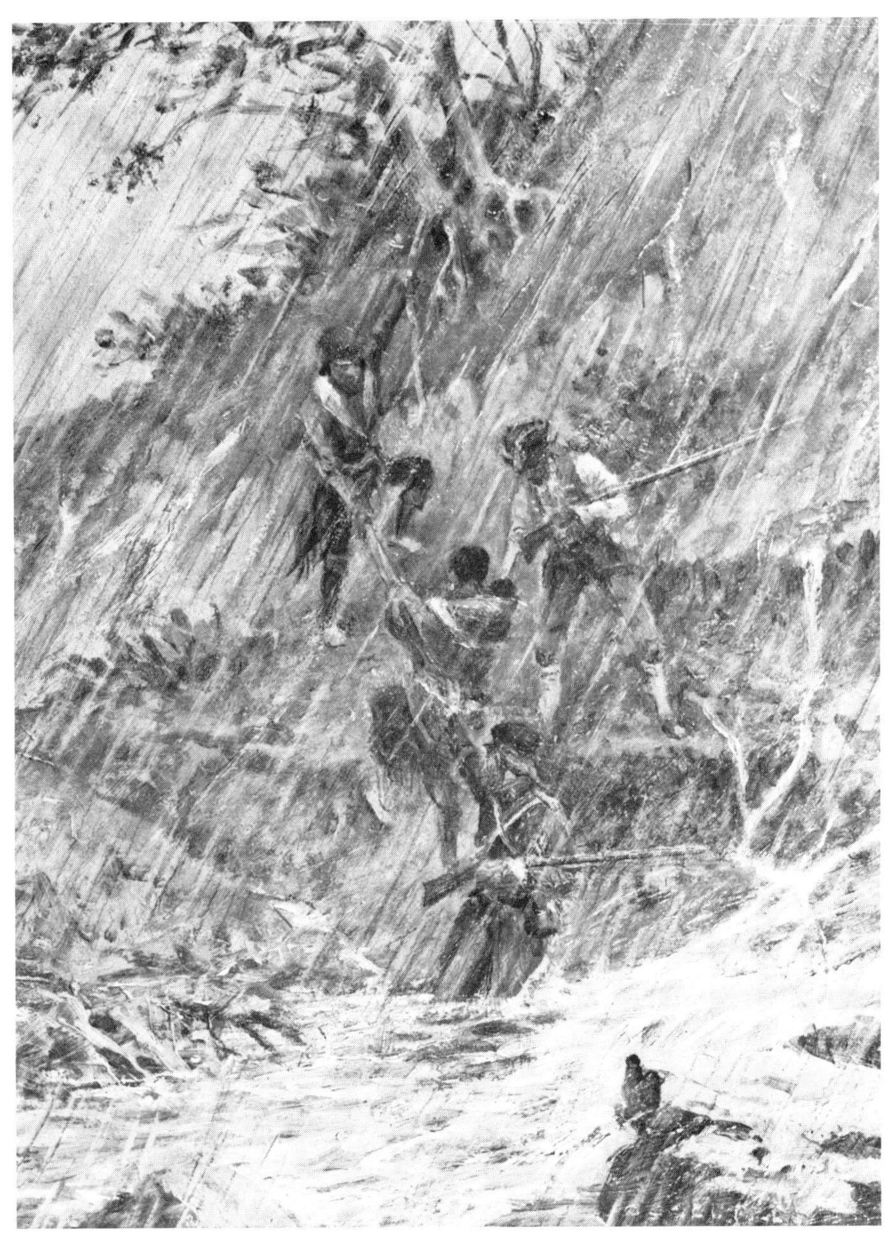

*Deluge at Colter's Falls*
1935
Miniature oil

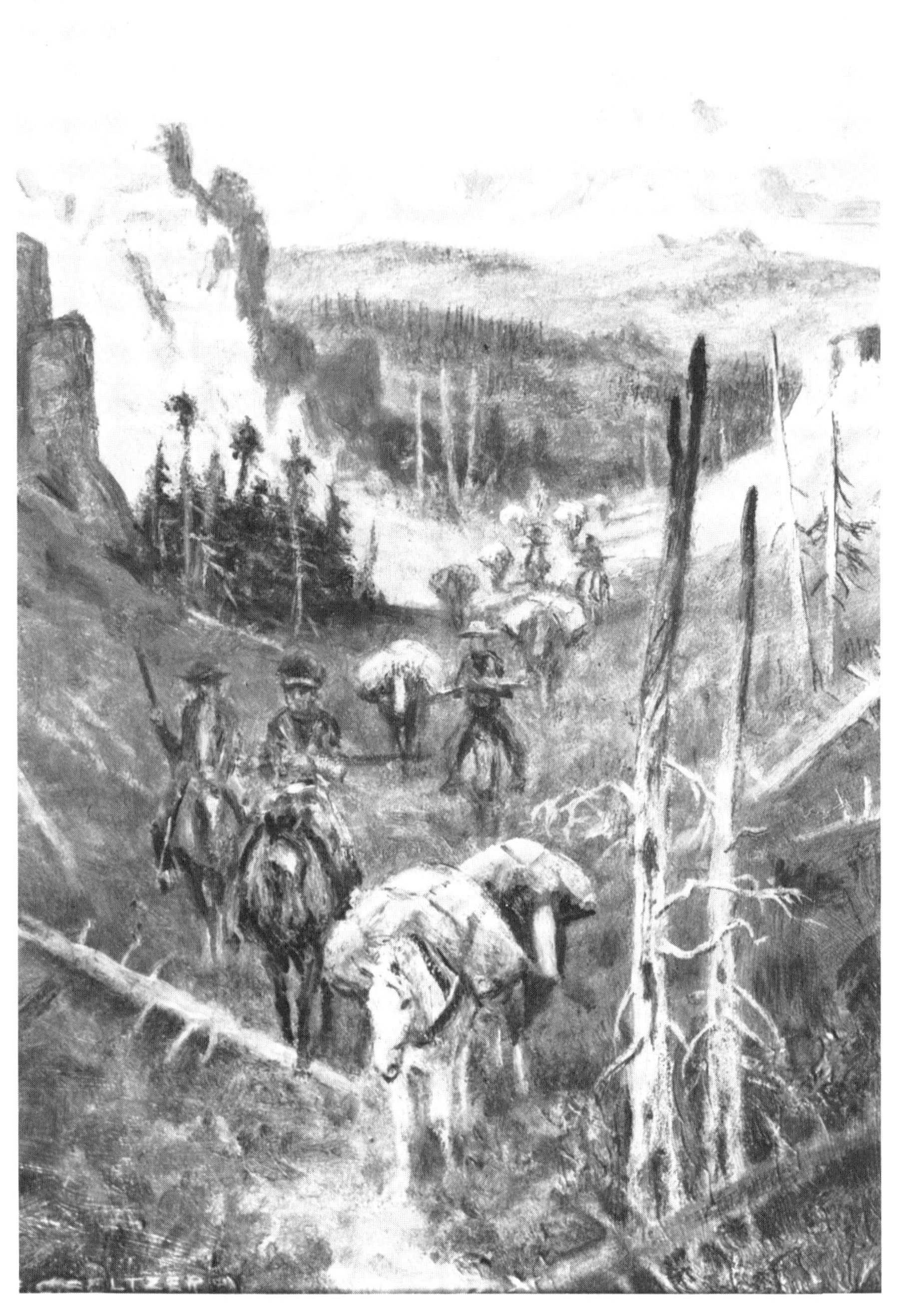

*The Lolo Pass*
1934
Miniature oil

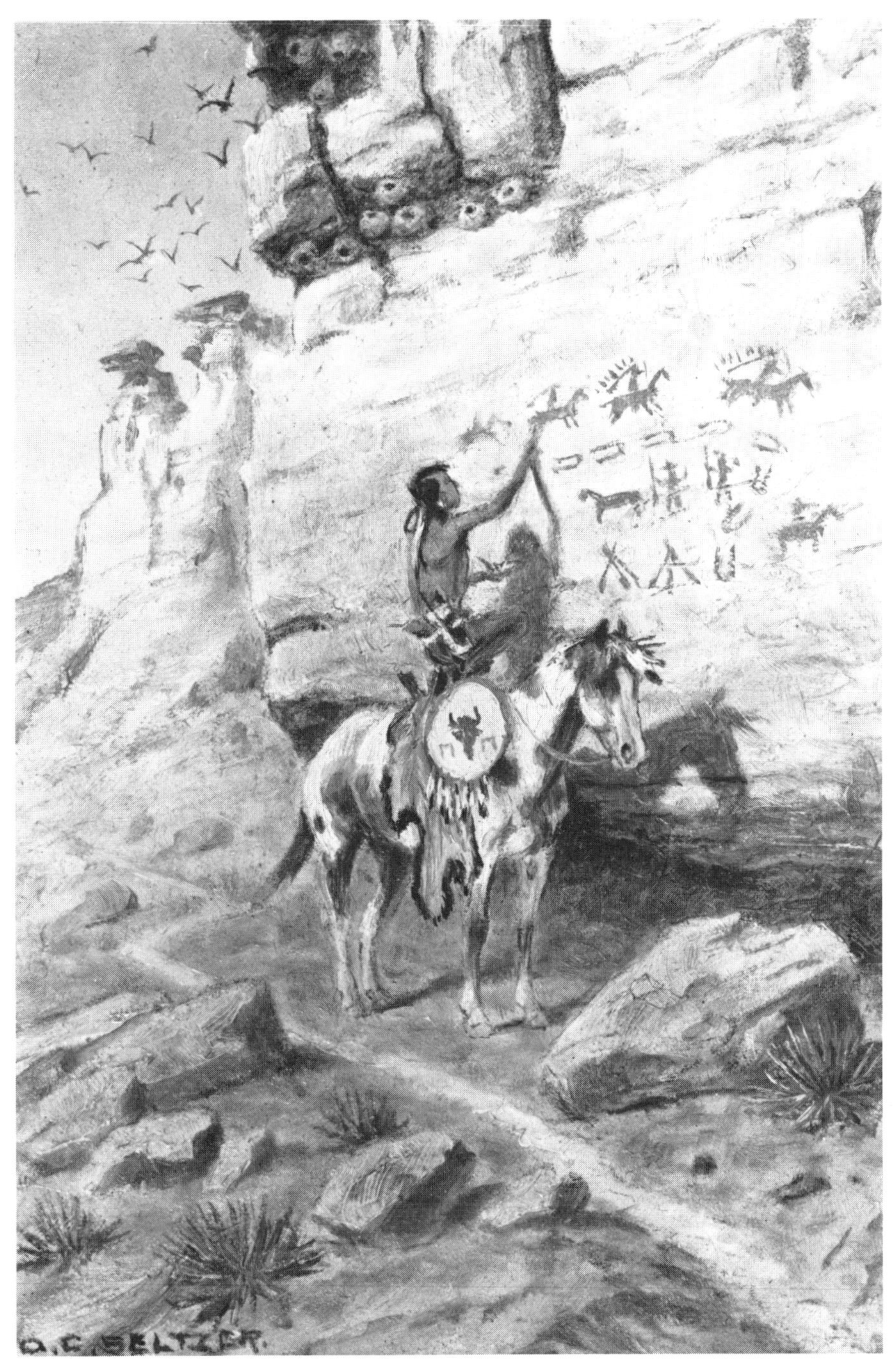

*The Picture Writer*
1935
Miniature oil

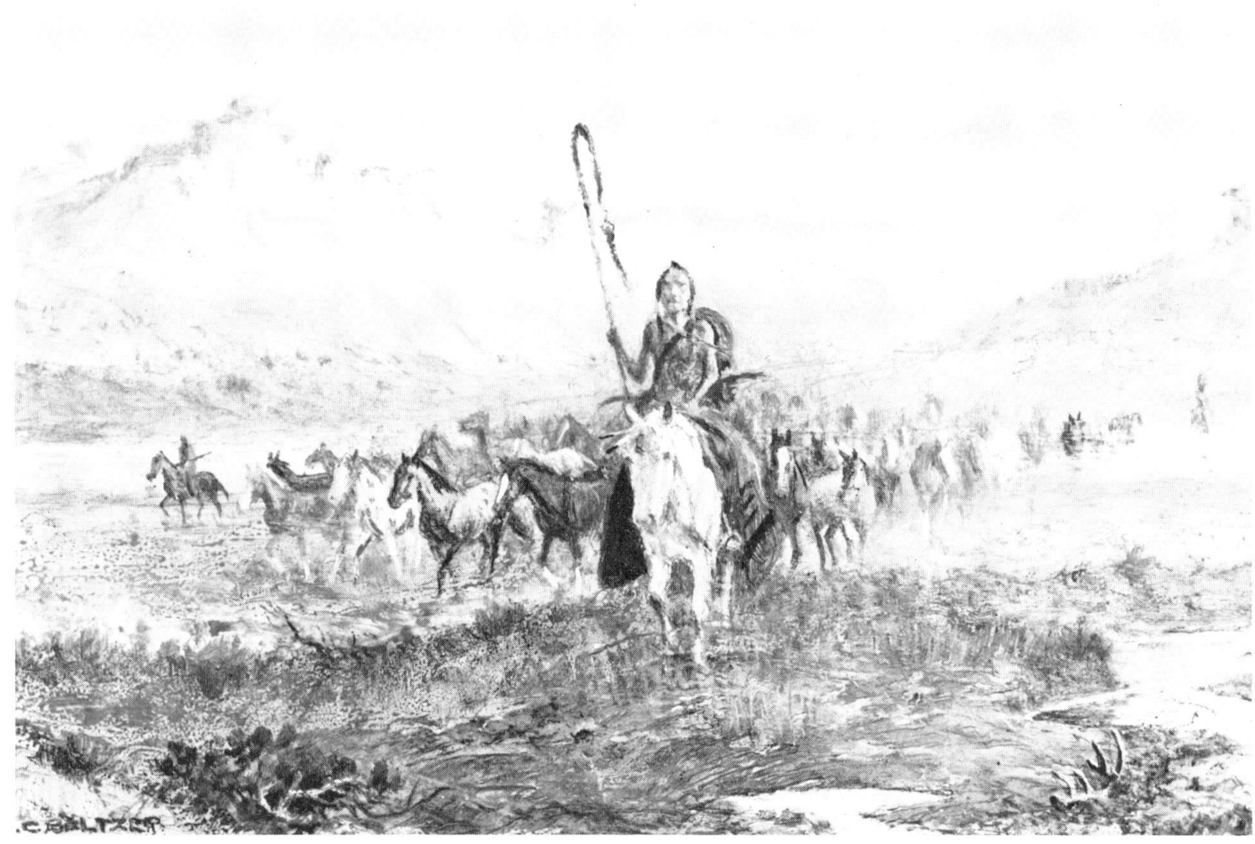

*Horse Thieves*
1934
Miniature oil

seem ominous and hostile as the hunters bend over the fallen prairie giants that are about to be skinned.

Three miniatures tell the story of the infamous road agent and murderer George Ives. In the first, his bold holdup of a stagecoach takes place in the soft light reflected from distant peaks. Ives's recapture is the subject of the second painting. The third relates Ives's nighttime trial on December 21, 1863, in Nevada City, with Colonel Wilbur F. Sanders conducting the prosecution and an advisory jury of twenty-four men deciding Ive's fate. The text lauds Sanders as the "hero of this hour," saying:

*Any desperado present (and there were many) would have felt honored to become his murder-er. But fearless as a lion, Col. Sanders confronted and defied the malice of his armed adversaries.*

*The verdict given—Col. Sanders mounted the wagon and recited that George Ives had been declared a murderer and robber by those there assembled, moved that he be forthwith hung by the neck until dead.*

There is a fire-lighted scene depicting the organizational meeting of the Vigilantes, who banded together in the Virginia City–Bannack area for "mutual protection from the desperadoes who were throwing terror into the entire community." *The Vigilantes' Oath* features the redoubtable Sanders as official prosecutor, along with five recognizable compatriots. *Vigilante Ways,*

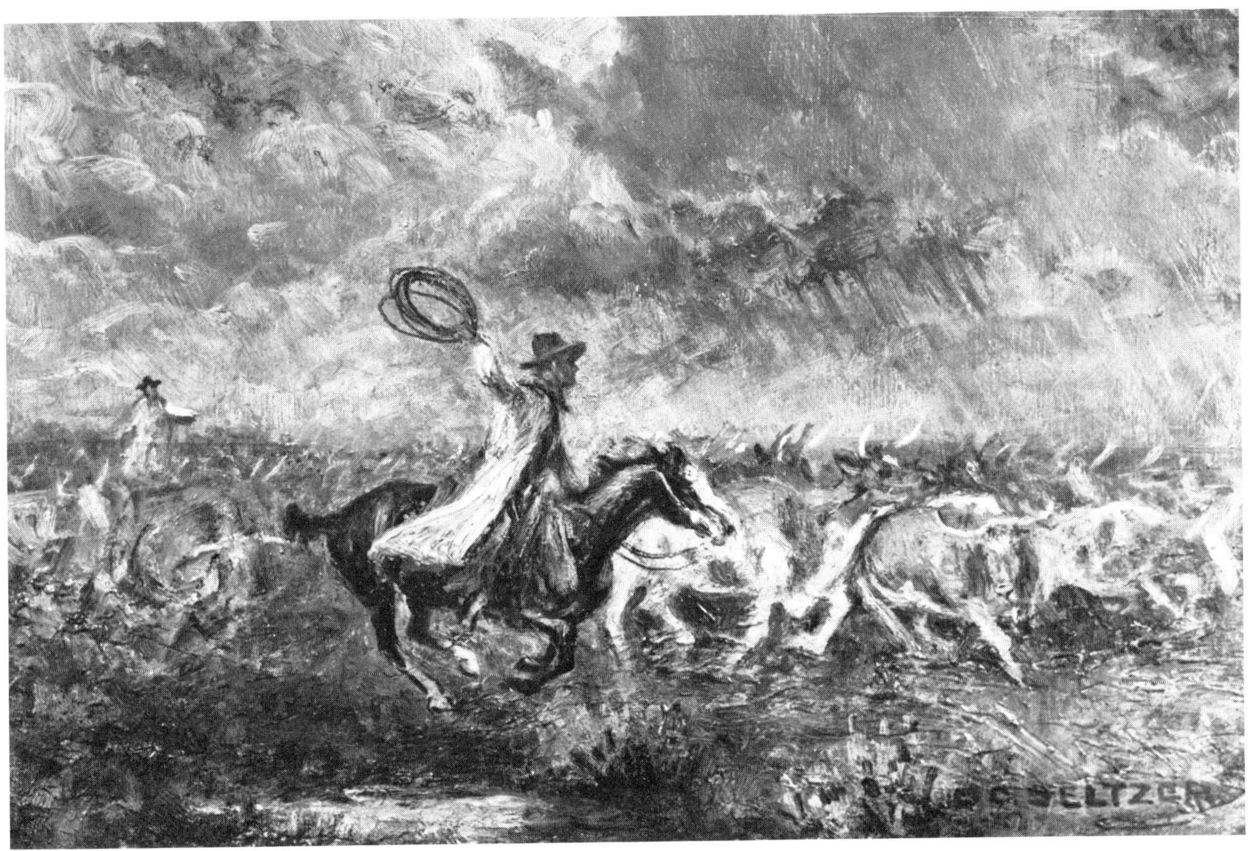

*The Cattle Stampede*
1934
Miniature oil

perhaps the most often reproduced of the miniature series, depicts four horsemen riding away from a hanging. The text explains:

"The Vigilante sign 3-7-77 chalked on the door of a suspect or nailed to a tree where holdups were accustomed to occur meant — 'You have 24 hours to leave this country otherwise yours will be a box 3′ wide, 7′ long, burried 77″ below ground.'"

This statement represents Cole's opinion; Seltzer was known to have held a different opinion, believing that the figures represented a more symbolic code.

Although he avoided violence, Olaf had no compunction about depicting gallows and hangings in the name of frontier justice. A third vigilante painting, *A Quintuple Hanging*, shows five nooses suspended from the roof beam of an unfinished building, destined to be a Virginia City drugstore. The sky is painted in a harsh eerie yellow green, against which the nooses are starkly silhouetted as the vigilantes lead their bound victims to the gallows.

So intriguing is the wealth of historical detail accompanying the Montana miniatures that the reader tends to overlook the rare and delicate beauty of the paintings themselves. Many of them are pastoral in feeling. *Saint Mary's Mission* shows a herd of sleek horses grazing in front of an old church. There is the thrust of springtime green in *Lewis' First Glimpse of the Rockies*; turbulent clouds obscure the mountain peaks in *The Elk Hunters*; a full moon bathes the scene of the discovery of the *Wrecked River Boat "Chippewa" Found by Crow War Party on the Missouri*

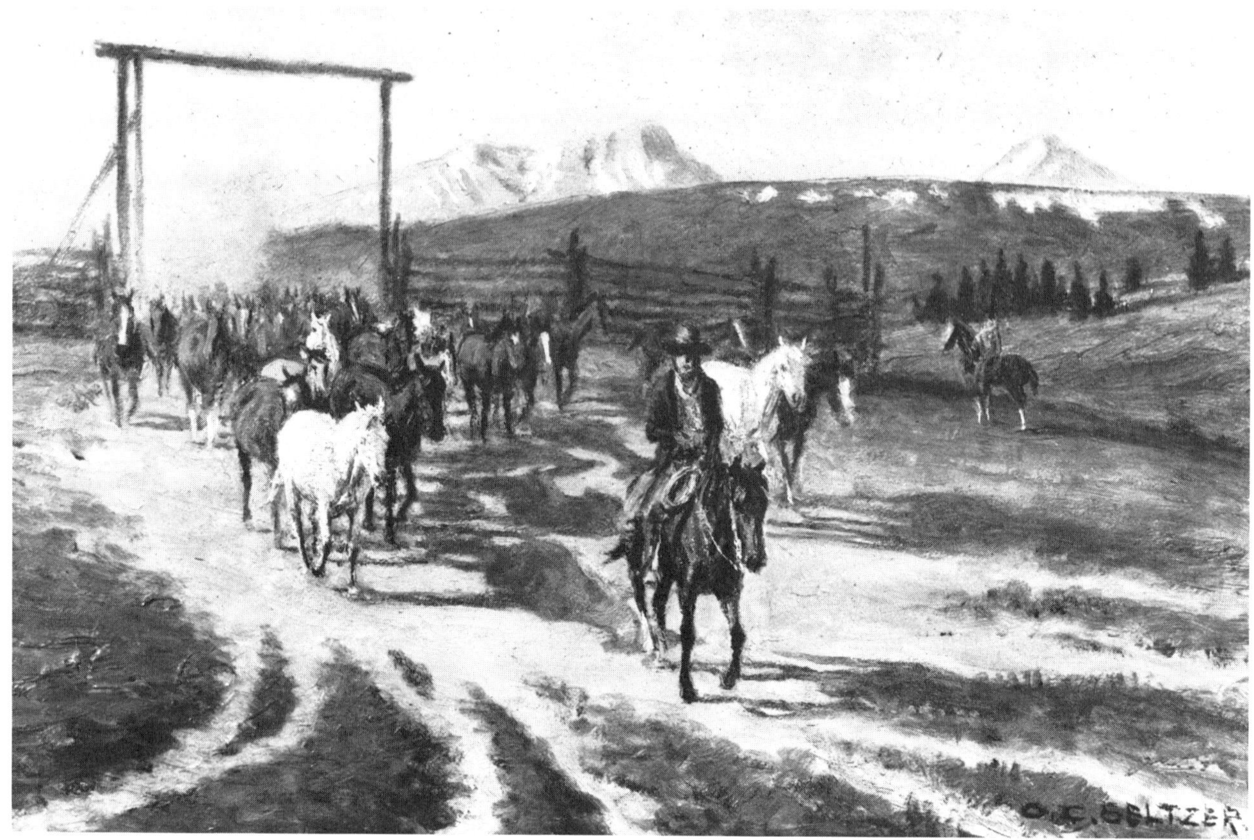

*The Remuda*
1935
Miniature oil

*River* (only a few additional lines were necessary to elaborate on this title).

*Fording Cattle on the Milk River* takes place against the seared vegetation of autumn, while in *The Swing Station at Box Elder* the loft area on the crude wooden stable is gilded by an evening sun that casts a glow on the distant mountains.

There is a distinctly textured effect on both *The Battle of Little Big Horn* and *The Hayfield Fight*. Mere specks of color provide detail, as in the distant campfires of the *The Circle*, the horse's trappings in *The Picture Writer*, the Stars and Stripes flown by *Kenneth McKenzie*.

*The Parley* is replete with minute detail, from discarded whisky bottles to playing cards, while *Cow Island Indian Fight* has about two dozen discernible figures.

Perhaps in no other area is Olaf Seltzer's mastery of color variation more noticeable than in his treatment of snow-shrouded scenes. All of his tricks of reflections from slanted light are brought into play, so that the viewer can almost tell the exact time of day from the hue of the snow. Particularly memorable for its nighttime lighting is the snow scene of *Portugee Phillips' Arrival* at Fort Laramie on the Christmas Eve, 1866, painted to memorialize a heroic three-day ride through a blizzard and hostile Indian country to rescue a cavalry post. Seltzer has caught the drama of this historic ride by showing Phillips's horse collapsing at the entrance to the stockade.

From a few feet away the surface of each of the miniatures appears to be as smooth as enamel. *The First Furrow* and the sentimental *In*

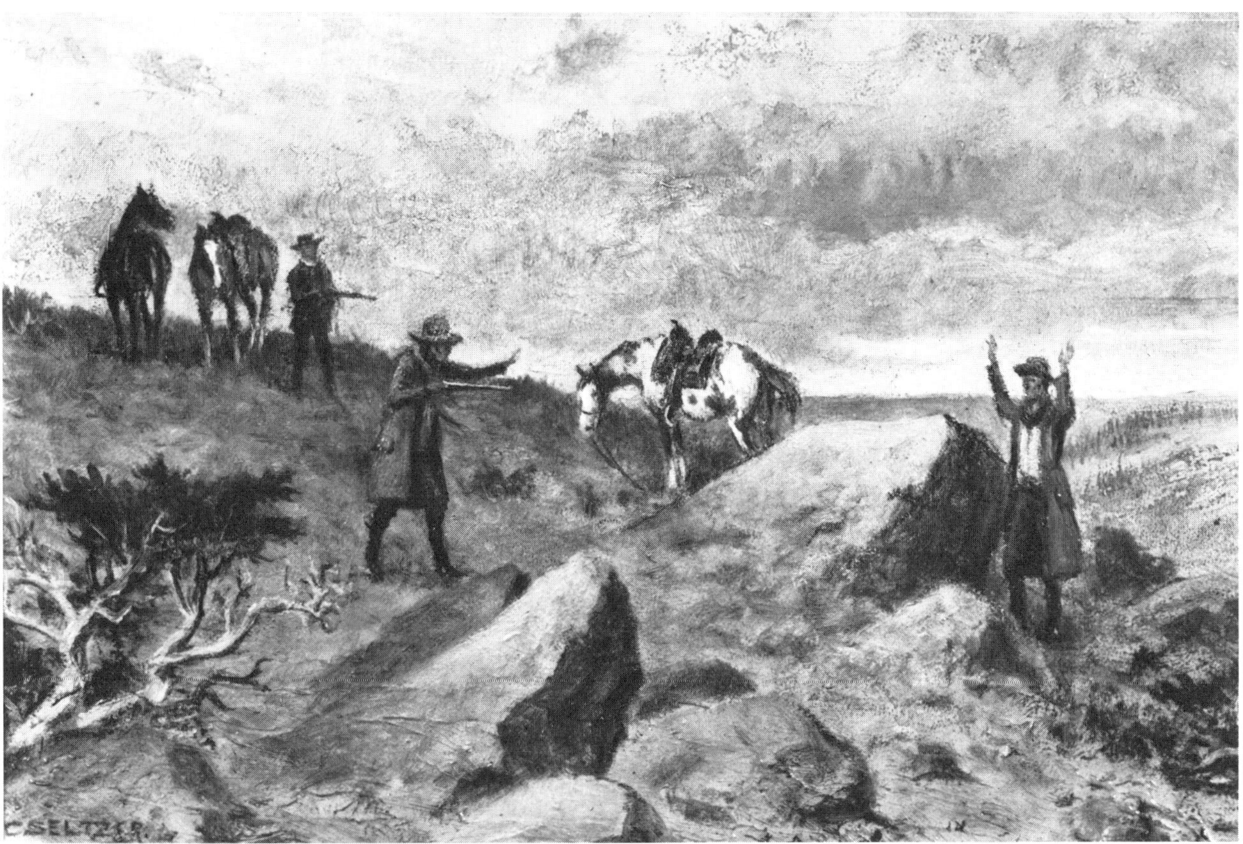

*Recapture of George Ives—1863*
1934
Miniature oil

*Memoriam*, with its hulk of a prairie schooner surrounded by the skeletons of a wheel mule and lead mule, give the calm, peaceful effect of a cool, enamel surface.

Usually a painter in the realistic tradition, Seltzer managed to instill mood into his brushwork. *A Black Robe Pioneer* imparts a sense of peace and serenity through the delicacy of coloring and the softness of atmosphere. *Chief Joseph's Surrender to Colonel Nelson A. Miles (October 4, 1877)*, painted so that the imposing shadows of the cavalry riders fall across the superbly lighted scene, is a rendition worthy of the chief's poignant words: "Hear me my Chiefs—I am tired, my heart is sick and sad. From where the sun now stands I will fight no more."

The deep empathy that Olaf Seltzer felt for his subjects is expressed through his perceptive use of color—deep salmons, ochres, desert tans, a subtle range of blues. It flowed through his brush, even when the brush bore but one sable hair and the artist's eyes were dim with age.

While Olaf was immersed in the joys and trials of creativity, Phil Cole was intrigued by his correspondence with old-timers who raised questions about fine points in the historical background of the miniatures. As collector of documents Cole corresponded with men who had studied some of the early Montana skirmishes. Among them was E. H. Brininstool, an authority on Custer and the events surrounding his defeat. In a letter discussing inquiries Cole had made about the Battle of the Little Big Horn and the episode covered by the miniature *Curley, Crow Scout, Bringing the*

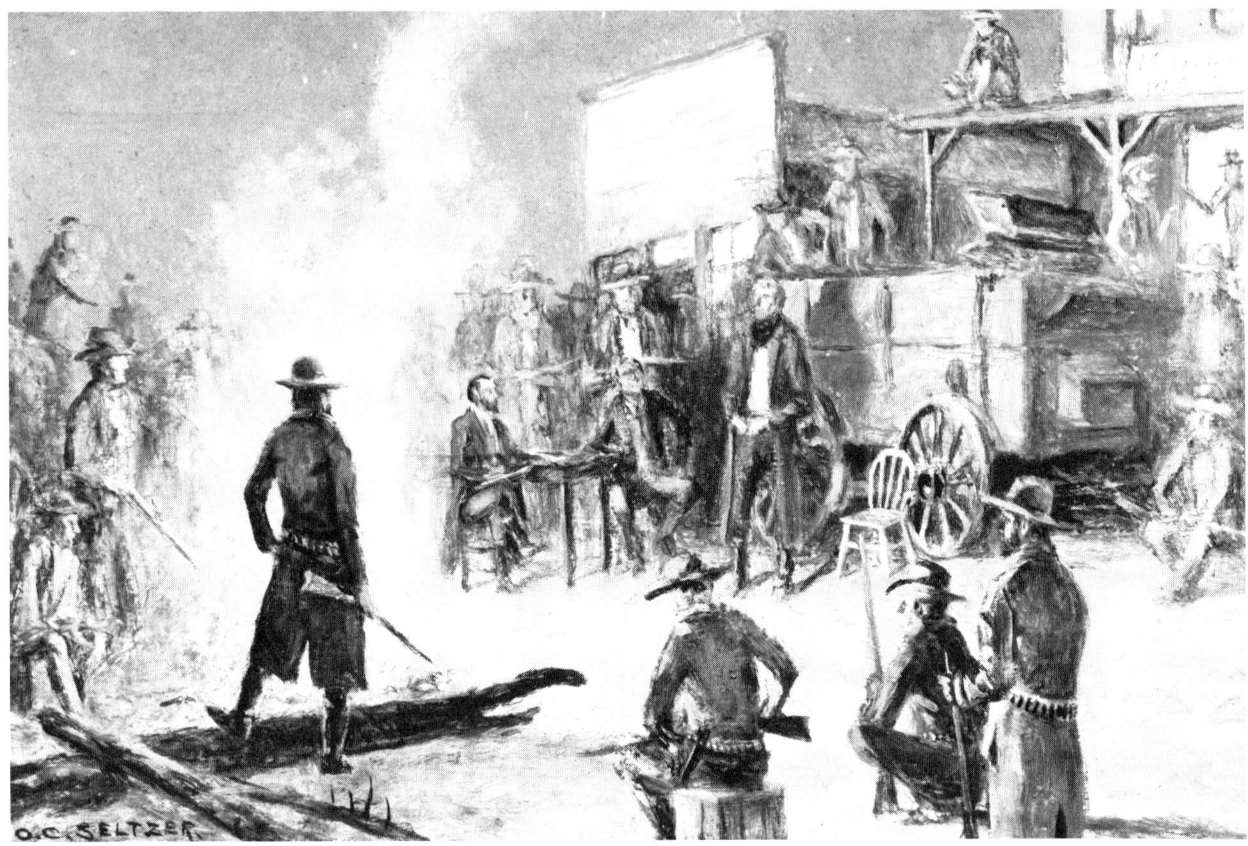

*Execution of George Ives—1863*
1934
Miniature oil


*News of the Custer Massacre*, the western historian, in May, 1933, offered some unsolicited advice:

Let me give you one tip right now before you make a big mistake. You say you are having Seltzer paint a picture depicting Bill Cody killing Yellow Hand. IT NEVER HAPPENED. Bill Cody had no more to do with the killing of Yellow Hand than you or I did. . . . Several troopers with the 5th Cavalry also claim that THEY killed Yellow Hand. Gen. King himself . . . told me "I did not see any duel between Cody and Yellow Hand."

. . . Just for your amusement I am sending you an account of that little affair which I got from a Cheyenne Indian who was the companion of Yellow Hand that day. His name is Beaver Heart, and he yet lives on a Northern Cheyenne reservation. . . . I also got the statement of Yellow Hand's sister at the same time. The superintendent . . . had Beaver Heart and the sister of Yellow Hand come to his office, and in the presence of Billy Rowland, official interpreter on that reservation, they told me their accounts of the War Bonnet skirmish. It was sworn to before a notary and signed by the thumbprints of the two Cheyennes. I have these official documents. . . . They are almost priceless—if you want the TRUTH.

. . . I can give you no information regarding the other events you mention that Seltzer is to paint for you—but gee, don't let him have Bill Cody doing something that never happened!! . . . Cody was a great showman. . . . He was genial, openhanded, a "good feller" and a royal entertainer.

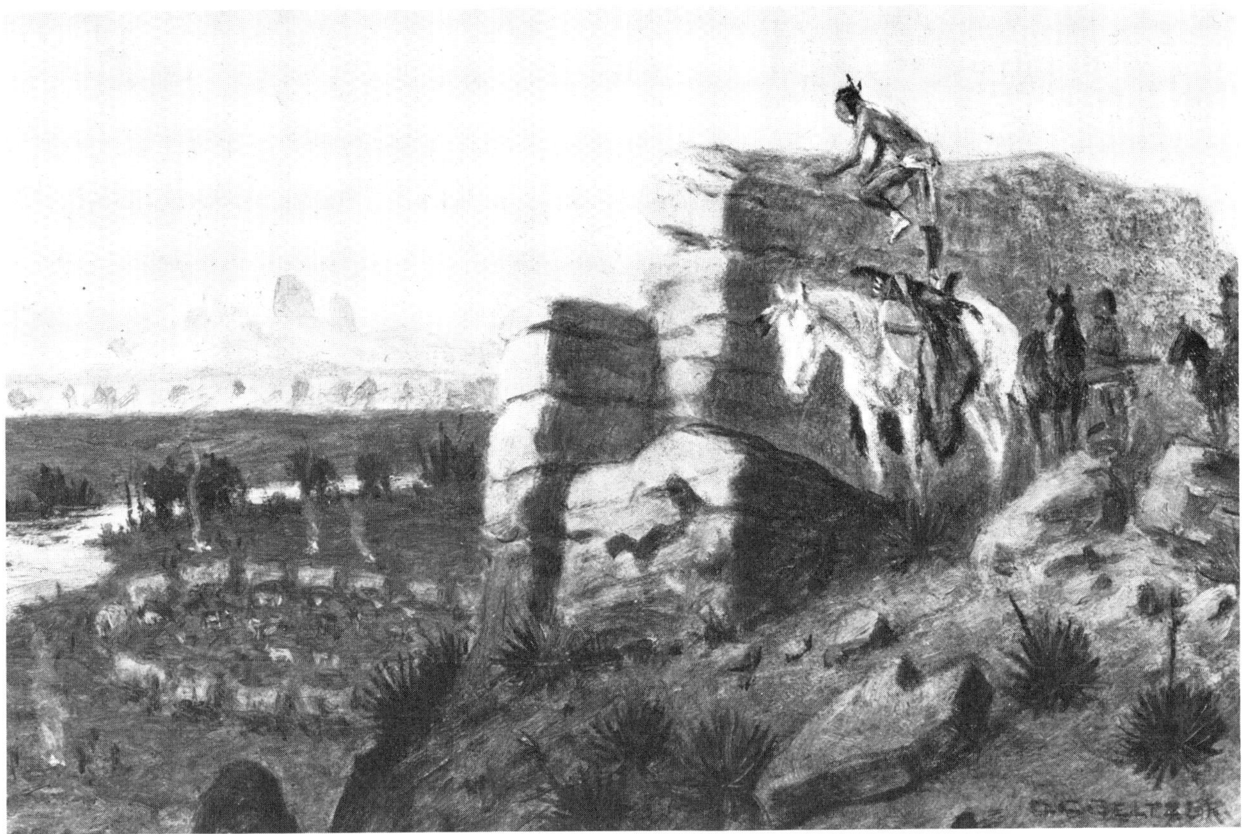

*The Circle*
1935
Miniature oil

Beyond that, well, the less said, the better. Ask any old timer like Cook or Luke North. Remember—don't take MY word for any of this.

Despite the advice Cole decided to go along with the accepted version of the story. The *Montana in Miniature* text describing *Buffalo Bill's Duel with Yellow Hand* states:

*On July 17, 1876 at a fork of Hat or War Bonnet Creek . . . Buffalo Bill (Col. Wm. F. Cody) serving under Gen. Merritt with the 5th Cavalry, was ordered to choose fifteen scouts and intercept a band of 800 Cheyennes who were on their way to join Sitting Bull on the Big Horn River. Successfully routing the Indians back over the hills, Buf-falo Bill was challenged to a duel by one of the Indians.*

*The band of soldiers, including Gen. Merritt, and the band of Indians remained in their respective positions as the duel took place before them. Charging on their horses, Buffalo Bill and the Indian fired their guns simultaneously, Buffalo Bill wounding the Indian's horse causing the Indian to be thrown to the ground. The Indian's bullet missed, but Buffalo Bill was dismounted by his horse stumbling in a gopher hole. Again each fired at the other, the Indian's bullet missing, while Buffalo Bill's bullet struck the Indian in the breast. Buffalo Bill ran up to him, plunged his bowie knife to the hilt in the Indian's heart, jerked his war bonnet off, scalped him, and hastened*

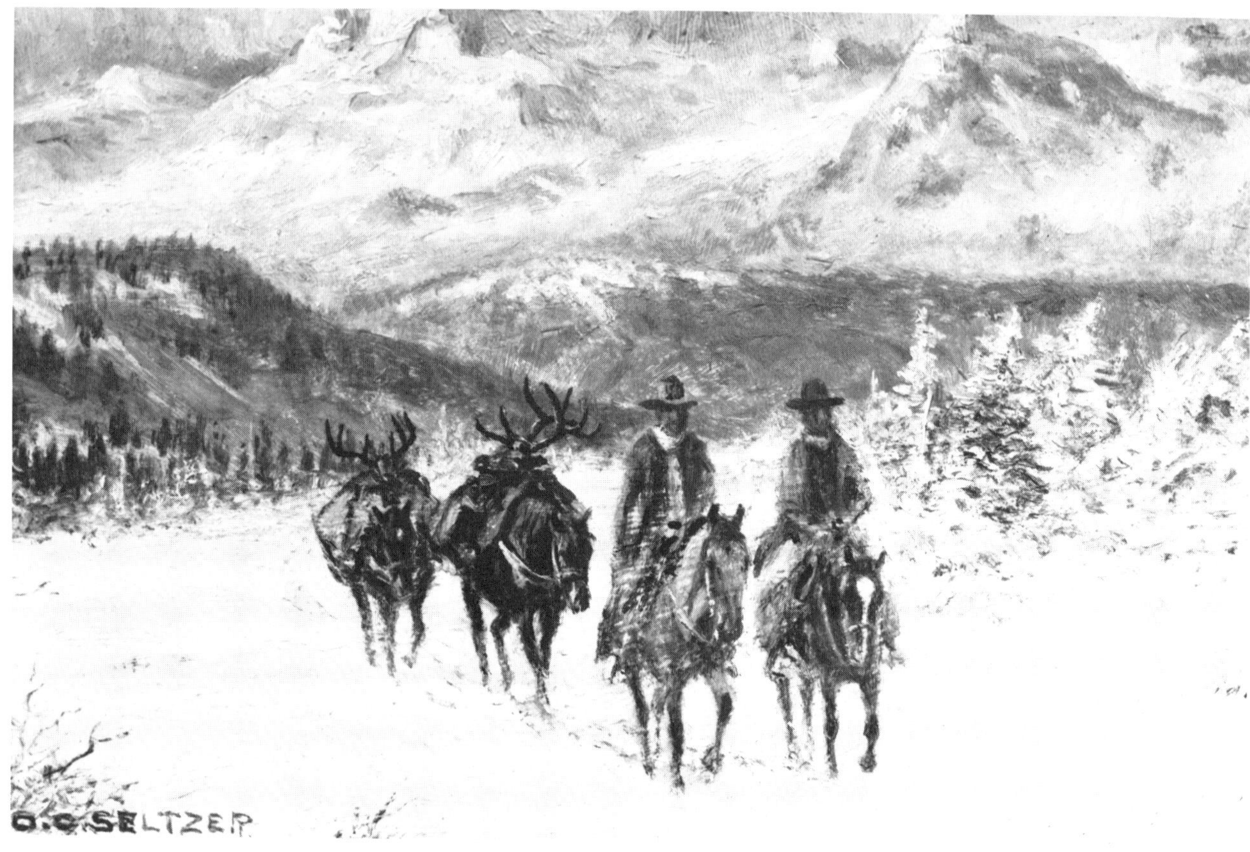

*The Elk Hunters*
1934
Miniature oil

*back to Gen. Merritt before the Indians could cut him off. The Indian was Yellow Hand, a son of old Cut Nose, a leading chief of the Cheyenne.*

The last of the miniatures were delivered to Cole in the autumn of 1935. *The Remuda, The Pow Wow,* and *The Stabbing of Crazy Horse* were entered on his records during October, followed by *Lewis on the Marias, The Deluge at Colter Falls, Cow Island Indian Fight,* and *Mike Fink—Double Crosser,* all registered in late November.

By the following May, Dr. Cole had completed photostating the miniatures and had assembled them into another suede-covered volume with a prefatory note explaining that the descriptions of true events of pioneer days in the West and the miniature oil paintings depicting them were crudely gathered in this fashion for the owner's convenience. "Some day I hope to put these paintings and such information as I have been able to gather in connection with them into book form," he wrote.

With this plan in mind Cole copyrighted his photostatic volume, *Montana in Miniature.* Several copies were made, including one for Olaf Seltzer, one for Dr. Butler, and one for Bill Marseglia, manager of the Cole estate.

Accompanied by his son Philip Gillett Cole, Jr., Dr. Cole called at Dr. Butler's home in Helena in 1937 to deliver personally Butler's copy of the book. The veterinary surgeon missed their visit, but he wrote his friend a glowing letter, praising the book as a classic. "I know that both my boys and I will read it over and over again and each time with added pleasure."[12]

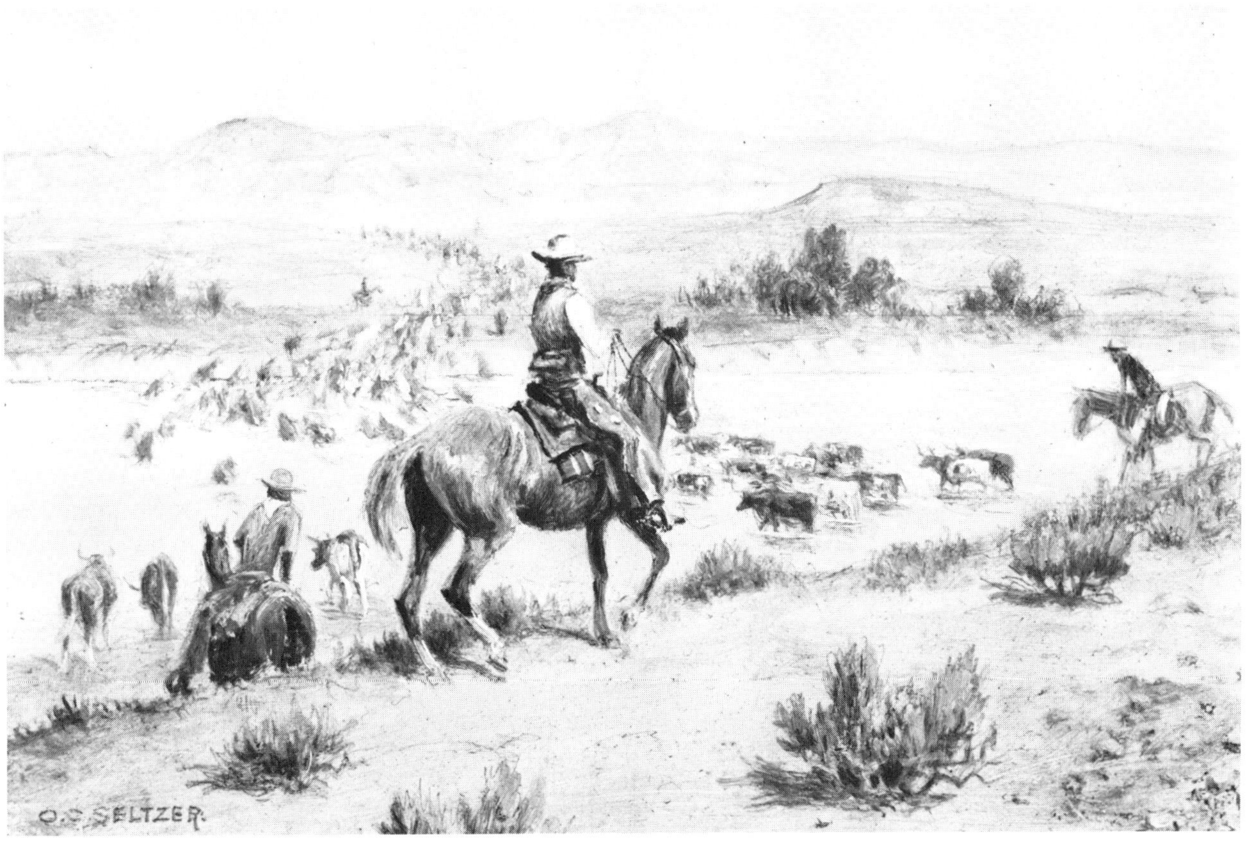

*Fording Cattle on the Milk River*
1934
Miniature oil

By the time this monumental series of historical miniatures was completed to Dr. Cole's satisfaction, Olaf Seltzer was wearing thick eyeglasses. He had severely strained his eyes painting the miniatures, and in his later years he could paint for only short periods of time during the morning hours. His limitations caused him to grow increasingly nervous.

Was the effort worth it? It is likely that if he had never painted another picture, he would be remembered for these gems of western history. So sharp and clear are the minute brushstrokes that the little paintings can be enlarged to three times their actual size and still show sharp detail. So rich and glowing are their colors that they are frequently compared to jewels; light seems to reflect in myriad fashion from their depth.

Though most of the scenes and characters he put on illustration board had passed through Montana before his time, Olaf Seltzer shared the enthusiasm of Frederic Remington and Charles M. Russell for western life. The miniatures comprise a documentary in oil of episodes that otherwise would become increasingly difficult to recall. They are indeed the crown jewels of Olaf Seltzer's career.

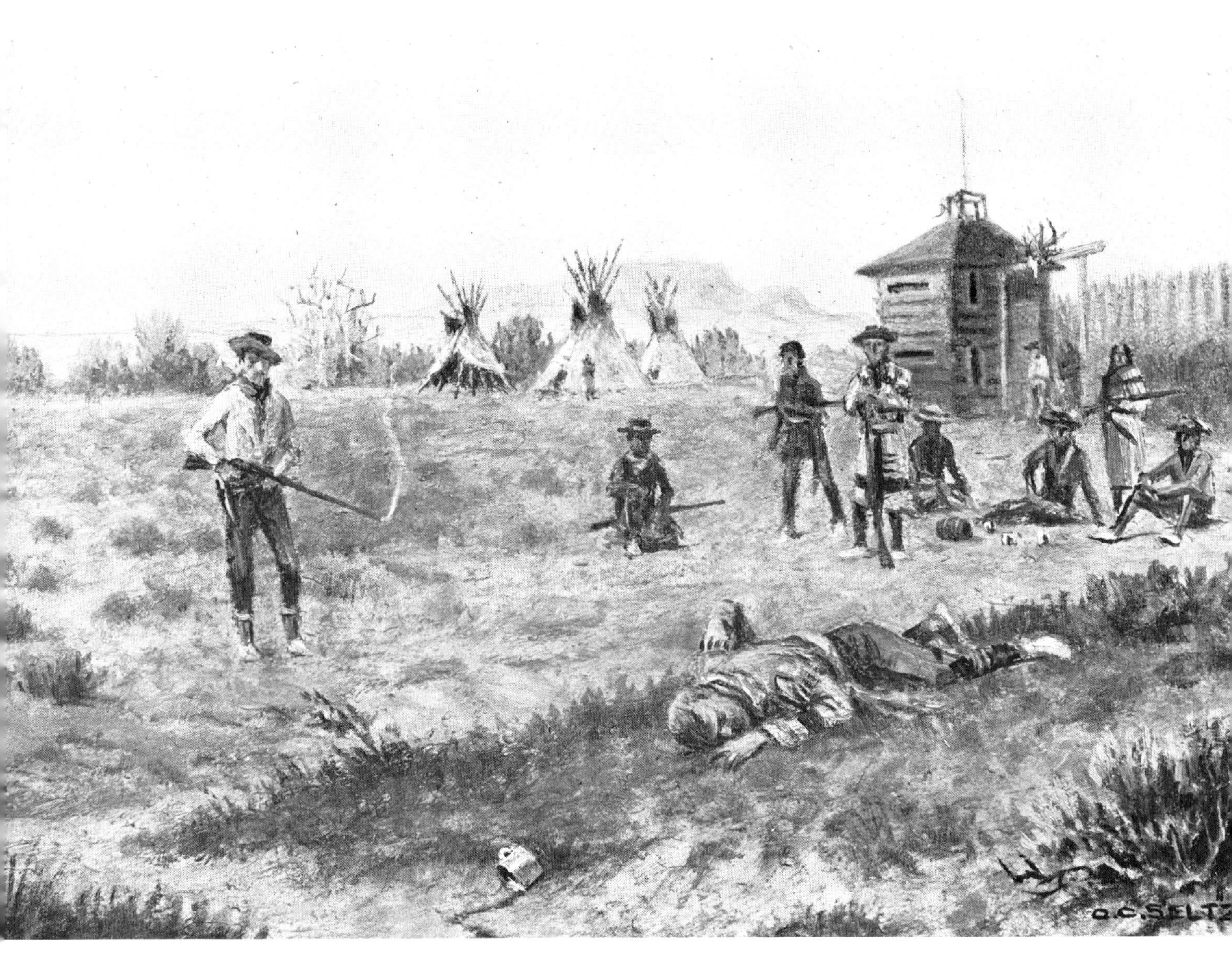

*Mike Fink—Doublecrosser*
1935
Miniature oil

# Chapter 10
# New Experiences

Now that the historical miniature series was completed and his reputation established, Olaf Seltzer could at long last work at a more leisurely pace. In June, 1936, he accepted Bill Marks's invitation to join him on a business trip through the Pacific Northwest, a trip that was to culminate in a Seattle exhibition devoted entirely to Seltzer's work. Nothing pleased the artist more than to have a longtime friend become a serious collector of his work; he was always eager to enhance such collections with illustrated letters and greetings. He was inordinately pleased when Marks arranged the exhibition.

For more than a decade the insurance broker whose roots were in Great Falls, had been quietly buying Seltzer paintings. To the eleven already in his collection he now added four oils inspired by a six-week motor trip the two friends took in 1934—*Sheep Camp on the Marias* and *The Peace Pipe* (both 24″ × 30″), a 20″ × 30″ picture called *Trouble Hunters*, and a 16″ × 24″ canvas entitled *Harlem River*. The backwater of the Marias River and Goosebill Butte are prominent in the first painting, which depicts a sheep camp in the springtime. *The Peace Pipe* shows a scouting party offering a calumet on a sage-covered hillside.

The five-day exhibition was held in the Green Room of the Washington Athletic Club in Seattle from June 19 to 23. It was publicized as an exhibit "depicting early Western life . . . shown through the courtesy of Mr. William H. Marks from his privately owned collection." Marks's interest was solely in spreading Olaf's fame. No paintings were offered for sale. Club members were invited to meet the artist at tea on the eve of the opening, marking the first time Olaf had ever been lionized before a large gathering. A reviewer for the *Seattle Times* told readers what they might expect to see:

*Lots of color, for the Indians of Montana are a colorful lot, from the trappings on themselves, to the paint on their horses, and the sunsets and sunrises of the Stubtoe State soften even the famous "badlands" with blues and golds and reds. Lots of action, for Mr. Seltzer has caught his scenes when "something was doing." Lots of understanding. . . .*

Referring to the long association of Marks and the artist, the *Times* pointed out that when Seltzer, Russell, and the Seattle resident took summer pack trips together "Mr. Marks was the 'kid' of the outfit, and [he] remembers the tricks these two artists used to play on him after a day of painting was over and everyone was full of Russell's cooking, for his dishes were as famous as his paintings."

Included in the exhibit were *Blackfeet Scouts, The Trail Boss, The Water Hole, The Range Mother* (an old cow attacking a skittish horse during calf branding), *Prowlers of the Prairie, Buffalo Hunters, Blackfeet War Party, The Buffalo Crossing, Crow Scout, The Forest Ranger,* and *The Bronc Buster.*

Some of Marks's oils had names identical to titles in Dr. Cole's collection and elsewhere. Seltzer increasingly had problems finding new names; he must have painted a dozen *Crow Scouts* in a decade. In one of his pocket notebooks he jotted down a list of names for future western paintings as they occurred to him:

*Horns and Hoofs, A Slick Ear, Rope's End, Impromptu Triangle, Stretching Rawhide, Nocturne, A Bad Actor (bucking bronco), Night-Hawk, Chuck Wagon—Night, Meat for the Chuck Wagon (antelope), Deer in Cottonwood River Bottom, dull moon, Squaws Traveling, the Salvagers, Blue Appaloosa Horse, Indian Camp (Young buck and squaw), Indians on Trail, Indian on horse (gold and cerulean), A Primitive Artist, Shooting out Stragglers, Roping Red Steer, Prairie Fire—buffalo, The Lone Wolf (road agent), Caught with the Goods, Enemies Country, Making War Medicine.*

Behind some of the titles Olaf jotted down proposed dimensions. A group of tavern names, including the Golden Key and the Blue Boar, appealed to him as titles for paintings of life in colonial America. There was a longer list for genre paintings, including:

*A Tribunal of War (old gate); The King's Jester, The Vulture's Nest, Conspiracy, the Scythmen of Kozioski, Danish Dragoons on March (mill); A Cuirassier (Danish horse guard), a Roundhead Trooper, A Cavalier, A Hallebardier, A Musketeer, Vedette (Pandour on Appaloosa), Output (French Dragoon with leopard skin), Sentinel (Danish Dragoon), the Mystic Shrine, The Strength of the Weak.* [1]

The mention of three Danish subjects for future paintings is the first sign of any nostalgic feeling that Olaf may have had for the homeland he had left forty-five years earlier.

Correspondence between Olaf and his New York patron was far less frequent now that the historical miniatures were completed. Dr. Cole found it necessary to devote more time to his business interests, even in retirement, as the Depression years wore on. "These are busy days, Olaf—too busy for lengthy letter-writing," Phil Cole concluded a note in 1937. Most of their correspondence now dealt with offers of additions to the Cole collection. Dr. Cole turned down most offers. He seems to have been both amused and annoyed by repeated attempts to foist on him work signed with Russell's name which he believed was faked.

True to what he forecast in his letters to prospective sellers while the miniatures were under way, Cole added only seventeen art works to his collection after receiving the last small historical painting, *Mike Fink—Doublecrosser*, late in 1935. The work he did acquire did indeed elevate the level of his collection. Included were a large (68½″ × 48½″) Leigh canvas, *An Argument with the Sheriff*, Russell's famous oils *Innocent Allies* and *Meat's Not Meat 'til It's in the Pan*, Remington's *Sitting Bull*, and a Russell black-and-white wash entitled *Custer's Last Stand*. There were also two Russell watercolors, *Beef for the Fighters* and *Pardners*, and six bronzes, three by Remington, two by Russell, and one by Fraser.

During the period when the historical miniatures were coming into his collection, Cole had purchased Russell's lighthearted oil *A Bronc to Breakfast*; his lyrical *Carson's Men* with its unparalleled western sunset, and the pathetic *Her Heart Is on the Ground* (registered in Cole's records as *The Mourner*), along with three bronzes by A. P. Proctor, two by Malvina Hoffman, and Remington's *Stampeded by Lightning*. According to Miss Ralston, Russell's *Lewis and Clark Expedition* was perhaps the last painting Cole bought. "He paid about $42,000 for it. It came from a private collection up for sale, and Dr. Cole had someone represent him at the auction." [2]

Lee M. Ford, of the Great Falls National Bank, offered Russell's *The Jerk Line* to Cole for $10,000. The collector wrote Ford that, although Olaf Seltzer, "as good a judge as I know of Russell's paintings," had spoken highly of this work, he was turning it down since "I know of almost no one anteing up this kind of money for any kind of painting these days." Always courteous and kindly, Cole offered to help the Montana banker find a New York art dealer to handle the sale of the Russell painting.

On November 18, 1937, Cole fired off a letter to Olaf:

I am hastening to get off these lines to you even though they are hurried, for I have some news which I feel you should know.

Within the past few days three paintings signed "C. M. Russell" and dated two of them I believe 1913 and one 1911, have been offered me for sale as beautiful examples of Charlie's work. Personally I am convinced that someone has been getting hold of some of your paintings and either changing your signature to that of Charlie's or possibly managing to get three unsigned ones and adding Charlie's signature.

Of course I don't know that they were painted by you, but I cannot think of anyone else except Charlie who could make such truly good paintings with so much good action, background, color, etc., etc. The dealers as a matter of fact raved over them.

I wish I had more information I could give you, Olaf. I am convinced that if you could see them you would recognize them as your own and want to help trace down the so-and-so who I feel sure is pulling a fast one. The only information I can give you is that one oil painting which as I recollect is somewhere in the neighborhood of 2′ long by 18″ high or so depicts two or three Indians at a waterhole, while coming toward it from the left-hand distance are several mounted Indians on a high bit of prairie land with some lovely pink buttes in the far background. This one is dated, as I recall, either 1911 or 13 or thereabouts. They seem to have no recognized titles but I am told offered for sale by somebody in Philadelphia. . . .

The other painting is a watercolor somewhere about the same size as the above mentioned ones with the date 1913 (this date I am sure of) and depicts in the foreground a cow frothing at the mouth with a cow puncher more or less standing in his left stirrup after having roped her, while to the right of the picture is another mounted cow-puncher about to drop a second loop over the cow's horn. In the background are a bunch of cattle with one rider approaching the scene of action, lovely pink buttes in the background, also there is a mudhole with tracks through it in the immediate foreground.

I am sorry I can't give you complete descriptions of the paintings but you know how it is to remember details. It is worth your looking into anyway, Olaf. If I get more information will be glad to pass it on to you.

My best.

As Always,
Phil

Olaf was out of town when Phil Cole's letter arrived. He answered it on November 30. Cole replied on December 6:

. . . I knew you would be as concerned as I am over who is apparently putting over some fast ones. Apparently the ones who have been taken in by the paintings are going to trace the thing down for they are reputable people and feel that they themselves have been "hooked." If I can do anything to help the friend from Long Island who

you are having represent you let me know, for as you know I will be glad to do everything I can in every direction.

Three days later the Fifth Avenue gallery offering the first two paintings sent Olaf photographs, as they did Nancy Russell, and a carefully worded letter in which they took the stance that the paintings were Russells. Seltzer was equally discreet. On December 15 he sent the New York gallery a brief typewritten letter:

. . . Dr. Cole has already written me about this matter. The two pictures look much like the real thing although the color scheme (in black and white photos) does not show, but I hesitate to give an opinion as I am well aware of the fact that much revamping of old, as well as later Russell paintings, some very extensively worked over, has been done in the past few years, which practice in itself would tend to confuse and make an opinion difficult. Hence my hesitancy.

Seltzer did not, however, claim the work as his own. It would have been in keeping with his integrity to have spoken up if he had reason to know the paintings were his. The New York incident reported by Cole would not be the only instance of an alleged attempt to change a Seltzer painting into a Russell. In an article on Russell forgeries Frederic G. Renner, an acknowledged expert on Russell, referred to three Seltzer paintings (the same trio or another group?) passed off as Russells:

*A number of years ago, three oils painted and signed by Olaf Seltzer, the fine Montana artist . . . were offered for sale in New York. A few months later, the same paintings were seen in other galleries; by this time Seltzer's name had been painted out and Russell's substituted, undoubtedly without Seltzer's knowledge. One of these paintings was unsold for several years. Finally a leading New York dealer made a comment about it that reveals a good deal of the philosophy about forgeries. . . . He said "It's too bad the blank Gallery is trying to sell that Seltzer painting as a Russell; but if they are going to do it, they ought to make it convincing and put the price up around $7,000. Trying to sell it for a measly $3,000 merely spoils the Russell business for the rest of us."* [3]

Early in 1937, Olaf Seltzer became involved in

a commercial venture, which was widely publicized over a seven-state area of the Northwest. Royal Mills, later a General Mills subsidiary, sponsored a contest to "Name the Oil Painting." Thomas D. Barry, manager of Royal Mills, commissioned Seltzer to paint the 32″ × 40″ canvas depicting a jerk-line freight outfit. Elegantly displayed in a gilt frame, the painting was offered as first prize for the best name. The winner was offered the option of taking $500 cash or the painting, for which the milling company paid Seltzer $225. Smaller cash prizes were offered for the next thirty-eight titles chosen, twenty-five of them being single dollar bills. Each winner was also awarded a print of the painting, making it one of the most widely distributed Seltzer works up to that time.

The prints were distributed in envelopes bearing a full description:

JERKLINE FREIGHTER OF PIONEER DAYS
*Theme of Spectacular Oil Painting by Famous Montana Artist*

*Your enclosed reproduction of the original oil painting by the famous Western artist, Mr. O. C. Seltzer, depicts a freighter with his jerkline freight outfit. Outfits of this kind carried every variety of merchandise from the few railroad points to even the most remote outposts in the broad state of Montana.*

*The team is guided by one line leading from the bit of the lead horse. The action shown by the lead horse in the picture tells us that the driver has just given two jerks, which to the intelligent horse indicates a right turn. The horses must swing to the right so that the wagon-train may be kept in the narrow road on the curve.*

*The driver is seen astride the horse near the lead wagon, where with his jerkline he not only guides his team but is in a position quickly to apply the wagon brakes.*

*These freighters traveled over the hills and prairies almost entirely on their own resources. The driver was the only human being in the outfit. He was everything from veterinary to cook. Twenty miles was a fair day's travel.*

*The artist, Mr. Seltzer, who has been painting Montana scenes and subjects for more than forty years, knew a different West than that of the wild and wooly legends. He knew a West full of color, a contented people working in peaceful surroundings yet enduring hardships with the sturdy for-*

*titude of the pioneer. Seltzer has blended the color and the expanse and the peace to give us a picture of the real West.*

*Notice particularly the contrast between the action expressed in the movement of horses and wagons and the majestic stillness of the rugged landscape. So lifelike is the fording of the stream that one can almost hear the creak and groan of the wagons as they splash through the water. In the background you see Mt. Helena, near Montana's capital city, Helena.*

*This picture is a brilliant example of Seltzer's superb use of color, and his perfection of detail. The typically Western landscape is remarkably lifelike. The color tones—from the grey-green clumps of sagebrush in the foreground to the cloud-filled aquamarine sky in the background —are a masterful blending of pastels and darker colors to produce a play of light and shade on the landscape and a remarkable illusion of depth. Seltzer has the true artist's feeling for color values. And these colors are beautifully reproduced in this print.*

DEPENDABLE REX *Flour, the oldest continuously active flour brand in Montana, was first milled at Great Falls in 1892. Many pioneers in Montana will still remember with gratitude these jerkline outfits which brought to them their necessities such as* DEPENDABLE REX *Flour, as well as the few luxuries available in those days.*

The contest ended in October. *Jerk Line Freighter*, the name submitted by George H. Lange, of Garrison, North Dakota, was chosen as first-prize winner by Lloyd D. Herrold, of Northwestern University, the judge. Lange decided to take the cash. Other winning entries came from the Dakotas and Minnesota, as well as Montana. When Barry was married, on June 11, 1938, the mill employes bought the canvas from the company and presented it to his bride as a wedding gift. Mrs. Barry has loaned it to the Museum of the Montana Historical Society.

Montana in general and Great Falls in particular had begun to know of Olaf Seltzer and to take pride in his work. On April 7, 1937, the *Great Falls Tribune* reported that Seltzer's latest painting, *The Jerky*, owned by Dr. E. D. Hitchcock, would be displayed in the show window of the local Paris Department Store.

In a rapturous description the *Tribune* reporter pointed out:

*The painting pictures the stage, drawn by six horses, which was in operation between Great Falls and Lewiston approximately 30 years ago, at a point on the old dirt road where it came up on the bench from Box Elder creek when traveling in the direction of Belt.*

*The distant background depicts a beautiful October sunset with its galaxy of gorgeous colors casting their rays on the Bird Rail Divide, silhouetted against the sunset back of Square Butte. Off to the northwest are the snowcapped peaks of the continental divide.*

*The bench from which the scene was sketched provides a most unusual panoramic view of the surrounding country. The horses pulling the stage are shying as they reach the top of the bench from a jackrabbit, which has just crossed the road.*

*One of the lead horses is white and the other a black, while the other four are bays. Every detail regarding the "jerky" as the stage was called at the time, the harness of the horses and the apparel of the driver and guard on the seat was carefully checked by Seltzer to insure accuracy.*

Memories of at least one ride on this particular "jerky" were permanently engraved on the consciousness of Olaf Seltzer.

On one occasion the Paris store held an exhibition of Seltzer's paintings, during which Olaf overheard a foreign-born couple explaining his work to their children in a language he could not understand. The family visited the exhibition several times. Finally Seltzer struck up a conversation with them and learned that they were Greeks and that they woefully missed the museums and art galleries of their native land. At the close of the show the artist presented the family one of his paintings.

It was typical of Seltzer that he would rather give a painting to someone he liked than to sell one to an ostentatious stranger or a pompous dealer. In spite of the poverty of his early years and the mark it left on him, Olaf valued his independence and artistic integrity above fame and fortune.

Olaf was discriminating in choosing his friends. He favored those who convinced him that their interest lay in the paintings themselves rather than in any commercial or speculative future value. Frugal by nature, he distrusted big spenders, even when their spending filled his own pockets.

Once Olaf called a man his friend, he remained loyal and generous, even letting himself be taken advantage of in the name of friendship. He frequently sent illustrated letters to complete strangers just because a friend asked him to do so. It probably never crossed his mind that these whimsical notes would someday become rare collector's items.

Seltzer distrusted both dealers and collectors who were too eager to snap up his offerings. Eventually he preferred to sell his output to middle-class Montanans—merchants, physicians, ranchers, ordinary townspeople—those with whom he felt at home. Outside buyers were received warmly in his home and studio only when they came recommended by trusted friends.

Seltzer drew great personal satisfaction from the reactions purchasers showed to the soft range of color he used in his western scenes, to his crystalline atmospheric effects, the shifting light, and illumined cloud formations. The way that admirers responded was more endearing to him than their ready cash.

Kermit Rasmussen, a Sunday painter and proprietor of the Hub, a men's clothing store in the farming community of Harlem, Montana, first visited the Seltzer home in the early thirties. At the time he had no money to spend on paintings, but the Seltzers made him feel at home and even invited him to bring his pet Sealyham Terrier. Rasmussen remembers the indignation that Olaf expressed in telling him about the West Coast industrialist who offered to pay him a thousand dollars, sight unseen, for any canvas he would paint. The insensitive would-be purchaser was shown the door, and Seltzer went on charging his customary prices.

"Olaf had a good sense of humor and at times was very witty," Rasmussen recalled. "But if he thought you were buying on speculation, he would run you off the place. He wanted you to buy his paintings because you liked them, and for that reason only. He never realized high prices for his work, and he was to blame for that."

In his declining years Olaf Seltzer grew very impatient if a buyer failed to pick up a painting immediately after it was ready to leave his studio. He called Rasmussen one day and ordered him to make the 165-mile trip from Harlem to Great Falls the following weekend to pick up a 16″ × 10″ watercolor of mountain sheep that Rasmussen had commissioned months earlier and that Olaf had only now finished. Rasmussen had other plans for that weekend, but he volunteered to come the following one. Olaf's temper flared.

"I'm a Dane, too," Rasmussen said. "So when he got mad, so did I. I didn't take the painting." The price agreed upon was under $200. Rasmussen paid for his Nordic temper a few years ago when he watched his mountain-sheep watercolor go for $9,000 at the annual sale sponsored by the C. M. Russell Museum in Great Falls.

Typical of Seltzer's uncompromising honesty is the tale of the oil painting that employees of the Great Falls Brewery asked him to paint as a farewell gift for their departing manager, Nick MacPhee, who was going to the Pacific Northwest. The committee raised $150 more than the price Olaf had agreed to take for the painting, and the artist put up fierce resistance to taking the full sum. He finally gave in. But on the subject matter of the painting he stood his ground. The donors had suggested a painting of a jerky and team; they got one of a jerk-line freight outfit.

Seltzer consistently risked losing sales because he refused to add touches to a painting if he considered them inappropriate. The Great Northern Railway once commissioned him to paint its excursion boat on Lake McDonald in Glacier Park. Then came a request to place in the prow the figure of the railroad's founder, James Jerome Hill, who had died in 1916. Olaf rejected the suggestion, bluntly telling the insistent rail executive that if he wanted Jim Hill on that boat he could paint him in himself.

But if he took a fancy to someone, Olaf might bombard him with illustrated letters or openhandedly present him with a painting. The Wagnerian tenor Lauritz Melchior was given a painting by Seltzer simply because Olaf enjoyed hearing the Danish operatic star sing on the radio. Melchior's thank-you note was written in the native tongue of donor and recipient.

Working at a more leisurely pace, Olaf Seltzer was still putting finishing touches on the Putnams' commissioned painting when word was received on July 3, 1937, that Amelia Earhart had disappeared at sea near Howland Island in the South Pacific. The artist had been attempting to make George Putnam's painting for Amelia a particular delight for her; the models he was using for the packtrain horses came from photographs (fur-

nished him by Amelia's mother) of the Putnams' own packhorses.

Olaf was disappointed but not surprised when Putnam decided not to buy the painting, entitled *The Fallen Monarch*, claiming that it would sadden him with the memories it evoked. The title refers to the trophy, an elk whose royal antlers boast seven heavy prongs to a side, the sole burden of a white lead packhorse accompanying a three-man hunting party.

Robert Elman, an authority on hunting, describes the 24" × 30" oil as having an

*aura of the past, yet even as late as the 1930's a mountain hunter was likely to carry a 30-30 Winchester or Marlin level action such as the rifle resting across the rider's saddle. In high country, an arduous stalk with a short-range woods rifle was still more common than a long shot with a powerfully-scoped bolt-action rifle.... The hunter seems to contemplate the bleached antler in the foreground, perhaps shed by the same animal or another in a previous year, perhaps a memorial to a less fortunate monarch—ill, winter-weakened, or injured, and then brought down by predators. Nature in this scene displays a poignantly dramatic symbol without revealing its true meaning.* [4]

By his adroit placement of the heads of the three lead horses in *The Fallen Monarch*, Seltzer managed to create an optical illusion. No matter what angle this magnificent painting is viewed from, the hunting party seems to be headed in the direction of the viewer. The painting remained in Olaf Seltzer's possession for many years before he agreed to sell it to his son Carl.

In 1938, Seltzer painted his largest canvas, a 9' × 15' oil commemorating the first Masonic meeting in Montana, held in September, 1862, on Mullan Pass, fifteen miles west of Helena. [5] The painting covers an end wall in the library of the Montana Grand Lodge building in Helena. After spending weeks of research, Olaf rented the Butterfly Room of the Elmore Hotel in downtown Great Falls and set to work building a stretcher large enough to hold the special canvas he had ordered for the painting. Thanks to the florid literary style of one of the three men with the Fisk Northern Overland Expedition—the men who held the Mullan Pass meeting—Olaf had the de-

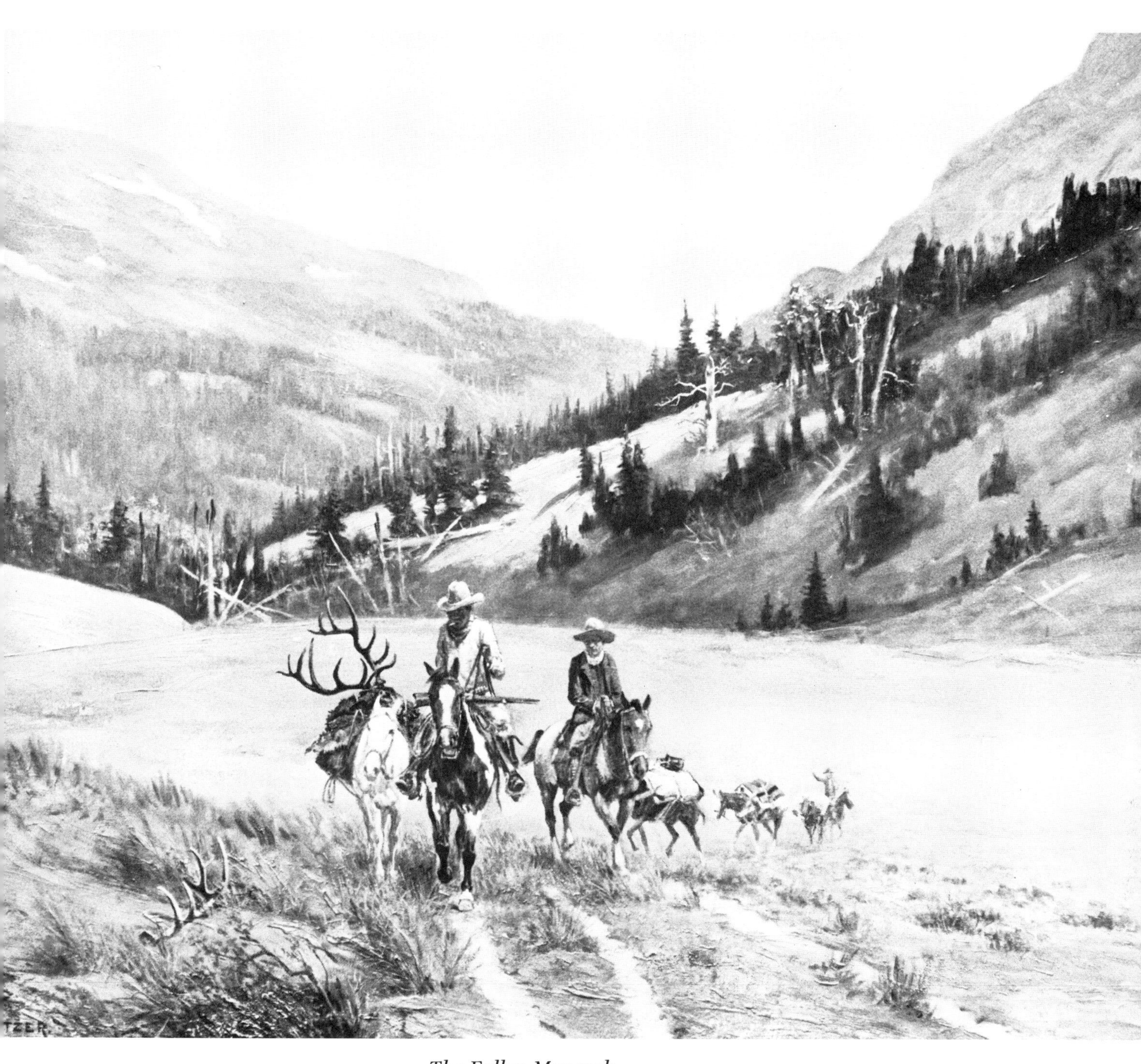

*The Fallen Monarch*
1937
Oil, 24″ × 30″
Copyrighted by Mr. and Mrs. Carl C. Seltzer.

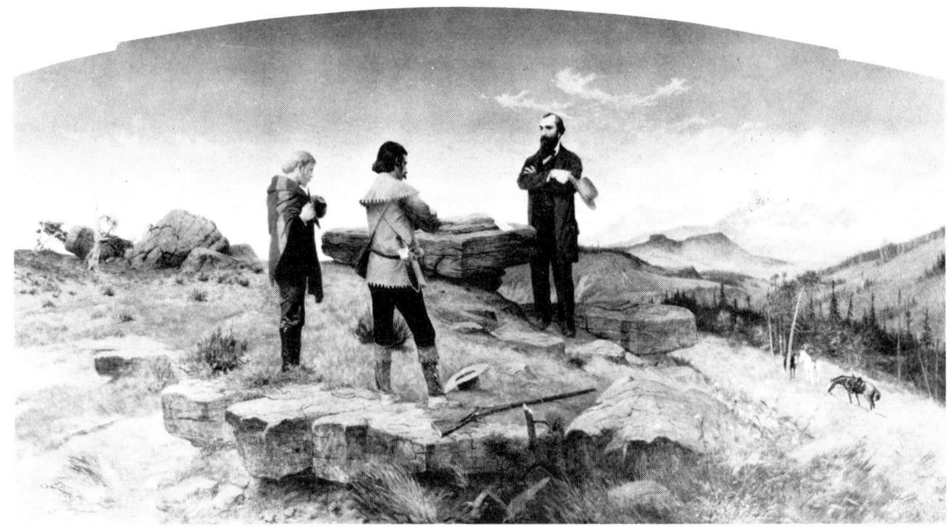

*First Masonic Meeting in Montana, on Mullan Pass, September, 1862*
1938
Oil, 9′ × 15′
Courtesy of Grand Lodge of Ancient, Free, and Accepted Masons of Montana.

scriptive material to stir his imagination. Nathaniel P. Langford, Grand Historian for the Grand Lodge session held in Virginia City, Montana, in October, 1867, gave a detailed account of the meeting, dwelling on the breathtaking beauty of the atmosphere in which it was held:

*I esteem myself fortunate in having . . . before I left the abodes of civilization, been raised to the sublime degree of a Master Mason. When the company, of which I was one, entered what is now Montana . . . a single settlement, known by the name of Grasshopper (now Bannack), was the only abode of the white man in the southern part of the Territory. Our journey from Minnesota, of fourteen hundred miles, by a route never before traveled, and with the slow conveyance of ox trains, was of long duration and tedious. It was a clear September twilight when we camped on the western side of the range of the Rocky Mountains. . . . The labors of the day over, three of our number, a brother named Charlton, another, whose name I have forgotten, and myself, the only three Master Masons in the company, impressed with the grandeur of the mountain scenery and the mild beauty of the evening, ascended the mountain to its summit. . . .*

*I had listened to the solemn ritual of Masonry an hundred times, but never when it impressed me so seriously as upon this occasion. . . . Our long journey and its undeviating round of daily employments had, until this occasion, been wholly unalleviated by any circumstance calculated to soften or mellow the feelings subject to such discipline. . . . Never was the fraternal clasp more cordial than when in the glory of that beautiful autumnal evening, we opened and closed the first Lodge ever assembled in Montana.*

Seltzer was not a Mason, but his artistic nature enabled him to visualize the scene and understand the emotional impact it had on the travel-worn men as he read further descriptions in Langford's speech:

*. . . The fact will render the spot sacred—it will never be forgotten, that the first Lodge in the Territory was opened and closed upon the summit of the Rocky Mountains.*

*I might dilate upon the beauty of the evening upon which we met; the calm radiance of the moon and stars; the grandeur of the surrounding scenery. We exchanged fraternal greetings, spoke*

*kind words to one another, and gave ourselves
up to the enjoyment of that elevation of spirit
which Masonry, under such circumstances, alone
could evoke....*

In his subsequent book, *Vigilante Days and Ways*, Langford named his first comrade as David Charlton, a member of a lodge in Hennepin, Minnesota. The third man remained unidentified until 1966, when the *Great Falls Tribune* headlined a May 29 story: "Masons Solve Century-Old 'Third Man' Mystery." The unknown Mason was George E. Gere, a member of a lodge in St. Paul.

Seltzer studied a photograph of the full-bearded Langford in creating his likeness, but he had to draw on his imagination to paint the other two men. He painted Langford full face in city clothes; the second Mason is portrayed in profile, while the "Third Man" is posed so that only a portion of his face is visible. Heads uncovered, they stand as in prayer on some table rocks in a glorious twilight that illumines the snow-covered mountains in the distance. Their riding horses graze peacefully in the open meadow below the rock-strewn summit.

As an artist who reveled in handling the effects of shifting light, of sun glint and afterglow, Seltzer was delighted with the Masons' commission—and with the $3,000 fee. But work on the oversized canvas in the empty public room at the Elmore was beset with frustrations. There was no humidity control; each time it rained, the canvas sagged in the stretcher, and work would have to be suspended until the air became drier. He had difficulty painting the third man's rifle; he could not get it placed against the rock in what he thought was a realistic position. "Fighting a picture" always irritated Seltzer, and he became more and more tense as his frustrations built up. It was enough to make a man seek the solace of the bottle—and Olaf did.

In such a mood Seltzer would sometimes go off for several days of hard drinking. Mabel would not permit liquor in their home; during these interludes it was his custom to stay away until he had sobered up.

Sometimes Olaf needed no further excuse than meeting an old friend. One Friday afternoon in March he ran into Pete Petersen, a Dane whose companionship he had enjoyed in the locomotive shops. Olaf was waiting on a downtown corner for a streetcar. He had finished a research session in the public library and had shopped for some fresh vegetables Mabel needed to stuff a turkey for Carl's birthday dinner the following Sunday.

The reunion between the two former machinists called for a drink. Old-timers at the Central Avenue bars chuckle when they recall the ferocity with which Olaf clutched his onions, celery, and carrots as he made the rounds that Friday evening, refusing to put down the paper sack for fear he would forget it. Olaf and his vegetables made it home by Saturday afternoon, both considerably the worse for wear.

Under most circumstances Seltzer knew when to stop. He never hid his habit and frequently told stories on himself. Sometimes when asked what product he favored in thinning paint, he would answer: "Some artists use linseed oil and some use poppy seed oil and some use alcohol." If the unwitting straight man asked how painters used alcohol, Olaf would reply, "They drink it."

Always the family man, Olaf considered 1938 a landmark year, because his younger son, Walter, married Della Thomas, a registered nurse who in time became supervisor in charge of psychiatric nursing at the Great Falls Deaconess Hospital. Walt had lived with his parents until his marriage to Della when he was thirty-two. During the early years of his marriage Walt Seltzer painted a number of admirable 10" × 8" watercolors of Indian heads, based on sketches he enjoyed making at tribal ceremonies. Two of these are in the museum collection of the Montana Historical Society.

Another marriage within the year brought pleasure to the Seltzers. Their bachelor friend Bill Marks married Alice Green. The newlyweds made a trip to Helena in the summer of 1940 to view the Masonic mural, continuing on to Great Falls so that Alice could meet other members of the Seltzer family.

Weeks after their visit Olaf accepted an invitation to spend some time with them in Seattle. He was there for the last month of the summer. Alice Marks remembers that he enjoyed reminiscing with her about her husband's younger days and the good times they had with Charlie Russell but that Olaf was "very much the introvert" and never talked about himself.

Now in his sixties and enjoying a better income from his sales, Olaf Seltzer had settled in to spend his remaining years at the easel, working at his own pace for those who appreciated his art.

## Chapter 11

# New Patrons

Olaf seltzer was always delighted to hear from his friend and patron Philip Cole. The letter Cole wrote to him on March 17, 1941, was typical of their warm and easy correspondence.

> Just a few lines to let you know that your friend, Mr. Marks of Seattle, called up last Sunday and I had a very pleasant conversation with him. . . . He was anxious to see the paintings and I would have loved to have been able to invite him out to the house on Sunday but it was impossible on that day. I did invite him to come some other time however, for any friends of yours would be welcome.
>
> By the way, Mr. C. R. Smith, President of the American Airlines, Inc., who is something of a Western fan, has been out to the house several times lately and admires (as he should) your things greatly. I think he has already gotten in touch with you and am doing everything I can to encourage contact with you so he can get some of your works for his own collection.
>
> Everything is pretty good at home. I have several additions to the collection, in which I know you will be interested, but frankly am side-stepping the spending of money the way I used to. You know how it is with everyone these days.
>
> Here's hoping that everything is going well with you oldtimer. All good wishes and best regards from all of us.
>
> As always,
> Doc.

But not all was well with the writer. This would be the last letter in the fifteen-year correspondence between patron and artist, for on June 29, 1941, Philip Cole died at fifty-seven, victim of a massive stroke.

The stroke that proved fatal was not the first one, according to Alice Ralston, but it is doubtful that Olaf knew about his friend's declining health. He had not seen Cole since his last visit to Tarrytown in the late autumn of 1934. Martin Wiesendanger, at the time a customer's man for the prestigious Kennedy Galleries, remembers Cole's pallor and a tremor in his hand during a four-year period when "he looked like a sick man." The *Great Falls Tribune* telephoned the news to Seltzer, who called it a "great shock." He recalled his first encounter with Cole at Dr. Butler's home in Helena as "the beginning of a lasting friendship."

Mrs. Cole took the children to Last Chance Ranch at Lake Placid for the rest of the summer. Miss Ralston, after directing the household staff in the disposition of Dr. Cole's personal belongings, ended an association of fifteen years with the family and returned to Bozeman, Montana, where she settled in a picturesque cabin. She did not see any of the Cole family again until 1966, when Kay Cole Worden, accompanied by David C. Hunt, the art curator of Gilcrease Museum, visited her in a convalescent home a few months before her death.

Zeeview, Philip Cole's dream world on the east bank of the Hudson River, where he had recreated his memories of a childhood under the open skies of Montana, was put up for sale. Word soon spread in Manhattan art circles that the largest and finest single collection of western Americana would be available. But Pearl Harbor plunged the nation into a state of emergency only a few months after Phil Cole's death, and three years passed before the sale of Dr. Cole's beloved collection was completed.

What were Philip Gillett Cole's plans for the disposition of his collection? Thirty-five years later this question still provokes debate. The man who bought for the sheer pleasure of re-creating the West as he remembered it never exhibited much concern among his friends or within his family about the future of his possessions. E. E. MacGilvra, former Montana state senator who has served on the board of the Montana Historical Society for many years, confirms Alice Ralston's recollection that Dr. Cole had made overtures to the society with the idea of leaving the collection for the proposed state museum, provided that a special wing was built to house it. At the time the offer was made, it "would have been outlandish for the state to even consider as we had no building of our own," MacGilvra said. Most likely the matter did not seem pressing in view of Dr. Cole's age, and he may have planned to renew the offer at a later date.

The art collection and library were willed to the Cole children, who were too young and inexperienced at the time to form an opinion about its future. Mrs. Worden recalls that no one asked her. When Mrs. Cole, later Mrs. Dwight Mills, authorized the trustees of her husband's estate to sell the collection, she stipulated that it must be kept intact, probably acting on advice that a quicker disposition could be made on the whole lot. When this happened, C. R. Smith, who had hoped to buy some of the Seltzer paintings, lost his chance.

In like manner Seltzer lost his chance to be more widely recognized within his lifetime, although he probably was not aware of the significance of the sale. Much of his best work, including the three ingeniously conceived series of paintings dedicated to the settling of the West, was among the 340 Seltzer pieces inventoried by P. J. Curry Company when the collection was put on the market. As part of the entire collection, these paintings were transferred to an even larger collection, where they are viewed by a constant stream of visitors from all over the world.

Under the strain of the war years Olaf Seltzer missed his close friend but gave little thought to the future of the western art collection on which he had labored so long and lovingly for Cole. He had never heard of the oilman Thomas Gilcrease, who would be the next owner of the paintings Seltzer and Phil Cole had planned together.

Like Cole, Gilcrease was a gentle, unassuming man with a penchant for beautiful possessions.

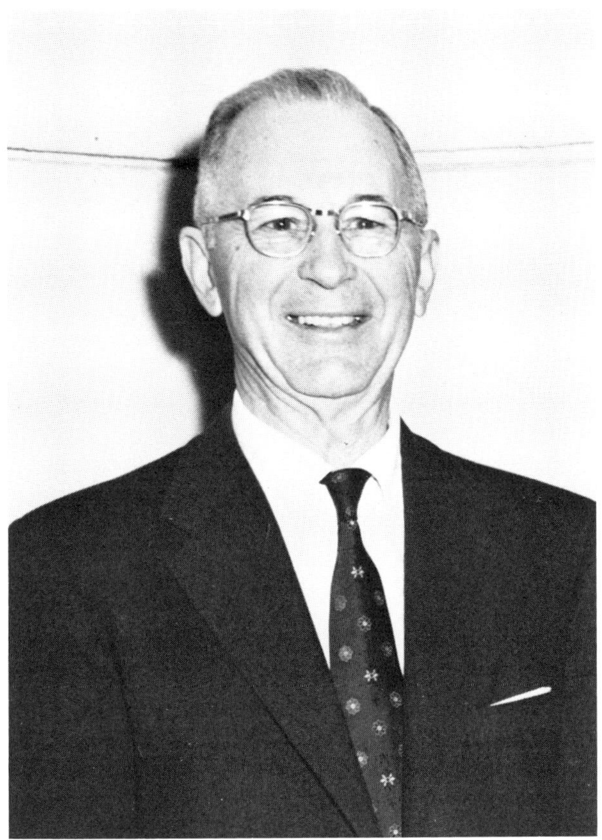

Thomas Gilcrease.
Courtesy of Gilcrease Library.

Their backgrounds, however, were poles apart. Unlike the squire of Zeeview, who enjoyed his possessions in the privacy of his palatial home and shared them only with intimate and appreciative friends, Tom Gilcrease began formulating plans for the public display of his art and artifacts as soon as he began making his many purchases.

The disciplined habits of a poverty-stricken childhood and an incredible stroke of good fortune combined to make Tom Gilcrease an independent oil driller by the time he was twenty. In 1912, when he was twenty-two, Gilcrease bought his first oil painting, Ridgway Knight's sentimental *Rural Courtship*, from a New York art dealer displaying his wares at the Hotel Tulsa, then a gathering place for wildcat oilmen like Gilcrease.

In later years Tom Gilcrease would accept compliments on his tremendous collection of Americana with a shy smile and the comment, "A man must leave some sort of track." His track was an impressive one—more than 4,000 paintings, several hundred pieces of sculpture, a library of 60,000 rare manuscripts and books, and an artifact collection so immense that the task of registering it has only recently been completed. Each of his acquisitions—and he bought entire collections—was related to the development of the Americas, with emphasis on Indian culture and history and on trans-Mississippi settlement.

William Thomas Gilcrease, the oldest of William and Elizabeth Vowell Gilcrease's fourteen children, was born in 1890 in Robilene, Louisiana. His father was of Scotch-Irish and French descent; his mother was one-fourth Creek Indian, and young Tom was listed on the Final Roll of Creek Citizens by Blood as No. 1505. Shortly after Tom was born, the Gilcreases moved to the Creek Nation in territory that would become part of the state of Oklahoma. A sensitive and introspective lad, Tom walked with a limp that could be traced to babyhood. When he was five, he was taught reading and writing, but his schooling was fragmentary. From childhood he helped his father on the farm and in the operation of the family's cotton gin and gristmill.

In 1899, William Gilcrease received 160-acre tracts of land as allotments for the Creek citizens of his family, his wife and each child. A neighbor pointed out an oil seep on the Gilcrease land; it would come in handy for greasing harnesses, he said. When the fabulous oil strike was made at Glenpool, Oklahoma, Tom Gilcrease's land allotment was only four miles away. The twenty-year-old assembled some crude drilling gear and began drilling operations on his own acreage. His labors eventually yielded thirty-two producing wells, and he became an independent oilman. With his first royalties he underwent surgery to correct his limp and enrolled at Bacone College for Indians in Muskogee, Oklahoma, where he remained for a semester. Most of his education came from the books he treasured and read on his own. Through such reading and personal observation Tom Gilcrease formed deeply held convictions about the effects of exploitation and liquor on his brother Indians. He determined early that he would not be a victim to either. This decision added to his strength as a bargainer.

By the time he was thirty-five, Gilcrease had fathered two sons, divorced his first wife, Belle Harlow Gilcrease, and possessed such wealth that he was casting about for some philanthropic project to absorb his interest. For a while he toyed with the idea of establishing a writer's colony. On a trip to Europe he began buying *objets d'art* and rare books, which he brought to his imposing stone home on a wooded hillside in the Osage Nation, overlooking the growing Tulsa skyline. After his stormy second marriage to Norma Smallwood, a former Miss America, and the birth of his daughter, DesCygne, Gilcrease moved his operations to San Antonio, Texas, where he began collecting art and manuscripts in keeping with his special interests. By the time he heard of the availability of Cole's art and documents, Tom Gilcrease was buying whole collections of American Indian material in London, New York, and Philadelphia. Yet so quietly was his purchasing done that his name often passed unrecognized.

Martin Wiesendanger, Swiss-born cousin of Mrs. Herman Wunderlich whose husband owned Kennedy Galleries, was aware of Tom Gilcrease's preoccupation with western American art. The first time they met, Gilcrease had written a $35,000 check to cover his purchases from Kennedy. Another customer of Wiesendanger's was Dr. Philip Cole, who often dropped by the galleries to purchase fine prints and etchings as wedding gifts. Wiesendanger and Cole also shared an interest in rare stamps.

When Wiesendanger learned that Mrs. Cole was offering her late husband's collection for sale, he was already in San Antonio, cleaning and restoring Gilcrease's paintings in preparation for their first exhibition. He urged Gilcrease to investigate the offering and to move quickly if he was interested in buying the Cole collection, because Wiesendanger had heard that the trustees of the estate wanted to meet a tax-filing deadline of December 15, 1944. The two men made a trip to New York City in early December, but Gilcrease refused to be hurried or pressed on terms. He balked at putting securities in escrow while negotiations proceeded, accustomed as he was to sealing deals with a handshake. The oilman and his first museum director returned to San Antonio empty-handed.

The broker for the sale, Daniel B. Browne, and Wiesendanger exchanged several frantic communications. Browne wrote to Wiesendanger, "... Mr. Gilcrease may be a proud and imperious person, but so are the Trustees, who said that they would require a deposit in escrow from the Rockefeller Foundation were they the potential purchasers."[1] Gilcrease and Wiesendanger returned to New York, but once more negotiations ended abruptly. The oilman wanted to pay the $250,000 purchase price in four equal installments for tax purposes. This was unacceptable to the estate trustees. In the end, however, Gilcrease's seeming indifference paid off, and the sale was consummated. Leonard A. Lombardo, of the Fairfield Antique Gallery in New York, was working through an attorney for the purchase of the collection. He came in with a bid of $400,000 for the R. W. Norton Foundation, of Shreveport, Louisiana, but just after Tom Gilcrease had made his deal.[2] An untutored, soft-spoken Oklahoma Indian, Tom Gilcrease, had made the art deal of the era. He purchased 560 paintings and 62 pieces of sculpture, plus valuable historical materials, for $250,000, a price that some individual items in the inventory would command today. Half of the paintings were by Olaf Seltzer.

Gilcrease had one further stipulation. He wanted the sale to be kept quiet until he finished making the payments and the collection was legally his. Two more years elapsed before public mention of the sale was made. In the interval the new owner decided to build his museum on the brow of a hill stretching north from his Tulsa home. Work was begun on a long-house structure of native stone to fit the contour of the hill and to provide the proper setting for Gilcrease's newly acquired treasures.

Tom Gilcrease's museum was opened in 1949. From then until his death in 1962 he derived great pleasure from the public appreciation of his treasures and the growing fame of his collections. During the early fifties Gilcrease overextended his obligations, and the art work and library were rumored to be in danger of being lost to Tulsa. Several noted institutions, most of them outside Oklahoma, made offers. A hastily assembled "Keep Gilcrease" committee financed a special election to authorize $2.25 million in bond funds. In return Gilcrease turned over his precious collection to the city of Tulsa and assigned future royalties from certain oil properties up to the limit of the bond issue to help in the maintenance and operation of the museum. Additional gifts to the museum have been made from the independent Thomas Gilcrease Foundation.

It is here that some of the finest works of Philip Cole's good friends Olaf Seltzer and Charlie Russell have found a permanent home, along with many works by George Catlin, Albert Bierstadt, Alfred Jacob Miller, Frank Tenney Johnson, Joseph Henry Sharp, William R. Leigh, Charles Schreyvogel, Frederic Remington, and Thomas Moran.

After he became familiar with his new treasures, Tom Gilcrease was intrigued by the human-interest appeal of Olaf Seltzer's work, particularly the Western Character sketches and the delightful letters Olaf illustrated for Dr. Cole. Returning from Helena by private plane in 1949, Gilcrease made a sudden decision to land in Great Falls and call on the Danish-born artist. The oilman was accompanied on the visit by his private secretary, Eudotia Teenor.

Seltzer was housebound at the time, crippled by an attack of the rheumatic condition that plagued him in his last years. He received his distinguished guest warmly, however, and took great pleasure in showing his current work to the collector and to Mrs. Teenor. She recalls that artist and collector took to each other immediately. Seltzer seemed pleased by the knowledge that the largest single collection of his paintings was in the hands of a man who planned to share it with those who found their way to the hilltop museum.

Soon after this visit Gilcrease mailed Seltzer an art catalogue and a clipping from a Tulsa newspaper describing an exhibit of paintings by Joseph H. Sharp at the museum. The oilman treasured Seltzer's reply, in which the artist commented on the authenticity of Sharp's paintings on the Crow Reservation. It was a brief but happy association between Seltzer and the oilman who felt a compulsion to leave some sort of track for those who followed and by so doing preserved the tracks of such creative artists as Seltzer.

The war years had been painful ones for Olaf. At sixty-four, an age when most men face retirement, he had undertaken to become a teacher in order to carry his part of the burden of the war effort. In October, 1941, Seltzer had become an instructor in a National Defense Training project at Great Falls High School, some blocks down the street from his home.[3] For most of the ensuing year Olaf taught lathe operation at evening classes, training prospective machinists and mechanics. He gave up teaching toward the fall of 1942 to return to the machinist's bench himself. Fired with patriotism, he went to work at the Great Falls Iron Works in August, 1942. His time

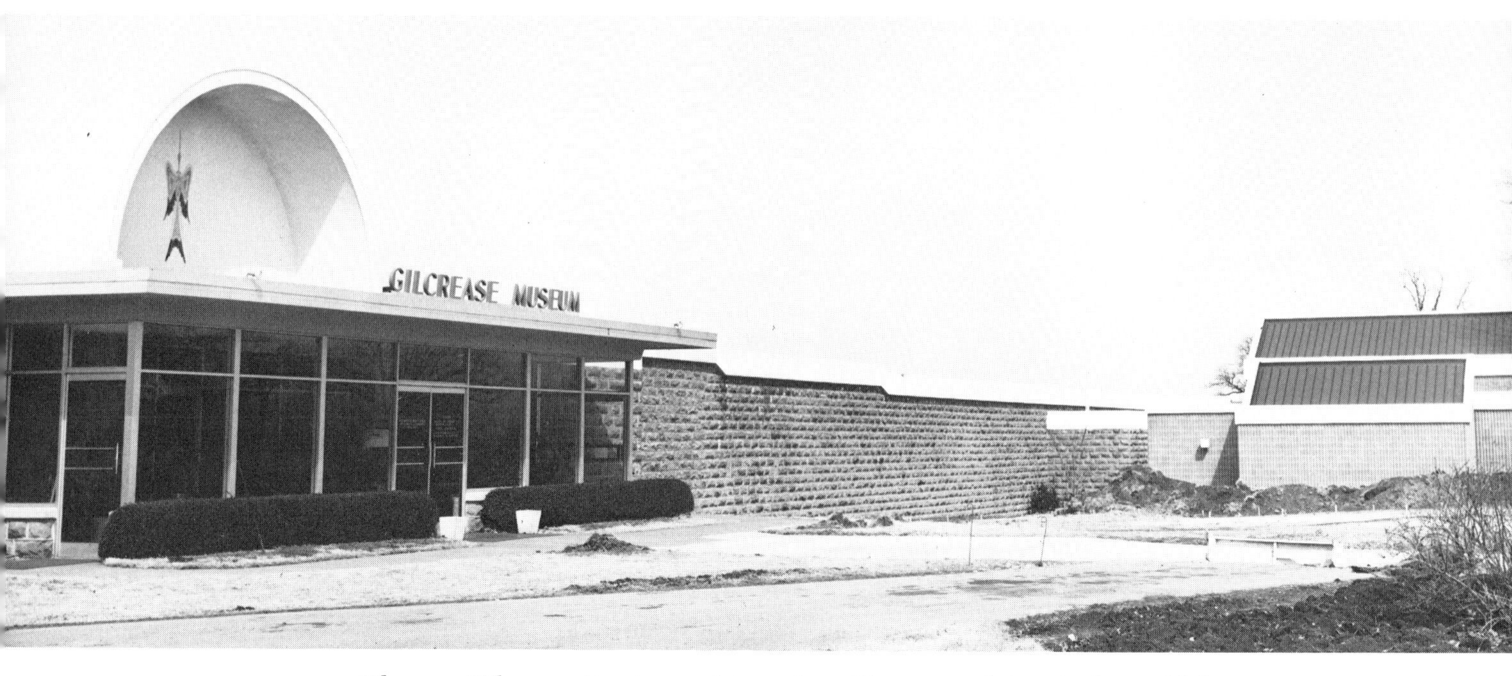

Thomas Gilcrease Institute of American History and Art, Tulsa, Oklahoma.
Courtesy of Gilcrease Library.

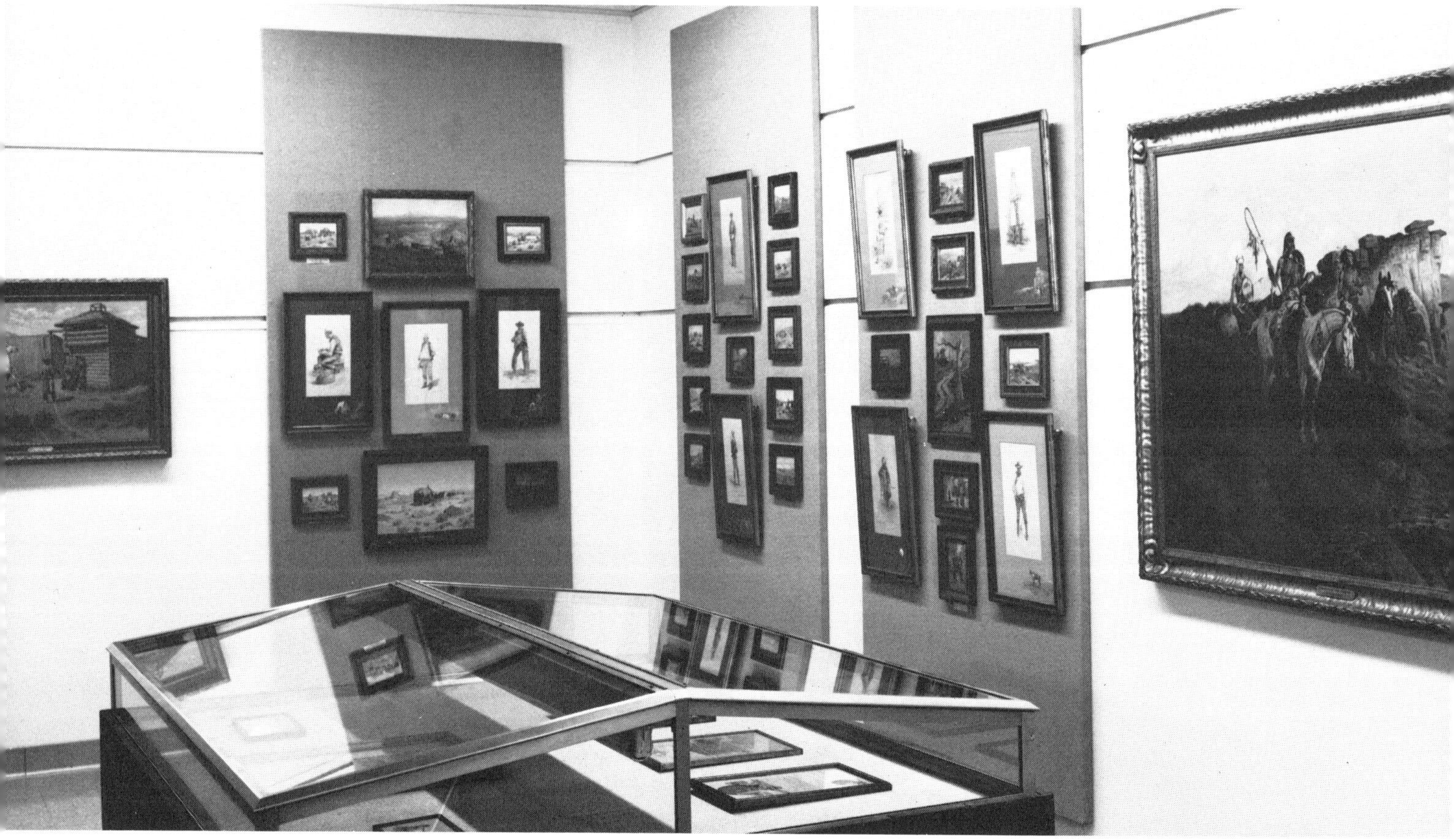

Seltzer Gallery, Gilcrease Museum.
Courtesy of Gilcrease Library.

there was brief, for on the last Saturday in November, while lending a hand to some friends in a machine shop, Olaf's wrench slipped as he was adjusting a large shaper. He was thrown backward, dropping four feet to the concrete floor. His right arm was broken just above the wrist, but he considered himself lucky not to have suffered more severe injuries. This accident may have triggered some of the arthritic problems he was soon to have.

During his eight months of convalescence, Seltzer continued to paint, learning to handle his brush in his left hand. Most of his output consisted of small genre paintings, the kind he liked to do for his own amusement. He gave an 11″ × 13″ watercolor, *Street in Oran*, to his "washerwoman," daughter-in-law Lillian, in gratitude for the household chores she was assuming for him and Mabel.

In August, 1943, Olaf was fully recovered from his injury and eager to take another war-related job. He reported to Malstrom Air Force Base, outside Great Falls, as a lathe operator. Among many satisfying experiences he had on the job was being able to make a speedy replacement for a broken worm gear on a plane loaded for Alaska, allowing the flight to continue without a long delay. Seltzer won a citation for helping design a mounting that enabled a thirty-millimeter machine gun to be used on a plane in place of a fifty-millimeter, saving the cost of higher-caliber ammunition. The idea originated with a co-worker, but Seltzer did the blowups and presentation, and the two men shared a citation presented by the commanding officer.

The artist began working at the air base at an annual salary of $2,200, and was given modest raises routinely. There is no question about his motivation. Daily he plunged hands capable of remarkable delicacy with brush and paint into the grime and muck of a heavy-machinery shop. Financially he could have done better in his studio, but he would have been frustrated had he not been able to demonstrate his loyalty to his adopted country. He sincerely believed that it was his duty to serve where he could contribute toward winning the war, though he had been away from the machinist's bench for twenty years.

"A painter of wide renown . . . has put aside his canvas and brush to take up the arms of our civilian army," Staff Sergeant Leo M. Crane reported in the *Machinists' Monthly Journal*, a union organ, in January, 1944. After reviewing

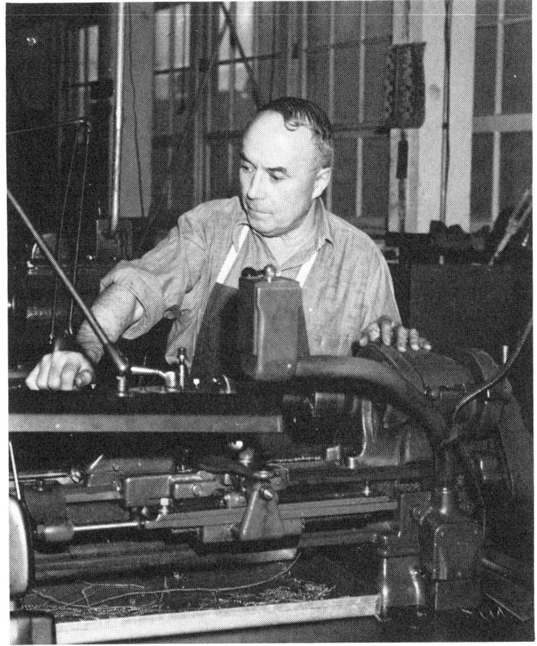

Seltzer at the machinists' bench during
World War II.
Courtesy of Carl C. Seltzer.

the artist's wartime efforts, Crane concluded: "Seltzer intends to continue working there until the war is won. Then he will again take up his art."

Within a year after the end of hostilities Olaf had a new patron, one who found the artist's behavior perplexing but who was determined to win his friendship. E. B. Craney knew O. C. Seltzer's reputation. He thought it would be a good idea to have Seltzer do a sketch for the letterhead of the new Craney radio station in Great Falls, KXLK, when it opened in 1946. Several months later the station manager telephoned Craney in Butte, suggesting he come to Great Falls to inspect the sketch. Craney told the manager to use his judgment, but he soon learned that it was not that simple. Seltzer refused to release his design without Craney's personal approval.

On his next visit to Great Falls, Craney called on the artist and admired his pen sketch of a Missouri River falls with a black eagle soaring overhead, a depiction of the scene that inspired Lewis and Clark to name the area Black Eagle Falls. Craney paid the artist fifty dollars for his sketch and began inquiring about two pictures hanging on the wall of Seltzer's small studio. One was an Indian burial showing a decomposed horse in the foreground, a painting Olaf told Ed Craney he had made years earlier.

"How come you haven't sold it?" the radio executive asked.

"I sold that picture a number of times," Olaf answered. "Young fellows like you come around to buy the picture and take it home. Their wives won't let them keep it and I get it back every time."

Craney assured Olaf that he had a place for the painting and that no woman would want it sent back. Then he asked about a second, smaller scene.

"That doesn't amount to anything," was Seltzer's reply.

Craney said it looked like the west side of Glacier Park. Seltzer agreed, "That's where it is." Taken with the way the artist had painted the sunset along the mountain tops, Craney offered to buy both paintings if the artist would remove some deer from the foreground of the glacier scene. This irritated Olaf, who demanded to know what was wrong with the deer. Craney told him he had not seen any deer when he was hunting on the Canada–United States line just west of Glacier.

"There's nothing wrong with the deer," Olaf insisted. "If you want the pictures, take them home, and if you don't like them after you get them there, send this one back and I will take the deer out for you." Thus ended the first visit between the blunt artist and the radio chain owner, who would buy more than twenty of Seltzer's paintings in the next decade.

In 1964, when Craney and his wife, Connie, assigned their Seltzer collection to the Greater Montana Foundation with the stipulation that the collection remain in Montana, Craney dictated a personal account of this first meeting and subsequent sessions with Seltzer.[4] His narrative is an interesting profile of the artist in his old age.

Craney did return the Glacier picture. Seltzer then sent him an illustrated letter showing the snag of fallen trees he was painting in the foreground to take the place of the obliterated deer. Not one to give up without a struggle, Olaf painted a watercolor buck and doe on the envelope. Craney had learned his lesson; he planned to tread carefully in his future dealings

with Seltzer. But he soon suffered a setback in his budding relationship with the aging artist because of a project he became involved in.

The Mint collection was on the market, and public-spirited citizens across Montana were trying to raise the $65,000 that they had reason to believe would keep the Russells in the collection in the state. Craney's radio empire raised $20,000, devoting air time to the project and distributing sets of Russell prints. Seltzer viewed this effort as a slight to his work, although Craney claims that he had proposed a similar series of Seltzer prints but that Olaf had put him off by insisting that he was busy preparing a number of watercolors for a New York gallery.

Craney admittedly was somewhat reluctant about nationwide distribution of Seltzer prints, because an incident that took place before the Montana State Accident Board caused him to question how just well known Olaf's work was. The artist had got something in his eye at the air base and had asked for compensation. The request was refused, so Olaf went to Helena to present his appeal to the board. When the chairman asked what Seltzer did for a living, Olaf answered, "I paint." The chairman told him he could see well enough to paint since "you're walking around here with no trouble." The embarrassed official later told Craney that he took Seltzer to be a house painter.

On a return visit to Seltzer's home Craney tried to buy several of the small tavern paintings but was turned down. On his next visit he brought his wife. Seltzer immediately agreed to sell the tavern paintings to Connie, along with a 20″ × 30″ western of three Indians at a water hole. Because the Craneys wanted to buy several paintings on this occasion, Seltzer offered them a reduced price!

Craney refused, telling Seltzer that he had a proposition to make to him. Craney thought Seltzer's 5½″ × 7½″ painting of a knight standing by his horse before a Moorish arch depicted the most beautiful horse he had ever seen. If Seltzer would make him a gift of this picture, the Craneys would see to it that all their Seltzer paintings would stay in Montana. Olaf agreed.

Craney wondered about the inspiration for the knight and his horse. The painter told him that the arch was from the *National Geographic* and that he had researched the knight's armor and the horse's trappings to make sure they were the style worn at the time of the Crusades. The Craneys then tried to buy a watercolor hanging on the wall of the Seltzers' living room. It was another Moorish arch with a flock of pigeons before it. In turning down their offer, Olaf explained that this arch also was from the *Geographic* but that the birds were "Great Falls' pigeons."

"I went downtown one day and sketched every pigeon I saw and there they are," Seltzer explained.

The Craneys began to feel more at home with Olaf as time went by, particularly after he did two watercolors that Connie ordered as a Christmas gift for Ed in 1948. To make sure the gift would be a surprise, Seltzer offered to bring the water-colors to Butte personally. In his letter of November 18 he gave Mrs. Craney explicit instructions for framing and hanging:

> . . . If they are not just as you would like, do not hesitate in returning them to me. The pictures speak for themselves, the old Medicine Man with his Coup Stick (Coo-stick) riding across the sagebrush flat at twilight, and the Scout on his good looking cayuse scanning the rolling prairie country. The pictures should be hung facing each other, say one on each side of your big oil at the end of your living room. Should you care to keep just one, it is OK to split the two, for I can always make some other companion piece. A delicate pattern in dull gold and not more than one inch wide would make a nice frame. ¾ inch I think would be even better, for a havey frame on a watercolor has a tendency to kill the whole setting.

Craney brought a New York entertainer and artist named Jacques Romano to call on Olaf Seltzer. Romano had come out to entertain at a dinner for KXLK advertisers. Craney remembers Romano as "a first class old faker" who "could make his pulse stop and do a lot of card tricks and all that sort of thing."

Seltzer came hobbling to the door with a cane. According to Craney, Romano put one hand on the artist's stomach and another on his back and asked, "Don't you feel any heat?" Then he told Olaf that there was nothing wrong with him and ordered him to throw away his cane. For a moment Craney held his breath. Seltzer "jumped around and decided he was perfectly okay. I figured I had finally made a hit with the old man by being able to do something for him."

But Craney's relief was short-lived. Once in the studio Romano told Seltzer that he wasn't getting the features right on a watercolor. "Jacques reached over, took a pencil out of the old man's pocket. . . . I knew I was in for trouble," Craney recalls. Romano drew a little picture of an Indian's face on a piece of paper he was holding in his palm and told Seltzer, "If you want to cheat a little bit with a good hard pencil you can get features into these watercolors that you can't get otherwise."

Contrary to Craney's fears, the flamboyant entertainer made a hit with Seltzer. Romano later sent the artist a broad-humored sketch based on a current Pentagon joke and a bottle of medicine "for whatever ails me," Seltzer wrote to Craney, adding, "Mr. Romano is a good scout."

At the time of the Romano visit the closet door in Olaf's studio-bedroom stood wide open. Craney noted that it was "filled right to the door" with rolled-up brown wrapping paper.

> *I asked Seltzer, "What in the world do you have in there?" and he said, "Oh, I'll get rid of that. The kids won't have to. That's filled with sketches from when Russell and I and occasionally others would go out and get on a horse and fall off just to see how arms and legs would look."*
>
> *If I had had an ounce of brains, I would have made the old man an offer for that batch of brown paper right then and there. I had always wondered how he had put the same snag on the Glacier Park pictures that he had put in the letter he wrote to tell me that he had taken the deer out and if I knew anything about art I would know that something had to be in the foreground and he wanted to put the snag there. Later on I purchased another Seltzer picture that had been in the Mint Collection and lo and behold—the same snag is in it. He simply had to have that snag and others, along with arms and legs and rock piles and everything else that went into pictures, in that closet.*

When he enjoyed a buyer's company, Olaf was inclined to demand that the customer come by to see the work in progress. Perhaps this was an old man's attempt to bring the outside world into his own preserve. "He was a peculiar fellow to try to do business with," Craney recalls. "If you gave him an order by letter he never seemed to want to get started on it. He always wanted to talk to you in person about it although he would write letters back to you."

Bothered increasingly with sciatica and eye trouble, Seltzer wrote to Connie Craney in October, 1950, to tell her why he and Mabel could not accept the Craneys' invitation to visit them on their ranch at Saint Ignatius, Montana:

> . . . I am sorry to tell you that I have not done any painting for some time past, and I have been on a cattle ranch up in the Sweet Grass Hills, visiting with a friend of mine. I am again in the clutch of sciatic neuralgia, beside having trouble with my eyes. . . . so I am just trying to get back to normal and am going back to the ranch this coming Thursday the 12th to get away from town and forget about pictures.

"Mrs. Seltzer is feeling fair, in fact, a whole lot better than I am," Olaf concluded.

The impatience that accompanied Seltzer's nagging pains became more pronounced. The Craneys were away from Butte a good bit, traveling on business in Washington and Oregon as well as across Montana. Olaf had difficulty keeping up with them. On June 5, 1951, he complained to Connie Craney: "I have tried to locate the whereabouts of Mr. Craney, but have had no luck. Last week I went to the KXLK office at the Park Hotel to ask a few questions, but I found I might as well have gone down to the City Gas Works to inquire."

This lack of communication and Seltzer's short fuse stood in the way of the Craneys' efforts to add to their collection. "His failing health and [our] inability to go and talk with him personally and to call back on him numerous times deprived us," Craney explains. "One oil he did complete for us—and by the time I got a check to him he had decided we didn't want the picture and sold it to someone else."[5] The only Seltzer paintings in the Craney collection not purchased from the artist himself were six watercolors of animals that had been in the Mint Saloon collection. These the Craneys bought from a dealer.

Although Olaf grew to enjoy the visits of the Craneys, whose thoughtfulness included gifts of cigars for him and candy for Mabel, he always signed his letters to them "O. C. Seltzer" or "Seltzer," and addressed them as "Mr. and Mrs." There was none of the close camaraderie with them, or with any of his other admirers and collectors in his later years, that there had been with Phil Cole. There never would be.

## Chapter 12
# The Declining Years

Shortly after world war ii, Olaf Seltzer fell while alighting from a bus and broke his right leg. The leg healed, but the injury left him with a sciatic condition that caused intermittent pain during the last decade of his life. For a while he used two canes, and eventually a wheelchair, but he never lost his habit of spending regular morning hours at his easel, even when he painted from the wheelchair, steadying his hand with his mahlstick.

Pain and frustration caused Olaf to become more testy and even more selective than he had been in deciding which customers he would accept. Punctuality was one of his determining factors in judging character. One of the many instances showing how Olaf felt about tardiness is Frank Curry's recollection of being asked by an official of the smelter to set up a way for him to meet Seltzer so that he could order a western painting. Curry made an appointment with Olaf for seven o'clock in the evening, but the smelter man didn't show up at Curry's home until close to nine o'clock. Frank suggested they cancel the arrangement for that night. His friend, unaware of Seltzer's temperament, insisted they ring the bell at 2715 Central Avenue. Olaf had retired. He opened the door long enough to deliver a scathing lecture on the rudeness of being late, then slammed it in his visitors' faces.

In spite of his feelings about touching another artist's work, in the autumn of 1946, Olaf agreed to restore a pair of Russell paintings that were Great Falls landmarks. They were destined for the C. M. Russell Museum. He spent the better part of a month working painstakingly over the unique pair—*The Buffalo Hunt* and *The Indian Camp*—that Charlie early in the century had painted directly onto the surface of circular plate glass. The two had been commissioned by Theodore Gibson, manager of the Park Hotel and were later purchased by O. S. Warden, publisher of the *Tribune*, for presentation to the Trigg-Russell Foundation that built the museum. The *Tribune* reported:

*During their years behind the cigar counter, the paintings had become dirty and smoke-begrimed. Wipe rags of well-intentioned janitors had worn a well-defined track down the glass around the circumference.*

*Later years also took their toll, the paint checking and peeling until the pictures were marred by glassy glints in certain light and apparently doomed to early disintegration unless they were given expert attention.*

*. . . With infinite patience, Seltzer cleaned, sized, and restored the paintings to a condition that insures a long future life.*

*Seltzer's restoration of "The Indian Camp" painting, showing an Indian on horseback with teepees in the background, proved revealing. Cleansing brought to light a turquoise blue stream meandering behind the teepees—a stream lost for years behind an accumulation of smut and grime.*

Seltzer the perfectionist was troubled by one detail of the restoration. Charlie had painted the buffalo with red tongues. Later, in a letter to an Oklahoma City collector, Olaf complained about artists who ignored details of this nature, exclaiming, "By God, the tongue of a buffalo is not red, but *blue-black*."

On May 12, 1950, Great Falls residents by the thousands turned out at the railroad station on the occasion of a campaign visit by President Harry S Truman. Governor and Mrs. John W. Bonner presented the President with a 17½″ × 21½″ western oil painting by Olaf Seltzer named *Indian on Horseback*.[1] It had been given to the Bonners for this purpose by Jean Toole, daughter of the Shelby rancher on whose Sweet Grass Hills ranch Olaf was soon to spend some time recuperating. The artist was not in the crowd at the station.

But not all was pain and cynicism for the aging artist. Increasingly he drew joy and consolation from his family and took his mind off his trials by spending his housebound hours poring over his butterfly and stamp collections. A new set of grandchildren had come along to grace the Seltzers' later years. Walt and Della's firstborn was a girl, Helen, nicknamed Tudy (a few years later, as a gift for her mother to mark the event, Olaf made a charming sketch of a little girl departing for her first day of school). Then came three sons: William, Walter Steven, and Richard.

The Carl Seltzers' girls were grown. In 1949, fifty years after Mabel Cleeland Seltzer was graduated in the initial class from Great Falls High School, her oldest grandchild, Ruth, wore her grandmother's class pin on her own commencement gown. Ruth married shortly thereafter and moved with her husband, Ed Teddy, to Peoria, Illinois. On October 15, 1951, shortly before they started back to Great Falls, the young couple received an elaborately detailed illustrated letter showing a brave and his wife with travois before a road sign that indicated 97 miles to Peoria and 1203 to Great Falls. Seltzer wrote:

> In about two Moons, you'll be starting to break up your camp at Peoria, the Indian village on the Illinois River, taking down your Teepe and get the old "Travaux" packed up, and your motive power fed and watered, ready for the long back-trailing "Trek" westward to the old camping grounds on the Prairies of the setting sun. The above sketch, done by the well-known "Medicine Man"—Old Chief "Never Sweat"—who is also often referred to as "Gramp"—shows the pair of you well on the trail, via Minneapolis, Bismarck, Miles City and other points west. I know you regret leaving your good friends in Peoria, but the best of friends must part sometime. Those you left behind when you went so many Moons ago, are waiting to welcome you both home to the

"Medicine Lodge" and perhaps celebrate with a "Scalp Walk-Around." Until then,

> "Na-Koo-Se"
> Gramp

The other "little devil" was not forgotten in her grandfather's correspondence. In the late summer of 1951, when Sue was in Denver working for the Federal Bureau of Investigation, her grandfather made her a beautiful illustrated letter:

> My Dear Sue:
> The sketch on the envelope I am sending you depicts a young Blackfeet Scout on his sorrel bald-faced pony. He has on a beaded buckskin shirt and striped blanket of many colors. The buck on this painting is a Cree Indian by name— 'Man Child'—whom I knew years ago. You could always see him on some street corner wrapped in his faded three-point Hudson Bay blanket, trying to sell a set of highly polished Buffalo Horns, which was all that was left of the thousands of Nature's Cattle that roamed the Prairies long ago, the livelihood of the Plains Indians, Blackfeet, Piegans, Bloods, Crees and Crows. This bottom Indian I know not much about. He is one of the Southwest tribes with a decided Spanish look, the Navajo, Apaches, Comanches, Kiowas & Ute Indians, some of them often referred to as the Pueblo Dwellers.
>
> Love and best wishes from old
> Gramp Seltzer

Sue was particularly close to her grandfather. As a child she would sit quietly for long periods watching him paint. In high school she worked part time as an elevator operator at the Great Falls National Building. She opened a checking account on her first payday and wrote her first check to buy her grandfather's painting *The Arabians*, an 8″ × 10″ oil showing an Arab watering his horse at a wall fountain. Olaf never cashed her check, but was flattered to receive it. Sue came home to work for the commandant at Malstrom Air Force Base and married a California-born officer she met there, Joe Erwin. Olaf took a liking to both his grandsons-in-law and enjoyed reminiscing with them about his early days in Montana.

The Walter Seltzers' children were younger and more boisterous—three of them boys— during the highstrung artist's declining years. Helen, the oldest, was given several small watercolors of horses, which she has generously shared with her brothers. Seltzer was more accustomed to the ways of granddaughters. Steve is particularly regretful that he was not old enough to watch his grandfather paint and to study his technique. All that he remembers of his grandparents is that Grandma Seltzer always had candy for the boys when they came with their father to do the yardwork and that she seemed concerned that they would disturb Grandpa. A graduate of Montana State University at Bozeman, Steve has made a hobby of turning up as much information as possible about his grandfather's style of painting. In mid-1974, he left the real estate business to become a full-time artist in Hermosa Beach, California, and has established a name for himself as a painter of the western scene.

When he was not painting or enjoying family visits, Olaf puttered with his collections. Across the years he had added beetles and butterflies brought back or ordered from New York dealers, or gathered by him and the boys in Montana and Idaho. His collection included such colorful varieties as the Goliath beetle from Africa, the rhinoceros beetle, and the walking leaf. With customary meticulousness he mounted the larger ones on pins and kept them in a three-drawer chest, with a glass over each drawer. He kept the small beetles and butterflies in cigar boxes. It was the color of the insects that attracted Seltzer, rather than their rarity or scientific value; he was less concerned with labeling his acquisitions. Like Doc with his pictures, Olaf drew pleasure from them at the moment and showed little concern for the identification problems of any future owner. The limitless range of color and the translucency and iridescence wrought by the changing quality of light fascinated Seltzer.

Beauty, rather than market value, also guided his selection of stamps. Issues that showed birds or animals intrigued him. He wrote to dealers to track down rare stamps that he read or heard about, such as the canceled "Puffin" stamp from Lundy Island. He filled four notebooks with stamps, mounting his treasures with infinite care on paper gridded in gold ink and arranging them according to geographic regions.

Seltzer no longer had the chance to add to the glass-animal zoo, nor did he expand on his gathering of such old-time Montana brands as Mill Iron, Hash Knife, and 7-Up. These had served their purpose as markings in the details he used on

western paintings. Briefly, while at the machinist's bench in World War II, he had taken up jewelry making, turning out a ring in which he mounted a cat's-eye. To have beauty, in his opinion, a stone need not have monetary value.

Among Olaf's other hobbies was his collection of postmarks, neatly mounted in their own scrapbook and classified according to subject matter. He would clip the stamped ends from envelopes and, after mounting, draw neat panels around each, usually with gold ink. Although the stamps were not the reason for the collection, many of those kept for the postmark have also become valuable.

Since Carl Seltzer's sales work took him across the state, he was a heavy contributor to the postmark collection. He made a point of mailing his father an empty envelope from each hamlet that had an amusing or colorful name. Friends did likewise. Hence the scrapbook contains canceled stamps bearing postmarks of Emerald, Wisconsin; Diamond, Washington; Garnet, Ruby, and Sapphire, Montana; Salmon, Idaho; and Whitefish, Fishtail, and Mussel Shell, Montana. There are postmarks from Cuba and Copenhagen, New York; Turkey, North Carolina; and China, Maine. Six Lakes, Michigan; Number Four, New York; Twenty-six, Kentucky; Seventy-six, Missouri; and 96, North Carolina, are represented, along with Two Harbors, Minnesota; and Twenty-nine Palms, California. Larkspur, Colorado; and Rosebud and Iris, Montana, share a page. Sleepy Eye, Minnesota, and Medicine Hat and Seven Persons, Alberta, are included. Old Glory, Texas; Liberty, New York; and Justice, West Virginia, are in a class by themselves. There are postmarked two-cent stamps from What Chew, Iowa; Zigzag, Washington; Sweet Horse, Oregon; and Bird in Hand, Pennsylvania. Olaf added to this inexpensive collection from 1919 until the late forties.

Beginning in 1947, when he was seventy, Olaf formed the habit of noting all sorts of random information, such as his trouser size, the names of visitors and the day when the price of haircuts went up. His awareness of nature was as acute as ever; his notes ranged from hearing a mourning dove to the date on which the last of the iris bloomed. Typical entries read:

*Thursday, Sept. 16—Heard over at the flour mill a meadow lark first time this year and saw this*

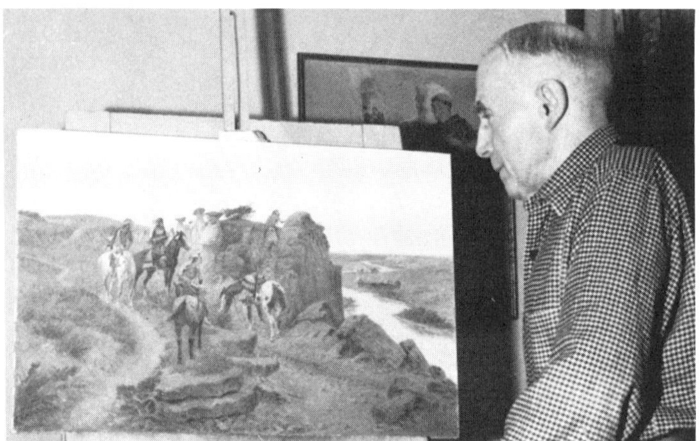

Seltzer in 1954.
Courtesy of Carl C. Seltzer.

*afternoon in the back yard one of those pretty Tortoise-Shell butterflies. Have seen no two-spots this year.*

*Friday, Oct. 15—first snow this fall. Nice, with gentle big flakes. Not cold . . . some of the Rust-colored Dragon flies were around in back yard.*

Such observations were interspersed with remarks that may have given him a chuckle: "Sometimes a clear conscience merely indicates a poor memory," or "Pack my box with five dozen liquer jugs."

Some of the entries in his little black book were tinged with poignancy. There was a page of death dates, each name followed by a tiny cross. Bill Marks's name was there, and Pearl Hynote's. Sylvia Bryant had died on January 14, 1944, at the age of seventy-four, Olaf noted. Maurice Weiss, former manager of the Placer Hotel in Helena and witness for him and Mabel when they exchanged their vows, died in 1948 at the age of eighty-two. Working backwards, Olaf put down the date of Doc's death and that of C.M.R. On a separate page, he memorialized family pets, noting the passing of the cat Sally, the collie Fox, and one simply mentioned as "the bobtailed cat." Those who knew and loved him were aware that behind his often cantankerous exterior was a kind and gentle and sentimental man. It is regrettable that it never occurred to him to collect and organize his jottings as he did his stamps and postmarks.

It is sometimes characteristic of the elderly to endow memories of things past with new significance. Olaf Seltzer, painfully aware of the fullness of his years, jotted down his views on art and life. In his last decade of life Olaf spent more time noting his reflections and convictions on life, writing in pencil on scraps of foolscap or on the backs of used envelopes. His once-robust health gone, he ruminated in his notes about what a man carries with him as the end approaches. "Memory is the only beautiful thing in life, for pleasant memories no one can take away from us," he wrote. "To drift along on the tide of remembrance, old faces, old scenes, old incidents, old triumphs, old failures, all of which pass before your mind's eye in kaleidoscopic panorama, now drab, now brilliant, ever changing"

On the back of a discarded letter, he wrote in his fine hand:

*The remembrance of something past, the beauty of some thing or of some personal relationships or of a certain country has always seemed to me to be the staff of life.*

*The present cannot be held, it slips through our fingers and becomes immediately the past. The future may be neither beautiful nor interesting. . . . But what has happened is ours and cannot be taken away from us, and the mind transmutes in retrospect almost everything into loveliness. Remembrance is the only sure immortality we know.*

Olaf had much to remember of "a certain country," of capturing some fleeting moment of pristine beauty and transmuting it in retrospect into a canvas of everlasting value through his skill with brush and palette. As might be expected of a creative artist, in his sixty-five years of painting he had experienced his moments of greatest happiness at his easel. He once told an interviewer that his pleasure came in the creation of a picture, not in the finished product. When a work in progress was moving well, he would be seized with a kind of exaltation. When things were going badly, he would be plunged into despair, his spirits brought down by the bleak prospect of his work being only mediocre.

In spite of the compliments Seltzer received on his linear composition, he seemed most confident in his mastery of color, of light and shadow, and particularly of reflections. Here he was able to exhibit his incredible delicacy in the handling of color to lend a soft, atmospheric effect to his paintings.

"There is no element in our sensuous nature which yields us a greater, or perhaps I should say a more varied, pleasure than the perception of brilliant and beautiful colors, hence our appreciation of Russell's art," he wrote in the draft of a statement commemorating his painting colleague.

Seltzer's chief contention with contemporary art instruction was that too much stress was placed on color alone at the expense of proficiency in draftsmanship. For all his love of color and his years of experimenting with it, his Old World discipline would not permit him to countenance what appeared to him to be unstructured work. Seltzer once told his friend Frank Curry about a promising lad in Great Falls who had gone east to school, and was now painting in the prevailing avant-garde style. "That kid had talent but they sent him back east to study with some painter who broke his own style," Seltzer said. "If his dad hadn't had the money to send him off to school, he'd be a fine painter."

He was ruthless in his criticism of trends in painting: "The terrible art efforts of today are a disgusting travesty on the ideals of true art. [They are] the dead-pan mummeries of certain deranged individuals who cannot draw or model and are trying to pass off delirium tremens monstrosities as a mysterious kind of art."

To his sons as boys he often emphasized the beauty to be found in commonplace objects, even in a garbage can. "It all depends on the lighting," he pointed out to Carl on one occasion, noting the delicate shadows along the grooves of the fluted surface.

For one of Olaf's makeup, the loss of acute eyesight must have been an excruciating experience. He now wore thick bifocals for normal work. At the easel it was necessary for him to use full-view magnifying glasses, but he followed the habits of years, rising with the first rays of light to make himself a light breakfast of coffee and toast before beginning a painting session of three hours or more by his north window. If his hand trembled a bit as it rested on the mahlstick, Olaf made up for his unsteadiness by taking unlimited time to achieve his desired effects.

His paintings now hung in almost every major city in the United States and in western Canada.

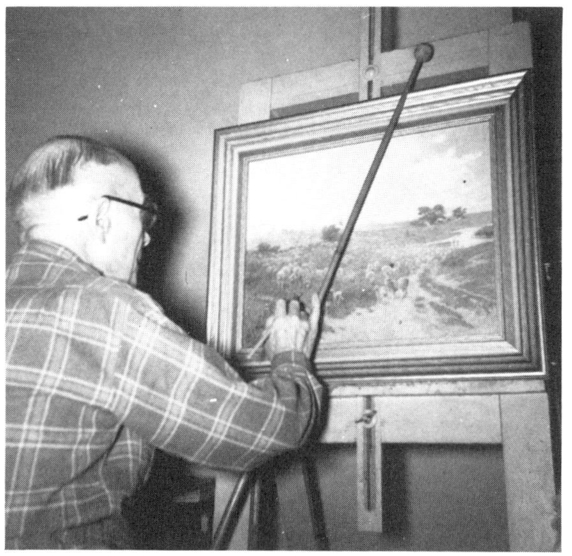

The last photograph made of Seltzer.
Courtesy of Carl C. Seltzer.

Visitors came from both coasts to admire and to buy, providing some gratification—and considerable irritation—for the nervous shut-in. A four-day visit from Alice Marks was worthy of mention in his pocket notebook, along with mention that she returned to Seattle in an October snowstorm. George Montgomery and Dinah Shore came by during Montana visits. On one such occasion they signed their names on the back of a favorite painting, an 11″ × 13″ oil, *The Charger*.

Will Rogers, Jr., and Olaf were photographed together when Rogers came to Great Falls for the Montana premiere of his movie about his famous father, *"The Boy from Oklahoma."* Olaf enjoyed answering the many questions Rogers asked about his father's good friend Russell, and he showed him some of the rough sketches he and Charlie had made of each other on their pack trips. The two men were photographed together by Seltzer's granddaughter Sue.

An unexpected visitor was Frederick R. Downer, of Vancouver, British Columbia, son of the Lethbridge hotelman. Downer had grown up in Westminster House in Lethbridge, where his father had so proudly displayed Seltzer's first oil painting on the stair landing. At the time the younger Downer made his visit, the still untitled picture was hanging in his den in Vancouver. He was considering naming it either *Indians in the Sun Valley* or *Blood Indian Scouts on Crow's Nest Pass*.

Olaf gave Downer a print of *The Jerkline Freighter*, which he signed for him. The son of his first Canadian patron subsequently presented the artist with an unidentified butterfly of rare beauty that his uncle, a tea merchant, had sent from England. Olaf reciprocated with an illustrated letter and detailed information on the species, which was native to India.

Eventually Seltzer grew more weary of visits from strangers. He made an arrangement for the newly opened Charles M. Russell Museum to handle all of his work through its sales desk. "People don't bother me so much now. . . . I just tell them to see the gallery," he commented afterward.

When Olaf and Mabel Seltzer quietly celebrated their fiftieth wedding anniversary in 1953, Mabel was petite and wiry, her white hair carefully coiffured. She filled the role of grandmother gracefully, dispensing her good cooking and a wealth of advice to the six grandchildren.

Mabel was fond of quoting a quaint saying of her mother's: "You've got to winter and summer someone before you know him." She had wintered and summered an impatient perfectionist for half a century, often with anxiety but always with faith in his extraordinary talent and the deep personal conviction that she was married to a genius. In recent years she had often served as a buffer, making up with her considerate ways for her husband's bluntness.

Although his hair had thinned, and its brindled color of late middle age had given way to silvery-white, Olaf was described as looking younger than his years in a profile that appeared in the *Great Falls Tribune* just before his seventy-seventh birthday in 1954.

Two years later the Seltzers found new joy in the fourth generation of their family, when Sue and Joe Erwin became the parents of twins. The proud great grandfather enjoyed playing with the twins in spite of his physical discomforts.

Olaf Seltzer's last year was marked by pain and lengthy stays in the hospital before he was moved to a convalescent home, where he died on De-

cember 16, 1957. It was Mabel's seventy-sixth birthday. The cause of his death was listed as arteriosclerosis and heart disease.

Old friends Frank Curry, Emile C. Fischer, Wray Miller, Chester B. McNair, Robert D. Warden, and Jack Toole were his pallbearers. Hanging over his casket at the funeral home was his last oil, *The Trouble Hunters*.

Among the artist's papers was found this scrap of verse:

> I thank Thee, Life, for many precious gifts
> For peace of mind, and tender thoughts
>    that lift
> My soul beyond Life's rock strewn path above
> But most of all, I thank Thee, Life, for love.

Two years later North Dakota Stark and his wife came back to Great Falls on a visit from their home in Vancouver, Washington. The man who as a teenager took the photograph of a rakish Seltzer and Russell in their heyday wrote of this visit:

> *Oh! my heart was sad. For now Olaf had followed Charlie. His home waited in the same location . . . but the people living there had never heard of a Seltzer family.*
> *We found Mabel . . . in a hospital with a broken wrist, but in pretty good spirits. . . . In the Sand Hills south of town we visited the graves of Charlie Russell and Olaf . . . two giants among western artists.*

Because of Mabel's injury, she was delayed in answering a query from James Taylor Forrest, then director of Gilcrease Museum, who was preparing an article for an early issue of the museum's magazine, the *American Scene*. When she did write, she concluded her letter to Forrest with her husband's oft-repeated statement, in which he found consolation during the long years when he was waiting for recognition: "If there is in my art anything of lasting value, it will live; if not, it will perish."

In January, 1960, a month after celebrating her seventy-ninth birthday, Mabel Cleeland Seltzer was laid to rest beside her husband.

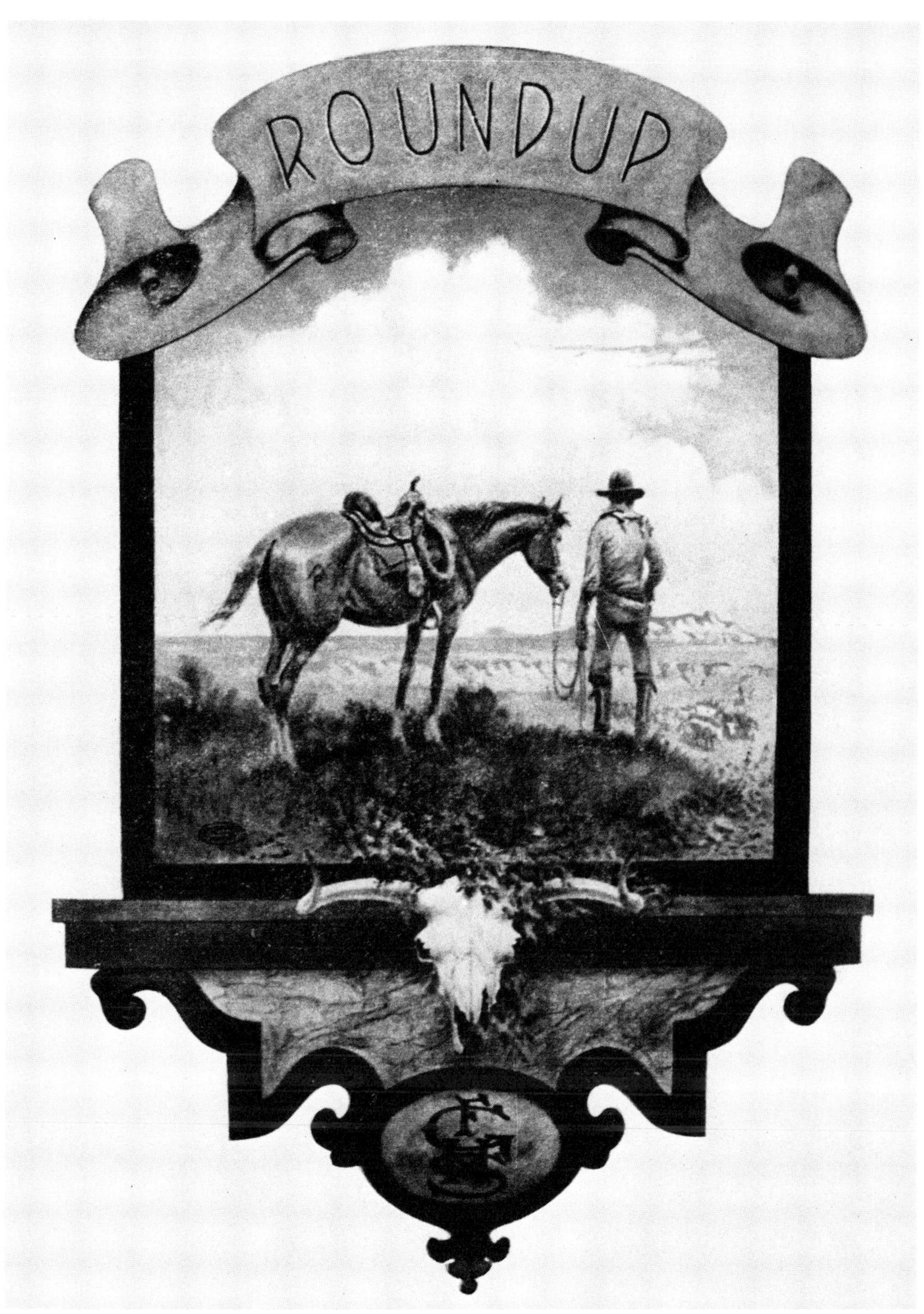

*Roundup*
1922
Watercolor, 15½″ × 13″

# Epilogue

Had olaf seltzer lived for another decade, he would have witnessed scouts from the New York and West Coast art galleries making regular visits to Montana to cultivate the artist's old friends in the hope of picking up an oil painting here, a watercolor there, or even a Christmas greeting or illustrated letter. Today there is as much chance of finding a Seltzer painting for sale for a paltry sum in rural Montana as there is of coming across a buffalo skull on the open prairie. Montana has been picked clean of art bargains; dealers contend that the asking prices for Seltzer-signed paintings are as high there as in Manhattan.

Were he to walk the streets of downtown Great Falls today, Seltzer would find his paintings, on loan from Frank Curry's collection, decorating the executive offices of the First National Bank. At the Northwestern Bank he would face a group of fourteen Western Character sketches hanging behind the tellers' wickets, and recall that these were originals on which Phil Cole wanted changes made. He had painted new ones and sold the originals at something off to Doc Hitchcock and other old-timers.

Walking into Ed Teddy's jewelry store on Third Street North, Olaf would be dazzled by the array of Seltzer prints for sale there. Ed gets them through Gilcrease Museum in Tulsa, where the demand for Western Character prints is so great that the museum is assembling a second limited edition of twenty-four in a folder, with a photograph and brief biography of the artist.

At the Great Falls Clinic, where he consulted his doctor, Olaf would see the four 20″ × 30″ oils bought from him in 1928 for $600 still prominently displayed, in spite of the $60,000 offer the clinic reportedly turned down a few years ago. His dark eyes beneath beetling brows would light up at the Alex Gordon collection that created so much excitement when Gordon and his family loaned their Seltzer paintings to the C. M. Russell Museum in 1974. Gordon, former owner of the City Art Store, did a lot of Olaf's framing in the old days. More than forty oils and watercolors comprise the Gordon collection. Almost as many more hang in various areas of the two-level Russell gallery, some of them bequeathed to the City of Great Falls by their original owners.

Olaf might have been entertained by the discovery late in 1975 of the watercolor he donated for the 1922 issue of *Roundup*, the yearbook of the Great Falls High School. The watercolor has since been used now and then as a frontispiece. Richard J. Heck found the original in a box of old clothing under the floor of an apartment building in downtown Great Falls. Upon taking it to the Russell Museum for an appraisal, Heck learned that the school district was the legal owner, but unearthing the original made him eligible for a one-thousand-dollar finder's fee.

School Superintendent Harold Wenaas suggested the reproduction of a thousand numbered prints to be sold at ten dollars each with proceeds to cover the costs of reproducing, the finder's fee, and the establishment of an O. C. Seltzer Scholarship. The artist would have been pleased with this solution, including the decision by the school district to keep the 15½″ × 13″ watercolor on permanent exhibition in the Russell Museum. Reduced for publication, the print is a postcard-sized watercolor-within-a-watercolor. The framed scene features a cowboy, horse on lead, looking out over a softly colored prairie toward a herd of cattle on a distant range. The scene, framed in black, is placed on a mantelpiece that bears emblazoned on a plaque beneath the shelf the interlocking initials *GFHS*. On the shelf is a longhorn skull and an arrangement of dried red oak leaves.

More than two thousand dollars has accrued in the scholarship fund. The requests for the print have come from all over the country.

Given the chance once more to stroll along Fifth Avenue in New York, he might catch a glimpse of his 20″ × 30″ oil *Round-up in the Judith Basin* in the Berry-Hill Galleries window and recall that he took a liking to Bob Heffernan of Oklahoma City, for whom he painted it in 1950. The two-page letter he wrote to Bob explaining the brands on the critters and the action taking place is mounted on the back of this painting, which is much admired for its depth of color and the adroit handling of the action during branding.

Over at the Kennedy Galleries, Olaf would learn that some of his paintings are featured in the western room at all times and that the June, 1974, issue of the *Kennedy Quarterly*, which was devoted to paintings of the West, placed him fourth in its listing of the "major names in this field of painting . . . Charles M. Russell, Frederic Remington, Henry Farny, Olaf Seltzer, Oscar Berninghaus, Thomas Moran and Albert Bierstadt."

At J. M. Bartfield's Galleries on West Fifty-seventh Street, Olaf would come upon the four framed panels of the cartoon-card he once made for Charlie Russell at Christmas. Bartfield featured the card with seven oils and watercolors in his *Catalogue of the American West*.

He would find commuter trains still gliding along the east bank of the Hudson River to Tarrytown. Were he once again to prowl around in Mrs. Cole's split-level studio among the rhododendron bushes where he worked so contentedly on the historical miniatures, he would discover that it is now a training classroom for followers of Dr. Sun Myung Moon's Unification church. Zeeview, long since renamed Belvedere, is owned by the Korean evangelist. The rolling slope on which Dr. Cole built his private world of the Old West has held as many as ten thousand of the Moon adherents for evangelistic services during summer holidays.

Olaf would find that there is a file with his name

on it in the New York Public Library's art room, one of his favorite haunts. He would learn that many recent books include full-color reproductions of his work and critiques of his painting style—Robert Elman's *Badmen of the West* and *The Great American Shooting Prints*, Frank Getlein's *Lure of the Great West*, *Harmsen's Western Americana*, the Reader's Digest series on the West and *The Art of the Old West*, which used forty-seven pieces of his work. His fame has spread abroad, leading to a series of five articles about him in *Politiken*, the Copenhagen newspaper he often bought and read in New York.

Turning westward, he would find the mural-sized oils that once hung behind the bar in the Mint Saloon, along with other of his paintings on display in the Rockwell-Corning Museum at Corning, New York. In the Midwestern Galleries in Cincinnati, run by Norma and Harry Lockwood, he would come across many old favorites, although the one best remembered—the painting of Charlie Russell astride Monte—is on five-year loan to the Museum of Native American Culture at the Pacific Northwest Indian Center in Spokane, Washington. It is part of the Lockwoods' "Two Hundred Years of the American West" exhibit that toured the state of Washington in 1976 under a grant from the American Revolution Bicentennial Commission. Its itinerary included the Frye Free Public Art Museum in Seattle.

The Amon Carter Museum of Western Art in Fort Worth also has two of the Mint Collection oils. The Whitney Gallery of Western Art in Cody, Wyoming, usually has several Seltzers on display, while in a spectacular mountain-top gallery at St. John's College in Santa Fe, New Mexico, Olaf could view his poignant snow scene, *The Lone Wolf*, loaned by the Fenn Galleries.

Olaf would have had many other satisfactions and a few heartaches in the past twenty years. He would view with ambivalence granddaughter Ruth Teddy's keen analysis of his motivations (she worked for a psychiatrist) and the experience of his second "little devil," Sue Erwin, as a Junior League docent at the Russell Museum. He would be inordinately pleased that his second grandson, Steve, and Steve's wife, Carol, gave up secure positions in Great Falls so that Steve could study art and paint in southern California, and that Steve's oils and acrylics are now being snapped up by discriminating collectors of western art. The young artist, his wife, and their daughter now occupy their recently built home and studio in the rolling countryside near Great Falls.

Had Olaf and Mabel lived a few years longer, they would have been crushed by the loss in the early 1960's of their oldest grandson, William Ross, a victim of leukemia in the closing weeks of his college years. Bill had hoped to enter medical school. With his respect for learning, Olaf would be pleased to know that his granddaughter Helen was a teacher before her marriage and that both Steve and Richard (Rick), the third grandson, married teachers.

After Olaf's death Mabel sold his prized entomology collection to Paul Buck, biology teacher at Great Falls High School, who arranged the butterflies and beetles, mounted on pins, in ten $12'' \times 16''$ glass-covered boxes for classroom use. A generation of Great Falls science students had access to O. C. S.'s beauties before Buck's death. Now the insects and Lepidoptera are in the possession of Buck's daughter, Janis, and her husband, Rick Seltzer. Rick plans to tackle the task of proper labeling.

Olaf would have taken an interest in his son Carl's progress in local politics, first as a Great Falls alderman and now in his fourth term as assessor for Cascade County. Since his assessor's office was the first in the state to use computers, Carl is in demand around the state. When at home, he spends countless hours corresponding with art collectors, dealers and writers, answering requests for information about his father. Carl is a collector, too. His basement is a veritable museum of railroading, a hobby Olaf took into account when he painted the $16'' \times 24''$ oil *Kid Curry Holdup* for his son. One of his most frequently reproduced works, the painting depicts the 1901 robbery of Great Northern No. 1 at Exeter, Montana, west of Malta, in which Kid Curry reputedly got away with $48,000.

Carl is often asked to clean and authenticate his father's work, for with recognition of an artist's works comes the problem of fakes—"the most accurate index to prevailing taste is to be found in the field of fakes."[1]

When a gala two-day celebration was planned in April, 1974, to mark the twentieth anniversary of the operation of Gilcrease museum by the City of Tulsa, Olaf Seltzer's Western Character *Reservation Buck*, was selected to grace the invitation. Carl and Lillian Seltzer were special guests for the

dinner at which the artist's son was called upon to answer repeated queries from avid admirers about his father's work. In addition to "mixing with the face cards," as Olaf would have considered participation in this gathering, Carl pinned dozens of buffalo skull emblems on youngsters during a Sunday communitywide open house at the museum.

In the fall of 1975 a Seltzer gallery was opened at Gilcrease as one of only six galleries dedicated to the work of a single western artist. (The others are the Moran, Catlin, Russell and Remington galleries, and one devoted to the work of the contemporary Oklahoma Cherokee wood sculptor, Willard Stone.) Burlap-covered panels in the Seltzer gallery hold three of the transportation oils, a dozen or more Western Character sketches and ninety-three miniatures. Several of his letters, cards, and illustrated envelopes addressed to Phil Cole are exhibited in a standing case. Between the panels, against dead white walls, are hung three foremost oils: *Prowlers of the Prairie, Disputed Trail*, and the oil which most typifies the mellowness of color for which Seltzer is famous, *Herald of the Robe Trade.*

Although Gilcrease is the first museum to put in an exclusively Seltzer gallery, the Museum of the Rockies, in Bozeman, Montana, will open its Seltzer gallery in the spring of 1979, on the strength of Ed Craney's promise that his collection of the artist's work will always remain in Montana. "The largest one-man Seltzer show ever assembled" was held in 1960 when the Montana Historical Society exhibited 142 paintings borrowed from thirty owners. Museum director Michael Stephen Kennedy prepared a monograph, "O. C. Seltzer: Meticulous Master of Western Art,"[2] as part of the catalog.

While Tom Gilcrease was alive and it was possible to remove paintings from his collection, several of Seltzer's works were sent to an exhibit at the American Indian Exposition at Anadarko, Oklahoma. Gilcrease himself attended the exposition, held in the summer of Olaf's eightieth birthday. In 1961 four Seltzer oils were included in "The Artist in the American West 1800–1900", an exhibition sponsored by the Fine Arts Museum of New Mexico in Santa Fe in connection with meetings of the Western History Association. The Goodwin Chases lent their watercolors for the exhibit "Art Prospective of the Historic Northwest," sponsored by the Eastern Washington

State Historical Society in Tacoma. There were exhibits at the C. M. Russell Museum in 1966 and 1969.

Not only has the demand for Seltzer's western scenes mushroomed, but the small-genre oils he painted for his own relaxation are much sought after. At the sixth annual C. M. Russell Art Auction in 1974, after the first three hours of bidding, the leading individual sale was Seltzer's *English Nobleman*, which brought $5,800 for its Bozeman owner.

A Seltzer pen-and-ink sketch, *Stretching Rawhide*, was chosen by the Franklin Mint in 1974 to be used on the Montana ingot in the fifty-state collection, issued through the Western Montana National Bank in Missoula.

At the 1973 "Rendezvous of Western Art" in Helena, Carl Seltzer accepted from the historical society a bronze plaque in the shape of the state of Montana, on which is engraved:

OLAF C. SELTZER<br>
HONORED ARTIST<br>
1973 RENDEZVOUS OF WESTERN ART<br>
A MAN OF MANY TALENTS WHO<br>
METICULOUSLY AND FAITHFULLY<br>
PORTRAYED THE WEST<br>
AN ADOPTED SON OF MONTANA<br>
WHO LOVED IT UNTIL THE END

A reproduction has been placed on the artist's grave.

O. C. Seltzer had once made the fatalistic statement: "If there is anything of lasting value in my art, it will survive. If not, it will perish." Was the artist justified in making this statement?

Seltzer was a paradox. He thought in terms of the epic scene, and he was happiest sketching in countryside that stretched for miles toward serrated snow-capped mountains, yet much of his work was on a small scale. His historical record, for the most part, appeared on postcard-sized miniatures, and in his witness to the past he preferred to commemorate the customs of the aborigines and early settlers rather than battle scenes.

Two men changed the course of the young Dane's life after he left the crowded tenements of Copenhagen for the open skies of Montana; a third would become the steward of his work. Yet even without their influence, Seltzer would have painted with quiet enjoyment all the years of his life.

From Charles M. Russell he drew inspiration, encouragement, comradeship and a glimpse of what might lie ahead for him. Philip Cole's sincere admiration, supportive friendship and open-handed patronage spurred him on to record the history of the Old West while it was still possible to use some primary sources.

Each was his benefactor and each unwittingly impeded his progress. Had Olaf Seltzer painted under different skies, away from the mystique and flamboyance of an overwhelming personality like Russell, his work might have received more recognition within his lifetime, for he gave to Russell as much as gained from him. The cowboy artist's paintings became alive with color after he began riding and sketching with his younger and more academically trained friend. Michael Stephen Kennedy calls Russell "master and nemesis" of Seltzer:

*The suggestive painted details so brilliantly done by Russell in an easy light manner were meticulously and laboriously spelled out by Seltzer. The action—even to the point of distorted anatomy—which gave Russell so much acclaim, was captured in slow-motion camera sequence by Seltzer. Russell's subtle mountains, hazy prairies and suggestions of wind-swept sage were brought into bold, almost photographic focus by Seltzer. In effect, they complemented and supported each other. The West was fortunate that both artists were there together.*

*Thank God for the unreconstructed, uncommon genius of Russell. . . . Thank God, too, he had the counterpart—a silent, sincere, devoted disciple—yet an artist with his own deep conscience, his own ideas and his own disciplined techniques —a master in his own right, the meticulous Dane, Olaf Carl Seltzer."*[3]

Philip Cole unwittingly held back Seltzer's recognition by buying up so much of his work over the fifteen-year period when Seltzer was in his prime as an artist. For many years Cole had as his private preserve the only major collection of Seltzers outside of the mountain states. Yet the Montana-born collector's knowledge of old ways and old days enabled Olaf to paint a remarkable historical record of the West in his miniatures. Cole talked about Seltzer to all his art-buying friends, and was solely responsible for the small-but-enthusiastic following the artist had in the East during the thirties.

It remained for a remarkable man, whom Olaf Seltzer met years later, to provide assurance that the artist's work would survive. Tom Gilcrease, by taking over Philip Cole's holdings and adding them to his other sizable acquisitions, became the steward of the greatest western art collection assembled. Holding in this unparalleled collection, the bulk of work painted during Seltzer's prime, however, has meant that little of it is available on the open market. The result is that the artist's fame has spread slowly and his work still has not achieved as wide an audience as it deserves. Tom Gilcrease planned well for the future, passing on his treasure to his beloved city of Tulsa, and it is here principally that a constant stream of visitors from all parts of the world are exposed to the creative efforts of Olaf C. Seltzer.

James Taylor Forrest, director of the art museum at the University of Wyoming, suggests that the best criteria by which to judge Seltzer's work are the questions posed by Hendrik Van Loon:

*'What is the artist trying to say? Does he succeed in getting his message across? Were the results worth the effort?' In Seltzer's work, the message is not obscured for it is always simply executed in a straightforward manner. His colors are generally true to nature—although to the viewer not accustomed to the clear vaporless air of the high country his palette seems overly strong. This is especially true of his watercolors. Yet his watercolors are gems of perfection in detail and color harmony. He was obviously one of the best draftsmen to work in the West at any time in the one hundred-year history of painting in that region. His ability as a draftsman had led some critics to claim a stiffness in his work, yet a careful analysis will indicate that the artist with the seemingly freer style is guilty of distortions never found in Seltzer's paintings. . . . Only future generations can tell, but it would appear that this is one of the West's great artists.*

O. C. Seltzer has at last come out of the shadow.

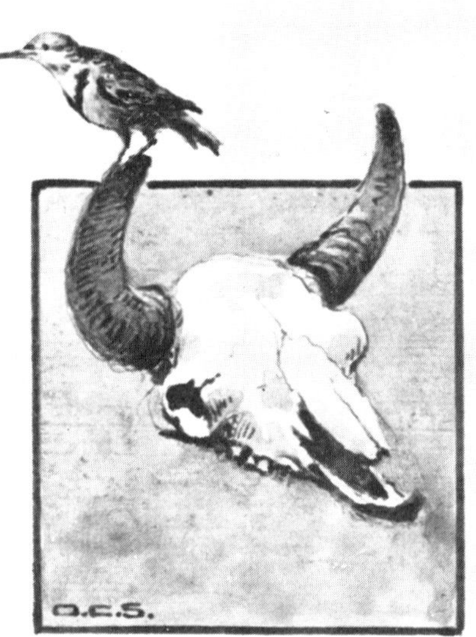

*Prairie Lark and Skull*
1926
Watercolor, 4″ × 4″

# Notes

## CHAPTER 1

1. According to the Danish archives, Ludwig and Caroline Seltzer were living alone at Adelgade 113 in the year of their grandson's birth. An 1881 census fails to list the Seltzers. There is no further record until the turn of the century, when the widowed Caroline applied for Danish citizenship. Her husband and son had never done so.

2. A letter from Sigurd Jensen and Jeppe Rasmussen, of Købenshavns Stadsarkiv, dated November 11, 1974, discloses that the signature "M. Børreson" on Olaf Seltzer's report cards from 1885 through 1890 was that of Olaf's widowed maternal grandmother, who concocted a new name for herself from her middle name and her husband's name, Børre. By 1893 she had resumed use of her previous name.

3. Letter from Hans Sode-Madsen, assistant keeper, Rigsarkivet (Record Office), København, May 3, 1974.

4. O. C. Seltzer claimed that his Uncle Louis never learned that Laura had anything to do with his sudden removal from Copenhagen to the United States.

5. Letter from Halder Hansen, *True West*, February, 1963.

6. Walt Coburn, *Pioneer Cattlemen in Montana*, p. 139.

7. *Ibid.*, p. 137.

8. Theodore Roosevelt and Frederic Remington, *Ranch Life in the Far West*, p. 39.

## CHAPTER 2

1. Seltzer undoubtedly studied M. N. Forney's *Catechism of the Locomotive*, published in 1879 by the Railway Gazette. Forney's manual set out to make "plain to the plain people" through a series of questions and answers, complete with line diagrams, the complexities of the steam locomotive.

2. The Charles M. Russell Museum was built in 1953 in compliance with the bequest of Miss Josephine Trigg, daughter of the saloonkeeper and close friend of Nancy Russell, who left her collection of Russell paintings and memorabilia to the people of Great Falls. The adjoining log-cabin studio is operated by the city.

3. Lola Shelton, *Charles Marion Russell, Cowboy, Artist, Friend*, p. 159.

4. Letter to Dr. Philip Cole from C. M. Russell, dated September 26, 1926. The letter follows a half-page scene of elk grazing against snow-capped mountains. The two-page text includes a report on Russell's recent hospitalization: "Iv got no kick coming Iv been trimed my self but the medicine men at Rochester onely took from me things I didn't need and was glad to get rid of I look and feel better but I'm still verry weak if you see Olaf Seltzer give him my regards." This letter, on display in the Russell Gallery at Gilcrease Museum, Tulsa, was written exactly a month before Russell's death. It also appears in Russell's book *Good Medicine*, pp. 160–61.

5. Con Price, *Memories of Old Montana*, p. 149.

6. Titled *The War Party*, this collaborative effort hangs in the Montana Historical Society Museum, Helena, on loan from E. E. and Edna MacGilvra, of Butte, Montana. Russell evidently enjoyed the idea of collaborative efforts with his painter friends. According to the *Montana Post*, the newsletter of the society, Russell and Ralph Earll DeCamp, who together formed the Helena Sketch Club, had contemplated collaborating on a painting. vol. 14, no. 1 (February–March, 1976), p. 1.

7. *The Scout* is the property of the Montana Historical Society. The painting was purchased from Downer's son in Vancouver, British Columbia, after the director of the society inquired about borrowing it for the state's centennial display. According to an official Montana Historical Society listing, dated October 21, 1977, the painting is now known as *Indians Watching the Wagon Train*.

## CHAPTER 3

1. The Seattle owner from whom Jean and Obert Undem, of Fayetteville, Arkansas, bought *Flagging Antelope* in the early 1960's claimed that Seltzer said that he was painting himself and Russell at one of their favorite pursuits while on pack trips. This watercolor was sold at auction by Parke-Bernet in 1973 for ten thousand dollars.

2. Amon Carter Museum Newsletter, n.d.

3. *Saloon Keeper*, owned by the Northwestern Bank of Great Falls, is on display in the banking area. *Barkeep* is in the Gilcrease Museum, and is included in Seltzer Portfolio I

of prints issued by the museum.

4. Curry Tape, July, 1974.

## CHAPTER 4

1. Seltzer's friend Frank Curry recalls an incident in Olaf's declining years when the two men and their wives visited the Montana Historical Society Museum in Helena shortly after the MacGilvras loaned *War Party* for permanent exhibition. The placard identified the work as a collaboration by "Charles M. Russell and Oscar Seltzer." When he called the error to the attention of the guard, Curry was assured that no mistake had been made. Curry introduced Seltzer to the guard, so the latter might explain to Seltzer that he had been mistakenly using the wrong name. The placard was corrected.

2. Carter V. Rubottom, "I Knew Charles M. Russell," *Montana Magazine of Western History*, Winter 1954, p. 24.

3. Seltzer's Montana Miniature *Scaffold Grave* bears the following explanation: "In former times before the Indians were forced to use coffins and practice interment, tree and scaffold burial was common. One of the many reasons being that thus removed from the ground he was not subject to the ravages of the coyote or the wolf. When all hope for the sick person was abandoned he was painted and dressed in his best costume. After death the body was wrapped in a blanket or robe and buried within a few hours. No effort was made to mark the spot and fear kept the mourners away.

"The dying usually made requests of their family that certain personal belongings were to be buried with them. Sometimes this request was a horse, in which event the horse was killed at the burial place. It was also quite usual for the tail and mane of the man's favorite horse to be cut at his death."

Scaffold graves intrigued artists of the West as far back as Thomas Moran, who made his first trip west with the Hayden Expedition in 1871.

4. In the material accompanying Seltzer's Montana Miniature *Counting Coups, Blackfeet vs. Crows*, it is explained: "Among many of these tribes the first warrior to touch an enemy or his body was credited with a 'coup' or deed of honor. The social rank of an individual was largely dependent upon the number of 'coups' to his credit. Thus Red Cloud claimed 80 'coups'—an unusual number, since four 'coups' were generally considered sufficient to achieve distinction."

5. Seltzer mounted a print of this photograph in a matting embellished with an iridescent dragonfly and a red-striped bug and presented it to Charlie and Nancy Russell. It is on display in the log-cabin studio.

6. Austin Russell, *CMR: Charles M. Russell, Cowboy Artist*, p. 120.

7. North D. Stark, "Two Giants in Western Art," *Frontier Times*, June–July 1964, p. 54.

8. *Ibid.*, p. 15.

9. Letter from North Dakota Stark to Mildred D. Ladner, November 7, 1974.

10. *Great Falls Tribune*, July 18, 1954.

## CHAPTER 5

1. Lars Rostrup Bøyesen, director of the North Jutland

Art Museum, in *Denmark: An Official Handbook*, p. 738.

2. The movement began with John Constable and his English contemporaries in the early nineteenth century, and was adapted by the French Impressionists to achieve new effects in landscape painting.

3. "Color Versus Form in Art," *Great Falls Leader*, February 8, 1937.

4. A few years later Olaf sent a painting on consignment to a Los Angeles art dealer, suggesting that he would like to get $250 for it. When an acquaintance returning from the coast reported that the painting was being exhibited in the gallery window with a price tag of $1,800, Seltzer exploded: "Does he think some damn fool is going to pay that?"

5. This screen is among the memorabilia in the Montana Historical Society Museum in Helena. Of the New York painters, Austin Russell (author of *C. M. R.: Charles M. Russell, Cowboy Artist*), wrote: "A generation later, after World War II, I went through the card index in the art room of the New York Library. No mention of either Krieghoff or Philip Goodwin—two good artists, both New Yorkers, and nothing to show they existed" (p. 197). Of Seltzer, the hometown artist, he wrote, "Years later, I suddenly saw his paintings on 57th Street, New York, and recognized the coloring even before I stepped close enough to see the name" (p. 120).

Bull Head Lodge is now owned by a prominent Montanan who has kept intact the lodge and nearby studio, complete even to the dishes and toiletries left behind by the Russells. Nancy sold the cabin after Charlie's death without returning to remove their personal effects. The clearing around the cabins has now become overgrown, and the location of the lodge is a well-kept secret.

6. When Walt Seltzer took part in Round-Up Day festivities at Great Falls High School just before his graduation in the spring of 1923, he proudly wore Charlie Russell's own chaps.

## CHAPTER 6

1. Another veterinarian with whom Seltzer spent time, accompanying him on his rounds to learn more about the physiology of cattle, was Dr. B. O. Fisher, the district federal veterinarian in Great Falls.

2. The J Bar ("Phil called it a meat hook," Olaf Seltzer wrote to Dr. Butler in an illustrated letter) was branded on the left ribs of Dr. C. K. Cole's cattle and on the left shoulder of his horses. The "Reverse See-Kay" brand was used on the right ribs of the cattle and the left ribs of the horses. The brands, along with a longhorn steer and an Appaloosa horse, appear in a watercolor Seltzer made for Cole during the early months of their acquaintance.

3. *Quinquennial Record of the Class of 1906, Princeton University* (Quinquennial Record Committee, 1912), p. 47.

4. *Ibid.*

5. *Good Medicine*, pp. 160–161.

6. In autumn of 1974 the Russell Room of the Montana Historical Society Museum in Helena was renamed the Mackay Gallery of Russell Art in appreciation of the Mackay family's placement of thirty-five Russell paintings and drawings in the museum on permanent loan.

7. Mackay's book about his Alaskan hunting experience was never published. He died in 1932 at the age of fifty-one.

## CHAPTER 7

1. *Great Falls Leader*, June 18, 1927.

2. Cole apparently believed in trading with dealers. By the time his collection was sold to Thomas Gilcrease, it no longer included any of the H. A. McNeil, A. A. Weiman, or A. P. Proctor bronzes or oils by John Fery or Charles W. Eaton. Nor is the single watercolor by Elizabeth McG. Knowles or any work by Colombi in the acquisition inventory. By mid-1927, Cole's tastes had become more sophisticated, and fewer of the lesser-known artists' works appear in the album.

3. Unfortunately, no comparable effort was made to catalogue Cole's holdings of original letters, documents, and journals.

4. Vigilantes organized for mutual protection against desperados in the Virginia City–Bannock area used the sign "3-7-77." Some believed that the sign indicated, "You have 24 hours to leave this country, otherwise yours will be a box 3′ wide, 7′ long, buried 77″ below the ground." Others believed that it was a more complicated code. There are still differences of opinion in Montana over the meaning of "3-7-77."

5. Several small paintings including these figures would appear in the later Montana in Miniature series.

6. The reference to the check for a hundred dollars is the only mention of price in any existing correspondence between artist and art collector. There may have been letters concerning financial agreements, for Olaf Seltzer preserved only a small portion of his correspondence. This particular letter probably was kept because of the artist's pleasure in his patron's glowing praise. It would have been consistent with Olaf's makeup not to have set a definite price, trusting Cole to be fair with him. His affection for Phil and the enjoyment the two men derived from working together on projects mutually pleasing to them made price a secondary consideration. It would never have occurred to the artist to raise his prices because of Doc's eagerness. Cole paid only as much as, and sometimes less than, local collectors in Great Falls, for the pragmatic artist held the cheaper-by-the-dozen concept of pricing. Carl Seltzer has no recollection of any family discussion about what his father expected Cole to pay him. "My father was very old-fashioned about matters of that sort. He would have considered that to be nobody's business but his own."

7. There are a few pen-and-ink character sketches of a similar nature by Russell, each with a vignette in the lower-right-hand corner of the sheet, just as Cole suggested to Seltzer. Olaf was undoubtedly seeking a format for his watercolors that would be uniquely different from the earlier characters done by Charlie Russell. He would continue with the vignettes on the matte as he originally planned.

8. A portfolio of twenty-four prints in the Western Character series, along with a photograph and brief biography, was issued in a limited edition by Gilcrease Museum in 1974. It immediately became a collector's item.

9. The Northwestern Bank owns fourteen character sketches, which are on display in the area behind the tellers' cages. This is the only known collection apart from the seventy-nine at Gilcrease Museum. There are a few scattered character sketches that were the prototypes before Seltzer settled on the format he would use.

10. *The Art of the Old West*, p. 101.

11. *Ibid.*, p. 102.
12. *Ibid.*, p. 149.

## CHAPTER 8

1. Bronzes by Frederic Remington.

2. Art curator's report compiled from notes made in Billings and Bozeman, Montana, in October, 1966, from interviews with Alice Ralston and Kay Cole Worden, Gilcrease Museum Library, p. 13.

3. The Cole version of *The Disputed Trail* occupies a place of prominence in the Seltzer gallery of the Gilcrease Museum. *The Disputed Trail* in the Mint Collection is reproduced in Robert Elman's *The Great American Shooting Prints*, plate 37.

Paul T. DeVore, a reporter for the Great Falls Tribune in the late 1920's, contends, in his article, "First Russell Gallery a Saloon" (*Pacific Northwesterner*, vol. 21, No. 4 [Fall, 1977], pp. 50–62), that the Mint catalog was published in 1928. The catalog itself bears no date.

DeVore's article includes a detailed floor plan of the Mint drawn from memory by Carl Seltzer, who was provided the following description:

"The Mint was on the ground floor of a two-story red brick building erected on Central Avenue in the 1880s. Originally it occupied only the bottom portion.

"I'd say the Mint . . . was about 50 feet wide by 90 deep. The plastered walls must have been 12 feet high. A partial basement, with sandstone walls, opened with a trap door about 20 feet from the alley. The building was steam heated and the wooden floor kept clean.

"There were no pool tables in the old days. To enter, you went through the front door, then two swinging doors. . . . By crowding, perhaps as many as 50 men could belly up to the bar. . . . The back bar is in the Montana Historical Society Museum in Helena.

"There were tall show cases beyond the cigar counter as you came in, and others less than half as high around the cigar counter and a front corner of the main room. They were filled with Indian artifacts, small paintings and models. Above them hung large oil paintings (mostly) by Charlie Russell and my father. . . .

"Speedy Swift used to have charge of the cigar counter, and Sid Willis sat on a stool near it and the front door. Guy Harris, the office man, cashed pay checks for customers through a small window near the door to the gambling room.

"When I was a kid I sold papers in front of the Mint. It was such a good spot I had to fight to keep it. Several times I sneaked in to sell papers in the bar, but always they'd kick me out."

4. Monte, named after the Mexican card game, was the Indian pinto pony Russell bought from the Blackfeet on the Piegan Reservation in 1881. He kept the horse until he was nearly thirty years old. Red Bird was a sorrel. Seltzer painted his friend on both of these horses, as well as on Gray Eagle (a gray), and on Neenah, the mount Russell had purchased from their Cree friend Young Boy.

5. This brand features a square with an eyebrow-shaped arc over it.

6. A group of thirty-four portraits of Blackfoot Indians made by Winold Reiss were sold from the Cole holdings by

the P. J. Curry Company, of New York, during the process of organizing the collection at Zeeview.


## CHAPTER 9

1. Johnson's portrait is one of only a few not painted by American artists or not in this country in the Gilcrease Museum. It is included because its subject was John Smith's patroness.

2. Catalogue of the *Family Collection of Miniatures, the Property of J. Pierpont Morgan*, Christie's, June 24, 1935.

3. There is confusion about the exact number of paintings in the Montana in Miniature series. Gilcrease archivists counted 110 officially in 1978. In a 1967 Gilcrease museum inventory 117 Seltzer oil paintings were considered to be miniatures. This count probably included several slightly larger pictures of a western subject, but of the kind the artist termed "genre." A third inventory, made by the P. J. Curry Company, of New York, in connection with the sale of the Cole collection (indicating in which of the Zeeview rooms each of the Seltzer paintings was hung), refers to a "set of 102 Miniature Paintings 'Historical Series' average size 4 × 6" hanging on the staircase to the second floor but also mentions six additional paintings that are usually included in the series, four of them in a guest room and two in Dr. Cole's study. The count, according to photographs and index in Phil Cole's suede-bound album, puts the total at 112.

4. Art Curator's report, p. 12.

5. Lighton's collection was left to his sisters in Fayetteville, Arkansas.

6. According to the *New York Times* of June 30, 1941, Dr. Cole's stamp collection was sold at auction in 1939 for $38,000, with a single stamp going for $5,300.

7. This letter and envelope were given by Miss Ralston to the Montana Historical Society Museum in Helena.

8. Mrs. Worden's most abiding memory of Seltzer is tied to a persisting sense of guilt. As a child of about eight, she was laboring over a pastel drawing she was doing to please her father. She had drawn a house with a path leading to it. Seltzer peered over her shoulder and suggested, "Why don't you put in an Indian?" Then he quickly sketched one in. Dr. Cole was more than surprised with the handiwork of his youngest and extravagant in his expression of appreciation, but he asked, "You didn't put in that Indian?" The child glanced at Seltzer for assurance. His smile gave her the courage to nod gravely and accept credit. To this day, according to Mrs. Worden in a telephone interview with the author, she feels sorry about her fib, although she now realizes how hard it must have been for the two men to keep straight faces.

9. *The Art of the Old West*, p. 109.

10. The Black Eagle (Montana) Chapter of the Daughters of the American Revolution is planning to erect a historical marker on the site of this painting. It will feature a reproduction of Seltzer's interpretation of the event.

11. "Old Bill Marks" was Louis Marks, father of the Seattle insurance broker Bill Marks, who was Olaf's friend.

12. In 1966, Cato Butler, son of the veterinary surgeon, coedited with Dr. Van Kirke Nelson a reprint of *Montana in Miniature* published in Kalispell, Montana.


## CHAPTER 10

1. *The Strength of the Weak*, a 42″ × 68″ oil, was unfinished at the time of Olaf Seltzer's death in 1957. It is a strangely moving depiction from the brush of one who belonged to no church, for it portrays a priest apprehended by bandits in a South American setting. The priest's only protection—"the strength of the weak"—is his cross. Only the guns and the horses' reins remain to be put into the unsigned canvas, now owned by Seltzer's son Carl. It is not as defined in its linear work as his earlier paintings, probably because of Seltzer's failing eyesight.

2. Curator's report.

3. F. G. Renner, "Bad Pennies," *Montana, the Magazine of Western History*, vol. 6, no. 2 (April 1956), pp. 7–8.

4. Robert Elman, *The Great American Shooting Prints*, p. 51.

5. The commission was awarded in a competition. Sketches by six Montana artists were submitted with names of artists concealed. Seltzer's sketch was chosen unanimously. The painting was presented to Helena Lodge No. 3 by Jesse Stem Stoner.


## CHAPTER 11

1. David Randolph Milsten, *Thomas Gilcrease*, p. 177.

2. Letter from Leonard A. Lombardo to Mildred D. Ladner, October 6, 1975.

3. Walter Gustav and Birtell Foresman, brothers who came to Great Falls from Tracy, Montana, to take this course, recall that five of the original class of fifteen took jobs with Boeing Aircraft Company in Seattle. Birtell Foresman was one of the five. His brother operates a summer book-and-print shop at Apgar, just inside the west entrance of Glacier National Park, only a mile or two from the spot where his former machine-shop teacher once painted with Russell.

4. In 1978, Craney placed the collection in the Museum of the Rockies, Bozeman, Montana.

5. One of the oils that got away from Craney was sold to Goodwin Chase, of Tacoma, Washington, who, with Mrs. Chase, loaned their Seltzer watercolors in 1963 to the exhibition of western art held in Tacoma by the Eastern Washington State Historical Society.


## CHAPTER 12

1. According to a letter dated February 26, 1976, from John R. Nesbitt, chief of museum and audio-visual programs for the Harry S Truman Library in Independence, Missouri, *Indian on Horseback* has been on exhibit several times in the museum gallery.


## EPILOGUE

1. Aline B. Saarinen, *The Proud Possessors*, p. 70.

2. Michael Stephen Kennedy, *The Life and Times of Olaf C. Seltzer, 1877 to 1957*, Montana Heritage Series, no. 10.

3. *Ibid.*, p. 19.

4. "Olaf Seltzer . . . Artist of the High Plains," *American Scene*, vol. 2, no. 2 (Summer, 1959), p. 8.

# Bibliography


### BOOKS

Arnold, Bruce. *A Concise History of Irish Art*. New York: Oxford University Press, 1977.

Bøyesen, Lars Rostrup. "Painting." In *Denmark: An Official Handbook*. Copenhagen: Royal Danish Ministry of Foreign Affairs, 1970, 1974.

Churchill, Allen. *The Splendor Seekers*. New York: Grosset & Dunlap, 1974.

Coburn, Walt. *Pioneer Cattleman in Montana*. Norman: University of Oklahoma Press, 1968.

Cross, Henry H., and A. W. Schorger. *The T. B. Walker Collection of Indian Portraits*. Madison: State Historical Association of Wisconsin, 1948.

Davenport, Cyril. *Miniatures—Ancient and Modern*. London: Metheun & Co., 1907.

Elman, Robert. *Badmen of the West*. New York: Ridge Press, 1975.

——————. *The Great American Shooting Prints*. New York: Alfred A. Knopf, 1972.

Fischer, Erik. "Drawing and Engraving." In *Denmark: An Official Handbook*. Copenhagen: Royal Danish Ministry of Foreign Affairs, 1970, 1974.

Forney, Matthias N. *Catechism of a Locomotive*. New York: Railway Gazette, 1879.

Getlein, Frank. *Lure of the Great West*. Waukesha, Wis.: Country Beautiful, 1973.

Harmsen, Dorothy. *Harmsen's Western Americana*. Flagstaff, Ariz.: Northland Press, 1971.

Linderman, Frank B. *Recollections of Charlie Russell*. Norman: University of Oklahoma Press, 1963.

London, Hannah R. *Miniatures of Early American Jews*. Springfield, Mass.: Pond-Ekberg Co., 1953.

McCracken, Harold. *The Charles M. Russell Book*. Garden City, N.Y.: Doubleday & Co., 1957.

——————. *The Frederic Remington Book*. Garden City, N.Y.: Doubleday & Co., 1966.

Mackay, Malcolm. *Cow Range and Hunting Trail*. New York: G. H. Putnam, 1925.

Mayer, Ralph. *A Dictionary of Art Terms and Techniques*. New York: Thomas Y. Crowell, 1969.

Milsten, David Randolph. *Thomas Gilcrease*. San Antonio: Naylor Company, 1969.

Møller, Jan. *Citizens in the Old Copenhagen*. Copenhagen: Perspectiv Bøgerne, 1969.

Morgan, Neil. *Westward Tilt: The American West Today*. New York: Random House, 1963.

Moynahan, J. M., and Andy Tromp. *The West of Sandy Ingersoll*. Cheney, Wash.: Art of the Northwest, 1974.

Myers, Bernard S., and Shirley D. Myers. *Dictionary of Art*. 5 vols. New York: McGraw-Hill Book Company, Inc., 1969.

Nelson, Van Kirke, and Cato Butler, eds. *Montana in Miniature*. Kalispell, Mont.: O'Neil Printers, 1966.

Nørlund, Poul, Erick Struckmann, and Leo Swane, eds. *Danish Art Through the Ages*. Copenhagen: Tidsskriftet Danmark, n.d.

Price, Con. *Memories of Old Montana*. Hollywood, Calif.: Highland Press, 1945.

Renner, Frederic G. *Paper Talk*. Fort Worth: Amon Carter Museum of Western Art, 1962.

Roosevelt, Theodore, and Frederic Remington. *Ranch Life in the Far West*. Flagstaff, Ariz.: Northland Press, 1968.

Rosenberg, Holger. *Smuthans*. Odense, Denmark: Miloske Boghandels Forlag, 1905.

Rossi, Paul A., and David C. Hunt. *The Art of the Old West*. New York: Alfred A. Knopf, 1971.

Russell, Austin. *C. M. R.: Charles M. Russell, Cowboy Artist*. New York: Twayne Publishers, 1957.

Russell, Charles M. *Good Medicine*. Garden City, N.Y.: Doubleday & Co., 1929.

——————. *More Rawhides*. Pasadena, Calif.: Trail's End Publishing Co., 1946.

——————. *Trails Plowed Under*. New York: Doubleday Doran & Co., 1931.

Saarinen, Aline B. *The Proud Possessors*. New York:

Random House, 1958.

Shelton, Lola. *Charles Marion Russell: Cowboy, Artist, Friend.* New York: Dodd, Mead & Co., 1962.

Taft, Robert. *Artists and Illustrators of the Old West, 1850–1900.* New York: Charles Scribner's Sons, 1953.

Wehle, Harry B. *American Miniatures 1730–1850: 173 Portraits.* Garden City, N.Y.: Doubleday Doran & Co., 1927.

Wilkins, Thurman. *Thomas Moran.* Norman: University of Oklahoma Press, 1966.

## MAGAZINE ARTICLES

Clark, Helen: "The Artist Montana Almost Forgot," *Wild West*, vol. 2, no. 1 (March, 1970).

————. "Olaf Seltzer, Montana Artist," *Western Horseman*, February, 1967.

————. "Three Frontier Artists of the Northwest," *Big West*, February, 1968.

Crane, Leo M. "Artist in War Work," *Machinists' Monthly Journal*, January, 1944.

DeVore, Paul T. "First Russell Gallery a Saloon," *Pacific Northwesterner*, vol. 21, no. 4 (Fall, 1977).

————. "The Mint Collection," *Montana: The Magazine of Western History*, vol. 27, no. 4 (Autumn, 1977).

Dippie, Brian W. "Brush, Palette, and the Custer Battle," *Montana: The Magazine of Western History*, vol. 24, no. 1 (1977).

Dobie, J. Frank. "The Art of Charles M. Russell," *American Scene*, vol. 3, no. 2 (Summer, 1960).

Forrest, James Taylor. "Olaf Seltzer, Artist of the High Plains," *American Scene*, vol. 2, no. 2 (Summer, 1959).

Hamilton, Charles. "Art and Autographs: Collecting Illustrated Letters," *Hobbies*, April, 1952.

Hansen, Holder. Letter, *True West*, February, 1963.

Hunt, David C. "The Old West Revisited—The Private World of Doctor Philip Cole," *American Scene*, vol. 8, no. 4 (Winter, 1967).

Johnson, Dorothy M. "Number, Please: Confessions of a Teen-Age 'Central,'" *Montana: The Magazine of Western History*, vol. 23, no. 4 (1973).

*Kennedy Quarterly*, vol. 1, no. 4 (October, 1960); vol. 13, no. 2 (June, 1974).

Ladner, Mildred D. "Olaf Carl Seltzer," *American Scene*, vol. 15, no. 4 (Winter, 1974).

Mac, 'Tana. "O. C. Seltzer, Montana's Second Genius," *True West*, October, 1962.

*National Geographic*, vol. 127, no. 5 (May, 1965).

*Playgrounds of the Rockies*, vol. 7, no. 1 (April, 1964).

*Reader's Digest*, April, 1973.

Renner, F. G. "Bad Pennies," *Montana: The Magazine of Western History*, vol. 6, no. 2 (April, 1956).

Rosenstein, Harris. "Painters of the Purple Sage," *Art News*, Summer, 1968.

Rubottom, Carter V. "I Knew Charles M. Russell," *Montana: The Magazine of Western History*, vol. 4, no. 1 (1954).

Seltzer, O. "A Bear Story," *Rocky Mountain Magazine*, vol. 1 (January, 1901).

Stark, North D. "Two Giants of Western Art," *Frontier Times*, June–July, 1964.

## NEWSPAPER ARTICLES

*Copenhagen Politikens Ugeblad.* Feb. 20, 1954.

*Great Falls* (Mont.) *Leader.* June 18, 1927; "Thirty-two Years Ago," June 17, 1931; "Color Versus Form in Art," Feb. 8, 1937; "Dr. Philip Cole... Succumbs," July 2, 1941; "Tribune Gives Russell Gallery Artist's Paintings on Mirrors," Jan. 21, 1955; obituary, Dec. 16, 1957; funeral item, Dec. 19, 1957; "All Seltzer's Works Weren't Western," May 2, 1967.

*Great Falls* (Mont.) *Tribune.* "Cole Gives Art Book," Oct. 13, 1927; "Leaves for Coast," June 2, 1936; "Shows Work in Seattle," June 27, 1936; "Painting of Old Stagecoach on Display Here," Apr. 7, 1937; "Dr. Phil G. Cole, Montanan," July 2, 1941; "Lethbridge Hotelman Owns Early Seltzer Oil Painting," Jan. 2, 1949; "6,000 Greet Truman Here," May 13, 1950; "Artist Helps Gallery," June 11, 1954; "Montana Parade" section, July 18, 1854; "18 Seltzer Paintings Displayed in Russell Gallery One-Man Show," Sept. 15, 1954; "Two Russell Paintings on Mirrors Presented to Russell Gallery," 1960; "Four More Character Sketches," Jan. 15, 1961; "Masons Solve Century-Old 'Third Man' Mystery," May 29, 1966; "Stenzels' Gift," June 18, 1967; "Danish Paper Has Series on Seltzer," Dec. 10, 1972; "Seltzer Oil Goes for $5,800," Mar. 16, 1974; "Seltzers Back from Tulsa Art Institute," May 5, 1974; "Seltzer Sketch Featured," May 15, 1974; "Black Eagle DAR Plans Marker at Historic Site," Jan. 27, 1975; "Russells, Seltzers Help Illustrate 'Badmen of the West,'" Feb. 9, 1975; "Seltzer Art Stamp Proposed," May 18, 1975.

*Helena* (Mont.) *Independent Record.* "Dr. W. J. Butler, Prominent Montanan," Oct. 30, 1948.

*Inland Empire.* "The Spokesman Review" section, Nov. 25, 1962.

*Lethbridge* (Alta.) *Herald.* "A Frontier Painting That Changed a Life," Dec. 14, 1948.

*Montana Post.* August, 1963.

*New York Herald-Tribune.* "An Artist's Impressions of the Last Night of the National Horse Show," Nov. 15, 1934.

*New York Times.* "Miss Earhart Flies Pacific from Hawaii," "Aviatrix Started Her Career in 1918," Jan. 13, 1935; "Book Review" section, Nov. 30, 1971.

*New York World.* "The Disputed Trail," Apr. 21, 1929.

Ringsted, Henrik V. "Who Was the Dane in the Wild West?" *Copenhagen Politikens*, Apr. 2, 1972; "The Truth About Olaf Seltzer," *ibid.*, Apr. 15, 1972; "The Saga of Seltzer," *ibid.*, June 17, 1972; "The End of the Saga of O. C. Seltzer," *ibid.*, Nov. 25, 1972.

*Seattle Times.* "Seltzer's Art Exhibit Brings Old West Back," June 18, 1936.

*Tarrytown* (N.Y.) *Daily News.* "Patrolman Charles Schneider," Jan. 10, 1934; "O. Seltzer, Western Artist, Here," Nov. 23, 1934.


## MANUSCRIPTS

Cole, Philip G. "Montana in Miniature." Tarrytown, N.Y., May, 1936.

Downer, Fred. "My Life." Montana Historical Society Library, Helena, Mont., n.d.


## PAMPHLETS

*Amon Carter Museum of Western Art Newsletter*, vol. 2, no. 1 (n.d.).

Mac, 'Tana. "O. C. Seltzer, Montana's Second Genius." Butte, Mont.: Ashton Printing and Engraving, 1962.

*The Curator* (Gilcrease Institute of American History and Art), vol. 2, no. 5 (October, 1974).

*Great Falls Diamond Jubilee Book, 1959.*

*Lighton Memorial, SPG* [Screen Producers' Guild] *Newsletter*, no. 92. Beverly Hills, Calif., Feb. 4, 1963.


## CATALOGUES

*An Art Perspective of the Historic Pacific Northwest.* Montana Historical Society, September, 1963.

*The Artist in the American West 1800 – 1900.* Fine Arts Museum of New Mexico, Santa Fe, 1961.

*Bartfield Art Galleries' Catalogue*, no. 120, New York, 1973; no. 140, New York, 1976.

Christie's *Catalogue of the Family Collection of Miniatures: The Property of J. Pierpont Morgan.* London, June 24, 1935.

*An Exhibition of the Work of Charles M. Russell.* Fort Worth: Amon Carter Museum of Western Art. Summer, 1961.

*Exhibit of Paintings Depicting Early Western Life.* Seattle: Washington Athletic Club, June, 1936.

*International Auction Records* (Paris) vol. 7 (1973); vol. 8 (1974).

Kennedy, Michael Stephen. *The Life and Times of Olaf C. Seltzer, 1877 – 1957.* Montana Heritage Series, no. 10. Helena: Historical Society of Montana Press, 1960.

*Latendorf's Catalogue*, no. 27. New York.

Seltzer, Carl C. *Olaf C. Seltzer, 1877 – 1957.* Rendezvous of Western Art. Helena: Montana Historical Society, 1973.

*O. C. Seltzer Exhibit.* Great Falls, Mont.: C. M. Russell Gallery, April, 1966.

*O. C. Seltzer Retrospective Exhibition.* Great Falls, Mont.: C. M. Russell Gallery, 1969.

*Pacific Northwest Historical Pamphlet*, no. 3. Tacoma: Washington State Historical Society, April, 1963.

*Painter of the West Memorial Exhibition, Charles Marion Russell.* New York: Grand Central Galleries, November, 1927.

*Parke-Bernet Catalogues.* 1970, 1971.

*Souvenir Illustrated Catalog: Mint Saloon (Works of Charles M. Russell, Charles A. Beil, and O. C. Seltzer).* Great Falls, Mont., n.d.

<h1 style="text-align:center">Index</h1>